Caribbean
Hidea...

D0406389

Caribbean Hideaways

by IAN KEOWN

Illustrated by Claude Martinot

Prentice Hall Travel

New York • London • Toronto • Sydney • Tokyo • Singapore

Published by Prentice Hall Travel
A Division of Simon & Schuster Inc.
15 Columbus Circle
New York, NY 10023

First published by Harmony Books, a division of Crown Publishers, Inc., and represented in Canada by the Canadian MANDA Group

Library of Congress Cataloging-in-Publication Data

Keown, Ian.
    Caribbean hideaways/by Ian Keown; illustrated by Claude Martinot.
        p.   cm.
    Includes index.
    ISBN 0-13-116856-8
    1. West Indies—Description and travel—1981-   —Guide-books.
    2. Caribbean Area—Description and travel—1981-   —Guide-books.
    3. Hotels, taverns, etc.—West Indies—Guide-books.   4. Hotels,
    taverns, etc.—Caribbean Area—Guide-books.   5. Resorts—West
    Indies—Guide-books.   6. Resorts—Caribbean Area—Guide-books.
    I. Title.
    F1609.K46   1992
    917.2904'52—dc20   91-25240
                                                            CIP

Manufactured in the United States of America

Designed by Irving Perkins Associates

10 9 8 7 6 5 4 3 2 1

Contents

The French West Indies 215

The Queen's Windwards 247

St. Vincent–Grenadines and Grenada 283

The Dutch Leewards 315

Map List

Acknowledgments

As they say in Bonaire, *masha danki* (thank-you) to scores of friends and colleagues for tips and suggestions; to readers who took the trouble to send me comments and critiques; to island hoppers in airports and bars who shared their experiences; to innkeepers who took time, reconfirmed flights, and helped me get to the airport on time.

There are too many people to name individually, but for special efforts I'd like to offer a special thank-you to the following (in, of course, alphabetical order): Joan Bloom, Barbara Brooks, Dave Fernandez, Susan Hannah, Ralph Locke, Yvonne Maginley, Marcella Martinez, Marilyn Marx, Joan Medhurst, Madge Morris, Barbara Newfold, Alan O'Neal, Joe Petrocik, Meredith Pillon, Nick Thomas, Gillian Thompson, Hilary Wattley.

Likewise, I herein acknowledge the professionalism and what-would-I-do-without-her dependability of Lynn Woods who did most of the dirty work—editing, proofreading, keeping track of bits of paper and brochures, deciphering my scribbles, and even the tedious chore of checking out some hotels.

Finally, to colleagues and contributors who braved the midday sun to visit yet one more hotel and flush one more toilet: Eleanor Berman is the author of several books, including the *Away for the Weekend*® series of guides published by Crown; her byline also appears frequently in leading magazines and newspapers throughout the United States. Sharon Flescher has a Ph.D. in art history from Columbia University, writes scholarly articles on the French Impressionists, and works for a philanthropic/arts foundation. Elizabeth Murfee has her own public relations company and is closely involved with the arts in New York. Cynthia Proulx was my coauthor on *Guide to France for Loving Couples* and has contributed her peppy prose to several of my other guidebooks.

A Note about Prices   The author has made every effort to ensure the accuracy of the prices appearing in this book. However, prices may be affected by inflation or by changing circumstances, and it is not possible to guarantee the prices quoted.

A Disclaimer   Although the travel information in this book is based on the most reliable data obtainable, information may change under the impact of the many factors that affect the travel industry. The reader should keep in mind that changes can affect anything and everything—resorts, schedules, transportation, and more.

Safety   Incidents have been reported on some of the Caribbean islands, so whenever you're traveling, especially in an unfamiliar area, stay alert. Be aware of your immediate surroundings. Wear a moneybelt and keep a close eye on your possessions. Be particularly careful with cameras, purses, and wallets, all favorite targets of thieves and pickpockets.

Introduction

Introduction

You've dreamed the dream a hundred times: you, someone you love, a quiet beach, a row of palms; warm sand beneath your tummy, sand in your toes, sand in your ear; that delectable sensation of hot sun and cool breezes playing hide-and-seek on your back, the first chilly glop of suntan lotion, playful fingers spreading the glop around and around; the murmur of surf, sun flares in your eyes when you roll over, the heat in your cheeks long after you've moved into the shade; siestas, love in the afternoon, the quiet whirring of a four-bladed fan; rum punches at sundown, a table for two beneath the palms, candles flickering in the trade winds, tree frogs courting; after dinner, a walk on the beach, barefoot through the surf, the moon shimmering on the sea; early to bed, early to love.

For all you dreamers and lovers, here is another book of nice places, a guide for lovers of all kinds and inclinations—Romeo and Juliet, Romeo and Romeo, Juliet and Juliet, rich lovers, poor lovers, newlyweds and newly unweds, actresses and bodyguards, moms and dads who would still be lovers if only they could get the kids out of their hair for a few days. In other words, it's for anyone who has a yen to slip off for a few days and be alone in the sun with someone he or she fancies, likes, loves, has the hots for, or simply wants to do something nice for.

Whatever your tastes or inclinations, you'll probably find something that appeals to you in these pages. This is a fairly eclectic selection. Some of the resorts are on the beach and others are in the mountains; some are on big islands and some are on islands so small you won't find them on a map; some large resorts are included because there are lovers who prefer the anonymity a large resort affords (but none of them so vast as to be tourist-processing factories); some have nightlife of sorts but most of them don't even have a tape recorder; some are for lovers who want to dress up in the evening and others are for lovers with cutoff jeans and beat-up sandals. But these hotels and resorts all have something special going for them. It may be seclusion (Palm Island Beach Club or Petit St. Vincent Resort, both in the Grenadines), it may be spaciousness (Caneel Bay on St. John, Casa de Campo in the Dominican Republic) or nostalgia (Avila Beach on Curaçao, Pasanggrahan on St. Maarten), charm (Golden

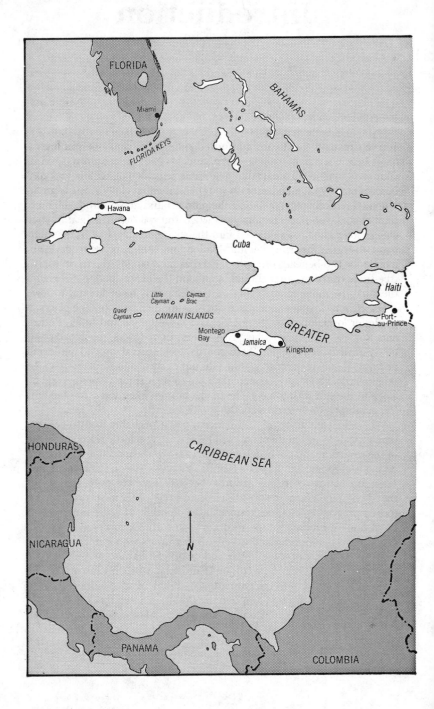

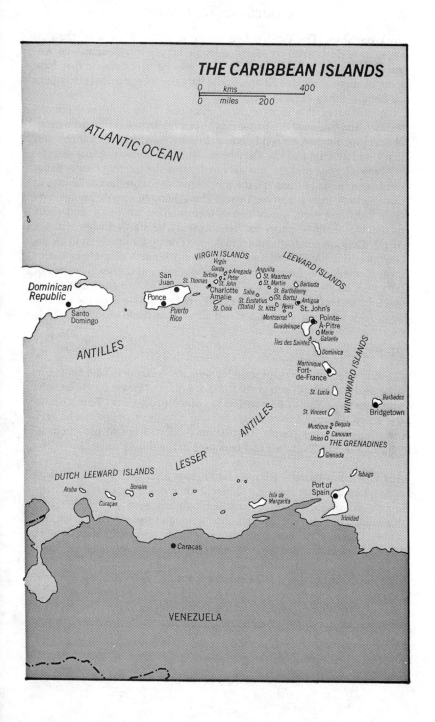

THE CARIBBEAN ISLANDS

0   kms   400
0   miles   200

ATLANTIC OCEAN

VIRGIN ISLANDS
Virgin
Gorda *Anegada*   Anguilla
Tortola   *Peter*   St. Maarten/
San   *St. Thomas*   *St. John*   St. Martin   Barbuda
Juan   Charlotte   St. Barthélemy
Ponce   Amalie   Saba   (St. Barts)   Antigua
      St. Eustatius   St. John's
Puerto   *St. Croix*   (Statia)   St. Kitts   Nevis
Rico   Montserrat   Pointe-
Dominican   Guadeloupe   À-Pitre
Republic   *Marie*
          Îles des Saintes   *Galante*
Santo   *Dominica*
Domingo
            Martinique
ANTILLES   Fort-
            de-France

LEEWARD ISLANDS

WINDWARD ISLANDS

      St. Lucia   *Barbados*
                 Bridgetown
     St. Vincent
    Mustique   *Bequia*
LESSER   *Canouan*
     Union   THE GRENADINES
ANTILLES
            Grenada

DUTCH LEEWARD ISLANDS   *Tobago*
Aruba   *Bonaire*   Port of
                Isla de   Spain
Curaçao   Margarita
                     Trinidad

       Caracas

VENEZUELA

Rock on Nevis, The Golden Lemon on St. Kitts), a sense of the past (Plantation de Leyritz on Martinique), or luxury (Malliouhana on Anguilla or Jumby Bay on Antigua). They may be here because they have some of these qualities and are, in the bargain, inexpensive (Frangipani on Bequia, for example).

In most cases, they're a combination of one or more of these characteristics, and in almost every case they're places where you can avoid neon, plastic, piped music, air conditioning, casinos, conventions, children, and that peculiar blight of the Caribbean—massed cruise ship passengers.

Above all, none of these hotels try to disguise the fact that they're in the Caribbean; none of them try, the minute you arrive in the Caribbean, to transport you instantly to back-street Hong Kong or ye olde pubbe in Ye Olde Englande (well, one or two of them maybe, but you'll read about their follies in these pages so that you won't be startled when you get there). They are hotels that don't make you line up for breakfast in an air-conditioned dining room and then line up immediately afterward to make a reservation for the first or second seating at dinner. They're not the sort of hotels that entice you with promises of soft air and trade winds, and then seal you into a box where you're not allowed to leave the balcony door open to let in the promised soft air and the trade winds.

PET PEEVES

Curmudgeons of the world unite! There are innkeepers who believe in some of the standards you try to uphold. I quote: "Please do not let your wife wear those ghastly hair curlers out of your room"; or "Tennis whites *does* mean wearing a shirt on court"; or "Transistor radios can be very disturbing to other people. Guests are requested not to play them in public areas"; or "No jeans and tank tops in the dining room."

Air Conditioning   For me, and I'm sure for a lot of you, louvers and ceiling fans are more romantic than whirring, dripping, throbbing, rusting, shuddering, grinding air-conditioning units, so most of the hotels in this guide either do not have air conditioning or use it only as a backup system. There is, of course, another side to the air-conditioning debate: In some hotels, the gadget is necessary to block out extraneous noises such as stray dogs, roosters, and roisterers, and on occasion you may welcome the background hum to keep your own noises *in*; moreover, one of my colleagues, who shall remain nameless, claims air conditioning is a necessity for after-lunch lovemaking in the tropics. Therefore, when a hotel has air conditioning as a backup system the fact is noted in the listings—but please don't take this as being a commendation at the expense of hotels without air conditioning.

Cruise Ship Passengers Presumably you're going to the Caribbean to find a quiet, secluded beach that won't remind you of Coney Island on the Fourth of July, but you can forget that idea if a few hundred old salts arrive in ankle socks and T-shirts. Some hotels encourage these visits because they represent instant profit; others ban them unequivocally, and still others are beginning to learn that after they've cleared up the litter and tallied up the missing souvenirs, cruise ship passengers aren't worth the trouble. ("They buy one Coke, then use the toilet, and the profit on the Coke is less than what I pay for the water.") Most of the hotels in this guide ban cruise ship passengers—or at least limit the numbers.

Piped Music If you take the trouble to search out a hideaway, as opposed to a big swinging resort, you probably don't want your peace and quiet to be disturbed by piped noise, especially when it's music that has no connection, harmonic or otherwise, with the setting—such as dining by candlelight on the veranda of a centuries-old inn and having to listen to a record of a chanteuse singing, "It's so-o goo-oo-ood."

Other Music Piped noise is not the same thing as discreet background music that's carefully selected by the management to match the mood of the guests or the setting; but any kind of music, taped or live, combo or steel band, should be avoidable (that is, if you don't want to listen, you should be able to go to another lounge or patio where you can't hear it), and it should never keep guests from their sleep. Also, any hotel that plays "Island in the Sun" more than six times in one evening should lose its license. Another ubiquitous blight these days is Bartender's Radio. He's bored, standing around all day serving drinks to a bunch of frolicking foreigners, and he wants his music—usually noisy with an insensate beat. It's a pain for owners, too: "I can see the bartender scurrying to turn down the radio every time he sees me approaching; I agree with you, guests shouldn't have to listen to the bartender's music." The "all" in "getting away from it all" includes other people's radios. That wish should be respected. Worst offense of all, of course, is amplified music—singer, combo, native band or, horror of horrors, steel band. Quite apart from the fact that the music is often so loud you can't hear yourselves whisper sweet nothings, the sound systems usually distort the music itself—too much *kaBOOM-kaBOOM*, not enough *trala-trala*. Too often, I suspect, loud music is managerial camouflage to distract guests' attention from the wishy-washy food.

In this guidebook, loud music is tolerated (but with the greatest reluctance) only *if* the hotel offers alternative facilities for imbibing and dining away from the noise; but if the kabooming follows guests all the way to their beds or balconies, or lasts beyond, say, 11:00 p.m., that place loses points. Hotel people often boast about the days when their guests were entertained by impromptu performances by a Noël Coward or a Cole Porter, but Coward and Porter never went *kaBOOM-kaBOOM*. Yet presumably people still managed to enjoy their vacations back in the days before combos carted their own power stations around.

Please, please: When you resent the music or the volume of the music, take the manager aside and explain that you paid all that money and took that long journey to get some peace and quiet. Remind him or her, gently, that it's considered bad manners to talk so loudly that people at the next table can't enjoy their own conversation. Ditto a band that plays too loudly.

Paging Systems   Even worse than intrusive music is the paging system around the swimming pool and bar; if you're trying to escape telephones and reminders of the office, it doesn't do much for your spirits to know that the people around you are wanted on the phone. Any man or woman who tips a telephone operator to be paged at the pool should be sealed in a phone booth! I can think of only one hotel in this guide with a paging system, and even then it's used sparingly.

Children   Some hotels ban them altogether, as they do cruise ship passengers; others shunt them off to a far corner of the property and feed them separately. It's not really the children who are the problem. It may be the parents, who are trying to have a vacation themselves and have allowed family discipline to break down until it reaches the point where it can be restored only by a public shouting match—usually on the beach or around the pool. As one innkeeper puts it, "Kids around pools mean noise—so we don't allow them at the pool." In any case, many couples in hideaways are parents trying to get away from their own families for a day or two, so they're hardly enchanted to be surrounded by other people's youngsters. Rowdy families are less of a bother in the Caribbean than they are back home because parents can't just pile everyone into a car and drive off to the islands. Sometimes there's a lot to be said for stiff airfares.

Conventions   The object of a convention or sales conference is to whip people into a frenzy of enthusiasm; but frenzied enthusiasm is something you don't need when you're trying to escape the business or urban world. Very few of the hotels in this guide accept conventions; if they do, the groups are either small enough to be absorbed without a trace, or so large that they have to rent the entire hotel. However, most of the hotels in this guide will accept small, seminar-type groups in the off-season, and in many cases they have to do so to stay in business; but that kind of group shouldn't interfere with your privacy and pleasure. In some cases, it's an advantage: While the group is cooped up studying or discussing its specialty, you have the beach, sailboards, and tennis courts all to yourselves.

SIGNING IN

"If we worried about whether or not our guests were married, we would lose maybe one-third of our clientele," seems to be a fairly general attitude among innkeepers in the Caribbean.

So, in these hotels you can sign in as Mr. and Mrs., or simply sign in with your own names if you are not married. Some hotels don't even bother to have you sign a register; few of them, if any, will ask to see passports or other identification.

Some managers prefer that you sign in with your real names, even if they don't match; others prefer you to sign as a couple because it's simpler for the staff. Unless you have strong views one way or another, the simplest procedure is to write the noncommittal M/M—that is, M/M John Smith, M/M Ian Keown, and so on.

However, at least one of you should use your real name. If it's absolutely imperative that you both travel incognito, then at some point you'd better take the manager aside and explain that "Mr. John Smith" will be paying the bill with checks or credit cards in the name of whatever your name is.

If you want to be anonymous and don't want anyone to find out where you were six months later, before you leave the hotel ask the manager to make sure your name does not appear on any mailing lists for Christmas cards, newsletters, and such.

THE RATES

This is the most hazardous chore in putting together a reliable guide-book. Most of the hotels in this guide were visited during the fall and winter of 1990–1991, when many managers or owners had not yet established their rates for winter 1991–1992. Unlike some guidebook writers, however, I feel that rates are indispensable in such a publication; therefore, to simplify the production of the guidebook and ensure that you get the most up-to-date figures possible I've listed all the latest rates in a special section at the end of the guide (except for hotels listed as "Added Attractions," where you'll find the rates at the end of each listing). This way you can scan the list more easily and compare resort A with resort B. Moreover, to give you some indication of what sort of place you're reading about, I've also included, with the description of each hotel, a symbol ($) for *approximate* costs (see page 17.) The symbols (please note this carefully) are based on *high season MAP rates for two people, with breakfast and dinner*—that is, the cost of room plus breakfast and dinner. They are high season rather than summer rates because they happened to be the most reliable figures available when the guidebook was compiled; please remember, the dollar symbols would look much less ominous if they represented summer figures, and if you are considering a summer trip, I suggest that as a rule of thumb you chop off one $, except in the case of the lowest category.

RESERVATIONS

It's nice to pack a bag and just go on the spur of the moment, and if the moment happens to spur in the off-season, you may be able to drop in on some of these hotels and get the best room without a reservation.

But is it worth the risk? Think of it: You fly down there, take a long, costly taxi ride to the other side of the island, only to discover that by some fluke this happens to be the weekend when a bunch of people have come over from an adjoining island and have filled every room, or that the owners decided to close down for the weekend because they had no reservations. For the impetuous, I've listed telephone numbers, most of them direct-dial (first three digits are area codes for the island). Call ahead at least. In any case, at peak seasons it's imperative that you also reserve your flight weeks in advance.

For lovers who think ahead, there are several alternatives:

1. Travel Agent   The agent who books your flight can also arrange your hotel reservation, probably at no extra charge; he or she will also attend to the business of deposits and confirmations. However, travel agents often have their own favorite islands and resorts, sometimes places involving no complications in terms of flights or reservations; if your agent tries to sell you a bigger island or resort, by all means consider it, but if you feel strongly about your own choice, dig in your heels.

2. Hotel Representative   You pick up the telephone, call someone such as David B. Mitchell & Company or Ralph Locke Islands, tell them where you want to stay, and they can let you know (often right there and then) if your hotel is full or otherwise; they'll make your reservation, and, if there's time, send you confirmation—at no extra charge, unless they have to fax or telephone. You'll find a list of the leading hotel reps (who handle two or more of the hotels) at the end of this guide; individual hotel representatives and phone numbers are listed under the hotel itself.

3. Fax   This is now the most efficient way to make a reservation direct, since you will receive your confirmation quickly—and in writing. Most hotels and resorts in the Caribbean now have facsimile equipment, and I have included the numbers where the service is available.

4. Letter   The least efficient. You could be senile by the time you get a reply.

Whatever method you choose, you must be specific: Know the number of people in your party, date of arrival, time of arrival, and flight number if possible; number of nights you plan to stay, date of departure; whether you want a double bed or twin beds, bathtub or shower, least expensive or most expensive room or suite, sea view or garden view or whatever; whether you want an EP, MAP, or FAP rate (these terms are explained at the end of this guide). Finally, don't forget your return address or telephone number.

DEPOSITS

Once you get a reply to your request for a reservation, assuming there's time, you'll be expected to make a deposit (usually one, two, or three days, depending on the length of your stay). Of course it's a nuisance—what if you want to change your mind? That's just the point. The smaller hotels can't afford to have reservations for a full house, turn down other reservations in the meantime, only to have half of their expected clientele cancel at the last minute.

From your point of view, the deposit guarantees your reservation. People sometimes make mistakes, especially with reservations, but if you have a written confirmed reservation in your hand *with proof of a deposit* you're not going to be turned away from your hotel.

If you're going in the peak season, you should always allow yourself time to send a deposit and get a *written* confirmed reservation. Again, you're better off using a fax, which gives you and the hotel a reservation/confirmation record.

HOW TO LICK HIGH COSTS

So long as people insist on scuttling south to the sun at the first hint of frost or snow, hotel rates will remain astronomical in the Caribbean during the winter months. The period from December to April is the island inns' chance to make a profit and they grab the chance with a vengeance (remember, the owners have to pay wages and overhead in spring, summer, and fall, too—even if *you're* in Maine or Europe).

Here are a few suggestions for keeping your budget within bounds:

1. Avoid the Peak Season   Obviously, it's great to get some Caribbean sun when the frost is nipping up north, but March and April are not so hot in northern climes either, and it's often very pleasant to escape to the islands in October, November, and early December. Some people head south in May and June to get an early start on a suntan. Even during summer, the Caribbean has its attractions, and more and more people are discovering them. Oddly enough, summer in the Caribbean islands can be *cooler* than in stifling northern cities. While northern beaches and facilities are overcrowded in summer, the beaches in the Caribbean are half empty, and while the northern resorts are charging peak-season rates, the Caribbean is available at bargain rates. So remember that the peak season lasts only four months (usually December 15 through April 15), *and for eight months of the year rates are one-quarter to one-half less.*

2. Choose Your Resort Carefully   Some resorts throw in everything with the rate—sailing, waterskiing, tennis, snorkeling gear, and so on; others charge extra for almost everything. Compare, for example, Curtain Bluff and St. James's Club on Antigua—free scuba-diving and waterskiing at the former; you pay for scuba at the latter. Obviously, if you don't want to scuba-dive or waterski, you may be better off at St. James's Club. But this sort of situation also occurs with tennis, windsurfing—even with snorkeling gear.

3. Dodge Taxes   Some islands have no tax on tourists and others are as high as 11 percent; not much as a percentage, true, but on a two-week vacation it can add up to a few hundred dollars. Taxes are listed in the section on rates at the end of this guide. So are service charges: Read tnese details carefully for they can save you a small bundle. Not simply because some service charges are 10% and others are 15%, but because in many cases the service charge relieves you of the need to tip. For example, this reminder from Antigua's Curtain Bluff: "A 10% service charge is added to all accounts. Therefore, TIPPING IS NOT ALLOWED"—their capitals. (This does not mean that guests cannot express their appreciation: "Curtain Bluff has a fund for the community of Old Road. If you want to donate funds, please see a member of the management.")

4. Drink Rum   On rum-producing islands, rum is less expensive than Scotch or bourbon, and in a thirst-building climate this can make a noticeable difference when the tab is tallied at the end of your stay. However, some island governments clamp such enormous duties on soda or tonic that your rum may cost less than its mixer. In that case, drink the local beer.

The best way around big bar tabs is to buy a tax-free bottle of your favorite liquor at the airport before you leave. This may be frowned upon in smaller hotels, but in any case you should never drink from your bottle in public rooms. Several of the hideaways in this guide have a bottle of rum and mixers waiting for you in your room—on the house.

5. Kitchens   No one wants to go off on vacation and spend the time cooking, but a small kitchen is useful for preparing between-meal snacks, lunches, and drinks, without running up room service charges. Several of the hotels listed in this guide have refrigerators and/or kitchenettes and/ or fully equipped kitchens, and a few of them have mini-markets on the premises. They can save a lot of dollars without a lot of extra effort.

6. Double Up   Consider the possibility of trotting off to the islands with your favorite couple and sharing a suite or bungalow/cottage/villa. If you do this in a place such as, say, Tryall in Montego Bay, you can enjoy a villa with kitchen, sitting room, and two bedrooms with two complete bathrooms. You'll find many examples of such cost-cutting options in this guide.

7. Packages   These are special rates built around the themes of honeymoons, water sports, tennis, golf. "We have people coming back every year for five or six years on the honeymoon package," sighs one hotel-keeper. In fact, some couples have arrived on a honeymoon package with all their children in tow, looking for reduced rates for them, too.

Honeymoon packages usually include frills such as a bottle of champagne, flowers for the lady, or a half-day sail up the coast. Check them carefully—you may be better off with a regular rate. Sports packages usually are a good deal. They will probably include free court time (carefully specified) for tennis players, or X number of free rounds for golfers. If you're a sports enthusiast, check with the hotel rep or your travel agent for the nitty-gritty details.

8. Tour Packages   Dirty words to some people but they needn't be. A tour package is not the same thing as an escorted tour: It can mean simply that 10 or 20 people will be booked on the same flight to take advantage of a special fare; they may be given their choice of two or three hotels on the island, so you may never see them again until you get to the airport for your return flight. Local sightseeing is sometimes included and sometimes it's an option; some packages include boat trips and barbecues. If you don't feel like taking part in these activities, you may still be ahead of the game because the special rates you will be paying for hotels and flights may be such good deals. The advantages of package tours are that you may qualify for lower airfares (always with conditions, but you can probably live with them), and the tour operator may have negotiated lower hotel rates; in winter, tour operators may have "blocked off" a group of hotel rooms and seats on jets, and package tours may be your only hope of finding reservations.

Few of the hotels in this guide are likely to be overrun with package tours, but some of them do in fact accept small tour groups, a fact that is noted under the P.S. at the end of each hotel listing. Look into the tour brochures of some of the airlines—say, American, BWIA, or Pan Am—and you may find special packages built around some of these hotels— the Half Moon Club in Jamaica, Cobblers Cove in Barbados, and Casa de Campo in the Dominican Republic.

THE RATINGS

All the hotels and resorts in this guide are above average in one way or another, but some obviously are more special than others. To make choosing simpler, I've rated the hotels (using symbols) for romantic atmosphere (stars), food and service (goblets), sports facilities (beach balls), and cost (dollar signs). The ratings are highly personal and subjective—the fun part of compiling the guide, my reward to myself for scurrying around from island to island and hotel to hotel when I could just as easily have been lying on the beach.

Stars represent the *romantic* atmosphere of a hotel or resort more than the quality or luxury or facilities. Of course, the two go together, and here we're talking also about the setting, decor, size, efficiency, location, personality, welcome—the intangibles.

Goblets evaluate not just the quality of the food but the overall emphasis and attitude toward dining, the competence of the waiters, the way the food is placed before you. *This is a specifically Caribbean evaluation*—it takes into consideration the special circumstances in the islands. In other words, any hotel that promises "the finest in gourmet dining" or "the ultimate in continental cuisine" almost certainly gets a low score because this is a vain promise: "The finest continental cuisine" is something you find at a three-star restaurant in France. Caribbean islands just don't have access to the market gardens and meat markets to match those standards. There are times, in fact, when you get the impression that all the meals in the Caribbean are coming from some giant commissary in Miami (even fish); so hotels that list local dishes, such as conch pie, *keshi yena*, or *colombo de poulet riz* on their menus, even if only occasionally, stand a better chance of getting a higher rating than most hotels trying to emulate continental cuisine (unless they do it really well).

Any hotel that forces you to dine indoors in an air-conditioned restaurant ranks badly (there are only two or three of them in this guide, and although one of them is Dorado Beach, which gets a three-goblet rating, at least it gives you the option of dining al fresco in a second restaurant, or on your room balcony). It seems to me that one of the great pleasures of dining in the Caribbean is to be in the open air, surrounded by the sounds of the tropical night or the sea, in an atmosphere of palms and stars—not in some third-rate interior designer's concept of an English pub or Manhattan nightspot. Wine does not enter into consideration in this guide. The conditions, usually, are all wrong for storing wine and caring for wine, and by the time it has been trans-shipped three times, it's overpriced. Most of the hotels that rate highly for food have passable to good wine lists; otherwise it's a hit-and-miss affair (except, perhaps, on the French islands, or in special cases such as Curtain Bluff hotel in Antigua, Malliouhana on Anguilla, and Biras Creek on Virgin Gorda, all run by oenophiles).

In the listings following each hotel, you'll occasionally find the term *family style*. This doesn't mean that you all sit down with the kiddies; it means, rather, that you don't get a menu: You take what's offered, and usually all the guests sit down to dine at the same time, perhaps at communal tables. Sometimes you will be offered a choice of dishes, sometimes not; if you have problems with your diet, check with the manager each morning, and if he or she's planning something you don't fancy, he or she'll probably prepare a steak or some other simple alternative. If you're fussy about food, skip places serving family-style meals. Moreover, you may not want to dine with strangers each evening.

While on the subject of dining, please note that under each hotel listing I spell out the evening dress code. I've seen too many hapless vacationers either laden with wardrobes they have no opportunity to show off, or, conversely, the male has to borrow tie or jacket to get into the dining room. Although most of these hideaways set their code as casual or informal, this does not mean sloppy—and for most places that means no shorts, no tank tops or T-shirts in the evening, cover-ups and no wet swimsuits at lunchtime. My personal preference is to have the option of dressing or not, depending on my mood; I have obviously included some places that expect guests to dress up every evening, but they either have alternative dining areas or can arrange for you to have dinner on your private patio or balcony.

Beach Balls   offer you a quick idea of the availability of sporting facilities, but you'll also find the actual facilities spelled out at the end of each hotel. I tried originally to include prices for each activity, but this became too cumbersome; however, you will learn from the listings whether a particular sport is free or whether you have to pay an additional fee.

Remember, no matter how well-endowed the hotel, sports facilities are less crowded in the nonwinter months.

Dollar Signs   Use these as a rough guide only, primarily for comparing one resort with another. For detailed rates, turn to the special chapter at the end of the guide. The $ symbols are based on *winter rates for two people*; since the most accessible rate for comparison between hotels is the *MAP rate*, this is the one that is used (that is, for room, breakfast, and dinner). Each $ represents roughly $100; where a hotel overflows into more than one category, I've used the lower category, assuming that this represents a reasonable proportion of the available rooms. For a quick guide to *summer rates*, you will not be far off the mark if you reduce the higher ratings by one $.

Here are the ratings:

☆   *A port of call*
☆☆   *A long weekend*
☆☆☆   *Time for a suntan*
☆☆☆☆   *A place to linger*
☆☆☆☆☆   *Happily ever after*

♉   *Sustenance*
♉♉   *Good food*
♉♉♉   *Something to look forward to*
♉♉♉♉   *As close to* haute cuisine *as you can get in the Caribbean*

➊   *Some diversions*
➊➊   *Lots of things to keep your mind off sex*
➊➊➊   *More diversions than you'll have stamina for*
➊➊➊➊   *All that and a spa or horseback riding, too*

$ *$250 or under, MAP for two*
$$ *$250 to $350 MAP for two*
$$$ *$350 to $450 MAP for two*
$$$$ *$450 to $550 MAP for two*
$$$$$ *$550 and above MAP for two*

ADDED ATTRACTIONS

A special feature in this guide is the "Added Attractions" sections at the end of the listings for some islands. These are, for the most part, hotels, inns, and resorts that we visited as possibilities but that didn't quite measure up; in some cases they are hotels that were rated in earlier editions of the guide but have since lost some of their appeal or changed management. But they may help fill a few gaps for you, especially since several of them are relatively inexpensive. If you visit any of them and think they deserve to be featured and rated, please let me know.

DOUBLE BEDS

Some Caribbean hoteliers seem to have installed twin beds in most of their rooms. However, most hotels of any size have some rooms with double, queen- or king-size beds, and all but the tiniest hideaways can arrange to push two twins together to make a double—if you give them advance notice. If this is the case, however, check before indulging in any trampolining, because if the beds are pushed together and sheeted lengthwise rather than crosswise they may part like the Red Sea and you may end up in a voluptuous heap on the floor.

CREEPY-CRAWLIES AND OTHER HAZARDS

Snakes, spiders, and tarantulas are no problem. Mosquitoes, no-see-ums, and sand flies have been sprayed almost to oblivion on most islands; however, they do sometimes appear in certain types of weather, so if you have the sort of skin that can rouse a dying mosquito to deeds of heroism, take along a repellent.

Sea urchins are a hazard on some islands, depending on tides or seasons or something I don't understand. Every hotel seems to have its solution, but, for what it's worth, here is the traditional remedy from the island of Saba: "Count the number of spines sticking in you; then swallow one mouthful of seawater for each spine." Since sea urchin stings are painful, check with the hotel staff before venturing into the sea.

Drinking water is not a problem on most islands, but it is chemically different from what you're accustomed to, and if your system is touchy about such things, ask for bottled water.

Sun is something else altogether. Naturally, you want to get a quick tan, and of course you love lying on the beach—but remember, your reason for slipping off together is love, and love can be a painful affair if you both look like lobsters and feel like barbecues.

Remember, too, the Caribbean sun is particularly intense; one hour a day is enough, unless you already have a hint of tan. Some enthusiasts forget they can get a sunburn while in the water; if you plan to do a lot of snorkeling, wear a T-shirt. If you do get a burn, stand in a lukewarm shower. Some people recommend compresses of really strong tea; one of the beach boys on Aruba has quite a sideline going rubbing on the leaf of the aloe plant; the Greeks recommend rubbing on yogurt. For heat prostration, Sabans again seem to have the endearing answer: "Rub the body with rum, particularly around the stomach."

MUGGINGS AND OTHER VEXATIONS

Each time I set out to research this guide, friends keep cautioning me about the horrible things that might happen to me in the Caribbean— robbery, mugging, assault, battery, anti-Americanism, fascism, racism, and other everyday hassles.

Nothing has happened so far. There are probably plenty of statistics around to prove that things can be unpleasant in the Caribbean, but it has never been immediately obvious to me. Nevertheless, travelers should always be alert, keep valuables in a safe place, and listen to any warnings given by hotel personnel or local people.

PIRACY ON THE HIGH ROADS

Caribbean taxi drivers. Now there's a motley, shameless, scurrilous bunch of brigands! They begin hectoring you the second you leave the plane, follow you, if they can, through customs and immigration, and before they take time to welcome you to their lovely island in the sun they're already trying to make you "reserve" them for sightseeing tours and the trip back to the airport. (There are, of course, exceptions, and I hereby apologize to the one taxi driver in a hundred who is pleasant, courteous, punctual, honest.)

Their gross behavior can get your amorous tryst off to an unpleasant start, and the way around this is to ask your hotel to assign one of its pool of "approved" drivers to meet you at the airport; the hotel will send you his or her name when confirming your reservation, in which case, you simply ask for Sebastian or whatever the name is when you get there. If there's no time to send the name before you arrive, the hotel may post a message for you on the airport notice board, telling you to ask for Sebastian. (This procedure is not the same thing as sending over a hotel limousine; you may still have to pay the regular taxi fare, but at least it will be the official rate and not whatever the driver thinks he or she can get away with.)

Taxis can cost you an arm and a leg in the Caribbean, and the driver may go for the shoulder and thigh too. That's why I've included the cost of the taxi ride from the airport in the list of nitty-gritty following each hotel.

The drivers' point of view is that their costs are unusually high—imported cars, imported gas, imported parts, highways that knock the hell out of the cars, stiff insurance rates, and so on. Fine. What's not so understandable is why island governments kowtow to the drivers, who won't allow anyone else to operate a bus or limousine service; the result is that you, the visitors, have to pay perhaps $10 to $12 for a taxi ride, when you could be paying only $2 to $3 for a mini-bus or limousine. On some islands authorities quite blatantly post lower rates for residents. In some cases, taxis operate on a "seat available" basis—that is, you pay a share of the cost with other people going in the same direction; but if only six people get off an interisland flight they may not be going in your direction, and in any case by the time the immigration officer has finished stamping your passport, all the "seat available" taxis may have mysteriously left. Your best bet, if you have a long taxi ride, is to ask your hotel to have a taxi and driver waiting for you at the airport.

SOME CARIBBEAN COMMENTS

Water   You'll be constantly reminded of the old Caribbean adage— "Water is the gold of the Caribbean," or as it's less eloquently phrased on some signs, "On our island in the sun we don't flush for number one." In deluxe resorts with their own catchments and reverse osmosis plants, the cost to the hotel for one shower may be $5—your two showers each per day account for $20 of your rate; hotels that have to import water will have a still higher bill. Be sparing. Shower together.

Hot Water   Most of the hotels in this guide supply hot water, but a few don't (noted in the listings for that hotel). Don't let that turn you off; the water pipes are just below the surface and the midday sun warms the water before it reaches the tap. In the early morning, just cling to each other.

Caribbean Service   Don't expect the staff to rush around. It's all right for you—you're there for only a few days, but the people who live there don't find the glaring sun so appealing day after day. They'll operate at a normal Caribbean pace no matter how much you tip, and at a less than normal pace if you shout and snap your fingers and stamp your feet. You just have to learn a few tricks. For example, always *anticipate* your thirst: Order your drinks about 10 minutes before you'll be gasping for them. Also, place your order in simple English; the islanders don't want to figure out what you're trying to say—it's too hot to bother.

ESCAPE ROUTES TO THE CARIBBEAN

There are several hundred flights a week from the North American mainland to the Caribbean islands, and it's about time you were on one of them. But which one? What with deregulation and mergers, it's a hassle trying to keep up with airlines these days. You'll find a quick summary of the major services to the various islands, or groups of islands, at the beginning of each chapter in this guide; please note that this information is based on *winter schedules*, and lists only nonstop or direct (that is, with no change of aircraft) flights from major North American departure points.

The major multidestination carriers to the islands are still *American, Pan Am, Air Canada*, and *British West Indies Airways (BWIA)*, but they have been joined by others such as *Delta, United, Continental*, and *TWA*. If you live in or transit via the northeast, American and Pan Am are the carriers with most flights to the islands, and they should be your first choice; most Caribbean flights from Miami are flown by American, Pan Am, and BWIA.

But overall, American is now *the* Caribbean carrier, with its major hub at San Juan and interisland services on its offshoot, *American Eagle*. American Eagle, and to a lesser extent *Sunaire* (until the demise of Eastern, it was known as Eastern Metro), are the best things that have happened to the islands in years. They blanket the islands with modern fleets of twin-engined prop or turboprop aircraft, and both have above-average consideration for matters that other Caribbean carriers seem to find tiresome—such as maintaining on-time schedules and honoring confirmed reservations.

Remember (and I've also said this elsewhere because it's important) when using regional services that the smaller aircraft do not have capacious overhead bins or racks for garment bags, so luggage that would normally be considered carry-on will have to be checked. That probably means a little more care in packing.

Of the Caribbean-based carriers, BWIA (known affectionately or patronizingly, as the case may be, as BeeWee) is a sort of national carrier; it probably has to serve too many islands (and, therefore, too many governments) for its own good—Antigua, St. Lucia, Barbados, Trinidad, and Tobago (and, off and on, St. Kitts/Nevis). *Air Jamaica* flies all up and down the eastern states and provinces and sometimes the West Coast, garnering passengers for Montego Bay and Kingston.

ALM (Antilleanse Luchtvaart Maatschappij) is the flag carrier of the Netherlands Antilles, linking Miami and New York with Aruba, Bonaire, and Curaçao (with occasional service to Haiti), with interisland services to St. Maarten, San Juan, and Trinidad.

AIRLINES WITHIN THE CARIBBEAN

Apart from Sunaire and American Eagle, mentioned above, it may be necessary to finish your trip to your chosen hideaway on a local island-hopper. Here's where the fun begins—if you have a bottomless sense of humor.

Windward Island Airways is my favorite interisland carrier. St. Maarten—based, it shuttles between Juliana Airport and Saba, St. Eustatius, St. Kitts, St. Barthélemy, and Anguilla. This very efficient little outfit, (30 years old in 1991), operates a complex "bus service" (more than a thousand flights a year to Saba alone) with a few DeHavilland Twin Otters, that short takeoff and landing (STOL) workhorse, the engines of which are washed every morning—inside and out.

Air Guadeloupe, *Air Martinique*, and *Air Barthélemy* are handy, fairly dependable commuter lines linking the French islands with each other and with outsiders such as Barbados, Antigua, St. Thomas, San Juan, and St. Vincent and the Grenadines.

The biggest operation in the Caribbean is *Leeward Islands Air Transport (LIAT)*. In terms of departures/arrivals per day it's actually one of the largest airlines *in the world*. It's always been a sort of laughingstock, and in an earlier edition of this guide I quoted some of the scathing comments associated with its acronym—Leave Island Any Time, etc. Truth is, LIAT is a much-improved airline. Serving so many independent islands with the kind of frequency (45,000 takeoffs and landings a year) LIAT has to maintain is a momentous task. LIAT now has a first-rate on-time record (officially, although it's hard to believe when you're on a flight, as I was once, leaving one hour early and heading north instead of south). Moreover, the line has recently introduced new aircraft—updated versions of its warhorse British Aerospace Avro 748s (you no longer feel like you're about to sink through the worn cushions to the floor) and nifty DeHavilland Dash propjets.

For short flights to the smaller islands, it may be smart to charter a small plane. The local hotels will make the arrangements for you, teaming you with other couples to cut costs. These shared charters are common practice in St. Kitts/Nevis and the Grenadines. For St. Kitts/Nevis or other islands around St. Maarten/St. Martin or Antigua, you can arrange to have a Beechcraft or Partenavia of *Carib Aviation* waiting for your jet. From Antigua to Nevis is a quick flight (10 minutes or so), costs only a few dollars more when shared, and can save hours waiting for a scheduled LIAT flight. In St. Vincent and the Grenadines, most hotels will arrange to have you met at Barbados by a representative of *Air Mustique*, who will escort you to your small plane and make sure your luggage is aboard. The alternative is probably a connecting flight via St. Vincent or Grenada, which could take forever.

Caribbean airlines may not have the sophisticated electronic reservations systems, or even the alert staffs of U.S. airlines, so always double-check tickets—date, flight number, check-in times, and so forth.

Even if you're taking a 10-minute flight with only half-a-dozen passengers to be boarded you'll be expected to check in *an hour and a half* before departure. I questioned this with one airline executive, and his disarming reply was: "Because the flight may leave early." He wasn't kidding, either. Moreover, to be sure of your seat, get to the check-in desk as early as possible, even if your ticket is reconfirmed—and make sure the check-in attendant sees it. Don't assume that being *in line* on time is enough to guarantee your seat.

Also, a reconfirmed ticket doesn't mean a thing until it's in the hands of the ticket agent. You can be standing politely in line, ticket in hand, and still lose your seat. The people huddled around the check-in counter may not have tickets—they may be waiting for someone not to show up. You, for example. Push your way to the front.

Always reconfirm your flight 48 hours before departure. This is very important, because some of the lines have a tendency to overbook, and some passengers have a tendency not to show up; so the airline may simply decide that if you don't reconfirm you're not going to fly and they'll give your seat to someone else. Many hotels will handle your reconfirmations, but there's nothing they can do if you wait until it's too late.

If you're taking along carry-on luggage, remember that what may qualify as carry-on size on a 747 may have to be checked on smaller island-hopping aircraft, so make sure it is locked and labeled. Also, luggage allowances on U.S. carriers may not be acceptable to local carriers, and you may find yourself paying excess baggage charges on some stretches. If you anticipate problems, see your travel agent before you leave.

ISLAND-HOPPING STOPOVERS

This is really something you have to take up with your travel agent, but I mention it here to remind you of some of the possibilities you may be overlooking for visiting several islands for the price of one. A full-revenue ticket from New York to, say, Barbados may entitle you to stop off for a few days in Antigua on the way down, in Martinique or Guadeloupe on the way back. Likewise, with a full-revenue round-trip ticket from New York to Haiti in your pocket you may be able to visit Santo Domingo and/or Puerto Rico, at no extra fare; a round-trip ticket from Miami to Tobago may also take you to St. Lucia and Trinidad. The actual stops will depend on the type of fare, day of week, season, and so on—but the prospect of seeing twice as much Caribbean for the same price is certainly worth the time it will take you to ask about island stopovers.

For serious island-hoppers, LIAT has special explorer fares, valid for 21 days or 30 days, offering up to 25 destinations from San Juan to Trinidad. They cost from around $180 to $380. For details, fax LIAT 809/462-3038.

BOAT TRAVEL

Several of the islands or groups of islands are linked by seagoing ferries.

In the Virgin Islands, the M/V *Bomba Charger*, M/V *Native Son*, and M/V *Speedy's Fantasy* operate 90-passenger, air-conditioned multihulls between Charlotte Amalie in St. Thomas and West End, Road Town, and Virgin Gorda in the British Virgins. Fares: $17 per person each way.

There are also regular services, by 20-passenger powerboat or catamaran, between St. Barthélemy and St. Maarten/St. Martin, some departures in the afternoon to connect with flights from New York and other northeastern destinations.

Cayman Islands

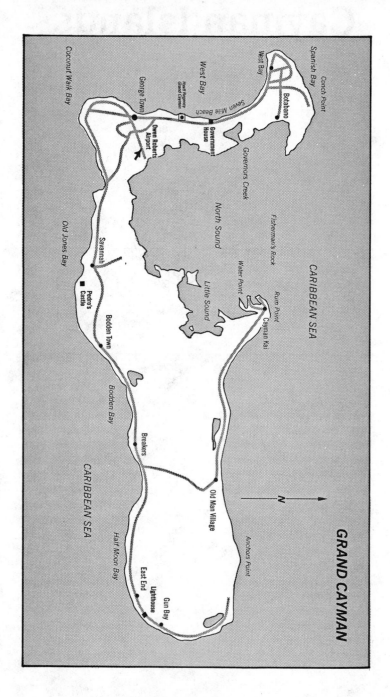

GRAND CAYMAN

Cayman Islands

There are three of them—Grand Cayman, Little Cayman, Cayman Brac. Together they're a British Crown Colony that will probably remain that way for some time because, as one local taxi driver put it, "If we got independence we'd only end up with a lot of politicians."

Otherwise, the Caymans can't seem to make up their mind what they want to be. On the one hand, the colony claims to be, as the brochures put it, "as unspoiled as it was the day Columbus sailed by"; on the other hand, a banking boom has "transformed George Town from a sleepy village into a dynamic financial capital." At last count there were about 400 banks for a population of less than 20,000 plus who knows how many mega-bucks wheeler-dealers skulking among the sea-grape trees searching for the perfect offshore banking. The islands are touted as a tax haven, but everyone seems to forget to mention that it's taxless only for people who live there or buy condominiums there; the poor visitors get zapped with a 6% tax on rooms, a $7.50 departure tax (but they *have* fixed up the airport nicely), another fee for a local driver's license, and the aftereffects of an import duty that has sent prices soaring alarmingly ($2 for a ginger ale, for example).

All of this would be easier to take if Grand Cayman, the largest of the trio, were something special. But this is no lofty, luxuriant Jamaica or St. Lucia. It's flat, swampy, and characterless (well, what else can you call a place whose prime tourist attraction is a turtle farm?). True, there are lots of beaches, most notably Seven Mile Beach running north from George Town, but they're lined with an uninspired collection of hotels and condominiums (none of them, it should be noted, higher than the palm trees, so no one can accuse the authorities of ruining the place).

What the Caymans do have—in abundance—are miles, fathoms, leagues of coral reefs, with water so clear you can spot an angel fish 200 feet away. I have it on the unimpeachable authority of world-class diver Helga Gimbel that diving in the Caymans is "AAA+ ... absolutely spectacular."

How to Get There   Daily nonstop from Miami on Cayman Airways, Pan Am, American, and Northwest; from Houston and Tampa on

Cayman Airways; from Dallas on American; in winter, charter flights once or twice a week from New York, Chicago, Detroit, Atlanta, Boston, Philadelphia, Tampa, St. Louis, and Minneapolis (and possibly others); flights once or twice daily from Grand Cayman to Cayman Brac.

Hyatt Regency Grand Cayman

Grand Cayman

☆ ♈♈ ◐◐◐ $$$

You won't find many chain hotels represented in these pages, but, like its sister resort at Dorado Beach in Puerto Rico, this $54-million resort eschews the Hyatt formula.

The architecture, described as British colonial, is really more birthday cake colonial, with white iron verandas and decorative trim "icing," a pastel-blue facade accented by flower boxes and decorative fanlights. After dark, the *mise-en-scène* becomes positively magical, what with a zillion lights gleaming through French windows, bathing the reflecting pools and fountains, spotlighting the fountains and festooning the ficus trees.

The Hyatt is just one corner of a 90-acre resort development known as Britannia, a tropical conglomerate with 1-, 2-, and 3-bedroom villas, its own beach club and marina, as well as the current hotel and one-of-a-kind golf course. The hotel itself is comprised of a courtyard of lawns, pools, and fountains surrounded by the seven wings of the hotel, the tallest of which is five stories high. At 235 rooms, it is, for my money, a hundred rooms too big, but it brings to the Caymans a touch of luxury hitherto found only in a few of the island's condominiums. The guest rooms are tastefully designed, as you'd expect from Hyatt, and equipped with all the trimmings, such as mini-bars and bathrobes. Color schemes reflect the aquas and corals of sea and sand, with flashes of lilac and pink tossed in; travertine marble layers the foyers, bathrooms, and oval bathtubs; the custom-designed furniture features mostly upholstered rattan and wicker (the only complaint here is that in the standard rooms a two-seat couch crowds the room without adding much in comfort or convenience, unless you plan to watch hours of television). For a view of the sea (about 300 yards away) you'll have to check into the top two floors; if you want private sunning space, ask for one of the 22 Terrace Rooms. The most attractive accommodations are probably the Deluxe Junior Suites (with sleeping galleries, brass beds, wet bars, and three telephone extensions); but for as much seclusion and privacy as you can muster in a hotel this size, check into the premium Regency Club and ask for a room overlooking the golf course.

Generous in all things, the Hyatt people give you a choice of dining spots—the veranda of the Britannia Golf Club & Grill, another restaurant at the beach club called Hemmingway's, and the Garden Loggia (the main dining room, stylishly decorated in bleached ash paneling with latticed ceilings, French windows opening to the al fresco garden extension). Menus are hardly predictable Hyatt fare, the English chef producing a masterly combination of continental, American, and Caribbean dishes— tenderloin of veal with braised bok choy and grilled swordfish with passion fruit butter. (Remember to make reservations for dinner: The Hyatt is the most stylish dining spot along Seven Mile Beach and popular with nonresident diners.)

Even Hyatt's water-sports facilities are a notch beyond the usual with a flagship 65-foot catamaran designed specifically for cruising around the Caymans and equipped with spacious decks, comfortable seating, stereo, bar, two restrooms, and underwater glass panels for fish watching.

But what heaps most attention on Britannia is its golf course. Jack Nicklaus not only designed the 9-hole links-style course but also designed the special Cayman Ball, a sphere that claims to do something my own tee shots have been doing for years—going half as far as they should. The advantage of the Cayman Ball in a resort like this is that players can get in 18 holes in half the time, on a course that requires space for 9 rather than 18 holes. Figure that out. The links (as beautiful as anything Nicklaus has designed) also function as an 18-hole executive course weekday afternoons and as a 9-hole regulation course on weekends. It may not be St. Andrews but at least it's another reason besides scuba diving for going to the Caymans.

Name: Hyatt Regency Grand Cayman
Manager: Malcolm Jennings
Address: P.O. Box 1588, Grand Cayman, BWI
Location: On the Britannia resort development, across the main road from Seven Mile Beach, 2 miles outside of George Town, 12 minutes and $10 from the airport
Telephone: 809/949-1234

Fax: 809/949-8528
Reservations: Hyatt Worldwide, toll free 800/228-9000
Credit Cards: All major cards
Rooms: 235, including 44 Regency Club rooms, 8 Deluxe Junior Suites, 2 Luxurious Suites, some with terraces or patios, some with small verandas, all with ceiling fans and air conditioning, fully stocked mini-bars (wet bars in suites), satellite TV, clock/radios, direct-dial telephones, bathrobes, and hairdryers; suites are duplexes with sleeping lofts and canopy beds
Meals: Breakfast 7:00–11:30, lunch 11:30–2:30 (everything from sandwiches to complete meals, at any of 4 indoor/outdoor locations), dinner 7:00–10:00 (in the fan-cooled indoor/outdoor Garden Loggia, $60–$80 for two); light snacks until midnight; Sunday champagne brunch buffet 11:30–2:30; casual resort wear appropriate in all restaurants; piano player with breakfast; no-smoking area in dining room; 24-hour room service
Entertainment: 4 bars and lounges, live music all nights except Sunday
Sports: Beach (i.e., a section of the popular Seven Mile Beach across the road), 3 freshwater swimming pools, with swim-up bar, Jacuzzi, tennis (2 Plexipave courts, with lights), croquet—all free; snorkeling gear, catamaran and Sunfish sailing, windsurfing, parasailing, paddleboats, scuba and day sails on the resort's private 65-ft. catamaran for a fee; private 9-hole golf course that can be played three ways, including 18 holes with the Cayman Ball
P.S.: At any season (at least for the first few years) you may encounter groups that come perilously close to behaving like conventioneers

Added Attractions

Cayman Kai
Grand Cayman

Cayman Kai's 42 rooms are known as Sea Lodges because of their unusual design—triangular screened patios and white tentlike roofs that make them seem like something out of a concrete Arabian Nights. But their tiled floors, ceiling fans, louvers, hammocks, loungers, and island decor are a perfect backdrop for Caribbean nights. You can spend most of your time in your tent, since they all have kitchens (deliveries made from the local supermarket upon request) and venture into the sunlight only for water sports and strolls along Cayman Kai's 1½-mile-long beach (wild, undeveloped coral strand). If you feel in the mood for dining out, you don't have to walk more than a few paces to the resort's modest bar/lounge and restaurant, and you don't have to dress up to go there, either. (You could go farther afield for dinner, of course, since you have the freedom of a room-only rate—but you would spend about $40 in taxi fares getting to and from the nearest dependable restaurant.) Avoid numbers 1–10 (which do, however, have air conditioning) as they are too close to the public areas; ask for numbers 11, 17, 18, or 24 (but maintenance is not always what it should be). 42 suites. Doubles: $130 to $250. *Cayman Kai, P.O. Box 1112, Grand Cayman, BWI. Telephone: 809-947-9056, 9055; fax: 809-947-9102.*

Divi Tiara Beach Resort
Cayman Brac

The brac is the rugged bluff that distinguishes this particular Cayman; the Divi Tiara is just the sort of hotel to help you enjoy the quiet and solitude of this unspoiled island. Since the main attraction of this small Divi hotel is the Peter Hughes Dive Center, most of the guests are underwater nuts, and the colorful room decor seems to be trying to outdazzle the reefs. Besides scuba, there are sailboards, paddleboats, a tennis court, beachside pool, and bicycles. Cuisine is undistinguished, but even the divers surface for the Sunday buffet brunch, with every dish cooked al fresco beside the pool. A new 3-story complex with 18 rooms has been added to the original 59 air-conditioned, balconied rooms and luxury apartments. Doubles: $140 to $245. *Divi Tiara Beach Resort, Cayman Islands, BWI, reservations via Divi Hotels in Ithaca. Telephone: 607/277-3484 (reservations toll free 800/367-3484); fax: 607/277-3624.*

Jamaica

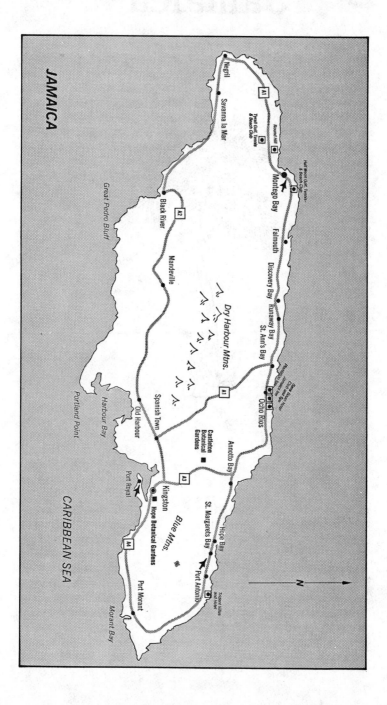

Jamaica

It's the stuff travel posters are made of—rafting down the Rio Grande, frolicking in waterfalls, limbo dancing and reggae, aristocratic plantations, and elegant villas.

Where to go in Jamaica? Most flights from North America touch down in Montego Bay before continuing to Kingston, so MoBay's the place to begin. Once a quiet honeymooners' haven, it's now crowded with tour groups, cruise ship passengers, and honky-tonk. But there's still much to enjoy—in town and in the surroundings—so begin with a few days at one of the three classy resorts just outside town. Two hours east along the north shore, Ocho Rios is a scaled-down version of MoBay, with three more of the island's top resorts and oodles of activities, from scrambling up Dunn's River Falls to touring Prospect Plantation to polo—spectating or playing—at not one but two locations. Port Antonio is the least developed of the three resorts, although visitors drive from all over the island to go rafting down the Rio Grande. You can also go horseback riding on the estate of Patrice Wymore Flynn, the widow of movie star Errol Flynn.

A tip on planning: If you find choosing where to stay as difficult as I do, you may want to look into Elegant Resorts of Jamaica's *Platinum Plan*—an all-inclusive sampler where you'll enjoy the hospitality of six of the hotels mentioned in this chapter. You might begin with a few days at one of MoBay's top resorts, with a day trip to Negril. Then, since your plane is probably going to stop at Kingston anyway (where you'll probably have to disembark while the aircraft is serviced), I suggest you sightsee your way to the airport—driving along the north shore, spending a night or two in Ocho Rios and/or Port Antonio on your way to the airport in Kingston. If you stop over in the capital itself, be sure to visit the new national gallery and the crafts boutiques, café, and restaurant at Devon House.

The selection in these pages begins on the north coast, near Montego Bay, and moves east toward Port Antonio.

How to Get There   Jamaica is now one of the easiest islands to get to from North America. Air Jamaica has nonstop or direct flights from Atlanta, Baltimore, Los Angeles, Miami, New York, Philadelphia, Washington, and Toronto (not all daily but at least frequently); American and

Continental have daily nonstop flights from New York, Pan Am has several flights a week from Miami, and there's additional service from Toronto on Air Canada.

Tryall Golf, Tennis & Beach Club

Near Montego Bay

☆☆☆☆ ♇♇♇ ➊➊➊➊ $$$

Tryall is 2,200 acres of lush Jamaican plantation that long ago switched from sugar to the sweet life. The 155-year-old Great House is a stylish 52-room inn, perched on a low hill a few hundred yards inland from the beach and surrounded by championship fairways and sumptuous villas (individually owned, uniquely individual, and oftentimes available).

Golfers know Tryall well—they've seen it past winters in live telecasts of the Mazda Seniors Tournament and, last January, in the LPGA "Jamaica Classic." It's an appealing layout: waterholes lined with coconut palms, a sixth fairway that skirts a centuries-old, still-turning waterwheel. And there are so many fruit trees lining the course—star apple, orange, breadfruit, mango—the caddies are not only expert in which clubs to play but also in having perfect timing when it comes to knowing which fruits are ripest.

Other guests never leave their knolltop for days on end. Why should they? A few paces from their Great House they have nine well-tended tennis courts. A few steps in the opposite direction, they can plunge into one of the Caribbean's most spectacular swimming pools, complete with waterfall and swim-up bar.

Tryall's guest rooms flank the driveway leading to the Great House, linked by wooden arcades draped with morning glories. The so-called Garden Terrace rooms look out on lawns and fairways; the pricier Junior Suites frame views of seashore, fairways, and the coast all the way to distant Montego Bay—distant enough to preserve Tryall's seclusion, accessible enough for occasional junkets into town to shop, dine, or hit the reggae clubs. Upper-level deluxe rooms have private balconies; lower-level rooms have lawn patios.

Recently refurbished, all 52 rooms are different, yet each is spacious, comfortable, practical. New marble bathrooms have been added to the suites, which boast large sitting areas, king-size beds, and chintz-covered furnishings. The Hibiscus and Garden Terrace rooms also have been redone in chintz, and each bathroom has been modernized.

Even the shingle-roofed, native-stone Great House, designated a national monument in 1989, has had a facelift, with furniture reupholstered in chintz, marble floors, and a new porte cochere at the end of the elliptical drive. The former card room has been transformed into a formal reception area, where guests can relax with a welcome drink as they check in. The dining room has been enlarged, with a new traditional-style "tray" ceiling, which harmonizes with the house's Georgian architecture. The al fresco terrace has also been extended to take advantage of the magnificent view. Best of all, a new bar room, with stone walls and picture windows, is currently under construction. Adjoining the eastern wing of the house, it will provide a spectacular, 180-degree view of the coastline. None of these innovations are at odds with the house's traditional elegance. If anything, they enhance it.

Guests are so pampered here they don't even have to make a reservation for dinner (villa guests and outsiders most certainly do). Early-bird sunrise watchers find Jamaican Blue Mountain coffee waiting for them on the veranda at 6:30 a.m. And even that lovely championship golf course is now reserved exclusively for villa owners and Tryall guests and the occasional visitor from nearby Round Hill.

Name: Tryall Golf, Tennis & Beach Club
Manager: Robert Raedisch
Address: Sandy Bay Post Office, Hanover Parish, Jamaica, WI
Location: On the north shore, 12 miles west of Montego Bay, 35 minutes and $40 by taxi from the airport
Telephone: 809/952-5110/1
Fax: 809/952-0401
Reservations: Robert Reid Associates
Credit Cards: All major cards
Rooms: 52 Great House rooms, some with balconies or patios, air conditioning *and* ceiling fans, direct-dial telephones, amenities baskets; most of the 52 villas, beside the beach or in the hills, are available for rent as complete, staffed units, a few with 2 bedrooms, most with 3 or 4 bedrooms
Meals: Breakfast 7:00–9:30 (continental 9:30–10:30), lunch noon–3:30 (in beachside pavilion; salads and sandwiches at Ninth Hole Bar 11:00–5:00, pool or golf clubhouse), afternoon tea 4:00–5:30, cocktails/

hors d'oeuvres 6:00–7:30 (Great House), dinner 7:00–9:30 (in the open dining terrace, approx. $70 for two); Friday evening barbecue on the beach, jackets in the evening in winter; room service during kitchen hours (Great House only); small combo or calypso trio most evenings at the Great House

Entertainment: Lounge/bar, manager's cocktail party on Monday (guests and homeowners), music for dancing every evening, VCR in meeting room, parlor games, cabaret on some evenings during the winter

Sports: Freshwater pool at Great House, pools at all the villas, beach, snorkeling, Sunfish sailing, windsurfing, paddleboats, glass-bottom boats, tennis (9 Laykold courts, 5 with lights, pro shop), golf (18 championship holes, full pro facilities); scuba, sport fishing, horseback riding, day cruises to Negril can be arranged

Round Hill
Near Montego Bay

☆☆☆☆☆ ♉♉♉ ➊➊➊ $$$$

The sweeping, casuarina-lined driveway says "class." And when you get to the crest of the hill and take in the gardens and the view of coves and mountains, it's easy to understand why this elegant resort has been hosting the rich and famous for 36 winters.

Of all the resorts along Jamaica's fabled north shore this is probably the one that still comes closest to the glory years of everyone's memories. Its villas and servants have beckoned the likes of the Oscar Hammersteins, the Moss Harts and, in Villa 25, Adele Astaire. As if that weren't cast enough for one resort, Cole Porter and Noël Coward (Villa 3) used to entertain the entertainers. Ever since, the upper crust of show business, high society, and big business has been chauffeured up that driveway in loyal streams, among them Kennedys (Jackie's favorite, Villa 10) and McCartneys. One famous American fashion and home designer even named one of his lines after this idyllic spot.

Many visitors to Round Hill have to bed down in three two-story wings alongside the beach, hitherto known as The Barracks but now rechristened Pineapple House after what passes in these conservative parts as a major renovation (new pencil-post beds handcrafted from local mahogany, pale, cool, green walls, new clay tile floors, bigger windows for better views, more space by incorporating the balconies into the rooms). In other resorts, they'd probably be the most desirable rooms because of their beachfront location; but the true Round Hill is to be found on the bosky bowl rising from the beach, what seems to be 28 acres of tropical garden planted with villas rather than the other way around. Each whitewashed, shingle-roofed villa is privately owned, 17 of them have private pools, many have recently been outfitted with new kitchens, and each is designed in such a way that it can be rented as an individual suite, with a bedroom with louvered shutters opening to a covered outdoor patio framed by bougainvillea and croton and mahogany trees. Since they're privately owned, all the villas are different. Unless you book now for winters two or three years down the line, you will almost certainly have to settle for whatever is available, but if I were specifying lodgings these are some of the villas I'd bid for: number 8 (new owners have spent a bundle installing marble floors, silk rugs, walls hand-stenciled by a specially imported Japanese craftsman, a canopy bed with pink chintz); number 13 (also new owners, who have installed a large deck, pool, and the resort's only Jacuzzi); number 6 (frilly boudoir with chinoiserie living room); number 18 (a particularly attractive high-ceilinged, arched living room, with fabrics to match the anthurium and elephant ear in the garden).

But what sets Round Hill apart is probably the service. Life here may be the closest you can come in this hemisphere to experiencing the pampering of the British Raj in India. The staff numbers 250. When you rouse yourselves in the morning, your maid sets the terrace table and prepares breakfast. Your gardener (there are 40 of them!) has already cleaned the pool and positioned your loungers to catch the morning sun. If you opt for the cove, each time you paddle into the sea you'll find a beach boy has edged your chaise around to face the sun. At the lunchtime buffet, an army of waiters totes your laden plates to your table, whisks away the empties when you're ready for refills, recharges your water glasses, holds chairs for the ladies. Laundry? Just drop it in the basket and the maid will take care of it (no charge, other than tip). Room service? If you can't be bothered trotting down the hill, the dining room will send your dinner up. There are drivers to get you to and from your rooms when you don't feel like walking, ball boys to retrieve stray serves on the tennis courts.

Many people have misconceptions about Round Hill, so let me correct three myths: It's not formal; it's not stuffy; it's not prohibitively expensive. Black tie is requested for Saturday's gala evenings, but only a handful of men actually dress up; other evenings, dress is informal (but stylishly so, of course). Everyone who wants to mingle, mingles—marquises and marchionesses included. During the peak season, general manager Josef Forstmayr (formerly of Trident Villas in Port Antonio) makes a point of inviting hotel guests to the Tuesday evening cocktail parties sometimes put on by villa owners. And with the Jamaican dollar slightly groggy as of this writing, Round Hill's rates are almost a bargain. Compare rates here (and elsewhere in Jamaica, for that matter) with some other islands; for what some down-island resorts charge for room only, Round Hill throws in a suite, personal maid, and all meals.

There are only two drawbacks to all this. All those upper-crust guests lose interest in the Caribbean come April, so Round Hill goes full tilt for a limited season. However, during spring, summer, and fall the villas are still available for solitude seekers, complete with maids who'll prepare meals, beach boys who'll mix your piña coladas—and you might have the tennis courts all to yourself.

The other minor drawback: On weekends in winter regular jet services are augmented by charter flights that occasionally shatter your sense of seclusion (they're not supposed to fly over the resorts and the owners are trying to do something about it).

But that's no reason to forego the lap of luxury, because *once* in a lifetime at least everyone should sample a week in, say, Lady Rothermere's newly renovated hillside villa, with its plush outdoor living room, a pool shared only with one other couple, an enormous deck shaded by an even more enormous cotton tree, a gardener to move your lounger around with the sun, a personal maid to bring you afternoon tea.

Name: Round Hill
General Manager: Josef Forstmayr
Address: P.O. Box 64, Montego Bay, Jamaica, WI
Location: On a promontory west of Montego Bay, about 10 miles, 25 minutes, and $32 by taxi from the airport
Telephone: 809/952-5150/5
Fax: 809/952-2505
Reservations: Robert Reid Associates
Credit Cards: All major cards
Rooms: 101, including 36 rooms in Pineapple House plus 65 suites in 27 villas; rooms in Pineapple House have walls of shutters facing the bay, standing fans or ceiling fans, telephones; villas have maids and gardeners, ceiling fans (air conditioning in some bedrooms), balconies or patios, gardens or lawns, indoor/outdoor living rooms, direct-dial telephones, kitchens (for maids' use), private or shared pools

Meals: Breakfast 8:00–10:00, lunch 1:00–2:30, snacks 11:00–7:00, dinner 7:30–9:30 (on the beachside patio beneath the almond trees, $80 for two); bamboo torchlight picnic on the beach Monday evenings, barbecue Wednesdays; dress informal, except jacket and tie on Saturday (black tie is "requested"); room service, no extra charge; music (amplified until 11:00) for dancing most evenings

Entertainment: Local band for beach picnic and barbecue; library, parlor games, art shows, VCR movies

Sports: Private beach (60 or 90 yards depending on the tides), freshwater pool, 17 villa pools, snorkeling, floats, tennis (5 courts, lights, pro)—all free; waterskiing, windsurfing, Sunfish sailing, paddleboats from the beach at extra charge; golf at Tryall, horseback riding 40 minutes away

P.S.: Some children, some small executive groups at extra charge

Half Moon Golf, Tennis & Beach Club
Near Montego Bay

☆☆☆ ♈♈♈ ◑◑◑◑ $$$$

The beach is indeed an almost perfect half moon, shaded by sea grape onshore, sheltered by a reef offshore, and dotted with tiny black-and-white shells, like the Half Moon's symbol in miniature. The first vacationers settled around their half moon in the fifties in a cluster of private cottages, each one different from its neighbor. Later expansions included undistinguished two-story wings of beachside rooms and suites and, in the past year, the tastefully renovated studios and apartments that were once the neighboring Colony Hotel. The total tally, 208 rooms, is spread along 1½ miles of beach, which in turn is a mere corner of a 400-acre estate that includes riding stables, a working ranch, and a Robert Trent Jones golf course.

Which of these varied accommodations you stay in may depend on what you want to do with your days as much as with prices. If you like to step directly from your cottage into the sea, check into one of the original cottages around the beach (some of which also have semiprivate patio pools; some have picture windows facing a tiny patch of lawn—and a big stretch of beach); the two-story wings of rooms and suites are closest to the tennis courts; and the new suites in the neo-Georgian villas of the former Colony have private maid service and each has a kitchen, which can be stocked from the commissary across the driveway. Like the casuarina trees near the half-moon beach, the beachside cottages that were opposite the tennis courts did not survive the hurricane. However, the club has replaced them with 23 one-bedroom Royal Suites, complete with cable television and black-tiled bathrooms.

Despite the rambling nature of the place, the Half Moon staff still manages to offer service in the old Jamaican tradition, and chances are maître d's and waiters will have your name down pat on your second visit to their breeze-cooled beachside domain, even if it's not Bush or Steiger, to name just a couple of recent guests.

That lovely half-moon beach may have been the reason people were first lured to this spot, but the resort's sports facilities have to be a major attraction today. Where else do you get to play a Robert Trent Jones at no extra charge? And how many resorts that promise free tennis actually give you a chance to get in a game by providing 13 courts? And with lights, too.

The club has just emerged from a $1-million overhaul of the grounds. Kingston architect/decorator Earl Levy (owner of the Trident in Port Antonio) has totally transformed the public areas with striking success, adding cupolas and courtyards and bold tropical colors (some of which, like the roof on the main building, a few cupolas, and many of the gardens, have been replaced or replanted since the hurricane).

Whether you've spent your day lolling on the beach or lobbing on the courts, the Sugar Mill Restaurant is where you may want to spend your evening, dining under the trees, softly lit by wicker-shaded hanging lights, cooled by the night breezes, warmed by one of the restaurant's spicy, flavorful specialties like Jamaican curry pot or country chicken. Located close by the golf course, the Sugar Mill is independently operated by the affable Swiss chef Hans Schenk who will honor Half Moon guest cards—if you'd like a change from the Half Moon's terrace restaurant, you might just drive down the few yards and turn in where you see the great water wheel turning.

Name: Half Moon Golf, Tennis & Beach Club
Manager: Heinz Simonitsch (part-owner/managing director)
Address: P.O. Box 80, Montego Bay, Jamaica, WI
Location: 7 miles from town; 5 miles from the airport, 10 minutes and
   $12 by taxi

Telephone: 809/953-2211
Fax: 809/953-2731
Reservations: Robert Reid Associates
Credit Cards: All major cards
Rooms: 208, including studios and superior rooms, suites, and villas, all with air conditioning, some with air conditioning *and* ceiling fans, balconies or patios, refrigerators, direct-dial telephones, some with kitchens, some with private or semiprivate pools
Meals: Breakfast 7:30–9:30 (or you can leave your order the night before, wake up, and it's ready on your balcony or patio), lunch noon–2:30, dinner 7:30–9:30 (on the open beachside patio, new covered dining room, or the Sugar Mill at the golf course, $55 to $70 for two); long-sleeved shirts after 6:00 in winter, jacket and tie requested on Saturdays, otherwise informal (but "shorts, T-shirts and jeans are not allowed"); room service in most rooms, small extra charge; live music for dancing every evening
Entertainment: Bar/lounge/terrace, live (too live) music every evening (resident band, calypso, steel band), floorshows, crab races
Sports: Beach, 17 freshwater pools (13 private or semiprivate), tennis (13 courts, 7 with lights, pro shop), golf (18 holes, pro shop), sauna, Nautilus gym, squash (4 courts)—all free; water sports on the beach (windsurfing, new Mistral windsurfing school, Sunfish sailing, scuba, snorkeling), horseback riding (with guide), massage, aerobics, table tennis, bicycles—all at an extra charge
P.S.: Some children, some seminar groups up to 120

Plantation Inn
Ocho Rios

☆☆☆ ♙♙ ◑◑ $$$

For 25 of the last 30 years or so, Plantation Inn was one of the grand names in Jamaican resorts—on a par with Round Hill and Jamaica Inn. Then it slumped in the early 1980s. But now it's bouncing back with new owners and manager Roy Yallop, heading a seasoned team that includes many long-serving waiters and chambermaids.

There are two groups of accommodations here, and all the rooms in each have been refurbished during the last two years. Rooms in the original wings are tropical, with lots of hardwoods and louvers (they're also less expensive). To the left of the dining terrace is a walkway covered in flowering vines and leading to a four-story wing of rooms and suites right on the edge of the beach. It doesn't do much for the setting when seen from the beach, but from the rooms the views are impressive—east along the coast, across the bay to Jamaica Inn.

The white-columned porte cochere may strike you as more Carolinian than Caribbean; the tiny dark-hued lounge just off reception is more Mayfair than Antillean, but once you step beyond the lobby to the terrace the setting is pure Jamaica. Masses of hibiscus and bougainvillea drape walls and railings. Flights of steps lead to a small swimming pool, then continue down to an expanse of soft, white sand. And with beachside *bohio* bar, you don't even have to come up for lunch and piña coladas.

Name: Plantation Inn
Manager: Roy W. H. Yallop
Address: P.O. Box 2, Ocho Rios, Jamaica, WI
Location: Just east of town, 1½ hours and $84 by taxi from Montego Bay airport, or $32 per person round trip by air-conditioned mini-bus, making stops along the way
Telephone: 809/974-5601
Fax: 809/974-5912
Reservations: Robert Reid Associates
Credit Cards: American Express, Visa, MasterCard, Diners Club
Rooms: 77, including rooms, junior suites, and deluxe suites, all with new air conditioning and ceiling fans, balconies overlooking the sea, telephones, some with wet bars and refrigerators, 2 with Jacuzzis
Meals: Breakfast 7:30–9:30, consommé on the beach 11:00, lunch 1:00–2:30, afternoon tea 4:00–5:30, dinner 8:00–9:30 (on the terrace or in the covered dining pavilion, $70 for two); jackets required Monday through Thursday, jacket and tie Friday and Saturday in winter, jackets only on weekends in summer; room service at no extra cost; "breakfast on your private terrace encouraged"
Entertainment: Bar/terrace, calypso music, folklore show Thursday, VCR in main lounge, card room with parlor games, live and amplified music for dancing 6 nights a week
Sports: Beach (reef-protected for good swimming and snorkeling), freshwater pool, Sunfish sailing, windsurfing, tennis (2 courts, 1 lighted), new "jungle gym" cottage with Nautilus, aerobics, sauna—all

free; golf (free fees at Upton), scuba, horseback riding, and polo nearby

P.S.: No children under 12 nine months of the year, no children under 7 in summer; some groups and seminars year-round

Jamaica Inn
Ocho Rios

☆☆☆☆ ♀♀♀ ☻☻ $$$

The loggias alone are larger than rooms in most hotels. Better furnished, too, with padded armchairs, ottomans and overstuffed sofas, breakfast tables, desks, desk lamps, fresh flowers, and drying racks for soggy swimsuits and beach towels. Have a swim before lunch and you'll find a fresh supply of big, bulky beach towels waiting for you in your rooms; have a nap or something after lunch, then a dip and, sure enough, the maid has straightened out your mussed-up bed by the time you get back. Your nap or whatever may take place in a romantic little pencil-post bed, in a tropical boudoir of cool pastel blues and greens and yellows, the sunlight filtered by green and white drapes, the breezes filtered by louvered windows and doors, the terrazzo floors softened by white rugs.

The West Wing is best—with your loggia right on the edge of the water, your front door facing the beach and garden. If you want to be right on the beach, choose the Beach Wing and you can step from your patio over a shin-high balustrade right onto the sand. If you can afford the best, ask for the Blue Suite, a self-contained cottage right on the beach; if the *very* best, then ask for the White Suite, where Winston Churchill stayed in the 1950s—it has its own small pool with a circular ramp, and a path over a private promontory to a very private sun terrace right above the sea.

The inn, once the private hideaway of a Texas millionaire, has two one-story and two two-story wings, all a pretty pastel blue, strung out along a private 700-foot beach, on 6 acres of lawns, wild banana, sea grape, hibiscus and bougainvillea, and very tall coconut palms. The covelike beach (one of the most beautiful on the island), the clear water (as cool and inviting as the bedrooms), the placid tempo and elegance of the place have been attracting devoted fans for more than a quarter of a century. Service is exemplary, mainly because one of the Morrow family, the owners, is sitting right there in the "Morrow Seat" on the terrace, with an uninterrupted view of reception, lounge, bar, dining terrace, and beach.

But ask the fans what they like most about Jamaica Inn and they'll probably tell you the food. For 28 winters, chef Battista Greco has crossed over from Europe to supervise the kitchen here, turning out meals with a cosmopolitan choice of cuisines—American, Italian, French, Jamaican (his renowned lunchtime buffets are bountiful and beautiful). He leaves again in the spring, but his spirit and recipes stay behind to satisfy less affluent off-season palates. It's not just the food, though, that makes dining at Jamaica Inn so pleasurable; dinners are served on a broad lamplit terrace with an ornamental balustrade by the edge of the sea, beneath the stars. It's the classic Caribbean setting—and you're expected to dress accordingly. With the Jamaican coconut pie or zabaglione, there's dancing under the stars on that balustraded terrace. Nondancers often retire to the croquet lawn for a moonlit duel. But there's always that big tempting loggia with the big, comfy sofa, sheltered by wild banana and serenaded by the surf.

Name: Jamaica Inn
General Manager: Rudi Schoenbein
Address: P.O. Box 1, Ocho Rios, Jamaica, WI
Location: On the eastern edge of town, $84 by taxi from Montego Bay (alert the hotel and they'll have a reliable driver there to meet you)
Telephone: 809/974-2514
Fax: 809/974-2449
Reservations: Caribbean World Resorts, toll free 800/243-9420 or 804/460-2343
Credit Cards: American Express
Rooms: 45, all with air conditioning plus fans plus breezes, large loggias, telephones; all facing the ocean
Meals: Breakfast 8:00–10:00, lunch 1:00–2:30, dinner 8:00–9:30 (beneath the stars, approx. $80 for two); jacket and tie (and often, by preference of the guests, black tie) in winter, jackets only in summer; $3 charge for room service (off-season) 8:00 a.m.–10:00 p.m.
Entertainment: Dancing to a moderately amplified four-piece combo every evening, library/lounge with masses of jigsaw puzzles
Sports: Beach (good swimming and snorkeling), freshwater pool, Sunfish sailing, croquet—all free; 1 tennis court (no charge) at adjoining hotel; scuba, boat trips, golf, horseback riding, polo (for players,

learners—and sometimes the managers cart all the guests off to a match for a jolly afternoon of spectating) nearby

P.S.: No groups, no conventions ever, no children under 14

Sans Souci Hotel Club and Spa
Ocho Rios

☆☆ ♉♉♉ ◑◑◑ $$$

From the driveway it looks like a very pink, very private hideaway on the Italian Riviera; from the sea it's a great, multitiered palazzo—splashes of pink stucco in 35 cliffside and beachside acres of tropical greenery, gazebos, and traceried terraces. Steps guide you gently past fountains and lawns, mineral pool, and freshwater pool to the waterside play area with its giant chess set.

This is the "spa" part of Sans Souci, which seems to be heavily promoted by the management—and heartily approved by many hotel guests. Jamaican owners Maurice and Valerie Facey turned one gazebo, on a promontory overlooking the ocean, into an airy but private massage room. A second suite of cabanas became Charley's Spa, where you can get everything from a rigorous exercise plan to a relaxing facial. A new beachside pavilion has a wall of mirrors so you can watch the waves as you work through a low-impact aerobic warm-up; downstairs the open-to-the-breezes exercise room has hand-held weights and Nautilus equipment. *Sans souci?* Apparently for some.

On the same level, the mineral pool, the core of the spa, is fed by a secret stream that emerges from a grotto with a big and venerable green turtle called Charley.

There's another pet in the lobby, a raucous Brazilian macaw with, apparently, a tin ear: When flautist James Galway stayed here he serenaded the feathered fool with one of his golden flutes but Sir Walter Raleigh merely squawked louder than ever.

Raleigh's domain is your first glimpse of the $4-million restyling of Sans Souci—an inviting, curving salon with French doors opening to the patio, and a raftered ceiling hung with oversized white baskets, all 16 of them trailing greenery that's replenished once a month. Beyond, a pair of arches lead to the Balloon Bar and dining room, but the most popular spot for sampling the kitchen's homemade pasta (or "spa" cuisine; the light, healthy dishes with a turtle symbol and a calorie count next to them) is the big cliff-top terrace, level with the tops of lofty flame trees, the tables shaded by umbrellas of coral pink and white stripes.

This is real snuggly-poo territory, and the owners keep nudging your thoughts in the right direction: The restaurant, for no apparent reason, is called the Casanova, there's the mineral pool and spa for toning up your muscles—and big bouncy beds for showing them off in. Plumply uphol-stered guest rooms come in one of two color schemes—bananaquit yellow or the ubiquitous Sans Souci coral pink. Valerie Facey, a decorator by profession, had the fabrics custom designed and printed right here on the island and redesigned the bathrooms with marble (and the quietest flushers you've ever heard). A one-bedroom suite, D20, is one of the hotel's most desirable aeries, sort of a penthouse with 30 feet of red-tiled terrace, loungers at one end, dining table for six beneath a wooden pergola and views past the palms to the sea *and* westward to the moun-tains and sunsets. Since Sans Souci's guest rooms are spread along paths and stairways, it might be smart to ask for lodgings, depending on your tastes, closer to the beach and tennis courts or closer to the pools and spa.

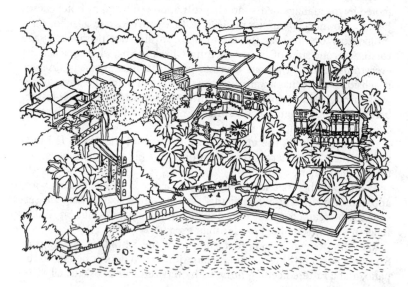

Beachside accommodations are probably the quietest. The "E" wing is a bit too close to the amplified terrace band and exercise pavilion. Unless you keep the air conditioning on, you may be bothered by strains of "My Way" (definitely not sung Sinatra's way), and if you're on your terrace, breakfasting on those delicious (and caloric) jams and fresh muffins, do you really want to hear "Stretch, 2, 3, 4"?

Name: Sans Souci Hotel Club and Spa
Manager: Werner Dietl
Address: P.O. Box 103, Ocho Rios, Jamaica, WI
Location: 2 miles east of town, 60 miles from Montego Bay airport, $84 by taxi
Telephone: 809/974-2353
Fax: 809/974-2544
Reservations: Robert Reid Associates
Credit Cards: American Express, Visa, MasterCard
Rooms: 71 rooms and suites in 5 two-story and three-story wings, all ocean views, but 1 with balcony, ceiling fan, *and* air conditioning, telephones, tea/coffee makers
Meals: Breakfast 7:00–10:00, lunch noon–3:00, afternoon tea 4:00–5:00, dinner has 2 sittings 7:00 and 8:30 (approx. $80 for two, on the terrace beneath the stars or in the fan-cooled Casanova Restaurant); jackets in winter ("no shorts or jeans"); room service 7:00 a.m.–9:00 p.m., no extra charge; music (amplified) from the next terrace down
Entertainment: Piano player in Balloon Bar, live music in band shell, folklore shows, backgammon, chess, Scrabble, cable TV/VCR in separate lounge
Sports: Small beach, 2 pools (1 mineral spring), tennis (4 Laykold courts, 2 with lights, pro shop)—all free; water sports concession on beach (waterskiing, sailboats, windsurfing, scuba, snorkeling trips, paddleboats, picnic cruises), spa (sauna, weights, 2 whirlpools [1 mineral], massage, facials, exercise programs), extra charge; golf (18 holes), horseback riding, and polo (clinics, instruction, rentals) nearby
P.S.: Some children during holidays, a few seminars, special pro-am tennis week in mid-January
P.P.S.: At presstime, Sans Souci had been bought by new owners, who plan major changes.

Trident Villas and Hotel
Port Antonio

☆☆☆☆☆ ♀♀♀ ◑◑ $$$$

White breakers come plunging through, under, and over the craggy coral. A winding pathway leads to a gazebo for two that seems to float in the middle of the sea spray. Farther along the coast, scores of waves spume and fume, the Blue Mountains crowd the shore, the narrow road winds among villaed coves and lush green headlands. This is one of the more dramatic corners of Jamaica and Trident makes the most of its setting. Of all the small luxury hideaways along Jamaica's north shore, here is the one that most magically puts you into another world. Screened from the roadway by garden walls, it's a whitewashed, shingle-roofed enclave of gardens and courtyards, with most of its villas strung out along the edge of the shore, cuddled in bougainvillea and allamanda. At one end of the garden, a big circular swimming pool sits atop the coral; at the other, a columned doorway leads to a secluded cove with private beach and lagoon.

The main lodge has something of the look of one of those whitewashed, black-trimmed staging-post inns in England's Lake District. Even the interiors are more English country house than Antillean resort, the drawing room decked with striped fabrics and wingback armchairs, the dining room with Oriental rugs and Baccarat flambeaux. The villas and rooms display many of the grace notes associated with its owner, Jamaican architect Earl Levy—peaked shingle roofs, roughcast stucco, lattice window grills and ornamentation, gazebos, and clay tile patios.

Villa 1 is still my favorite nest here, 20 paces from the lodge, screened from its neighbors by hedgerows and shrubbery. The French doors of the living room open to a patio for wave watching, a dainty gazebo (lovely spot for breakfasts for two), a patch of lawn separated by a low wall from the coral. In the bedroom, a bay window forms a sunny reading nook with an armchair, foot stool, and reading lamp. The living room sports color-coordinated wicker chairs and sofas (custom-made on the Patrice Wymore Flynn estate), tile floors, louvered windows, and an antique desk and end tables, every flat surface a potential setting for vases of fresh tropical flora, plucked that morning by the maids. Colors and furnishings vary from suite to suite, but each is a minor masterpiece, no concessions to untropical carpeting or air conditioning. The most impressive accommodation is the Imperial Suite, a 2,000-square-foot duplex in the Tower Wing—dining room and living room downstairs, a twisting white stairway swirling to a capacious bedroom where three more mahogany steps put you onto the mammoth four-poster bed.

In previous editions of this guide I questioned whether vacationers would want to dress up every evening, dine indoors in an air-conditioned, chandeliered salon, consuming seven-course, fixed-menu dinners served by white-gloved waiters. Well, apparently they do. Even Monty Python's John Cleese and actor Kevin Kline, Broadway stars Betty Buckley and Tommy Tune, fashion stars Klein and Blass, princes, princesses, and duchesses. (The meals are nicely paced, with small portions, classic cuisine accented with local variations such as ackee pâté, smoked blue marlin with capers, and red snapper patties; the menu is posted each morning in the lobby; if you're on a diet you can order substitutes.)

Perhaps Trident's distinguished guests enjoy their dinner hours because here's a resort that doesn't feel obliged to regale you with amplified music. A pianist plays in the drawing room; a local trio known as the Jolly Boys—guitar, rumba box, and banjo—plays on the terrace. (They have an amazing repertoire, including their own compositions, which are both jolly *and* wicked.)

And that's about it as far as nightlife is concerned, unless you trot into town for a night of reggae at the Roof Club, or guests like Betty Buckley and Tommy Tune entertain you after dinner in the drawing room.

It's not unknown for the manager to round up a party of guests and take them rafting on the Rio Grande, riding on the Flynn ranch, or hiking to a secret waterfall for a picnic and swim. But wherever you disappear to by day, be back on the terrace by 4:30, when Mrs. McHardy, a gracious Queen Mum of a lady, oversees afternoon tea. Silver pots. Wedgwood china. Finger sandwiches and home-baked cake. Peacocks and peahens preen expectantly—Oscar, Otto, Ophelia, Ozzie, and offspring. It's all very civilized, very garden partyish. Even the breakers calm down.

Name: Trident Villas and Hotel
Manager: Louis Karer
Address: P.O. Box 119, Port Antonio, Jamaica, WI
Location: A few miles east of Port Antonio, 2 hours and $84 by taxi from Kingston, 20 minutes by air ($100 per plane, included in the hotel rate if you stay 7 nights or more); the Port Antonio airstrip is about 15 minutes from the hotel
Telephone: 809/993-2602, 2705, 2809, 2838
Fax: 809/993-2590
Reservations: Robert Reid Associates; Flagship Hotels & Resorts
Credit Cards: All major cards
Rooms: 30 rooms, including 15 villas, 13 junior suites, and 2 deluxe suites, all with ceiling fans and louvers, balconies or patios, telephones; all villas have refrigerators and wet bars, some have kitchenettes
Meals: Breakfast "from 7:30 on," lunch "whenever," afternoon tea 4:30–5:30 (all served on the awning-covered terrace), dinner 8:00–10:00 ($80 for two, in the main dining room, cooled by fans or air conditioning); Jamaican buffet Thursdays; jackets required, jacket and tie preferred; room service for breakfast and lunch only, no extra charge
Entertainment: Bar/lounge, piano player, calypso trio every evening ("no amplification ever"), occasional folklore shows, parlor games in drawing room

Sports: Beach, freshwater pool, snorkeling, Sunfish sailing, tennis (2 courts, no lights)—all free; massage, windsurfing, scuba can be arranged, horseback riding (with guides) on the Patrice Wymore Flynn Ranch

P.S.: "Children any age, any time," but it's not really suitable for young children

Added Attractions

The Admiralty Club
Port Antonio

Trembly Knee Cove is, according to the welcome brochure, a "clothes optional beach."

Crusoe's Beach, the alternative, is a stretch of windswept, reef-rimmed sand with a palm-thatched bar, a wooden jetty with a sundeck at the tip and steps into a sandy-bottomed swimming hole.

To get to either beach you have to walk—four or five minutes maximum—because the only vehicle on this islet is a beat-up blue Jeep used for hauling luggage and furniture. ("We're getting a new Jeep . . . maybe next week.")

In other words, you're not basking in the lap of luxury here, except for those ineffable luxuries of seclusion: a private cay, secret pathways through your own mini–rain forest, coral outlooks you share with only 30 or so fellow escapists.

Half of those guests check into seven beachside studios—individual wood-framed bungalows with two walls of louvered shutters that fold right back to join the veranda as one large living space. The sturdy wooden furniture is handmade, right there in the workshop beneath the clubhouse; the beds are topped by canopies of mosquito netting (more romantic than functional). Remaining accommodations are in wood-and-louver cottages with two or three bedrooms.

Getting away from it all, however, doesn't mean that you should have to sleep on uncomfortable beds, looking at dusty ceilings, then go for an early morning walk through uncleared hurricane foliage debris. The Admiralty Club needs to get a bit more shipshape.

Still, there's the pleasant dining room and yacht-clubby bar/lounge that rises on stilts above the water's edge, with just the right amount of fancying up for a castaway's cay. Three guest rooms, 6 deluxe studio, 2 one-bedroom, and 5 two-bedroom bungalow suites. Doubles (1989): $155 to $315 MAP. *The Admiralty Club, P.O. Box 188, Port Antonio, Jamaica, WI. Telephone: 809/993-2667; fax: 809/993-2041.*

The Jamaica Palace Hotel
Port Antonio

An alternative to Trident, just down the road, for any vacationer who insists on television, air conditioning, 24-hour room service, and a 114-foot swimming pool in the shape of Jamaica. This imposing 80-suite palace was built by an Austrian baroness with a hankering, it seems, for *Alt Wien* since she has decked it out with Meissen china, antiques, chandeliers, and other nonislandy touches like silken potted plants and concrete pedestals for the beds. The main road lies between the Palace and what the brochure refers to as "the Palace's private beach." Not everyone's idea of Jamaica (and certainly not Port Antonio), but the rates may make up for shortcomings on that score. Doubles: winter 1991–92, $120 to $310, room only. *The Jamaica Palace Hotel, P.O. Box 277, Port Antonio, Jamaica, WI. Telephone: toll free 800/423-4095 (reservations only) or 809/993-3459.*

Haiti

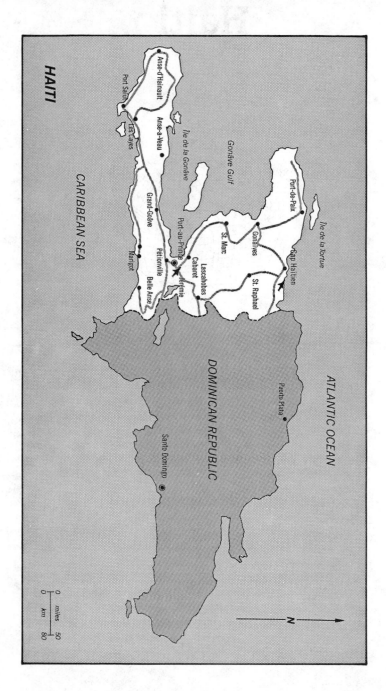

Haiti

As readers of previous editions of this guidebook well know, I'm a big fan of Haiti. It's everything people say it is. Mysterious. Vibrant. Hot. Spooky. Damp. Poor. Fun-loving. Sensual. Edgy.

Haiti, more than any other Caribbean island, is an *experience*. I wish I could exhort you to go there, but I hesitate to rate most hideaways in Haiti, especially with the demise of the beloved Oloffson. Because of the unsettled state of the nation, there seems to be little enthusiasm on the part of tourists to go there. (American tourists, that is. Haiti still has a loyal following among Europeans.) Consequently, most (but not all) hotels have been holding back on renovations and refurbishing. Since conditions there can change at any time, for better or worse, I skipped a research trip to Haiti this time around. What you have in the following pages, therefore, are reminders rather than recommendations, based on previous visits to the island.

How to Get There   From New York, daily nonstop flights on American, one-stop flights on Pan Am; from Miami, nonstop on Pan Am, ALM, and Air France; from Montreal, once-a-week nonstops on Air Canada.

Added Attractions

Le Relais de L'Empereur
Petit-Goâve

At first glance, it doesn't look like a hotel. Its imposing three-story colonial facade and the flag unfurled above the entrance seem to herald a town hall. But don't drive past; it is the ensign of the Relais de l'Empereur, the creation of Oliver Coquelin, inspired founder of the legendary but now defunct Habitation Leclerc. Once again, a precious if slightly impractical gem fit for an emperor (in this case, Haitian emperor Faustin I, who lived in this very building between 1849 and 1856).

Inside, it may remind you more of a French country inn than a tropical resort. Everything is solid and cozy, with only the terraces open to the breezes. There are just 10 guest rooms, each exquisitely furnished with antiques, their beige walls accented by ceiling beams and heavy, dark wooden terrace doors. Each room has a terrace facing either the mountains or the village square with the blue bay beyond. Ceiling fans spin softly in the rooms (there's no air conditioning, nor is it needed most of the time). There are no windows, only the louvered terrace doors, and when they are closed some people might find the effect a bit somber, even claustrophobic.

But no one will fault the marvelous king-size four-posters that dominate the rooms—some brass, others mahogany, all with plenty of room for maneuvering. As if that's not enough, the spotlight is shared by huge porcelain bathtubs ornamented with gold-plated fixtures. Real sybarites' dreams. In most rooms the tubs (and washbasins, also with gold-plated fixtures) are accorded a place of honor on a platform within the bedroom itself; but for those guests who want more privacy when bathing and mystery when dressing, or just don't like tubs anyway, there are two guest rooms with enclosed shower stalls.

The atmosphere is peaceful and serene, except, that is, when punctured by street noises. This is, after all, a *relais* in the heart of a typically Haitian town, charming, unspoiled, but tropical and exuberant.

There's not much to do in Petit-Goâve, which you can explore in half an hour. It's certainly no place for anyone who demands activity or lively nightlife. There's no swimming pool on the premises, only a lovely, leafy courtyard with caged birds and tables shaded by *ombrelles*. So, what do you do?

Board a powerboat for a half-hour trip to Cocoyer Beach, a long sliver of white sand with clear blue water framed by coco palms (or *cocoyers*). The only way to get to this Eden is by boat, and although a few day-trippers from hotels in Port-au-Prince usually go along, too, you can enjoy delicious privacy once you're there. The beach barbecue (free to hotel guests) is complemented with punch and fresh coconuts.

Back at the Relais, glowing from hours in the sun (and, perhaps, the bathtub), guests gather for apéritifs and dinner, elegantly served, and quite outstanding—real Haitian cuisine prepared by a local chef, François. You dine family-style at 8:30, seated with other guests, unless you request a table for yourselves.

The Relais, like Petit-Goâve itself, is not for everyone, but it most certainly is an experience for the special few who appreciate hideaways off the beaten track, who prefer the charm, say, of a mews house to the open space of a penthouse, who appreciate elegant appointments and the special mystique of Haiti. 10 rooms. *Le Relais de l'Empereur, P.O. Box 11399, Carrefour, Haiti, WI. Telephone: 509/350-810. No credit cards.*

Hotel Ibo Lélé
Pétionville

Entering the 70-room Ibo Lélé is like stepping into a Haitian painting: The salmon pink walls almost throb with brightly colored murals by local artists Antonio Joseph and Tamara Baussan, wife of the architect-owner. For some people, the atmosphere of Ibo Lélé may be almost as exuberant as the decor, but the guest rooms themselves are more secluded, staggered across the terraced hillside. Some of the most attractive (and least expensive) rooms are the "standard" accommodations in the entrance patio; some of them have striking doors and headboards hand-carved from local hardwoods, and small balconies overlooking the garden. There's not much to do here except relax in the springlike temperatures or make forays into Port-au-Prince; if you want to enjoy a more sporty life you can exchange a few nights here for a few nights at the Baussans' Ibo Beach resort on Cacique Island, where you'll find three lighted tennis courts, three pools, sailboards, pedal boats, and just about every water sport you could ask for, including scuba-diving. Accommodations are in small, basic but attractive "chalets" (each with private bath and terrace); but Ibo Beach is also a popular spot for day-trippers and on a busy day it is as peaceful as St. Tropez in August. Still, two days by the beach in Cacique and two in the hills of Pétionville make an interesting mix. 70 rooms. *Hotel Ibo Lélé, P.O. Box 1237, Port-au-Prince, Haiti, WI. Telephone: 509/370-845.*

Hotel Mont Joli
Cap-Haitien

At its best, the hotel lives up to its name, a pretty mountain setting of gardens and vine-covered terraces overlooking the bay, the town, and the great gleaming dome of the cathedral. The dome was constructed by the father of the Mont Joli's present owner, and Mont Joli was the family home until it became a hotel in 1956. The oldest (and prettiest) of the 30 rooms are furnished with 100-year-old French colonial beds, wardrobes, and chairs, mostly in sturdy mahogany; the remaining 6 rooms are in two-story wings, and a dozen new mini-suites in the terraced garden at the rear. Room 1, in the old wing, is particularly attractive, separated from the others by a porch, with a small terrace overlooking the sea; room 2 sports a canopied bed. All rooms have air conditioning (rarely necessary at this elevation—200 to 300 feet above the sea—for cooling but helpful for shutting out the sounds of crowing cocks and barking dogs). 30 rooms. *Hotel Mont Joli, P.O. Box 12, Cap-Haitien, Haiti, WI. Telephone: 509/320-300.*

Hotel Beck
Cap-Haitien

You've heard of hotels with their own nurseries, others that make their own furniture, but here's a remarkable little inn with its own nursery, workshop, and its own lime kiln. The rooms are constructed from stones dug up and fashioned by hand right here on the plantation; the furniture is handcrafted in the inn's workshop from mahogany trees grown on the estate. Even the drinks are cooled by "spring-fed" ice cubes, and the same spring supplies the water for the big swimming pool.

This self-sufficient hotel, like its near neighbor, the Mont Joli, started out as a private home for the family that has been running the plantation for four generations. The family chef has been here more than 20 years, and since the Becks were originally German, the menus are likely to feature *sauerbraten* and *marmorkuchen* alongside chicken Haiti-style.

The guest rooms are solidly comfortable, furnished throughout with estate-grown mahogany, the best of the batch being the half dozen new rooms above the pool area. All the rooms have air conditioning, although most of the time you won't need it. "This is the coolest spot in town," claims Kurt Beck, but even without the mellowing effect of the mountains, trees, and deep verandas, this is a refreshing garden to return to after an expedition up the Citadelle. 16 rooms. *Hotel Beck, P.O. Box 48, Cap-Haitien, Haiti, WI. Telephone: 509/320-001.*

Hotel Cormier Plage
Cap-Haitien

Your first impression says no-frills beachcombers' resort, and your second impression confirms it. The surprises come later. The parking lot seems to merge with the beach; the front office is a small *bohio* with screen walls;

the gentleman with Jacotte the parrot perched on his big toe is Jean-Claude the co-owner. Ahead of you, a massive almond tree shades a score of wooden loungers; a few hammocks are strung between the palms and sea grapes; and beyond them stretches half a mile of sand and reef, with a few native fishing boats hauled up on the beach. The 30 guest rooms (or most of them) are scattered among the garden's 26 varieties of hibiscus; 10 small thatch-and-wattle cottages modeled on the native huts you passed on the way from town, plus 20 rooms in two new wings, each with terrace. They're furnished with French colonial antiques, and have straw-matted doors; bedspreads and lamps are covered with voodoo motifs; each room is equipped with louvers and table fan.

While you're having dinner, a quartet of the fishermen you saw on the beach earlier in the day (and who probably caught the snapper or lobster you had for dinner) settle outside the lounge to play haunting Haitian songs. (Ask them to play "Ibo Lélé" and you'll see what I mean.) To top it all off, when you return to your cottage, you find that your chambermaid has turned down the bed, replenished your ice bucket, and put a match to the bug-repelling candle. Your first impression was right: Cormier Plage is a beachcombers' resort—but with many extra attentive little touches. 30 units. *Hotel Cormier Plage, P.O. Box 70, Cap-Haitien, Haiti, WI. Telephone: 509/321-000.*

Hotel Roi Christophe
Cap-Haitien

In a historic byway such as Cap-Haitien you may want to forego an inn by the beach or a room with a view of sea or mountains and check into a hotel that captures something of the character of this offbeat town. The Hotel Roi Christophe more than fits the bill. Built in 1724, once the home of the French governor, M. de Chatenoy, its sturdy stucco walls rise two stories from lush tropical gardens. Modern facilities, air conditioning, and private bathrooms complement old-world features such as ceilings and arcaded halls, wooden beams, and elaborate chandeliers. But it's the cloisterlike gardens that will surely capture your heart. Strolling in them or sunning yourselves beside the Olympic-size pool, it will hardly seem possible that this 18-room inn is right in the center of town. Although the inn is full of character and charm, not all of the rooms are what you would hope for: The "standard" rooms tend to be small and somber, more suitable for the governor's underlings than for his excellency in person.

The six superior rooms, on the other hand, are outstanding—yet still reasonably priced.

Many visitors consider the beamed dining room of the Roi Christophe to be the best in Cap-Haitien—its ambitious cuisine, a combination of Creole and French, beautifully prepared and presented. As a Frenchman, old Governor Chatenoy might well be proud of what's become of his home. 18 rooms. *Hotel Roi Christophe, P.O. Box 34, Cap-Haitien, Haiti, WI. Telephone: 509/320-414.*

Hotel La Jacmélienne
Jacmel

You reach Jacmel from Port-au-Prince by driving south past some of the greenest, lushest scenery in all of Haiti. First, the sugar plantations, then the mountains, with their dizzying, winding roads, clear air, and views that seem to go on forever. Not too long ago the trip took all day, but a new superhighway gets you there in about two hours. It's a demanding drive nonetheless, and once in Jacmel, you will probably want to stay a while. The perfect place: La Jacmélienne.

It's a sprawling, contemporary two-story structure directly on the beach at the edge of town. Everything about La Jacmélienne is light and airy and unpretentious—lobby and reception are open to the breezes; a covered dining room, on the second floor, is exposed on two sides; guest rooms are spacious and bright with private terraces facing the water. Even the spirit is open and expansive, due no doubt to the personality of owners/managers Erick and Marlene Danies. Crisply uniformed Jacméliennes take your order and graciously serve you lunch—simple, well-prepared Haitian specialties at reasonable prices.

La Jacmélienne can be a lively place, from the Haitian band that serenades you at dinner nightly and at lunch on weekends to the crowds who linger at the pool and beach. Although there are only 31 rooms, the hotel is a popular spot for day-trippers from Port-au-Prince, with the result that on busy weekends there might be upward of 150 people, including families, enjoying themselves. Beach and pool are both large, however, and there's plenty of room for privacy. In any case, the visitors clear out around sunset and you and the other guests have the place to yourselves.

The Jacmélienne's dark sand beach is unexceptional, but there are several white sand beaches nearby, considered to be among the best on the island. You can also explore the town with its colonial architecture (reminiscent of New Orleans) and art galleries. But best of all you can rent a horse, ride into the mountains, and spend an afternoon beside the waterfall of the *bassin bleu* (blue pool) looking for the nymphs who, according to legend, cavort in the mountain grottoes. 31 rooms. *Hotel La Jacmélienne, Rue St. Anne, Jacmel, Haiti, WI. Telephone: 509/224-899; fax: 509/465-778.*

Villa Creole
Pétionville

This is a favorite of many longtime visitors to Haiti. A sprawling (70 rooms) white structure high in the hills of Pétionville (near the deluxe El Rancho, without a harbor view), it has a large swimming pool, attentive staff, and restful atmosphere. The public and private rooms are tastefully decorated. The outdoor dining areas are charming. Guest rooms are a mixed bag. All are air conditioned (necessary), but the hot exhaust ruins too many of the terraces. If you do stay here, I recommend the three "special deluxe" rooms (509, 609, and 710) in the new wing, built in 1977 and recently redecorated with Haitian furniture and marble bathrooms. Each has two terraces to capture the sun at all angles. They're private and quiet. Nelson Rockefeller once stayed in room H in the old wing; its large terrace is, unfortunately, enclosed, but the room is big, comfortable, and quiet, and you can always imagine that the red carpet actually laid down for Rockefeller still leads to the door. 72 rooms. *Villa Creole, P.O. Box 126, Port-au-Prince, Haiti, WI. Telephone: 509/571-570; fax 509/574-935.*

Le Picardie
Pétionville

Yet another private home turned hotel, the Picardie has only 10 rooms, of average size and ordinary decor, each with private bath plus terrace or garden. Swimming pool and gourmet restaurant overlook Port-au-Prince and the harbor. One guest room has a huge terrace with the same view. Ask for it. This place rarely advertises (most people, even in Port-au-Prince, don't know it exists), but its rooms are always full by word of mouth. 10 rooms. *Le Picardie, P.O. Box 2150, Pétionville, Haiti, WI. Telephone: 509/171-822.*

Prince Hotel
Port-au-Prince

Like many of the most charming hotels in Haiti, the Prince was originally a private home. Located in the hilly residential area of Pacot, just behind the Oloffson, it has 33 rooms, all with air conditioning and small terraces (some with harbor views). There's a small swimming pool, a large public terrace with a magnificent view, and a pleasant if unextraordinary dining room. The public rooms are furnished with antiques and the walls are adorned with Haitian paintings. The private rooms, on the other hand, leave something to be desired—moderate size, small bathrooms, sturdy dark mahogany furnishings, and rather somber atmosphere. Still the place has great charm and character, a European ambience, and reasonable prices. 33 rooms. *Prince Hotel, P.O. Box 2151, Port-au-Prince, Haiti, WI. Telephone: 509/152-764.*

Manoir Alexandre
Jacmel

Perhaps the most adorable hotel in all of Haiti, the little Manoir Alexandre in Jacmel perches on a hill overlooking the bay, a private home before it was converted to a 6-room hotel. Outside, a large flower-decked porch faces the sea, while inside, family heirlooms and bric-a-brac tastefully decorate the dining room and drawing rooms. The bedrooms, though, are strictly for travelers who want real island atmosphere—sparsely furnished, no private baths, only two rooms with double beds, and they don't seem too sturdy. But for charm and price this *manoir* would be hard to beat. 6 rooms. *Manoir Alexandre, Jacmel, Haiti, WI. Telephone: 509/182-711.*

The Dominican Republic

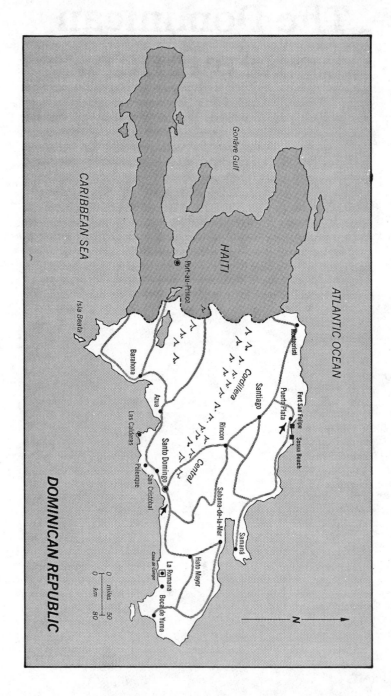

The Dominican Republic

It's the other part of Hispaniola, Columbus's favorite *La Isla Española,* which it shares with Haiti. The first permanent European settlement in the Americas was here, in a place called Montecito, founded the year after Columbus arrived in 1492. A few years later, Columbus's brother, Bartolome, founded a city on the banks of the Ozama River and named it New Isabella; we now know it as Santo Domingo. At one time Santo Domingo was the most important city in the Caribbean, and it was from here that renowned conquistadors set forth on their expeditions to colonize the surrounding lands—Diego Velázquez to Cuba, Hernán Cortés to Mexico, and Juan Ponce de León to Puerto Rico, which is less than 60 miles to the east. In recent years, the Dominican government has been forging ahead with an impressive program to preserve and restore the old colonial city. It's well worth a visit.

But Santo Domingo's surprises don't end with the old colonial section; it also has one of the largest botanical parks in the world, a zoological park with five miles of pathways and one of the largest bird cages in the world, and somewhere in the city there's a Museum of Miniatures with a fully clothed flea.

How to Get There   Daily nonstop flights from New York by American, Pan Am, Continental, and Dominicana de Aviación, and nonstop from Miami by American, Pan Am, and Dominicana; there are also flights direct to Casa de Campo from San Juan by American Eagle and Air BVI. (The Caso de Campo's airstrip is listed under La Romana in airline directories.)

Casa de Campo
La Romana

☆☆☆ ♈♈♈ ◑◑◑◑ $$$

The original "ambience" here was designed by Oscar de la Renta and the hotel brochure almost has you thinking that every last guest was designed by de la Renta.

True, many celebrities vacation here and several of them have built private homes on the property, but La Romana's "house in the country" is a pleasant, informal resort with few airs—designed not so much for beautiful people as active people. And how!

Two golf courses (one seaside, one inland) designed by Pete Dye are the pride of the project. With reason. Both are highly rated by pros, but for average duffers they promise more frustration than relaxation. A third Pete Dye course opened in 1989, but it is reserved for the exclusive use of the homeowners. Tennis facilities are so extensive they get a "village" all to themselves, across the main road, where you'll find both Har-Tru and clay courts (10 with lights), ball machines—even ball boys. There are, on a casual count, a dozen swimming pools, and 500 quarter horses and 500 polo ponies in the equestrian center. Even the polo fields come in pairs.

William Cox was the architect who pulled the whole thing together and created a sprawling complex that nevertheless manages to be compatible, more or less, with its Dominican surroundings. Buildings (never higher than three stories, mostly two) are finished in stucco, with red corrugated roofs, native stone and rough-hewn local hardwoods. Interiors sport floors of hand-fired tile, screened-glazed-and-louvered doors, local paintings, and boldly patterned fabrics. Every hotel room has a stocked refrigerator and patio or balcony; villa suites are larger and more luxuriously appointed.

All in all, Casa de Campo doesn't sound like the creation of a big, corporate conglomerate, but that's exactly what it is—or was. The Gulf + Western Corporation started the project in a corner of its 7,000-acre sugar plantation, but sold everything—sugar, land, hotel, horses, golf balls—to the Fanjul brothers of Palm Beach, Florida, a family also heavily into sugar plantations. As homeowners themselves on the Casa de Campo estate, they were probably eager to buy up a project 11 times larger than Monaco.

The problem is, Casa de Campo is getting to be more *casa* than *campo*, with new villas going up everywhere and a new 150-room hotel planned alongside an already crowded beach. Nowadays, you almost have to plan your travels around this hotel as diligently as you might plan a tour of Caribbean islands: Tennis is here, golf is there, stables thataway, and the closest beach somewhere else. So the first thing guests do when they get here is rent a "villa cart" or moped, to avoid standing around waiting for shuttle buses. (In fact, smart guests reserve their carts when they reserve their rooms.)

The hotel is organized around a handsomely designed core of restaurants, lounges, terraces, patios, courtyards, and a spectacular split-level pool with swim-up bar and thatch-roofed lounge. Grouped around it are the hotel "casitas." Golf villas are half a mile or so east; the equestrian center, polo fields, and tennis courts are across the main island road; Altos de Chavon, the resort's arts-and-culture village, with a range of restaurants, boutiques, and ateliers, is a few miles farther east. There are private homes on the hill (some for rent, others like the Pucci place strictly private) and private homes (like de la Renta's) down by the spectacular shoreline—and adjoining the resort's private airport. In all, there are more than 1,000 rooms for rent at Casa de Campo, half of them in casitas, half in private villas.

To fill all those beds, the resort has to haul in groups and conventions (a new convention center is in the cards), and since groups and conventions are unwieldy, many of them arrive directly at the airstrip—once the private preserve of corporate mini-jets.

With all those rooms, all those acres, and a staff of 2,000, management obviously can't keep an eye on every detail. Hence, some flaws in basic amenities: New villas with connecting doors between rooms are not soundproof; valet service is tentative (I had to bully a concierge—young and untutored but dressed by de la Renta—into having a pair of pants pressed, not even laundered); and how do you think Oscar de la Renta would feel if a waiter arrived at six o'clock the evening before he checked out to do an inventory of his refrigerator—then locked it? These gripes aside, it should be emphasized that the staff is pleasant even if not always polished, rates are reasonable, and you can eat well at modest prices (there you are, out there in the boonies, miles from the nearest cantina, and they don't try to gouge you—you can have a huge custom-made breakfast for just $7).

And even if you never catch so much as a glimpse of the polo-playing, party-giving, trendsetting socialites who fill the usual glossy articles about Casa de Campo, here's a place where you can never say you're bored. Ever.

Name: Casa de Campo
Manager: Luigi Fedele
Address: La Romana, Dominican Republic
Location: On the southeast coast, 1½–2 hours from Santo Domingo airport, 2–2½ hours from the capital itself; the resort has an air-conditioned lounge at the airport and hostesses to escort you to air-conditioned mini-buses for the ride to La Romana ($50 per couple round trip), but have your travel agent look into the possibility of flying direct to the resort via San Juan on an American Eagle 66-seater turboprop
Telephone: 809/523-3333
Fax: 809/523-8548
Reservations: Own Miami Office, toll free 800/8 PREMIER
Credit Cards: American Express, Visa, MasterCard
Rooms: 1,000, in casitas and in suites of various sizes in villas and homes of various sizes; all casitas have air conditioning, ceiling fans, and louvers, wet bars and stocked refrigerators, balconies or patios, direct-dial telephones
Meals: Breakfast, lunch, and dinner somewhere on the resort or at Altos de Chavon from 7:00 a.m. to midnight in one or other of the 9 restaurants (some with taped or live music); dinner for two anywhere from $25 to $80; informal dress, but long trousers for men everywhere after 6:00 p.m. and jackets or long-sleeved shirts in the hotel's Tropicana Restaurant; room service, limited menu, $5 extra per tray
Entertainment: Bars, lounges, taped and live music, dancing, disco, movies, folklore shows, occasional concerts and recitals at Altos de Chavon
Sports: 3 beaches, 19 pools (plus some semiprivate pools); you pay for just about everything else—boat trips to Catalina Island, snorkeling, windsurfing, Hobie Cats, Sunfish sailing, scuba, deep-sea fishing, waterskiing, tennis (13 Har-Tru courts, 10 with lights, full pro shop), an enlarged fitness center (squash, racquetball, massage, sauna, whirlpool, exercise equipment), 350-acre trap and skeet shooting club, 150-station shooting center, horseback riding (Western and English, with *vaquero* guides only), polo instruction and rentals, golf (2 superb Pete Dye courses), pheasant hunts

Added Attractions

Hostal Palacio Nicolás de Ovando
Santo Domingo

The *palacio* of Diego Columbus, the discoverer's son, is a few yards away at the end of Calle de las Damas; the Casas Reales, the former administration buildings, are directly across the street; a short stroll will bring you to the first city hall, the first university, the first hospital, and the oldest cathedral (where the remains of Christopher Columbus are said to be buried in a marble-and-bronze mausoleum) in the Americas.

The 55-room Hostal itself has been created from two 15th-century mansions and is one of the most charming small hotels in the Caribbean. Its weathered facade may look rather somber on arrival, but step into the lobby and you're in surroundings befitting the former home of the knight commander and governor for whom the hotel is named. Public rooms gleam with heraldic tapestries and bronze mirrors; guest rooms have hardwood furniture hand-carved in Spain to re-create the colonial era. Quiet patios echo with fountains, and one of them has been fitted with a full-size pool, sun terrace, and poolside bar overlooking the port. 55 rooms. Doubles: $40 EP. *Hostal Palacio Nicolás de Ovando, Calle de las Damas 53, Santo Domingo, Dominican Republic. Telephone: 809/687-7181.*

Hotel Gran Bahia
Samana

Samana is a relatively undeveloped region in the northeast, hugging a bay that also happens to be a popular breeding ground for whales. Now it has been slated as a new Casa de Campo, but on a much smaller scale, beginning with this 96-roomer. Scheduled to open after this edition goes to press, the Gran Bahia promises 24-hour room service, two restaurants (Antillean, French, Italian cuisine), horseback riding, tennis, fitness center, and water sports. 96 rooms and suites. Doubles: winter 1991–92, approximately $165 to $330. *Hotel Gran Bahia, P.O. Box 2024, Samana, Dominican Republic. Telephone: 809/562-6271; fax: 809/562-5232.*

The U.S. Islands

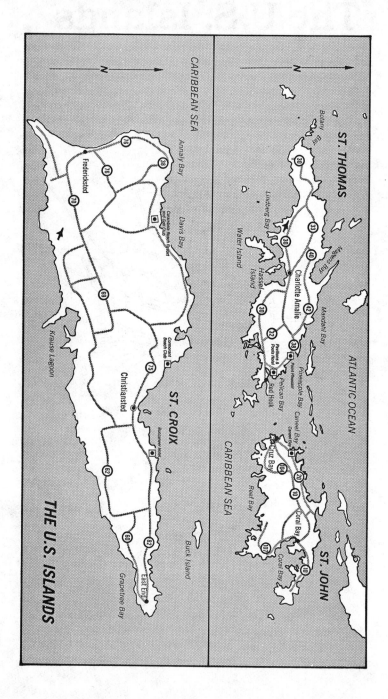

THE U.S. ISLANDS

The U.S. Islands

Suburbia south. With a few delightful exceptions, they're just about everything you're trying to escape—shopping centers, real estate billboards, telephone poles, traffic jams, crowded restaurants. However, since they are politically part of the United States and get a lucky break on airfares, Puerto Rico, St. Thomas, St. Croix, and St. John have their attractions, sometimes bountiful. Not least of these attractions is the fact that you don't have to worry about passports, don't have to fidget in long lines on arrival while some official thumbs his way through immigration formalities, don't have to stand in line at customs behind returning islanders laden with suitcases and cartons that have to be painstakingly inspected and evaluated. These islands need no introduction, but a few comments might be helpful.

When most people think of Puerto Rico they think of San Juan, which, impressive though it may be from a commercial and political point of view, is no longer a tropical hideaway. But how about *Old* San Juan? The old city, with its narrow streets and fortresses, is still one of the unique places of the Caribbean. Even the United Nations thinks so: It designated six sites in Old San Juan as World Heritage Monuments. Moreover, when you get beyond the city, Puerto Rico can be a stunningly beautiful island. Head for the rain forest. Try a drive along the roadway that runs east to west along the Cordillera Central. And the modern *autopista* from San Juan to Ponce is a spectacular but effortless route across the mountains.

St. Thomas and St. Croix have had more than their share of problems, not least of them Hurricane Hugo and its aftermath. The islanders blame a hostile stateside press for bad publicity, but you should read the lurid headlines in their own local papers. Both islands are low on the list of priorities for this guidebook, not because of any latent unrest but because they are just too overdeveloped for comfort. Charlotte Amalie is an almost constant traffic jam. Poor Christiansted should be one of *the* gems of the Caribbean, but instead its lovely old Danish buildings are almost swamped by masses of power cables and carbuncled telephone poles. Your best bet on either island is to get to your hotel and stay put. Otherwise you'll have to deal with their taxi drivers, who are not the Caribbean's most obliging fellows.

St. John is the delightful, enchanting standout—just 28 square miles, almost half of them national park. Cruz Bay, the main town, looks nothing like a suburb of Florida, and there are enough beaches and coves and mountain trails for everyone.

How to Get There San Juan's Luis Muñoz Marín International Airport is the largest in the Caribbean (they've spent millions in the past few years expanding and improving it), and it's served by nonstop flights from 17 cities in North America, one-stop direct service from as far away as Los Angeles. From New York alone there are almost 20 scheduled flights every day. American has expanded its activities at the airport, and it's now the hub of new interisland services on American Eagle, flying small, efficient aircraft. When using these services, remember that as carry-on, luggage may have to be checked for the smaller flight, so pack accordingly.

Both St. Thomas and St. Croix are served by frequent flights from San Juan, but there are also direct services from Chicago, Miami, and New York on American, Midway and/or Pan Am; the same three airlines have daily flights to St. Croix from Miami and New York. For St. John, the quickest route is via St. Thomas, then the ferryboat from Red Hook at the easternmost tip of the island. Flights to St. Croix usually stop first at St. Thomas, so you can probably visit both islands for the fare to either. Inci-

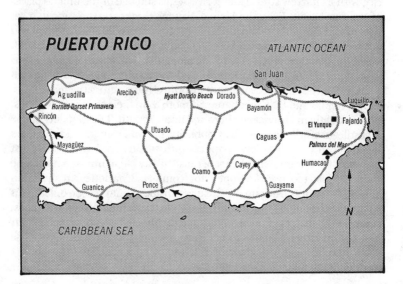

dentally, the new terminal on St. Thomas is an enormous improvement over the original, making St. Thomas a place to consider as a transit point to other islands.

Hyatt Dorado Beach
Dorado, Puerto Rico

☆☆☆ ♈♈♈ ◑◑◑◑ $$$$

Yes, despite the name it's the same classy, elegant Dorado Beach Hotel conjured up by the Rockresort people a quarter of a century ago.

But, it's been fiddled with during those 25 years.

Since it's now coming into its fifth full season under its latest owner (the fourth), perhaps it's more accurate to say it's *almost* the same classy, elegant resort.

The setting is still one of the most majestic of any resort in the Americas: an estate of 1,000 acres and thousands of coconut palms, of winding fairways and manicured lawns, and a pair of crescent beaches. The grounds have been replanted with a botanical bonanza of African tulip and almond trees, sweet immortelle and spiceberry, and fiddleleaf fig.

When I first came here in 1963, a few years after it opened, those crescent beaches were ringed with just 150 guest rooms, in decorous two-story wings hidden among the leafy palms; today, the room count has doubled. The first-rate sports facilities, once the playground of a mere 300, are now shared among all those extra guests *and* a local country club numbering 500-plus members.

Moreover, the 1,000 acres are shared with a sister hotel of more than 500 rooms, a mile down the coast. Nothing very new in that, of course: The eight-story Cerromar has been there for some time now and it, too, has come under the Hyatt banner (it's now the grandly named The Hyatt Regency Cerromar Beach Hotel). But since it's given over largely to groups and conventions, whose members have charge privileges at both hotels, the custom-built trolleys that shuttle between the two resorts seem to carry more bodies bound for Dorado than vice versa.

On a recent visit (admittedly out of season) I found the clientele at Dorado Beach was not at all what Laurance Rockefeller had in mind 25 years ago. The guests didn't add anything to the elegance of the original. They cluttered the dining facilities. To keep guests happy, slot machines have been installed in the casino.

But there certainly are pluses: When you include the sports facilities at Cerromar, you find you now have four championship golf courses (the two original Robert Trent Jones courses are still rated among the hemisphere's finest, and the Hyatt people have spent a small fortune rehabilitating them). There are now more than 20 tennis courts, a few lighted for night play. And it's still a rare pleasure to hop on a tandem and cycle along paths that weave between the fairways and the sea (although you're expected to return the bike to the rental people before 5:00 p.m.—just when the sun and the sea and the palms are at their most ravishing).

What the Hyatt people have also done is lavish about $5 million just on renovating the rooms, and almost everything they've touched is an improvement. Colors are sprightlier. New wicker and rattan furniture enhances the Caribbean mood. New additions to each room include mini-bars, safes, and terrycloth robes. The centerpiece of guest rooms on the upper floors is a sturdy bamboo four-poster; beach-level guests have to settle for a pair of double beds, but they have more floor space these days because the sliding glass doors have been repositioned halfway into the patios (which have dividing walls to maintain a sense of privacy).

The original deluxe beachfront rooms are the favorite of longtime guests, but the top-of-the-line accommodations are actually the Casita Rooms, located between the pool and the beach with split-level layouts and skylights above bath-size shower stalls.

Which room should you choose? The dozen or so "standard" rooms facing the fairways are the least expensive (and perfectly acceptable in terms of facilities); the "superior" rooms are closest to the swimming pool and dining rooms; "deluxe" designates rooms fronting the beach—with those in the East Wing (the originals) closer to the golf and tennis pro shops.

The Dorado kitchens are now in the care of a young Hyatt talent named Wilhelm Pirngruber. His Sunday buffet brunch of local specialties is not only stunningly presented in the classic Dorado manner, but at $30 it's an outstanding value. Especially good value, I might add, since your $30 includes seemingly endless flutes of Domaine Chandon *vin champenois* (the buffet officially lasts until 4:00 p.m. so you have plenty of time for seconds, on your plate and in your flute).

The Surf Room, where dinner is served, is hardly the most romantic room in the Caribbean, even with its 3,600 square feet of windows facing the sea. But Su Casa, the original estate house or *finca*, most certainly is romantic, with its candlelit tables, its cool courtyards, and foliage-draped stairways—a welcome holdover from the original Dorado.

Name: Hyatt Dorado Beach
Manager: Hendrick Santos
Address: Dorado, Puerto Rico 00646
Location: On the island's north shore, 22 miles west of San Juan, about 45 mostly untropical minutes by shuttle van from the airport ($13 per person each way, upon request)
Telephone: 809/796-1234
Fax: 809/796-2022
Reservations: Hyatt Worldwide toll free 800/228-9000; fax: 402/571-2094
Credit Cards: All major cards
Rooms: 208 rooms and suites in two-story and three-story wings, most of them strung along the beach; each with marble bathroom (bath and shower, bathrobes), lanai or balcony, air conditioning and fan, stocked refrigerator, safe, radio/alarm, direct-dial telephone
Meals: 4 restaurants—the 400-seat Surf Room, the redesigned Ocean Terrace, the Golf Pro Shop (if you don't mind cutely named dishes such as "sandwitches," etc.), and the romantic Su Casa (dinner only)—jackets in the Surf Room and Su Casa; room service, $2 per person extra
Entertainment: Small casino, music for dancing, beach parties, movies, VCR in lounge for special programs, plus the assorted lounges and disco at the nearby Cerromar; live music in the Surf Room and Su Casa (mostly Spanish-style ballads by strolling musicians)
Sports: 2 reef-protected crescent beaches and lagoons (good swimming), 2 pools (plus a children's pool), pedalos, walking/jogging trails—free; at extra charge: tennis (7 courts, 2 with lights, pro shop), golf (36 championship holes, carts obligatory, green fee $40 per day, pro shop), bicycles and tandems ($5 an hour); the golf and tennis facilities are augmented by additional courses and courts, with lights, at Cerromar; Spa Caribe at Cerromar
P.S.: In the slack months, the hotel hosts groups up to 300; in summer and during holidays there are lots of children, but youngsters from 3 to 13 have their own day camp

Palmas del Mar

Humacao, Puerto Rico

☆ ♈♈ ➀➁➂➃ $$$

Cobbled *plazuelas* with splashing fountains. Walls of tiles hand-painted by craftspeople in the village across the hill. A big free-form pool with tiles in a vivacious psychedelic design. It may not sound like a big sprawling residential/condominium development but it is—it's just that architect–developer Steve Padilla tried to keep the scale intimate by adding "visual delights," and decreeing that no building go higher than the palm trees. His 2,750 acres are located on a former sugar plantation, in an unhurried and scenic corner of the island, with the island of Vieques offshore and the rain forest an hour's drive up the coast.

This is a place for people seeking the outdoors—but with a dash of style and comfort. The 20 tennis courts are grouped in pairs, separated from each other by trees and flowering bushes, with a duck pond in front of the clubhouse snack bar. Hiking paths weave through bird sanctuaries and subtropical forests. Bridle trails and biking trails wind through nave-like stands of coconut palms. The fairways are as challenging and sporty as a golfer could hope for. The mile of beach and the marina between them allow for just about every water sport at pretty good values.

Accommodations come in a variety of villas and apartments (probably more suited to family than a couple) and a pair of attractive inns in Mediterranean style—the hilltop Palmas Inn and the Candelero Hotel (which is also, alas, the core of an executive conference center, but probably the best bet for one couple). Unlike so many resorts, Palmas del Mar has a room-only rate even in winter, allowing you to take advantage of the resort's varied dining facilities.

I lost track of all the dining spots—stylish French up the hill, Northern Italian in the inn, seafood at the marina, burgers and hot dogs by the beach and tennis center.

Don't expect unspoiled bliss, however; Palmas del Mar is still blossoming, so you can expect earth movers and concrete mixers around the property. But probably not on the beach. Not on the golf course. Not beside the psychedelic pool.

Name: Palmas del Mar
Manager: John Cruz
Address: P.O. Box 2020, Humacao, Puerto Rico 00661
Location: On the southeast coast, near the town of Humacao; an hour from the airport by mini-bus ($16 per person when sharing); by car take the *autopista* to Humacao and Yabucoa, then follow the skimpy signposts to the resort
Telephone: 809/852-6000
Fax: 809/852-6000, ext. 10344
Reservations: Own New York office, 212/983-0393 or toll free 800/221-4874; fax: 212/949-8084
Credit Cards: All major cards
Rooms: Several hundred rooms and suites, in villas, condominiums; 23 in the Palmas Inn, 102 in the Candelero Hotel; all with air conditioning (necessary much of the time), telephones, radios, and television; apartments also have full kitchens
Meals: Breakfast 7:00–11:00, lunch noon–3:00, dinner 6:00–11:00 (approx. $70 for two) in the hotel dining room; more extensive hours elsewhere; informal dress; no room service, except by individual restaurants
Entertainment: Bars, lounges, taped music, live music, depending on the location
Sports: 3 miles of beach and coves, 6 freshwater pools—free; tennis (20 courts, 7 lighted), golf (18 holes, designed by Gary Player), horseback riding (30-horse equestrian center), snorkeling, Sunfish sailing, paddleboats, deep-sea fishing, sailboat trips, bicycles
P.S.: Lots of groups and seminars, lots of children (especially on weekends) but there are special playgrounds and pools for youngsters

The Horned Dorset Primavera Hotel
Rincón, Puerto Rico

☆☆☆ ♈♈♈ ⬤ $$$

Here you are on the unspoiled western coast of Puerto Rico, where the jungly mountains give way to fields of sugarcane, surrounded by four

acres of tropical lushness dipping gently toward the sea—yet you're staying in a place named after a breed of English sheep? So let's get the
ungainly name out of the way.

Owners Harold Davies and Kingsley Wratten own a highly acclaimed
restaurant in upstate New York called the Horned Dorset; when they
opened a second inn on this island of perpetual spring they decided to
retain the goodwill of their Leonardsville original and tack on the Spanish word for spring, *primavera*. At least, I assume that's the reason—and I
assume they won't mind if I save paper and refer to it as the Primavera.
With that out of the way, let's get back to those four lush seaside acres.

Stateside, the owners have a reputation for meticulous care in
preserving old buildings, but here they called in a local architect with the
splendid name of Otto Octavio Reyes Casanova. Out of consideration for
the setting, he has spread the 24 suites over six two-story villas and a main
house, all in Spanish–Mediterranean style with stucco walls and red-tiled
roofs, mahogany, and wrought iron trimmings.

Each suite is decorated with native red-tile floors, four-poster beds, and
mahogany furniture custom-designed and hand-crafted in the city of
Ponce, farther along the coast. Louvered French doors open to balconies
and patios facing the sea; sitting rooms and bedrooms are separated by
classical Spanish archways; the bathrooms are almost too opulent (Italian
Carrara marble and a blaze of mirrors, with bidets and footed bathtubs
fitted with brass fixtures from France) with towels that are the thickest
anywhere.

The two-story main house, focal point for socializing and dining, is
flanked by a blue-tiled pool on one side, blue sea on the other. Downstairs,
the open-air terrace is the breezy rendezvous for breakfast and lunch; the
library doubles as bar and home for the live-in parrot. The second floor is
given entirely to the formal dining room (alas, air-conditioned), lined with
14 handsome mahogany doors, decorated with Jacquard tapestries and
softly glowing sconces and chandeliers. Dinner is a formal, but relaxed,
affair beginning at 7:00 and ending, six courses later, with rich desserts.

The Primavera cultivates an air of relaxation—and unabashed idleness
is exactly why you'd want to head out there. Granted, it's an ideal stopover
on a round-the-island tour (which I highly recommend), but make sure
it's a two-night stop at least.

By day, the popular agenda seems to be morning dip in the ocean;
lingering breakfast on the terrace—fresh mango and pineapple, fresh
coffee from the mountain plantations; an hour or two in one of the
bamboo loungers with a good book; light lunch, dip in the pool, siesta; an
hour by the pool; a rum punch at sundown; *tapas* in the bar at 6:30; and
an unhurried, elegant dinner to complete the evening.

Somewhere in the course of the day, tell the Messrs. Davies and Wratten you forgive the ungainly name—but thank them profusely for bringing Puerto Rico what it's needed for years: a stylish little inn beside the sea.

Name: The Horned Dorset Primavera
Owners/Managers: Harold Davies and Kingsley Wratten
Address: Apartado 1132, Rincón, Puerto Rico USVI 00743
Location: On Puerto Rico's west coast, just 15 minutes by car north of Mayaguez; you can get there by flying American Eagle or Sunaire from San Juan to Mayaguez (12 flights a day, 30 minutes each way), and from there it's a 15-minute drive to the hotel (you can arrange to be met at the airport); by car from San Juan, it's a 2½-hour drive along the north shore (you might want to consider stopping off at the Hyatt Dorado Beach for lunch) or 3 hours via the more scenic southern route through Ponce
Telephone: 809/823-4030, 4050
Fax: 809/823-5580
Reservations: Caribbean Inns Ltd.
Credit Cards: American Express, MasterCard, Visa
Rooms: 24, all suites, in 6 two-story Mediterranean-style villas, all with marble bathrooms, ceiling fans, four-poster beds
Meals: Breakfast 7:00–10:00, lunch noon–2:30 in the open-air terrace of the main house, dinner 7:00 in the formal, air-conditioned dining room (six-course dinner $80 for two); informal dress ("no shorts or bathing suits in the public rooms after 6"); taped classical music; room service for breakfast only
Entertainment: Bar/library, with *tapas* at 6:30 and stacks of vintage *Life* magazines; casino nearby
Sports: Freshwater pool, small beach; surfing and water sports at nearby Club Náutico de Rincón (Rincón is the site of world surfing championships); golf 25 minutes away; whale-watching, deep-sea fishing, and guided trips to the uninhabited island of Mona can be arranged
P.S.: No children under 12; no radios or television

⌒✦⌒

Caneel Bay
St. John

☆☆☆☆☆ ♇♇♇ ❶❶❶ $$$$$

Where else in the Caribbean, where else in the world, will $250 a day or thereabouts get you a resort with 7 beaches (each lovelier than the next), a private peninsula of 170 acres surrounded by 6,500 acres of national park on land and 5,600 acres of national park underwater; where you can hike along paths lined with flamboyant, tamarind, and shower of gold; snorkel among peacock flounders and trumpetfish; spot a yellow-bellied sapsucker or pectoral sandpiper, maybe even a bobolink; build up your strength on a five-course breakfast, buffet lunch, and five-course dinner in some of the best restaurants in the Caribbean, and then bunk down in a double-size love nest open to the breezes and birdsongs?

True, $250 plus a day is the summer rate, but you still get all the attractions that presidents, vice presidents, bank biggies, gospel biggies, French counts, and senators pay almost twice as much for in winter.

Caneel is Caneel 12 months of the year, in season or out of season—just about the ultimate in seclusion, tranquility, a sort of ecological euphoria. You almost have the feeling you're camping out here, but with a roof over your head rather than a tent, a bed under you rather than a sleeping bag, and real china rather than plastic plates.

There are 171 rooms at Caneel Bay (for every room an acre of landscaped parkland!) and most of them are right on beaches, a few are on headlands, 36 hillside rooms are in the Tennis Gardens, the rise behind the courts, with a few bungalows off by themselves on the edge of the national park. A pair of shuttle buses circle the grounds every 15 minutes, but it's still worthwhile to give some thought to *where* you'd like to be. Of the beaches, my preference is leeward Scott (single-story wing), but others prefer the windward Hawksnest (two-story, balconies for morning and afternoon sun) for its views of offshore islands. Rooms at Turtle Bay, perhaps the prettiest beach, are close to the old estate house restaurant (a few are actually in the estate house and may pick up the sounds of what passes as conviviality in these sedate parts, but room number 93 has a particularly bosky balcony).

The most secluded quarters are in the famous Cottage 7, once the home (*a* home) of the Rockefeller family, now the haunt of assorted VIPs (Kissinger, Bush, Mondale) since they can conveniently park their body-guards in the attached servants' quarters.

Adjoining Cottage 7, rooms 61 through 66 are on a headland, secluded from the rest of the hotel, with their own patch of sand; on Caneel Bay itself, rooms 26 through 29 are especially popular because they're farthest from the public areas yet close to the main dining room. Up in the Tennis Gardens, rooms 132 and 133 are particularly spacious.

Not that you're likely to feel claustrophobic in any of the accommodations here. Larger than usual, the Caneel Bay rooms each come with walls of louvers and another of glass opening onto a fairly private patio. No radios, no television, no room phones here (stocked mini-bars take care of your between-meal thirsts). Decor is low-key—"madonna gray" blends the exteriors with the environment. But the interiors have been getting a stylistic facelift and many of the rooms are now quite colorful—almost giddily so by traditional Caneel standards but still subdued and tasteful. Many of the bathrooms have been retiled, replumbed, and enlarged; some of the old fuddy-duddy furnishings have been replaced with rattans and wicker, and fabrics that echo the colors of the flowers rather than the soil.

The most recent innovation here is a new swimming pool—a traumatic step for Rockresorts, since Laurance Rockefeller always believed that if you're surrounded by some of the most inviting water in the world why would anyone want a pool? The answer is, most guests do not, except maybe for a few people staying in the Tennis Gardens where the pool is secluded behind a floral fence. The resort has also expanded its tennis park to include 4 new courts, bringing the total to 11—again, without detracting from the overall setting. And the Sugar Mill Restaurant has been restyled to incorporate a display kitchen featuring pastas and grilled seafood.

This flurry of activity can be attributed, in part, to the fact that Caneel Bay has been feeling the heat from newer luxury resorts and the Rockresorts management company has changed hands twice in recent years. Currently, the resorts are owned by a Chicago development corporation called VMS, which also has two or three other distinguished resorts under its conglomerate wing but seems to leave the everyday running of them to the people who do that best—in this case, the Rockresorts managers.

The question is how will regular guests such as Alan Alda, Mel Brooks, and Joan Collins react to all the changes? People don't encourage change here. That's why the managers went to great pains to point out that the new pool is only 4½ feet deep and therefore has no diving board to encourage boisterous leaps and shouts. That's Caneel for you.

Name: Caneel Bay
Manager: Martin Nicholson
Address: Virgin Island National Park, P.O. Box 120, Cruz Bay, St. John, USVI 00830
Location: 4 miles across the channel from the tip of St. Thomas; the resort has its own air-conditioned lounge at St. Thomas's airport and the host there will take charge of your transfer to the resort—by taxi to Charlotte Amalie, where you board a private 58-ft. launch, *Caneel Bay Mary II*, for the 45-minute trip direct to the Caneel dock (included in the rates)
Telephone: 809/776-6111
Fax: 809/776-2030
Reservations: Own U.S. office, toll free 800/223-7637
Credit Cards: All major cards
Rooms: 171 in a variety of one-story and two-story wings strategically located around the property, with a few suites in Cottage number 7; all with ceiling fans and louvers, balconies or patios, wall safes, refrigerators (in most rooms)—but no telephones, no television, no radios

Meals: Continental breakfast 7:00–7:45, full breakfast 7:45–10:00, lunch noon–2:00, afternoon tea 4:00, dinner 7:00–9:00 (approx. $90 for two), in 3 breeze-cooled dining pavilions, including the lovely hillside Sugar Mill; jackets for gentlemen after 6:00 p.m. in the Turtle Bay dining room, more casual in the main dining pavilion; "dry bathing suits and beach wraps and sandals at all times, no shorts or blue jeans after 6:00 p.m."; live music in the Turtle Bay dining room, some taped music in the Sugar Mill; room service for breakfast only, $2 extra per tray

Entertainment: Live music every evening (guitar, combo, "slightly amplified"), dancing most evenings, movies every evening, nature lectures, backgammon, Scrabble, chess (I still haven't succeeded in persuading them to install a putting green but I'm working on it)

Sports: 7 beautiful beaches, good swimming and snorkeling, new freshwater pool behind the tennis courts, Sunfish sailing, windsurfing, nature trails, tennis (11 courts, Peter Burwash pro shop, no lights)—all free; by arrangement: scuba (from the dock), sailboat cruises, boat trips to St. Thomas (popular for shopping) and Little Dix Bay; special package offering a few days ashore, a few days afloat in a Hinckley

P.S.: No children under 8 except at Christmas (but hardly a distraction), some small seminars ("but they have to fit in"), a few day-trippers (who are allowed to have lunch in the 90-seat Sugar Mill, which is why resident guests usually forego the daytime panorama from up there)

Point Pleasant

St. Thomas

☆☆ ♀♀♀ ◑◑ $$$

Guest cottages here are so artfully tucked into the crags and cactus gardens that at first you think you must have blundered onto someone's private estate. On second glance, a few cedar-shake roofs peek discreetly out of the greenery. Here and there, you spot a redwood deck, weathered to a sea-salty silver, jutting from the face of a hill that swoops 200 feet beneath you to an aquamarine bay.

Although Point Pleasant is only 15 years old, it has the ageless, settled look of belonging to its surroundings as rightfully as any gnarled old sea grape or mampoo tree. Colors, materials, designs are all just plain natural. From a 15-foot-high redwood ceiling, a paddle fan whirs above your king-size bed. Walls are mostly windows and glass doors, and can stay open to the trade winds, because there's nothing to screen out. At this height, both humidity and mosquitoes are conveniently blown out to sea.

Most of Point Pleasant's accommodations are in these airy hillside dwellings, usually two or three to a cottage. They range from a single room with either balcony or sunken garden to a five-room, three-bath villa.

A comfortable, affordable compromise might be what the management calls a "standard" suite—a sleeping-living room plus dining space, kitchen, and a deck with a gull's-eye view of St. John, Tortola, and various other Virgins undulating into infinity.

You, too, can do some interesting undulating—down and around Point Pleasant's boulder preserve. The route you take is a fantastic journey through what must have been a very big bang. In fact, you're standing precisely on the spot where, several billion years ago, a monumental volcanic eruption took place, the results of which look as if some psycho fire god had scooped up an acre of nice, quiet boulders, squeezed premature wrinkles into their skins, and petulantly flung them down like a handful of hot potatoes. And they're still sitting right where they landed, one balanced topsy-turvy on the tip of another, with organ-pipe cactuses and century plants sprouting out of them like Sassoon hairdos.

Point Pleasant has thoughtfully spiked your route along their new nature trail with some civilized stopping-off places. A woodland glade. A shady gazebo cantilevered over the abyss, where you can catch your breath and sip a planter's punch. Three freshwater swimming pools. A tennis court. A brand-new sea deck with comfortable redwood benches and chaises. And finally, at the end of the trail, an immaculate little white sand beach.

In the bargain, the hotel supplies you with free use of a car for a few hours a day—long enough to take you around the island to other sights, other restaurants, and back again to this very pleasant point.

Name: Point Pleasant
Owner/Manager: Ruth Pfanner; Maggie Day (general manager)
Address: Estate Smith Bay #4, St. Thomas, USVI 00802
Location: In the northeast of the island, overlooking Pillsbury Bay and the islands of Tortola and St. John, half an hour and about $9 by taxi from the airport
Telephone: 809/775-7200; toll free 800/524-2300

Fax: 809/776-5694
Reservations: Direct, toll free 800/524-2300 or Robert Reid Associates
Credit Cards: American Express, MasterCard, Visa
Rooms: 134 total: from standard to 2-bedroom suites, on the hill or by the beach; all with fully equipped kitchens, direct-dial telephones, breezes, ceiling fans, and air conditioning
Meals: Breakfast 7:00–10:00, Lunch noon–2:00, afternoon tea, dinner 7:00–10:00 in the Agave Terrace restaurant (approx. $50 for two), informal dress; two poolside cafés, open 11:00–6:00
Entertainment: Weekly managers' cocktail parties, island shows, rum tastings, jazz nights, shopping, Magan's Bay and evening shuttle bus service (small charge)
Sports: Beach, 3 freshwater pools (2 with poolside bars), complimentary snorkeling, Sunfish sailing, windsurfing, scuba lessons, tennis (1 court, lights)—all free; boat trips, golf; cars available to guests for 4-hour tours at no extra charge

Pavilions & Pools Hotel
St. Thomas

☆☆ ➊ $$$

The genies who designed this place proceeded on the premise that if we all had three wishes, they would be for (1) a tropical house on a tropical island, (2) a private swimming pool, and (3) no down payment, no mortgage. And, sure enough, they've made all three come true. More or less.

The pavilion part of their wish fulfillment consists of a suite (there are two basic designs, one slightly roomier than the other) of big, open rooms with one long wall of sliding glass doors. On the other side of the door lies the pool part: a completely private patio with a completely private swimming pool that's yours to do whatever you've always wanted to do in a swimming pool. A stout wall and plenty of tall spiky tropical plantings guarantee Peeping Toms can't peep.

Unlike most hotels with individual pools, Pavilions & Pools gives you one big enough (16 × 18 ft. or 20 × 14 ft.) for something more athletic than dipping your toes. And with most Caribbean hotels still frowning on topless tanning, you may be grateful for the chance to color in your white spaces without causing a riot. The rigorous privacy of the place, however, extends beyond your doorstep. To some, that's a plus. To others, a minus.

Because there is no central pool, no beach, and a bar with only limited meal service, you're scarcely aware of anybody but the two of you and the friendly people who run the hotel and happily help you arrange side trips, rent cars, call airlines, reserve tables at restaurants, etc. All activities outside your own room are at the hotel next door on Sapphire Beach. That includes tennis, any water sport you can think of, and meals (unless you prepare them in your own kitchen or drive around sampling the island's varied cooking).

P & P keeps right on being one of the Caribbean's most popular ways of getting away from it all. If you both agree that a king-size bed, a pool of saltwater, and thou are enough, come and join the crowd. Even though you'll never know they're here.

Name: Pavilions & Pools Hotel
Manager: Tammy J. Hurst
Address: Route Six, St. Thomas, USVI, 00801
Location: In the southeast, near Sapphire Bay, half an hour and $10 by taxi from the airport
Telephone: 809/775-6110
Fax: 809/775-6110, ext. 251
Reservations: Direct, toll free 800/524-2001 or Robert Reid Associates
Credit Cards: American Express, Discover, MasterCard, Visa
Rooms: 25 villas with private pools, king-size beds, kitchen, ceiling fans, air conditioning, telephones, some with "garden" showers, cable TV, VCRs
Meals: One-entrée dinner served nightly, except on Tuesdays and Fridays
Entertainment: You; cocktail party Tuesday nights
Sports: Private pools; snorkeling, tennis, golf, and water sports nearby

Carambola Beach Resort and Golf Club

St. Croix

☆☆☆ 🍷🍷🍷 ◑◑◑ $$$$$

Tree-clad hillsides plunge into the sea. A narrow roadway winds among mahogany and saman trees. Reefs and headlands shelter a secluded bay with a curve of white sandy beach. A tiny lighthouse pokes above a distant headland. And not a fast-food stand for miles around.

If this is not everyone's image of St. Croix that's because not many people venture to the still undeveloped northwest corner of the island light-years from downtown Christiansted.

Until recently, Davis Bay was a "secret" bathing Eden with few people. There must be a few Cruzan sun worshippers feeling miffed because their pristine bay now sprouts red-roofed villas among the coconut palms and saman trees. But not guests at Carambola. They seem to have few complaints.

This secluded resort (now operated by the company that runs West Virginia's renowned Greenbrier) tucks 150 rooms into a narrow 28 acres between hills and beach, its 24 villas ribboned among a grove of saman and coconut and mahogany trees. The porte cochere sets the architectural tone—red corrugated roof, steeply pitched roofline, hardwood ceiling with sturdy rafters from the entrance, and breezeways leading past the lobby, lounge, boutique, deli, bar and restaurants to end at a whimsical gazebo-cum-clocktower. By day it's part Caribbean, part Jutland, echoing the island's Antillean/Danish heritage; by night, it's pure Disneyland.

But in its quirky, understated way it all adds up to an attractive complex. The villas have the same red roofs and timber siding (except for one wall of pastel-colored concrete, presumably the "Caribbean" touch, but it looks almost as if the accountants gave the architect instructions to save money so he left one wall unfinished). Interiors feature masses of wooden louvers and brass fittings, screened doors, and tile floors. Each spacious (520 sq. ft.) room is quartered into dressing room/tiled shower, sleeping

area, sitting area, and (most attractive feature of all) screened porch with padded and cushioned banquettes around two walls—a reposeful, if not too practical spot for breakfasting on bananas in coconut cream and banana pancakes with mango-coconut syrup.

The furniture is custom-made—reproductions of somewhat staid Danish colonial sofas, chairs, rockers, and dressers. A nice idea—one designer's stand against plush-and-trendy California/Caribbean pastels—but it would work even better if the pieces were set off against weathered brick or wood rather than white concrete. Or if the pieces were comfortable.

A few of the rooms are just a tad too close to their neighbors' air-conditioned hum, but the lovely screened porches acquired "privacy panels" as part of a major post-Hugo renovation, which also included reading lights and breakfast tables on the porches. They all cost the same, but upper floors have an edge because of their cathedral ceilings, and although all rooms are designated "sea view," the reality is that some have obstructed views. My suggestions would be rooms 141–147, 161–167, or 251–267, if you want to be on the beach; 221–227 if you like to be next to the tennis courts; 71–77 if you want to be close to the hub. Rooms 11–61 form a separate wing on the opposite side of what the hotel calls the Greathouse (i.e., the lobby, breezeways, etc.), a few paces from the beach but very quiet.

The most impressive salons at Carambola are the dining rooms—the mahogany and the saman ceilings supported by massive tree trunks and festooned with scores (literally) of paddle fans. Air conditioning supplements the fans and shutters in the carpeted, elegant Mahogany Room. Cuisine is more formal here, too—traditional continental with island accents. Thus an active day on the beach, courts, or golf course might end sumptuously with coconut fried prawns and papaya lime coulis or herbed duck rillette with cassava bread; guava bisque with two tropical nuts or spice island coconut soup; steamed scallops with ginger nantua sauce or emince of chicken with pistachio and carambolas. All this is a sort of lead-up to bananas in armagnac caramel with chocolate granito and/or Caribbean lime mousse with papaya sauce. For the strict traditionalists the rack of lamb comes perfectly done. If service is sometimes slow, at least the staff is friendly, willing and, it seems, eager to measure up.

Name: Carambola Beach Resort and Golf Club
Manager: S. Lee Bowden
Address: P.O. Box 3031, Kingshill, St. Croix, USVI 00850
Location: At Davis Bay, on the unspoiled northwest coast; 20 minutes and $12 by taxi from the airport, about 25 minutes from Christiansted (shuttle bus daily, round trip $12 per person)
Telephone: 809/778-3800; toll free 800/447-9503
Fax: 809/778-1682
Reservations: Direct, toll-free 800/447-9503
Credit Cards: All major cards
Rooms: 150 in 24 two-story villas, all with oversized tiled shower only, dressing room, ceiling fan *and* air conditioning, stocked refrigerator, screened porch, telephone, clock radio; for suites, 2 rooms can be combined with a private entrance
Meals: Buffet breakfast 7:30–9:30, deli 11–5:00, lunch noon–2:00 in the Saman Room, 11:00–5:00 at the golf course clubhouse, dinner 6:30–9:00 in the fan and air-conditioned Mahogany Room or fan-cooled Saman Room ($80 for two); jackets for men in the Mahogany Room, casual but stylish (i.e., "no jeans") elsewhere; room service for breakfast only; no-smoking areas in both dining rooms
Entertainment: Bar/terrace, music every evening during peak season (low-key, mildly amplified), movies 4 or 5 times a week, billiards, parlor games and wide-screen television/video in the lounges
Sports: Beach, freshwater pool (not suitable for laps), two Jacuzzis, hammocks, snorkeling gear, tennis (pro shop, 4 courts, no lights, plus 5 Hydro Court clay courts, two with lights, at Golf Club)—all free; the resort's own Robert Trent Jones golf course 10 minutes away by shuttle

bus (18 holes, $45 per round); full-service dive shop; sailing and horse-back riding can be arranged; day charters on 42-ft. ketch

P.S.: Some seminar groups up to 120 ("but they have to blend in—no name tags allowed"); no restrictions on children, but the full rate is charged for kids over three, which effectively cuts down on numbers

P.P.S.: At presstime the resort had closed temporarily due to management contract disputes.

Cormorant Beach Club
St. Croix

☆☆☆ ♈♈♈ ◑◑ $$$

Hammocks dangle between the tall palms that rise straight from the sandy beach. Gentle trade winds skip ashore from reefs a hundred yards off the beach. Hi-tech mattresses float guests around the big freshwater pool.

And since there are never more than 76 guests at any time you never feel crowded, never have to "reserve" a hammock, never feel jostled at the breakfast or lunchtime buffet. You just while away your days in an air of total relaxation and contentment.

First, some background. This Cormorant was once a Pelican—the Pelican Beach Club, which lay moribund for several years before the original owners, Wally and Robbie Bregman, gave up their Connecticut/CEO life-style to plunge into the mad, mad world of Caribbean innkeeping in 1987. It's located on 12 quiet acres at the end of a rather domesticated drive from the airport, between a cluster of modest dwellings and a ribbon of beach that runs for probably half a mile in each direction. Not a *great* beach, but with its scores of palm trees (a few score more were swept away by Hugo) and bedazzling background of reefs and multihued waters, it's all very tropical and soothing.

The former Pelican's rather ungainly three-story lines have been soft-ened by trees and bougainvillea; the rooms have been brightened and light-ened, post-Hugo, with floral fabrics and rattan headboards, table, and chairs; the fitted carpet has been replaced by ceramic tile; and the louvered doors have built-in security bars. The lobby/bar and restaurant, trimmed with light wood, are open to the breezes and the beach; the bar-room tables double as backgammon boards; a tidy little library, just off the lobby, has enough paperbacks and hardcovers to fill a week of lounging in hammocks.

Because *lounging* is what this place is all about. It's a relaxing 12 acres where you can escape *or* mingle with like-minded idlers or find your very own corner or hammock. Apart from the earnest frolickers on the pair of tennis courts, guests move at a very, very lethargic pace; and with sprightly waiters to fetch your piña coladas or whatever, it makes more sense to loaf and lounge at the Cormorant than to go shopping or sightseeing in Christiansted.

Bathrooms have oodles of fluffy towels twice a day, bathrobes, and an amenities basket with shampoo and skin balm; there are fresh flowers in every room; for tennis players who've just finished a rigorous set there's a canvas-covered shelter and a cooler full of complimentary beers and soft drinks right at the courts.

The kitchen is thriving under San Franciscan Catherine Plaw; the dining room staff has polished its collective skills, but the staff in general seems to have taken its cue from the hardworking, cordial manager, Larry Bathon, so the welcome here is noticeably warm, smiles are genuine, tips are shunned. This is St. Croix? This is the Cormorant.

Name: Cormorant Beach Club
Manager: Larry Bathon
Address: P.O. Box 708, Christiansted, St. Croix, USVI 00820
Location: On the north shore, 20 minutes from the airport in one direction, 10 from Christiansted in the other, $8 for two sharing a taxi with two others to the airport, $5 to town
Telephone: 809/778-8920
Fax: 809/778-9218
Reservations: Direct, toll free 800/548-4460
Credit Cards: American Express, MasterCard, Visa
Rooms: 38, including 4 suites, in 2 two-story beachside wings, all with balconies or patios facing beach, baths and showers, bathrobes, air conditioning, ceiling fans, wall safes, direct-dial telephones that even dial your own wake-up calls; wet bars in suites
Meals: Breakfast 8:00–10:00, lunch 11:30–2:00, dinner 6:30–9:00 (approx. $65 to $70 for two), all beachside; island casual dress after 6:00; Caribbeau Grill Night on Thursdays; no room service, but tables with coffee and tea are set up in the breezeway of each wing from 7:00 a.m.
Entertainment: Steel band on Fridays, dance combo on Saturday (lightly amplified), steel band for Sunday brunch, VCR for new and old movies in meeting room

Sports: Half-mile beach, big hexagonal swimming pool, parcours trail, snorkeling gear, tennis (2 courts, no lights)—all free; scuba-diving, sailing, golf, and horseback riding (rain forest or beach) can be arranged

P.S.: No children under 16 from January 7 through Easter (at other times, age 5 and up); a few small but discreet corporate seminars

The Buccaneer Hotel

St. Croix

☆☆☆ ♈♈ ◐◐◐◐ $$$

Earlier editions of this guidebook were less than enthusiastic about The Buccaneer, but since the Armstrong family, owners since the hotel opened in 1948, spent a few million dollars on improvements in 1988–89, The Buccaneeer is now one of the most attractive resorts on St. Croix.

And if setting alone were the deciding factor, The Buccaneer would win hands down. Its rolling acres incorporate a challenging but not overwhelming golf course, tidy lawns, the stump of an old sugar mill on the hill, three coves of white sands lined by stands of coconut palms. Tropical flowers vie with the pink and white buildings to add occasional splashes of color. And every way you turn you have another glorious view of sea or bay and Christiansted (from this location, a pretty picture of pastel stucco without the unsightly spaghetti of utility poles and cables).

Guest rooms are deployed around the grounds in a variety of one-, two- and three-story buildings, some on the crest of the hill, some halfway down the hill, others beside the beach. Which you choose will probably be determined by whether or not you want a steady breeze, whether you want to be closer to the beach than the golf course, and so on; but let me suggest that you consider the Doubloons (a cabana-like colony beside Cutlass Cove) or the Beach Rooms that curve around the point between Cutlass and Beauregard Beach; on the ridge the choice lodgings, apart from room 212 in the main building, are the Ridge Rooms, a parade of little row houses looking across the fairways and sea to St. Thomas, 43 miles away. These rooms have now been rejuvenated with pastel colors, wicker and rattan, Italian marble tiles, and French windows leading to quiet patios shaded by mother-in-law's-tongue trees.

The public spaces haven't been overlooked by the painters and carpenters. The once-stodgy ridge-top lobby and Terrace dining room are now cheerier venues; the air-conditioned Brass Parrot, where guests gather for candlelit dinners, has a new chef, but the menu is still a play-safe list of New York–strip steaks and roast duckling.

In other words, this resort does not attract cosmopolites and glitterati, and despite the fact that its most secluded beach is named Whistle (as in whistle before you get there to let people know you're coming), The Buccaneer tends to have a fairly conservative clientele. But the real attraction here, besides those beautiful grounds, is the range of sports activities—golf (less expensive by far than at Carambola), 8 tennis courts, and water sports on your doorstep.

Name: The Buccaneer Hotel
Manager: Robert D. Armstrong
Address: P.O. Box 218, St. Croix, USVI 00801
Location: On the beach at Gallows Bay, about 10 minutes from Christiansted, $10 for two by shared taxi from the airport
Telephone: 809/773-2100
Fax: 914/763-5362
Reservations: Ralph Locke Islands
Credit Cards: All major cards
Rooms: 150, including 13 suites, in 8 categories, each with air conditioning and fan, refrigerator, direct-dial telephone, safe, balcony or patio; TVs available for rent
Meals: Breakfast 7:30–10:00, lunch 11:30–5:30 in a couple of beachside pavilions, dinner 6:00–9:30 in the beachside Mermaid, or the hilltop Terrace and Brass Parrot dining rooms, the first two cooled by the breezes, the last one by air conditioning (approx. $70 for two in the Brass Parrot), jackets required in the Brass Parrot, otherwise casual but "no shorts on the Terrace after 6"; room service all meals at no extra charge; piano player in the Brass Parrot
Entertainment: 2 movies and live music every evening, including steel bands, guitarists, and a combo featuring Duke Ellington's first clarinetist
Sports: 3 beaches, pool, health club—free; extra charge for tennis (8 championship caliber courts, lights, pro), golf (18 holes, pro, $24 per round), windsurfing, rowboats, Sunfish sailing, boat trips, seaweed wraps and massage; horseback riding nearby
P.S.: Lots of families, but no children under four; some small business groups in the off-season

Added Attractions

Ramada Hotel el Convento
Old San Juan, Puerto Rico

The love nooks here were once the cells of Carmelite nuns but don't let that inhibit your frolicking. The convent was established 300 years ago, when all those Spanish conquistadors were around and this sanctuary was probably the only place in town where a maiden could remain a maiden. The great mahogany doors of the convent still open onto the same tiny Plaza de las Monjas, which priests and penitents cross before disappearing into the tall blackness of the cathedral, and where old men occasionally play dominoes.

This historic convent in Old San Juan actually went through a period of martyrdom as a garage for sanitation trucks, before it was rescued more than 20 years ago by a group of brave and farsighted people, including a Woolworth heir and a pair of local brothers, Ricardo and José Alegría, whose passion it is to restore and preserve all the beautiful buildings of Old San Juan. They imported authentic antiques from Spain, and when they couldn't lay their hands on authentic pieces of the period, they had reproductions made specifically for El Convento. They decked the halls and galleries with paintings and tapestries, conquistadorean swords and shields, the guest rooms with hand-carved chests and high-backed chairs upholstered in satins and velvets, wrought-iron lamps, elaborate headboards and canopied beds, louvered doors and beamed ceilings (although the rooms were recently refurbished with a somewhat lighter touch—new fabrics, some rattan—to "combine modern comfort with Old World elegance"). The former cells are neatly spaced along graciously arched galleries around a central patio, which now sports a swimming pool.

Most visitors to Puerto Rico, of course, don't want to spend all their days in Old San Juan, and although El Convento has guest privileges with beachside hotels it has never become the great romantic hideaway it deserves to be. Nevertheless, this is a special place because of its location in miraculous Old San Juan, because of its historic overtones. Think of it not as a *gran hotel* but simply as a good first-class hotel, check into one of the remaining rooms with four-poster twin beds, dine at La Mallorquina a few blocks away, and El

Convento is still worth a couple of nights of your vacation. 100 rooms and suites. Doubles: $165 to $220 EP. *Ramada Hotel El Convento, P.O. Box 1048, San Juan, Puerto Rico, USVI 00902. Telephone: 809/723-9020; fax: 809/721-2877.*

Secret Harbour Beach Hotel
St. Thomas

No longer, apparently, a secret, judging by the private homes and low-rise condos that line the approaches. But secret enough to deter day-trippers, so once you're there, on a half-moon of sand studded with palm trees, you see only a few sun worshipers. This is basically a condominium resort with hotel services—maid service, restaurants, tennis, water sports. Accommodations, in four three-story balconied wings, are in air-conditioned studios and one-bedroom apartments, all facing the beach, all with kitchens and comfortable furnishings that vary to match the taste of the owners. (You want a studio or suite on an upper floor, since you can't see the sea from the lower level.) The Bird of Paradise restaurant comes in two parts, both beachside. The classier of the two pavilions entertains its diners with an entirely superfluous local radio station (complete with commercials), and while the food is more than acceptable it hardly measures up to the expectations aroused by the maître d's fancy duds. 60 rooms, including 9 studios. Doubles: $215 to $280 EP. *Secret Harbour Beach Hotel, P.O. Box 7576, St. Thomas, USVI 00801. Telephone: toll free 800/524-2250. No credit cards.*

The Mark St. Thomas Hotel/Restaurant
St. Thomas

The lights of Charlotte Amalie are right there at your feet (to be precise, 99 steps down one of the old city's step streets), but up here on the veranda of this 250-year-old, two-story home you're far from the bustle and traffic and fumes. Iron filigree frames the harbor and the cruise ships, lights sparkle, candles glow on the bluebitch stone and mahogany, and a player piano plays quietly in the background.

A former Wall Streeter, Jack Hepworth, turned this Danish colonial masterpiece (it's on the National Register of Historic Homes) into a distinctive eight-room inn in 1987 and filled it with just what you'd hope to find in such a setting—an eclectic, surprising, charming, sometimes witty blending of antiques and reproductions, of baldachins and authentic 1890 sinks, a sleeping nook notched into a massive chimney, ballast brick walls set off by bold (sometimes brash) colors and Robert Singleton paintings.

Two of the rooms—Red and Marble—may be too close to the kitchen for some tastes, but Red at least compensates by having a private terrace. Hepworth did not stint on luxuries—100%, 200-count percale cotton sheets ("We wash them ourselves"), air conditioning, ceiling fans, cable television, direct-dial telephones, hand-written bills, and an honor bar in the parlor.

The Mark's restaurant has become so popular with islanders and visitors that you have to make reservations well in advance, especially if you want to snag one of the veranda or window tables. In truth, the view probably outshines the cuisine (roast duck with a Cassis sauce fell short of its enthusiastic recommendation, although lemon curd with spring blueberries was a welcome change of pace). There's a tiny pool at the rear and the nearest beach (Magens) is just 10 minutes away by car, but The Mark is essentially an aerie for reading and dreaming in the terraced garden, among the sago palms and flamboyants, or for munching a leisurely breakfast while admiring the view. 8 rooms. Doubles: winter 1991–92, $105 to $150, with buffet breakfast. *The Mark St. Thomas Hotel/Restaurant, Blackbeard's Hill, Charlotte Amalie, St. Thomas, USVI 00802. Telephone: 809/774-5511; fax: 809/774-8509.*

Blackbeard's Castle Hotel
St. Thomas

Take the view from The Mark above and add a few more feet of elevation and you have the sweeping panorama from the pool deck of Blackbeard's. The two inns' garden walls abut each other, but there the resemblances end: Where The Mark has a tiny garden pool at the rear, Blackbeard's has a large pool at the front; where a house is the dominant feature of The Mark, here it's a circular watchtower dating from 1679 or thereabouts. The lookout may or may not have been used by the piratical Blackbeard, but over the years the site has been a Danish colonialist's plantation, a home and, since 1985, a hotel and restaurant (but be sure you don't confuse it with the larger *Blue*beard's Castle Hotel on a nearby hilltop). Guest quarters, in one-story wings around the courtyard, face east or west with only a couple enjoying harbor views; a few rooms have balconies or patios; all have ceiling fans, air conditioning, direct-dial telephones, and cable television. Again the restaurant and bar are prime attractions: Prices are moderate and the food is worth the hike up the hill. 20 rooms. Doubles: winter 1991–92, $140 to $190, including continental breakfast. *Blackbeard's Castle Hotel, P.O. Box 6041, St. Thomas, USVI 08804. Telephone: toll free 800/344-5771 (reservations only) or 809/776-1234; fax: 809/776-4321.*

Villa Madeleine
St. Croix

It's a villa complex rather than a hotel, but these new suites are among the most luxurious and most stylish lodgings on the island. Your hilltop suite is virtually a self-contained cottage (although they're so tightly packed in you'll hardly notice their separateness) with a private plunge pool in a walled garden. The interiors, by noted decorator Carleton Varney, are understated with light antiqued woods, subtle pastels, and rattan and wicker furniture; TV and VCR equipment is tucked into credenzas; bedrooms have custom-designed rattan four-posters; the sleek kitchens are fully equipped for *intime* dinner parties, including microwaves and dishwashers.

How often the microwave is utilized will probably depend on how many guests can resist the temptation to walk a few paces up the hill to the Cafe Madeleine in the Great House. This, too, was designed by Varney, but in one of his more dashing moods—with look-at-me colors, Japanese prints, a clublike library, and a billiard room where would-be diners can shoot pool while waiting for their tables. Meals, served on a spacious veranda beneath a floral awning, feature Italian dishes like pasta pie and *inventini* lamb (i.e., roasted leg stuffed with rosemary and garlic in a Barolo glaze); since you have to walk only a few yards rather than drive a few miles before tumbling between the sheets you can safely order the potent dessert known as The Hummer (a goblet of melted ice cream, Kahlua, and rum topped with chocolate chips) and take full advantage of the extensive wine list. Located at Gallows Bay, about 10 minutes east of Christiansted. 20 one- and two-bedroom suites. Doubles: winter 1991–92, $350 to $460, without meals. *Villa Madeleine, P.O. Box 24190, Christiansted, St. Croix, USVI 00824. Telephone: toll free 800/548-4461 or 809/773-8141; fax: 809/773-7518.*

Sprat Hall Plantation
St. Croix

The owner's family came here from England long before the first sugar mill was built and here they are, in a state of familial exuberance, still living in the island's longest-inhabited Great House. Start up a conversation here and you're swept into a rush of horse talk, island chitchat, family reminiscing, and more horse talk. You either love it or hate it. But it's genuine.

This 17th-century plantation consists of 25 acres of soursop and wild orchid trees, stables, and pastures, filling a hillside on the quiet western shore of the island, close enough to the rain forest for trail rides on the family horses—the inn's main attraction for many. There's also a beach across the street, with some basic water sports and a pleasant, breezy restaurant/bar. The 25 rooms are homey, furnished in a whimsical motley of family bric-a-brac, leatherette couches, ceramic pineapple lamps, and antiques culled from island homes and old Danish government buildings. One guest room has *two* massive four-posters, one Danish, one English. Dinner is served by candlelight, family style. 25 rooms. Doubles: winter 1991–92, $120 to $130, room only. No credit cards. *Sprat Hall Plantation, P.O. Box 695, Frederiksted, St. Croix, USVI 00840. Telephone: toll free 800/843-3584 or 809/772-0305.*

The British Virgins

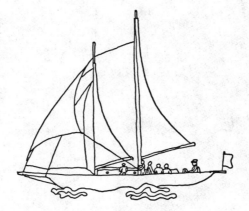

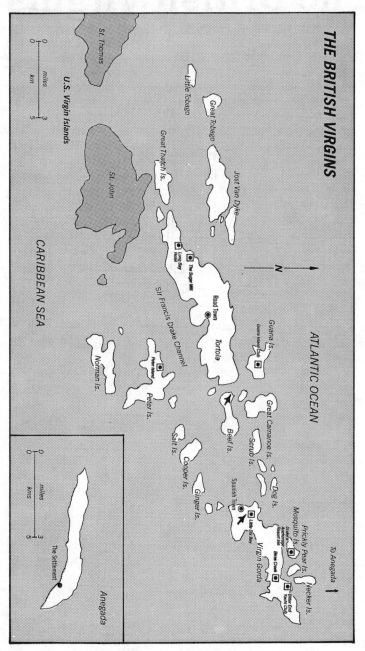

THE BRITISH VIRGINS

ATLANTIC OCEAN

CARIBBEAN SEA

U.S. Virgin Islands

St. Thomas

Little Tobago

Great Tobago

Jost Van Dyke

Great Thatch Is.

St. John

Long Bay Hotel

The Sugar Mill

Road Town

Tortola

Guana Is.
Guana Island Club

Sir Francis Drake Channel

Norman Is.

Peter Island

Peter Is.

Salt Is.

Cooper Is.

Ginger Is.

Great Camanoe Is.

Scrub Is.

Beef Is.

Dog Is.

Spanish Town

Little Dix Bay

Virgin Gorda

Biras Creek

Mosquito Is.
Drake's Anchorage Resort Inn

Prickly Pear Is.

Necker Is.

Bitter End Yacht Club

To Anegada

Anegada

The Settlement

N

miles
km
0   3   5

miles
Kms
0   3   5

The British Virgins

Where are they? When Winston Churchill was asked this question in the House of Commons he is said to have replied: "Presumably as far as possible from the Isle of Man." In fact, the British Virgins are more than 3,000 miles from the Isle of Man, but only 60 miles from Puerto Rico and a 20-minute boat ride from St. Thomas. There are 60 of them strung along Sir Francis Drake Channel, where the wily Elizabethan mustered his ships before attacking the Spanish garrison at El Morro in San Juan. The main islands are Tortola (Spanish for turtle dove), Beef, Peter, and Virgin Gorda (the Fat Virgin—named by Columbus, who had obviously been too long at sea by this point); none of them is as big as Manhattan, and if you squeezed them all together, they would still be smaller than, say, Nantucket.

These Virgins have no hangups. They're quite content to lie there drowsing in the sun, loyal outposts of Queen Elizabeth. Britain sends over a governor who nominally attends to matters such as defense and the law courts (which are operated on the British system). Otherwise, the islanders elect their own Executive Council and run their own affairs, such as they are. But they're no dummies, these islanders: Legal tender is the U.S. dollar rather than the British pound sterling.

These are quiet islands for quiet people. There's no swinging nightlife here. No casino. What little sightseeing exists is usually done by boat rather than car. But what the Virgins dish out in return is glorious sea, glorious scenery, glorious serenity.

How to Get There   Service has greatly improved in recent years with the introduction of dependable flights by Sunaire and American Eagle (and less dependable flights on Air BVI) from San Juan and St. Thomas, two or three times a day each way, getting you to the remotest hideaway in time for a stroll on the beach before dinner. Air BVI also flies from St. Croix, St. Maarten, and Antigua.

Two points to remember: Always collect your luggage at San Juan or St. Thomas, rather than checking it through. The new Sunaire and Eagle services have cut down on the delays in transferring baggage, but it's still wise to handle the chore yourself, rather than have to wait for delayed luggage to arrive on the next flight (which may be the next morning). Also, although the schedules may list Virgin Gorda as the first stop for setting down passengers, your flight will first stop at Beef; there you'll have to get off to clear immigration and customs, then re-board for the five-minute hop to Virgin Gorda. Tiresome, bureaucratic, pennypinching.

There's an alternative transfer to the BVI, longer (one hour) but less expensive (about $17 per person each way): by twin-hulled, air-conditioned ferryboats, each carrying 60 to 80 passengers. The *Bomba Charger*, *Native Son*, and *Speedy's Fantasy* leave from the ferryboat dock in Charlotte Amalie (about 10 minutes by taxi from St. Thomas airport) to West End or Road Town on Tortola, continuing, in some cases, to Virgin Gorda.

Long Bay Hotel
Tortola

☆☆ ♈♈ ◑◑ $$$

Long the bay most certainly is—one mile of placid, sand-rimmed sea proceeding in two gentle curves to a conical hillock known as Sugar Loaf. It's Tortola's prime strand, located at the far end of the island and tucked away from everyone else (although the resort is traversed by a narrow island road that serves a handful of summer homes and rental villas).

You enter this low-key, 50-acre estate beneath an old wooden viaduct that carried water to the sugar mill whose ruins now embrace one of the resort's two restaurants. Beyond the mill, tropical blossoms share the lawns with a nine-hole pitch-and-putt golf course, with half the guest quarters parked beachside, the others stacked on the slope behind the dining pavilion and bar. That description may be familiar to anyone who has ever visited Long Bay in the past, but anyone returning today will find that new owners have wrought change. Several of the Natucketty gray-wood beach cottages that give Long Beach its special character still stand on their stilts beside the sand, but they have been augmented, also overshadowed, by clusters of two-story townhouses in coral pink with white trim; the former dining room and bar have been completely redone; the cottages on the hill are scheduled for reconstruction. When I stayed there (January 1991) the place was still something of a construction site, but once the lawns are tidied up and the grounds are relandscaped Long Bay will again be an attractive escape—but not quite the beachcombery Long Beach of old.

However, the fancy new guest rooms have much to commend them—perky fabrics and island furnishing, refrigerators, wet bars, walk-in closets; ceiling fans and lots of louvers are supplemented by air conditioning, but the clunky units protrude from the windows and mess up the drapes. Perhaps the most appealing features of the new accommodations are the 120-square-foot wooden terraces, ceiling fans (yes, on the decks), and separate entrances to the showers so that guests don't have to trek sand through the sleeping quarters. (Avoid room 515, since its deck is too close to the walkway to the beach, at a considerable loss of privacy; in any case, it has no hooks for bathrobes and its clock/radio was a dud.)

Long Bay has always been noted for friendly service and the staff members are still indeed willing and able to cope with the basics. Dinner appears course by course without fuss or flash and the food is well-prepared and well-presented, but it's not going to start any trends. Ditto the Garden Restaurant—a split-level space with lights highlighting the greenery, but with no sense of the sea or the beach. For that you have to trot over to the Brigantine Restaurant in the old mill.

You may want to give the new Long Bay Hotel another season to settle down; on the other hand, there *is* that beach. And even with all the new construction the rates are maybe even more appealing than ever.

Name: Long Bay Hotel
Manager: Terence Ford
Address: P.O. Box 433, Road Town, Tortola, BVI
Location: On the north shore, $14 by taxi from Road Town, $20 from the airport
Telephone: 809/495-4252
Fax: 809/495-4677
Reservations: Direct, toll free 800/729-9599 or 914/833-3300
Credit Cards: American Express, Mastercard, Visa
Rooms: 63 in 5 categories, all with ceiling fans and air conditioning, balconies or patios, pantries or wet bars, refrigerators, coffee makers, toasters, clock/radios, direct-dial telephones
Meals: Breakfast 7:30–4:00, lunch 11:00–4:00 at the beach bar, dinner 6:30–9:30 at the beach or in the Garden Restaurant (approx. $60 for two) informal dress; no room service
Entertainment: Taped classical music in the bar, live music two or three evenings a week on the bar deck
Sports: Beach (at times too shallow for serious swimming), freshwater pool, tennis (one court, no lights), 9-hole pitch-and-putt—all free; snorkeling gear for rent; other water sports nearby

The Sugar Mill
Tortola

☆☆ ♥♥♥ ⓣ $$

You might think that travel writers and food critics, who hear endless accounts of the agonies and travails of innkeepers, would steer firmly clear of such a profession. *No.* Critics Jeff and Jinx Morgan came over from San Francisco in the mid-eighties, plunged into the deep end of acquiring this delightful 20-roomer, and forged ahead upgrading cuisine, service, and ambience. And still, come hurricanes come hassles, they manage to find time to *write.*

The Sugar Mill is the weathered stone ruins of a 300-year-old mill and distillery set in a hilly garden above the sea, surrounded by flamboyant and wild orchid trees. To this basic setting the Morgans have added three trellised gazebos beside the bar, where most of the evening mixing and chatting takes place. And when last seen the Morgans had blithely added a second restaurant in their beach bar, called Islands and featuring moderately priced Antillean fare like *rotis* and jerk chicken.

It's the reputation of the kitchen that lures vacationers and islanders over to this corner of Tortola. The setting is picture-perfect: candlelight flickering on stone, graystone accented by the colors of Haiti primitives, ceiling fans turning slowly beneath the hiproof ceiling, tree frogs singing, glasses clinking, and friends exchanging greetings. Dinner is a prixe-fixe of just three courses, and there must be many diners who wish it would last another course or two—just to sample some of the other dishes from the Morgans' own recipe book. Why settle for lobster and christophene curry and forego the coconut shrimp? Or fish baked in banana leaves and coconut cream instead of cognac mustard beef pie? The range of desserts makes you wish the Morgans would toss in the towel and start a neighborhood pastry shop: coconut cloud tart, cappuccino mousse with crème de Kahlua, piña colada cake, and meringue sea shells with banana cream.

There may be other fine restaurants on the islands, but few have such a congenial atmosphere. Sugar Mill is sort of the tropical equivalent of one of those tiny *auberges* in Burgundy, with fine food and a few rooms for staying over. But here you wake up to perfect days and sparkling sea. And no abbeys or châteaux or musty museums that *must* be visited. Here you just slip into days of lazing. Rum french toast on the breakfast terrace, a dip in the garden pool. Read a book and shuffle to the beach bar for a long, boozy lunch that slowly fades into a siesta. Another dip, a walk to the village, a piña colada, and before you know where you are it's time to be thinking about curried banana soup and quail with mango-papaya sauce.

Name: The Sugar Mill
Owners/Managers: Jeff and Jinx Morgan
Address: P.O. Box 425, Tortola, BVI
Location: On the northwest shore, near Long Bay, about 45 minutes and $25 by taxi from the airport, but only 10 minutes and $5 from the ferry dock at West End
Telephone: 809/495-4355
Fax: 809/462-8834
Reservations: Caribbean Inns Ltd.
Credit Cards: American Express
Rooms: 20 in various cottages in the garden, all with ceiling fans, balconies, some with pantries
Meals: Breakfast 8:00–10:00 on the terrace below the bar, lunch 12:00–2:00 in Islands beach bar, dinner 7:00–9:00 in the main dining room (approx. $60 for two), 6:30–9:00 in Islands beach bar (approx. $30 for two); casual dress, "though a touch of glamor is never out of place"; no room service
Entertainment: Bar, board games, library
Sports: Circular freshwater pool, small beach for sunning, snorkeling gear; other water sports nearby

Peter Island
Tortola

☆☆☆☆ ♉♉ ☻☻☻ $$$$

From the beginning, I never warmed to this place, a Norwegian ship-owner's dull little Bergen-in-the-sun on a private 1,800-acre Virgin, and I wrote some unkind comments about it in an earlier edition of *Caribbean Hideaways.*

Now, several million dollars (and a serious training program) later, there's been a complete turnaround. Now owned by the Amway Corporation, Peter Island still may not be the place most people think of as one of

the fashionable and exclusive resorts in the Caribbean, yet if you had been here in recent seasons, you might have found yourself shuffling through the buffet line next to a reigning monarch and his casually attired queen, or a Hollywood studio's grand panjandrum and her suntanned beau. Or you might have recognized the reclusive twosome in the hilltop villa as a movie star and a well-known violin virtuoso. Turnaround, indeed!

It's one thing to spend a bundle on building and decorating new accommodations (we'll get to them in a minute) and on planting hibiscus by the cartload, but the real surprise was the staff.

There was a period when service was a sometimes thing, the staff about as cheerful as a Bergen winter. Today the glowers and ineptness have been displaced by smiles, an urge to please and, by island standards at least, real competence. I assumed the old lot had been tossed into the channel and replaced. But no—same people. It's simply that they've been motivated, encouraged, trained (in some cases with stints at top-flight hotels and cooking schools in the States).

But the most striking difference between the old and the new Peter Island are the 20 deluxe rooms—at least for the lucky 40 who are able to book them—in 5 two-story bluestone-and-cedar villas tucked behind newly transplanted palm and sea grape trees in a quiet corner of Dead-man's Bay—without spoiling the looks of what is surely one of the most ravishing beaches in the BVI.

Let me tell you about my room there. The spiffy interiors are done in a style that might be called Island Sophisticate. Tiled floors, cedar walls, Brazilian walnut cabinets, wicker sofas, and peacock chairs establish the island ambience, but some of the wood surfaces have been painted cream in a misguided attempt to "brighten" the rooms.

Bathrooms come with fitted hairdryers, step-down bathtubs with floor-to-ceiling windows (and blinds), twin vanities, terry robes, and heaps of towels—hand, bath, and beach—and Amway soaps. The walk-in closets have coated wire baskets/drawers (to keep air circulating around your polos) and aerosols of Amway bug spray (about the only trace of the island's corporate ownership anywhere on the property).

If you ever want to have a pillow fight, by the way, this is a veritable Pentagon of pillows—overabundant, overstuffed, a dozen on the king-size beds, a dozen more on the sofas.

The really distinctive touch, though, is the tiny atrium garden between the floor-to-ceiling windows beside the bathtub; it creates a lovely sense of sleeping or bathing in a garden without going outdoors; it lets sunlight filter in yet screens you from the eyes of passersby.

One final note of extravagance: I counted 14 light switches in my room. Normally, on a Caribbean island, that would amount to overkill, if not overload; but so well did the Norwegian shipowner plan the infrastructure here that the problems plaguing many Caribbean islands are hardly a consideration: The electricity rarely (maybe never) gives out because the private generator is more than adequate for the demand, and when other islands are panting for water, Peter is drawing on enormous underground reserves—stored in earthquake-proof tanks—and a new desalination plant capable of producing 40,000 gallons of fresh water a day. So what are the 14 switches for? *Two* ceiling fans, *two* bedside lights, overhead lights, one light each for patio, entrance, desk, reading, closet, mirror. There's even a night-light in the bathroom, a spotlight over the toilet—and a dimmer switch for a lamp concealed among the greenery in the atrium.

The other new attraction at Peter is Deadman's Bar & Grill, the smart 60-seat beachside bar/restaurant halfway along Deadman Bay, open to the breezes with some tables in the shade, others in the open. It's a welcome alternative both for guests who don't want to dress for dinner every evening and for visitors from the charter yachts who don't want to look like landlubbers when they come ashore (*Little* Deadman Bay, beyond the headland, is a favorite mooring for charter yachts). Menus here are less elaborate than the five-course banquets in the main dining pavilion, where the original gymnasiumlike roughcast hall has been cleverly chopped into smaller, more congenial rooms.

If every dish here isn't a success, at least enough of them *are* to make dinner by candlelight something to look forward to. The best choices are, as you might expect, the fresh grouper and lobster or dishes with a local touch, such as the tasty breast of chicken stuffed with bananas, dipped in coconut, and served on a bed of orange-flavored pumpkin. The wine list, appropriate for the cuisine and climate, offers choices from $10 to $100.

And what of the original resort? Still a little Bergen, but much less dull than before because the 32 A-frames on the broad breakwater now sport the same cheery fabrics and furnishings designed for the beachside rooms. These Harbour House rooms will appeal to vacationers who want to enjoy the privacy and facilities of a 1,800-acre private island without paying top dollar. Or vacationers who prefer to be nearer the swimming pool than the beach (this pool is a beauty). Or vacationers who welcome the option of being able to switch on air conditioners to supplement the cross ventilation and ceiling fans. If you stay in the Harbour View, though, I suggest you ask for a room on the second floor (better view) and as far from the main pavilion as possible (to avoid post-dinner festivities).

The one feature I still find disconcerting here is the music that accompanies dinner and post-dinner dancing. It's amplified and too loud (for just 120 diners!) and in any case, neither solo guitar nor native flute sounds its best when processed by electronics.

But now, of course, you can avoid the loudest of the musical evenings by dining at the beach bar where the accompaniment is the gentle sound of surf and swaying palms. But best of all, if you're lucky, is to retire to your private beachside patio, fetch the champagne from your private bar, and settle down for a private session of stargazing.

Name: Peter Island
Manager: James Holmes
Address: P.O. Box 211, BVI
Location: Across the channel from Road Town on Tortola, a trip of 20 minutes aboard a 46-ft. or 65-ft. luxury power yacht (regular ferry service 9 times a day between the 2 islands)
Telephone: 809/494-2561

Fax: 809/494-2561, ext. 405

Reservations: Own U.S. office, toll free 800/346-4451 or 616/776-6456; or Preferred Hotels

Credit Cards: All major cards

Rooms: 50, 20 in the new Beach Houses, 30 in the original Harbour View, plus 1 villa; all rooms have private baths, mini-bars, balconies or patios, ceiling fans and split-unit air conditioning, telephones ("confidentiality cannot be guaranteed" because transmission is by radio wave)

Meals: Breakfast 8:00–10:00, lunch 12:30–2:00, dinner 7:30–9:00 (in 2 restaurants—main pavilion and beach bar, both cooled by the breezes); dress code casual at the beach bar, jackets in the dining room (in season); for nonguests, dinner for two $80 in the dining room (5 courses), $60 at the beach (3 courses); room service (breakfast only), no extra charge

Entertainment: Bar/lounge, parlor games, live entertainment (amplified) during and after dinner, for listening or dancing

Sports: Freshwater pool, several beaches (including isolated coves with transportation and picnic baskets supplied), windsurfing, floats, sailing (HobieCats, Squibs, Sunfishes), snorkeling, tennis (4 Tru-Flex courts, lights on 2)—all free; scuba-diving, charter boats for fishing and sailing can be arranged

P.S.: "Due to the special design and structure of our resort, children under the age of six are not encouraged"; some small seminars and high-level meetings

P.P.S.: The resort also has 1 hilltop villa for rent, with 4 bedrooms

Guana Island Club
Guana Island

☆☆☆☆ ♈♈ ☻☻ $$$$

The hotel boatman is waiting at Beef Island Airport to escort you the couple of hundred yards to the dock; there he stows your luggage and you step aboard the 28-foot Bertram *Double Eagle* or the 26-foot *Shamrock Sovereign* for the 10-minute ride to the island. Past Tortola and Great Camanoe, around the rock formation that gave the island its name and so into White Bay. There you're greeted by a dazzling sight—glistening water, glistening sand. But instead of the inn being buried among the palm trees it perches on the hill, in the midday haze, looking for all the world like a hilltop village in the Aegean. As you approach the private dock the boatman sounds the horn and a Landrover pickup winds down the hill to meet you. Step ashore and you're in another world: Even the run-of-the-mill Caribbean seems a long way from here. Guana Island Club was built in the thirties as a private club on the foundations of a Quaker sugar and cotton plantation. The native stone walls are two feet thick, graying whitewash with green shutters. The rustic library and lounge suggest the country home of a well-bred but overdrawn gentleman farmer; the dining terrace is a pair of tables beneath a ramada and framed by pomegranate and ginger thomas trees, cape honeysuckle, and white frangipani. From the Sunset Terrace, fragrant with jasmine and carpeted with blossoms from the pink trumpet tree, stone paths and steps wind through archways of trees and off into the hillsides. The loudest sound is a kingbird, perched on the highest bough of the highest tree. The views are stunning—hills and coves, slivers of white sand and polyblue bays, sailboats beating to windward, vistas of distant islands.

Guana Island is not a place you come to for stylish accommodations and luxurious conveniences (for that, head for Little Dix Bay or Biras Creek). Some people, indeed, may find it *too* rustic. Certainly (thank goodness) no one has made any effort to "style" the classic simplicity of the guest rooms. They are clean and comfortable, of course, with rush rugs, handwoven bedspreads, wicker chairs; bathrooms have showers only, and guests are discouraged from lingering and wasting precious water. The original 12 guest rooms, perched on a ridge above the beach, were once part of the original plantation. Of these, the Barbados is perhaps the most romantic—self-contained, spacious, with a very private balcony overlooking the Atlantic; guests in the Fallen Jerusalem have private terraces and share a common veranda, with stunning views all the way to St. Thomas. On the topmost hill, in the Villa, the views of islands, sea, and sailboats are also stunning, but the furnishings are more contemporary, the decor mocha-and-ecru modern; rooms here can be reserved *ensuite* with private use of the patio pool.

This is a place that either embraces you instantly or leaves you cold. It has something of the charm and coziness of the best small inns of New England or Burgundy. Guests mingle at sundown on the Sunset Terrace or in the rattan lounge for cocktails at seven. Dinner is served by candlelight, family-style, everyone gathered around the three tables (unless any couple happens to request a table for two—rare). Dinner is a fixed four-course menu. "If the cook's husband goes out fishing we may have fish,

otherwise roast leg of lamb with fried eggplant or Guana potatoes. . . ."
Continental cuisine (roast stuffed veal, chicken Marengo, roast leg of
lamb) comes with local home-cooking touches—Rita's Cold Curry Soup,
Rose's Conch Fritters, home-baked breads and rolls, cassava bread prepared specially by an old lady on Tortola. After dinner, the party atmosphere continues on the Sunset Terrace, where guests reassemble for
coffee and cognac and conversation.

By day, Guana Island is 850 acres of ineffable peace. Since the only way
to get here is by boat, the island's seven beaches are virtually private, and
two of them are so secluded they are accessible only to waterborne castaways. Indeed, so serene is the entire setting that when you finally hoist
yourselves from your loungers on White Bay's 600 feet of white sand and
peer across the dappled water, all you see is another deserted beach—on
the uninhabited side of Tortola. The meadow beside the beach is given
over to a croquet court and two tennis courts, one clay, the other Omni; the
Salt Pond in the center of the island is heaven for bird spotters—a preserve for black-necked stilts and red-billed tropics, plovers, blue herons,
and a small flock of flamingos.

The main beach, a quarter-mile sweep of the whitest powder, is a stiff
hike down the hill, a stiffer hike back up. Transportation is either by Landrover or on the not-too-padded backs of Jack and Jenny. Jack and Jenny are
the island's mules. Sad to say, even in this demiparadise you have to be
careful because things "disappear": apparently Jack and Jenny have developed an appetite for books. They're especially partial to the flavors of paperbacks with glossy covers (titles and authors irrelevant), so be warned.

As we were saying, this is not an everyday Caribbean island, but people
who enjoy a relaxed, soft-spoken, almost genteel atmosphere will love it
here.

Name: Guana Island Club
Manager: Juergan Keppeler
Address: Guana Island, BVI
Location: A private island northeast of Tortola, 10 minutes by boat ($50
for 2 round trip) from Beef Island Airport
Telephone: 809/494-2354
Fax: 914/967-8048
Reservations: The inn's stateside office, 914/967-6050, or toll free
800/544-8262
Credit Cards: None
Rooms: 15, cooled by breezes and ceiling fans, with private bathrooms
and terraces

Meals: Breakfast 8:00–10:00, lunch at 1:00, afternoon tea at 4:00, cocktails at 7:00, dinner at 8:00 (6:45 for children); informal (jackets optional, but often worn in January and February); no room service

Entertainment: Library, Scrabble, backgammon, conversation

Sports: 7 beaches (2 accessible by boat only), snorkeling cove (gear available free), tennis, (2 courts, 1 clay, 1 Omni, no lights), croquet, walking trails, 14-ft. Phantom and Laser sailboats, 16-ft. Hobiecat, windsurfing—all free; waterskiing, powerboats for rent (fishing gear available), Bertram cruiser for charter; scuba available

P.S.: Closed September and October; check with the inn about rules regarding children

P.P.S.: The entire island can be rented for groups of up to 30

Little Dix Bay
Virgin Gorda

☆☆☆☆☆ ♀♀♀ ◑◑◑ $$$$$

The Fat Virgin turned out to be Cinderella after all. Her Prince Charming—Laurance Rockefeller, no less. Between the two of them they've created an idyllic, dreamy loveaway; a half-mile, palm-fringed crescent of soft, white beach, a protective reef on one side, low-lying hills on the other, with 500 acres of conserved landscape to screen out the everyday world.

You could say that Rockefeller spent $9 million creating this 102-room resort, but that would be doing him a disservice. Lots of people spend lots of millions on resorts. What Rockefeller has done here, as he did at Dorado Beach and Caneel Bay, is instill his Rockresorts troops with a delight in environment, an appreciation of good taste, a commitment to peace and privacy.

What's so impressive about Little Dix is the tender, loving dedication. Twenty gardeners fuss over the trees and flowers as if they were paying guests; reception staff meet you at the airport, register you while you're collecting your bags, and drive you straight to your room; lights are deflected, signs are muted; no radios are allowed on the beach, no spear guns on the reefs, no hair curlers beyond the guest rooms. When you get to the beach you feel like you have the place all to yourself, and to make

sure no roving charter boats encroach on the peaceful setting, Rock-resorts built a 120-yacht marina to lure them to the other side of Cow Hill.

From the beach all you can see of Little Dix Bay are the four conical shingled roofs of the main dining pavilion rising above the trees. The guest cottages are cloaked by sea grape, tamarind, and calabash trees, and almost disappear among the scarlet cordia, frangipani, and fragrant Jerusalem thorn. The cone-topped, wallaba-shingled cottages blend natural stone and tropical hardwoods—red cedar, purpleheart, mahogany, and locust; the interior decor brightens wicker and cane with Caribbean fabrics and wall hangings and new accents of bright cushions and bedspreads the color of the flowers. Walls of screens and louvers admit the trade winds; ceiling fans boost the breezes. For the benefit of longtime devotees of Little Dix: During 1987 and 1988 many of the original rooms were overhauled, bathrooms and shower stalls enlarged, things generally livened up (nothing too drastic, of course, just enough to bring the rooms and facilities more into line with current trends while still retaining the resort's unique, and enviable, environmental harmony) and 20 new rooms in hexagonal two-story buildings were completed.

A few of the rooms have a view; others are coddled by greenery and flowers, but they all have a balcony, patio, or terrace. It doesn't really make much difference which room you stay in, but my preference would be one of the beachside 30 hexagonal hives, 15 of them on stilts, with patios on the garden level and hammocks swinging from the stilts. Rooms 121 and 122, at the Cow Hill end, up a few feet from the beach, are quietest; any room from 29 to 44 is closer to the boat jetty; rooms 27, 28, 33, and 36 are closest to the tennis courts; while 80, at the end of the beach, is the most secluded.

Little Dix is a place for doing lots of things in such a leisurely way you never have time to do them all. Swim out to the raft. Sunbathe. Swim back from the raft. Float around on a rubber float. Walk to the end of the beach. Skim across the lagoon in a Sunfish. Walk to the other end of the beach. Have a picnic on one of the untrampled beaches farther along the coast (the hotel will fix a picnic lunch and sunshade; a boatman will take you there in a Boston whaler and come and fetch you again a few hours later). Play a set of tennis. Go for a sail on Laurance Rockefeller's 49-foot Hinckley. Go scuba-diving. Take a walk up Cow Hill. Ride horses. Drive over to the Baths and swim in the grottoes formed by giant prehistoric boulders. Take a safari in a Jeep. Wrap yourselves up in your hammock. Sip a Pimm's Cup on the terrace. In some ways, though, Little Dix is at its most Cinderellalike in the evening, when the tiny lamps guide you between the fragrant Jerusalem thorn and scarlet cordia to the hotel's most distinctive feature—the four-coned roof towering over the big breezy pavilion housing the lounge and bar and dining room. This soaring masterpiece, supported by huge beams of purpleheart (hoisted by hand because there was no equipment on the island strong enough to lift them) adds a touch of Polynesian magic. Here, or in the adjoining 60-seat Sugar Mill, any meal would be a banquet, but the food and cellar here are first-rate to begin with—like everything else at Little Dix.

Name: Little Dix Bay
Manager: E. David Brewer
Address: P.O. Box 70, Virgin Gorda, BVI
Location: 5 minutes from the Virgin Gorda airport (in free shuttle bus), 5 minutes from the marina, light-years from real life
Telephone: 809/495-5555
Fax: 809/495-5661
Reservations: Rockresorts
Credit Cards: American Express, Diners Club, Visa, MasterCard
Rooms: 102 double rooms, various combinations of one- and two-story villas, plus 2-bedroom cottages, all breeze-cooled, all showers (no baths), all with stocked refrigerator, wall safe, balcony or patio (no telephones, no radios, no TV, no air conditioning)
Meals: Breakfast 8:00–9:30, continental breakfast 7:30–8:00, lunch

12:30–2:00, afternoon tea 4:30, dinner 7:00–9:00 (approx. $65 for two, in the Polynesian pavilion or the Sugar Mill restaurant, both breeze-cooled); jackets no longer required evenings in the pavilion (though this doesn't mean you should wear shorts), informal in the Sugar Mill and for barbecues; room service for continental breakfast only, no extra charge

Entertainment: Guitarist, steel band, combo, or dancing 6 nights a week, library, games parlor with VCR; local bars and bands a short taxi ride away

Sports: Half-mile beach, snorkeling gear, small sailboats (and instruction), waterskiing, snorkeling trips, water taxis to adjacent beaches, tennis (7 courts, pro shop, no lights)—all free; day sails on Laurance Rockefeller's 49-ft. Hinckley yawl *Evening Star* ($95 per person, including lunch and open bar); horseback riding (with guide) $13 per hour per person; scuba, Jeep safaris can be arranged

P.S.: Small groups (10–15) for lunch once or twice a week, usually from Little Dix's sister resort, Caneel Bay (a ferry runs between the resorts every Wednesday and Friday); no children under eight; reservations from December to mid-March are virtually family heirlooms

Biras Creek
Virgin Gorda

☆☆☆ ♈♈ ◑◑ $$$$$

It looks for all the world like a Crusader's castle when you first see it as you cross North Sound: a circular stone fortress with a peaked roof. But when you climb the hill, there's no mistaking it for what it is: a one-of-a-kind luxury hideaway for people who want seclusion without giving up too many comforts. The turretlike structure turns out to be The Clubhouse, bar, and dining room—three shingled roofs over a framework of heavy hewn beams, opulently furnished with custom-designed rattan chairs and tables, boldly patterned Caribbean fabrics, island ceramics, and a huge tile mural.

All the guest rooms are spacious beachside suites, two to a cottage, recently redecorated with gingerbread trim, expensive-looking furniture indoors and out, bright fabrics, tiled floors, appliqué and ceramic doodads, ceiling fans, big patios, platform rockers, coffee makers, small refrigerators (stocked with rum and mixers) and—the nicest touch of all—neat little outdoor shower patios with potted plants and tall walls to hide your hides. Two new "grand suites" (their words, not mine) have full walls of glass overlooking the sea and "three-room bathrooms" with sunken tubs.

The surrounding acreage is more than just scenery. It's a living, breathing nature preserve created with equal regard for the animals that live here and the people who come to look at them. Trails wind through a desert landscape so natural you can step right over a 3-foot iguana and it'll never blink. A saltwater lake twitters and flaps with waterfowl and wading birds. Even the docks where Biras Creek's powerboats plow in and out every day are clean enough to support baby lobsters and thousands of delicate tropical fish. Take a flashlight down to the pier after dark and you can do some spectacular snorkeling—without a snorkel and without getting your feet wet.

Since the beginning, the Biras Creek kitchen has always ranked among the best in the Caribbean, although more *local* seafood might be welcome. You'll be expected to make a reservation for a table in the evening, but it's a table for the entire evening. You can turn up whenever you feel like eating, not when they feel like serving. No one will hustle you to finish and make way for other guests, so you can relax and linger lovingly over your Château Montrose or Château Mouton Rothschild. Because what has really distinguished the dining experience here, what has always somehow justified that imposing Crusaders castle setting, is the wine cellar. Your choices are not merely good wines but—even rarer in the islands—good vintages.

Which is all the more remarkable when you see where Biras Creek *is*. Not even the dustiest road leads there. No airplane lands here. And boats are few and far between. So what do you do when you're up this particular creek? Well, you might start by wandering off together over miles of nature trails, by foot or by bike. Visit cactus forests and stands of turpentine trees (locally dubbed "tourist trees," because they're tall, bright red, and peeling). Admire the newly luxurious gardens, coaxed and cosseted into blooming by a scientific green thumb from Georgia. There's shell gathering on the long breeze-swept beach outside your cottage, and floating, wallowing, or swimming in another sheltered sandy bay. And then there's just winding down and savoring the cherished solitude. Sophisticated solitude. So much so that keys to the cottages "are available at the reception desk if required."

Name: Biras Creek
Managers: Nigel and Marion Adams

Address: P.O. Box 54, Virgin Gorda, BVI

Location: On North Sound, accessible only by boat; by air to Virgin Gorda airstrip, where you will be met by Mr. Potter's taxi, which will convey you over the hills to Gun Creek, where the launch will be waiting—a fairly efficient transfer organized by frequent two-way radio conversations; the new North Sound ferry also has regular connections to Biras from Tortola

Telephone: 809/494-3555/6

Fax: 809/494-3557

Reservations: Ralph Locke Islands

Credit Cards: American Express, Visa, MasterCard

Rooms: 32, all suites (including 2 "grand suites"), all directly on the bay except for 8 rooms, all with ceiling fans, refrigerators (unstocked), coffee makers, "garden" showers

Meals: Breakfast 8:00–9:30, lunch 1:00, dinner 7:30–8:30 (approx. $75 to $95 for outside guests), in the hilltop pavilion, except for beachside barbecue lunches; slacks and "long-sleeved shirts with collars" required after 6:00, but no jackets; no room service; live music twice a week ("quiet during dinner, louder later")

Entertainment: Mostly yourselves, except for the live music.

Sports: Virtually private, sandy beach called Deep Bay on leeward side (3–4 minutes from rooms by bike, 5–8 minutes on foot, with bar service), freshwater pool on windward beach (beside the rooms), tennis (2 courts, with lights), windsurfing, snorkeling, Holder 14 sailboats, motorized dinghies, hiking trails, garden walks, bicycles—all free; scuba-diving, waterskiing, and sailing trips can be arranged

P.S.: "While we welcome families, we regret we cannot accept children under school age"; closed September and October

Bitter End Yacht Club
Virgin Gorda

☆☆ ♈♈ ➊➋➌ $$$

The first thing you discover about this wonderfully windblown little place is how apt its name is. To get here from the United States involves two, maybe three, flights, followed by a powerboat ride almost straight to your doorstep

Well, getting to heaven isn't easy, either.

As for Bitter End, it's worth the trip. How often, after all, do you have a chance to spend your days and nights on land or sea—or both?

Choose sea and you get your own seagoing sailboat—a floating suite, fully equipped and provisioned even if you never leave your mooring. It's a Cal 27 or Freedom 30 sloop, easy to handle on voyages to The Baths, Peter, Norman, Treasure, and other nearby cays. Yet whenever you come back, all the landlubber conveniences of the hotel are waiting for you— from hot showers to waiters to live music and movies and camaraderie.

Choose land and you get a room or suite in a big airy guest cottage or chalet, fashioned from fir and topped with an Antillean-style red roof, outfitted in rattan and tile, decorated with serapes and batiks. Ceiling fans cool the interiors (the chalets also have air conditioning); acres of sliding glass doors open to semiprivate sundecks shaded by Mexican thatch. Some cottages stand on stilts a few paces from the shore; others are perched among hibiscus and hummingbirds on the boulders and have undisturbed views of sea and sails and islets; the chalet suites are two-to-a-bungalow on a hillside dotted with prickly pear and mother-in-law cactus.

Now, what happens if you can't decide between a sea or land vacation? You still get your days afloat because you have at your disposal an entire fleet of sailing craft—all day, every day, and at no extra charge. To Bitter End's credit, when they list windsurfing as an attraction, they don't mean just a couple of boards—they mean top-of-the-line Mistral Sailboards by the dozen. When they say they've added Freedom 30s to the fleet, they mean eight new Freedoms.

Although there are lodgings here for only 166 land-billeted guests, Bitter End is on nearly every seasoned sailor's Caribbean itinerary, which means that it's hardly ever a deserted little backwater, even in summer. The sea-breezy bars and dining pavilions flutter with hundreds of burgees left behind by the constant tide of salt visitors—from charter yachters lazing their way through the islands on a regimen of Mumm's to flinty Ahabs sailing single-handed around the world with nothing but Saltines and a sextant. Not to mention one of the resort's more memorable stopovers: a couple kayaking from Venezuela to Miami Beach.

If you don't consider yourself especially seaworthy, don't let that keep you away from Bitter End. Take a lesson from the Nick Trotter Sailing School, whose instructors are there for anyone who has never so much as hoisted a jib as well as for old salts who want to learn new tricks at the starting line. Start with a small Sunfish and work up.

Even the scuba-diving here ranges from the simple to the serious.

There's great coral hopping just about anywhere you stick your mask in the water. Deeper down, Horseshoe Reef is littered with the skeletons of doomed galleons. The resort will set up instruction, trips, and dives (but this you have to pay for).

And don't worry about missing anything when you're underwater. When you go back to the Clubhouse Steak and Seafood Grille, the sea dogs will still be sitting around under the burgees nursing their grog and swapping salty tales.

Name: Bitter End Yacht Club

Manager: Mary Jo Ryan

Address: P.O. Box 46, Virgin Gorda, BVI

Location: At John o'Point, at the east end of North Sound; fly to Tortola, walk a few paces to the jetty to board the new *North Sound Express*, powerboats with three 225-horsepower engines that carry up to 30 passengers and get you to the resort in about 20 minutes ($12 one way, last departure from Tortola at 7:15); otherwise, you can still get there via Virgin Gorda and a taxi ride over the hills to Gun Creek, where the club launch will meet you

Telephone: 809/494-2745, 2746

Fax: 809/494-4756

Reservations: Own U.S. office, 312/944-5855 or toll free 800/872-2392

Credit Cards: All major cards

Rooms: 98, including 38 suites, in a variety of villas, bungalows, and chalets dotting the hillside on both sides of the dock, each with private bathroom, tiled shower, refrigerator, balcony/deck, ceiling fan; suites, in the former Tradewinds Resort (now called the Chalets), have air conditioning and especially large bathrooms

Meals: Breakfast 8:00–10:00, lunch 12:30–2:00, dinner 6:30–9:30, in two beachside pavilions (approx. $50 to $60 for two); casual dress; no room service; some taped music

Entertainment: Taped music (jazz, pop, modern—sometimes loud), live music three nights a week, movies every evening in the Sand Palace

Sports: Beach (not terrific), snorkeling, windsurfing, sailboats (Sunfishes, Lasers, Rhodes 19s, JR4s), boat trips on the launch *Prince of Wales* to the Isle of Anegada or The Baths (lunch included), skiffs with outboard motors, rowing sculls, sailing and windsurfing instruction—all free; Cal 27 and Freedom 30 sloops, scuba-diving with the famed Kilbrides (their base is on the next cay) extra

P.S.: "We don't encourage preschool children"

Drake's Anchorage Resort Inn

Virgin Gorda Sound

☆☆☆ ♈♈ ◑ $$$

East-northeast from Tortola there's an island marked Mosquito on the charts—and bliss in the memories of escapists.

Now called Drake's Anchorage, it's all of 126 acres, each and every acre private, the playground of only 30 lucky sandaled sun worshippers. Three wood-frame, gingerbread-trimmed cottages perch on stilts along the shore, three or four rooms in each, all with white walls, tile floors, rattan furniture, wicker lamps, and hand-made cotton kimonos for each guest. Bathrooms are strictly functional; paddle fans and ample louvers take care of ventilation; spacious sundecks overlook the beach (or, at least, *one* of the beaches). The rooms with the best breeze are numbers 10, 11, and 12.

A few shuffling steps away among the casuarina and sea grape trees you come to the main lodge, a low-slung, timber pavilion where the sea laps at your feet and the trade winds waft through the driftwood decor—turtle shells and fan coral and stuffed snapper and dolphin. Yachters with the foresight to radio ashore for reservations will join you here for drinks and dinner, turning the driftwood pavilion into a merry salon. They've come ashore for the bounty of Brutus, a.k.a. Chef Martin Belmar, a longtime hero in these parts for a menu that's more sophisticated than you might expect in a backwater off a backwater. His personal recipe for chocolate mousse is guarded more zealously than pirate gold, and typical entrées are dolphin in curry sauce with bananas, rack of lamb (for two) and sauté of boneless duck in citrus sauce, served with fried cracklings.

And that's about it. Drake's Anchorage is strictly a place for the Five S's—sunning, snorkeling, snoozing, smooching, sailing. And with only 30 overnight guests there's plenty of room for all five pastimes. Plenty of nature trails lined with frangipani and barrel cactus. Plenty of beach— the one on your doorstep, three more a short walk away. The most idyllic is Honeymoon (10 minutes, over the hill), especially if you don't have to share it with yacht people. Offshore, gardens of staghorn coral and reefs boggle the eyes of snorkelers.

When you amble over to Lime Tree Beach you'll pass the island's big surprise: a pair of villas (belonging to the owners, MIT professors), as stylishly grand as the cottages are plain-Jane—with cathedral ceilings, fieldstone walls, bathrooms with sunken stone tubs, fully equipped kitchens, and stereo. They're rentable, by the week only, but at rates that work out to be *much* less expensive than a mere room in some of the snazzier resorts on bigger islands.

Of course, if all that sand and solitude begin to pall, you can always charter a Boston Whaler and skim across the Sound to Bitter End— Manhattan to Mosquito's Staten Island.

Name: Drake's Anchorage Resort Inn
Managers: Gary and Lisa Ashley
Address: P.O. Box 2510, Virgin Gorda, BVI
Location: On Virgin Gorda Sound. To get there, first fly to Virgin Gorda airstrip, then take a taxi (the resort can arrange to have it waiting for you) to Gun Creek, where you'll be picked up by the resort's launch (the boat ride is included in the rate)
Telephone: 809/494-2254
Fax: 617/277-5379
Reservations: Own U.S. office, toll free 800/624-6651; 617/661-4745 in Massachusetts
Credit Cards: American Express, MasterCard, Visa
Rooms: 10 (including 2 suites) in 3 cottages, each with shower, ceiling fan, and breezes, terrace, big rechargeable flashlamps for occasions when the lights fail; the suites also have refrigerators (in addition, the resort has 2 deluxe villas with sunken tubs and fully equipped kitchens)
Meals: Breakfast 7:30–10:00, lunch noon–2:00, dinner 7:30 ($50 to $60 for two), all served in a breezy surfside pavilion; informal dress; room service for continental breakfast only; taped background music (classical or jazz)
Entertainment: Darts, chess, backgammon, library, VCR, guitarist on Thursday (occasionally a steel band)
Sports: 4 beaches, snorkeling gear, 19-ft. Squibbs, motorized dinghies, windsurfing—all free; scuba-diving, sailing, and tennis can be arranged
P.S.: Closed September through November

Added Attractions

Sandcastle
Jost Van Dyke

Jost Van Dyke is the island off the northwest corner of Tortola—a Robinson Crusoe place with no airstrip, no electricity, not many inhabitants, and a few restaurants that cater mostly to people stepping ashore from charter yachts. Dinner is by candlelight, reading is by propane lamps, and water is heated, if at all, by the noonday sun. Which is, for many escapists, what the Caribbean is all about. Sandcastle is right on the beach (a beauty, shared with maybe a couple of private homes that lie empty much of the time). There's no dock. You just roll up your trousers or skirt and wade through the surf to get here, after a choppy ride by water taxi from West End (the hotel will make the arrangements). Activity revolves around the breezy beach bar, and the water sports—windsurfing, Sunfish sailing, snorkeling, rafts. But most of the time guests just seem to lounge around, wearing to dinner what they wore to breakfast. Menus feature West Indian fare at lunch, continental at dinner. A new owner from Tampa has made extensive renovations (new floors, new roofs, that sort of thing) and brightened the rooms with new beds, furnishings, and fabrics. 4 cottages. Double: $325 with all meals in winter. *Sandcastle, White Bay, Jost Van Dyke, BVI. Mailing address: White Bay Sandcastle, Suite 237, Red Hook Plaza, USVI 00802. Telephone; 809/775-5262; fax: 809/775-350.*

Paradise Beach Resort
Virgin Gorda

It's actually Mango Bay, a half-mile sweep of fine white sand just around the headland from Savannah Bay and screened by a ring of low hills from the occasional vehicles that pass as traffic in these parts. Eight sand-colored contemporary villas hide out in this flowering peaceful garden, but only four belong to Paradise—the others belong to Mango Beach Resort (don't ask me why, something about an Italian partnership that went sour)—with only one of them actually on the beach. But the owners/

managers are friendly and welcoming (they stock your refrigerator with enough provisions to see you through your first supper and breakfast), the furnishings are comfortable, the kitchens are well-equipped, and the indoor/outdoor living rooms are generous. 8 studios and suites. Doubles: 1991–92, $165 (studio) to $295 (one-bedroom suite), including the use of a Jeep. *Paradise Beach Resort, Virgin Gorda, BVI. Telephone 809/495-5871; fax: 809/495-5872. U.S. reservations: toll free 800/225-4255 or 212/696-4506; fax: 212/689-1598.*

Frenchman's Cay Resort Hotel
Tortola

The cay in question is located at the west end of Tortola, linked to its south shore by a narrow bridge and jutting into the sea so that guests may enjoy ravishing views of sea and islets and the Sir Francis Drake Channel. The villas are sited on the rise above the coral-fringed sea, each with a balcony for sea-gazing, kitchen, dining room, sitting room, attractive if undistinguished island furniture, air conditioning, and ceiling fan. The 12 acres of relaxing garden incorporate an Omniturf tennis court, six hammocks beneath a cluster of sea grape trees, a swatch of sand for sunning, a headland for snorkeling around, a swimming pool, and the octagonal pavilion that houses the reception, bar, dining terrace, and something like 200 paperbacks. 9 one- and two-bedroom villas. Doubles: winter 1991–92, $170. *Frenchman's Cay Resort Hotel, P.O. Box 1054, West End, Tortola BVI. Telephone: toll free 800/235-4077 or 809/495-4844 (for reservations only); fax: 809/495-4056.*

The Dutch
Windwards

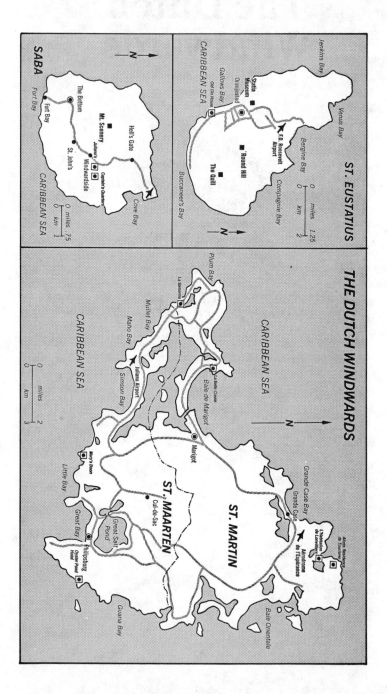

The Dutch Windwards

The Dutch West India Company that sent Henry Hudson scouting around the northeast coast of America also sent its ships and captains to the Caribbean; and Peter "Pegleg" Stuyvesant, the hobbling Hollander who became governor of New York City, tried to dislodge the Spanish from St. Maarten only to have the Spanish dislodge his leg. What 20th-century lovers will find in this corner of the Dutch Caribbean is a trio of islands—two totally unspoiled and serene (Saba and St. Eustatius), and one (St. Maarten/St. Martin) that offers only pockets of serenity since it tries to be a valid alternative to San Juan and the U.S. Virgins for vacationers who want hamburgers, casinos, and lively, varied nightlife.

Saba is the phantom silhouette you see on the horizon when you're sitting on the waterfront in St. Maarten. It's really the tip of a volcanic cone, a straight-up-and-down island with one roadway and a thousand inhabitants, completely unlike any other island in the Caribbean (it doesn't, for a start, have a beach). What it does have is a haunting, tranquil, otherworldly charm; but it's strictly for lovers who are content to be on their own (or, in recent years, for scuba-divers who crave a change of aqueous scenery).

St. Eustatius, likewise, except that you'll find beaches (sort of) here. Statia should be popular with Americans for historic reasons: The Dutch garrison of Fort Oranje fired the first salute to the brand-new American flag during the War of Independence. For its pains the island was zapped by England's Admiral Rodney, and Oranjestad, once the busiest harbor in the Indies, is now a half-submerged ghost town—but a treasure trove for snorkelers and scuba-divers.

Because the Dutch ended up splitting the island with the French, Sint Maarten is also St. Martin. When you go from one side to the other (there's no frontier, no customs), you're going from France to Holland—literally, because the French side is part of the Republic of France and the Dutch side is part of the Kingdom of the Netherlands. Between them, they offer you something like three dozen beaches—white, soft, powdery beaches, duty-free shopping, nightlife, scores of interesting restaurants, and more construction and concrete trucks than you probably want to encounter on your vacation.

131

How to Get There First, nonstop to St. Maarten by American, Pan Am, or Continental, from New York/Newark; from Miami, by Pan Am, Air France, and American. From St. Maarten, take Windward Islands Airways (Winair) to St. Eustatius or Saba, several flights daily, about $60 round trip to one or both islands. The 20-minute flight by Twin Otter DHT 6-300 to Saba is an experience in itself, because the only way the islanders could find a flat surface for a runway was by chopping the top off a hillock rising from the sea; touchdown here is like landing on an aircraft carrier, but no problem for an advanced STOL plane like the Twin Otter.

Note: If you're thinking of flying to any of St. Maarten's neighboring islands, buy your tickets before you leave home. The government of St. Maarten now imposes a stamp duty on airline tickets purchased on the island—not a token dollar or two, but $8 or thereabouts per ticket. Don't encourage them: Buy at home—you can always cash in your tickets if you decide not to use them.

Oyster Pond Hotel

St. Maarten

☆☆☆ 🍷🍷🍷🍷 ◐◐ $$$$

To get here, you have to drive all the way over to the other side of the island on a road engineered on the same basic principle as the roller coaster.

The final lurch brings you to the crest of a hill and your first heart-stopping glimpse of the eponymous pond—a circular lagoon with a circular hotel on the point of a promontory.

Until recently, that was about all you saw. That and St. Barthélemy off in the distance. But the island's concept of progress—where there's concrete there's cash—has been catching on even in this remote corner of the island, so there are now more homes, some condos, hotels, and restaurants strewn around the lagoon. Nevertheless, here are peace and seclusion in abundance. That hill you've just come over effectively shuts out the casual rubbernecker and bargain-hunting day-tripper. The background distractions of cars, planes, and tour buses are effectively eliminated, and the only distraction is more likely to be the occasional whine of an outboard motor hauling waterskiers around the pond.

Tranquility reigns once you step through the entrance to the hotel (formerly known as the Yacht Club)—a semicircle of natural stone with half a dozen arches, flanked by two square three-story stone towers. Within the arches, planters and white wicker with a scattering of antiques turn the lobby into a conservatory; jaunty sun umbrellas turn the circular courtyard into an al fresco café at lunchtime. Beyond are a plushly cushioned bar-lounge and a breezy candlelit restaurant with arched glass doors opening to the sea—and glimpses of aquamarine and azure every way you turn.

Guest rooms ring the courtyard, all but six of them on the second floor, around a white-walled gallery with dark wooden arches and balustrades, their names on shining brass plates—L'Oiseau des Iles, Passage, Monitor, Nirvana, Tantrum, and so on, echoes of ocean-going ships of bygone times. Decor is more or less identical throughout: New owners who took over six years ago installed Jacques Pergay wicker from France, white on white set against russet tiled floors, Pierre Deux fabrics, the walls decorated with prints by Rothko or Liechtenstein. Variations in rooms are minor—patios on the ground floor, balconies (and higher ceilings) on the upper level, a few extra cubic feet for deluxe rooms. Oddly enough, the duplex suites in the towers have no balcony, and the duplex gallery, accessible by steep wooden steps, is really practical only for reading or siestas. The best views (of the peaks of St. Barthélemy) are framed by the

windows of Monitor and Nirvana. Black Swan and Sea Cloud have practically no view but cost half the price of the Tower Suites.

But it's not just the pond that's expanding: The hotel itself has just
doubled its capacity by adding 20 new Oceanview Suites, farther out on
the bluff. Super location, super views (unobstructed sea and St. Barts),
super breezes. The new rooms (or "junior" suites, perhaps, rather than
full-scale suites) are larger than those in the main hotel and with more
luxurious amenities—cable television, refrigerators, direct-dial telephones, ceiling fans *and* air conditioning, despite the glorious breezes,
with sliding glass doors rather than louvers. Decor is stylishly island—clay
tile floors with scatter rugs, blue-and-coral upholstery on white wicker
armchairs, ottomans, sofas, and king-size beds.

Anita Adamski keeps the back of the house running smoothly; in the
kitchen, Paul Souchette (a protégé of La Samanna) turns out the kind of
cuisine (*soupe aux truffes, médaillons de langouste au gingembre, soufflé aux
framboises, marquise aux fraises et bananes*) that has dedicated gourmets
scrambling for reservations at one of the 14 Rosenthal-decked tables—
even though for outsiders dinner at Oyster Pond involves a helter-skelter
ride home on a roller coaster road.

Name: Oyster Pond Hotel
Manager: Anita Adamski
Address: P.O. Box 239, St. Maarten, NA
Location: On the southeastern shore, 35 minutes and $22 by taxi from
   the airport, 15 minutes and $12 from Philipsburg
Telephone: 599/52-2206, 2-3206
Fax: 5995-25695
Reservations: David B. Mitchell & Company, Inc.
Credit Cards: American Express, MasterCard, Visa
Rooms: 40, including 22 suites, all with ceiling fans, (4 with air condi-
   tioning), balconies or patios, showers only in the bathrooms; new
   Oceanview Suites have air conditioners, cable TV, refrigerator, balco-
   nies, direct-dial telephones
Meals: Breakfast 8:00–10:00, lunch noon–2:30, dinner 7:00–10:00
   (approx. $90 for two); informal dress ("but no shorts in the evening,
   proper attire at all times"); room service for continental breakfast only,
   no extra charge
Entertainment: Bar/lounge with taped music (cool jazz or classical),
   guitarist two evenings a week, parlor games
Sports: Mile-long beach a 2-minute walk through the gardens, stunning
   pool carved from coral rocks, tennis (2 mediocre courts, no lights)
P.S.: "No children under the age of ten years, please"

Mary's Boon
St. Maarten

☆☆ ♈♈ ◑ $$

The Mary with the boon was the late Mary Pomeroy, one of the Carib-bean's legendary innkeepers, but the inn is now owned by Rushton Little, known to many St. Maarten buffs as the long-term manager of Pasang-grahan.

It consists of six white-roofed bungalows with wraparound verandas and gingerbread trim garlanded with hibiscus, in a sandy garden of allamanda and shrubbery. It's right on the beach, practically in the water, on one of the longest stretches of sand on the island, and everything is designed to make the most of the setting. The sea beckons the minute you step through the main gate; lobby, dining room, and bar are all open to the breezes and framed by sea grape, coconut palms, and a wild cotton tree; the murmuring surf is right there all the time.

The rooms are really efficiencies, about half as large again as the average hotel room, fitted out with tile floors, ceiling fans, wicker furni-ture, a few antiques, original Dutch and Haitian paintings, and a few items that look as though they might have come from a millionaire's yacht. There's a kitchenette in case you feel like rustling up your own breakfasts, but the best feature of all is the bathroom: lots of toweling room, Italian white and sienna floor tiles, and tiled shower stalls. Since Rush Little took over six new rooms have been added (beside the bar) and the place has been spiffed up, top to bottom.

There's a great atmosphere at Mary's Boon. Pure beachcomber. The setting puts you in the mood for swimming and snorkeling, the exercise puts you in the mood for lunch, and lunch puts you in the mood for a siesta. Before you know where you are you're involved in the favorite pastime at Mary's Boon, sitting around the bar chatting with all sorts of interesting people—a French painter and his mistress; a pretty young woman who looks very innocent but happens to work for a think tank in California and knows all about supersonic jets; a few airline people; a few island people, old friends of Rush Little from farther down the islands. The bar is operated on the honor system and drinks (for house guests) cost only a dollar, so most guests are quite happy to have a few before dinner; and since coffee is served in the bar after dinner (damned good food, too), the drinking and conversation continue until the last guest goes home.

Mary's Boon is the almost perfect resort for young lovers except for one drawback—the airport. The runway is a hundred yards away, which means that half a dozen times a day you'll be bombarded by a few seconds of appalling whine, mostly midafternoon, never after 9:30 in the evening. But the agony really lasts for only 60 seconds and only half a dozen times a day, which leaves you another 23 hours and 53 minutes to enjoy all the good things about Mary's Boon.

Name: Mary's Boon
Manager: Rushton Little
Address: Airport P.O. Box 2078, St. Maarten, NA
Location: On the long, long beach at Simpson Bay, 5 minutes and $3.50 or more from the airport
Telephone: 599/55-4235
Fax: 599/55-3316
Reservations: Jane Condon, toll free 800/223-5608
Credit Cards: None
Rooms: 12 efficiencies, with showers, ceiling fans, and porches or verandas
Meals: Breakfast 7:30–9:30, lunch at 1:00, dinner at 8:00 ($50 to $70 for two, on the beachside veranda); casual dress
Entertainment: The clientele
Sports: Beach (more than 2 miles of it, one of the finest on the island), good swimming; water sports and tennis nearby
P.S.: No groups, no children, no cruise ship passengers, no outsiders for meals except by reservation; breakfast is the only meal served in August, September, and October

La Samanna
St. Martin

☆☆☆☆☆ ♉♉♉♉ ◑◑ $$$$$

A couple of decades ago a New York businessman named James Frankel went cruising in the Aegean Sea and found in those whitewashed Greek fishing villages the inspiration for his dream hotel, but what he's finally hatched, with the aid of architect Amos Morril, is Aegean with overtones of Marrakech, New Mexico, and Bel-Air.

Despite its seemingly jumbled pedigree, the 18-year-old La Samanna is a gorgeous spot, one of the most beautiful in the Caribees: gleaming white villas along a thousand yards of beach (a beauty in itself), rising in flower-decked terraces past a dazzlingly tiled swimming pool and the three-story main building to a pair of villas on a bluff above a cove. It's all arches and balconies and 55 acres of gardens, highlighted by blue doors and blue sun umbrellas (not the usual wishy-washy blue either, but a gutsy royal blue that makes even the Caribbean itself look sickly by comparison). The decor's artful blend of traditional wicker and rattan with contemporary lamps and chairs has stood the test of fashion (18 years ago, on reflection, it must have been well ahead of its time).

Rooms and apartments are divided among the three-story main lodge and villas strung beside the beach, among luxuriant tropical plantings. Most guests prefer ground-floor suites, presumably to be closer to the beach or pool; but aficionados of escapism opt for the second-floor suites with big tiled sundecks on their roofs—some so spacious they also have shaded patios topped by thatched ramadas. Pick, for example, a suite on the second floor of villas N and P (above the cove, to the left of the main lodge) and you get not only a dramatic view of the beach but on your rooftop deck you can do anything horizontally and only the pelicans will know.

Anyone wanting air conditioning as a backup for their fans should check into one of the 14 rooms in the main lodge, but the best room here (and the best value) is room 110, a corner nook newly redesigned to incorporate two terraces—one shaded by a ramada, the other an octagonal affair for taking in the sun, both furnished with armchairs and sofas of whimsical wicker.

Lounging on your sundeck. Lounging on your patio. Your room, your suite, your villa or whatever may be so appealing you never want to leave. But now and then shimmy into your smartest togs and head for the La Samanna dining terrace. If I had to name the Caribbean's 10 most romantic resort restaurants, this would surely be high on the list. It sits atop the coral cliff, open to the breezes, with frangipani and cup-of-gold framing glittering views of beach and sea. With its thatched ramada, red quarry tile floor, and rush chairs, it's a setting that conjures up memories of long leisurely luncheons on Mykonos. Or St. Tropez. But the Rosenthal china and replica Orient Express table lamps whisper Monte Carlo, and the cuisine is unabashedly French: *pavé de saumon mi-cuît au beurre de romarin, rouelles de langouste à la vapeur de verveine,* and *côte de veau poelée en cocotte, jus parfume à la sauge.* Bernard Malassenet, sous chef at La

Samanna since 1979, presides over the kitchen now that Jean-Pierre Jury has left to start his own restaurant. And there is a 20,000-bottle wine cellar to enhance the cuisine.

Sure you hear snide remarks about La Samanna not being what it used to be. About things slipping. Some people have been saying the same things about Pavarotti and Sutherland and Rysanek almost since they started singing. Some critics mumble about La Samanna's guests being too flashy. Flashy? Peter Ustinov? Richard Nixon?

On various visits to La Samanna, I've spotted Billy Graham and Jackie Onassis, but I've never been especially impressed by most of the guests here. When, after dinner, you stroll through that lovely low-arched lobby and lounge for a nightcap, it's the taste and flair that impress—the low-lit seven-sided tented lounge with its hand-sewn Indian embroidery. And the gleaming white terrace. And the striking blue-tiled swimming pool. The stars, the moonlight on the sea. The white villas peeking above the glistening palms. Gorgeous.

Name: La Samanna
Owner/Manager: Jan Beaujon
Address: B.P. 576, 97150 St. Martin, FWI
Location: On Long Beach, 15 minutes and $10 by taxi from the airport, about the same from Marigot
Telephone: 590/87-5122
Fax: 590/87-8786
Reservations: David B. Mitchell & Company, Inc.
Credit Cards: American Express
Rooms: 57 rooms, suites, and apartments, in a variety of one- and two-story villas or the main lodge, all with balconies or patios, telephones, kitchenettes, breezes and ceiling fans, some with air conditioning, some with rooftop decks
Meals: Breakfast 8:00–10:00, lunch 12:30–2:30, dinner 7:00–9:30 (approx. $100 for two), in an indoor/outdoor terrace overlooking the beach; informal but stylish dress (cover-ups at lunchtime); room service for continental breakfast only
Entertainment: Parlor games, soft taped music in the bar/lounge, which sometimes doubles as a low-key discotheque; VCR and movies in new TV room; casinos 5 minutes away
Sports: Mile-long beach, freshwater pool, snorkeling gear, Sunfish sailing, waterskiing, tennis (3 courts, no lights), new exercise pavilion with Stairmaster, Gerstung aerobic floor, Precor treadmill—all free
P.S.: No groups ever, some children during holidays

La Belle Creole
St. Martin
☆ ♀ ◑◑ $$$$

This is the hotel everyone seems to want to tag with the word "legendary." "A legend before its time," the resort's brochure proclaims. The vision of the "legendary" Claude Philippe of the Waldorf-Astoria we're told. Back in the sixties, Philippe wanted an ultraexclusive resort, in the style of a Mediterranean village, where he could entertain his rich and famous, royal and patrician Waldorf clientele. He finally managed to open the doors for a one-night stand before running out of money. For the next 20 years or thereabouts, the desolate village/resort squatted on its peninsula, a spectral pink stucco hamlet with a five-story campanile, being ripped off and ravished, waiting for a white knight. Along came Barron Hilton, head of Conrad International Hotels, the overseas division of Hilton USA (not to be confused with Hilton International, if you follow).

Now La Belle Creole has finally, after countless fits and startups, opened—but alas, the only thing "legendary" about the place is that it may have set the world record for the resort that took the longest to build.

Granted, it has a handsome setting, on the romantically named Pointe des Pierres à Chaux, a 25-acre promontory jutting into Marigot Bay; granted, the pink stucco and native stone buildings echo something of the allure of a Mediterranean village, complete with *plazuelas* and winding cobblestone paths shaded by flamboyant and sea grape trees. The problem is it's all so lifeless. Handsome the setting may be, but on an island blessed with beautiful beaches, one of Belle Creole's is narrow and windswept and unswimmable; the other is an overgrown sandlot alongside a manmade lagoon. And though the guest rooms are more spacious than usual in this part of the world, and the furniture *has* been imported from France, they still look like they've been decorated by committee.

Over its years of "graceful maturing," as the brochure puts it, La Belle Creole had acquired a patina of charm, even authenticity, but the Conrad crews seem to have scrubbed and flushed away the patina, trimmed and pruned the slightly overgrown shrubbery and flora, and arrived at something pristine and pretty but stark.

The 156 guest rooms and suites are deployed in 21 buildings of one, two, or three stories. They have all the basics (including, I'm happy to say, flow-through ventilation in addition to the ceiling fans and air conditioning), as well as frills like mini-bars and television to complement the antiqued pine desks and wardrobes, tile floors, and wicker and rattan chairs and sofas. The most inviting quarters are the split-level Loft Suites, but you want to avoid rooms on the ground floor of buildings 21 through 29; otherwise your patio may be looking directly into someone else's back wall. Next to the Loft Suites, the choice accommodations are the rooms identified as beachfront, in single-story villas lining the windward beach.

It would be gratifying to report that the "legendary" torch had been passed along from the "legendary" Philippe to the present-day staff. It hasn't. They're young and friendly (although not necessarily fluent in English) but decidedly unpolished. (I shudder to think what the young porters must feel about Claude Philippe's vision when they have to struggle up single-file staircases laden with overstuffed suitcases—he may have been an outstanding maître d' but he had no idea about the nitty-gritty of designing a hotel.) With sandwiches at $10 and up, you expect something better than the kind of service you normally get in a corner coffee shop back home. And what would the legendary Claude Philippe have to say about his dining room being cluttered with bottles of unlegendary Heinz tomato ketchup and A.1. sauce?

I'd still give this place a few more years to mature.

Name: La Belle Creole
Manager: Alan Stegman
Address: B.P. 118, Marigot 97150, St. Martin FWI
Location: On Marigot Bay, 5 minutes from Marigot, 20 minutes and $12 by taxi from the airport
Telephone: 590/87-5866
Fax: 011/590-875666 (ask for fax)
Reservations: Own office, Conrad International 212/980-6680; fax: 212/888-6557
Credit Cards: All major cards
Rooms: 156 rooms, including 14 suites, distributed among 20 buildings; all with private bathrooms (hairdryers, Lancôme toiletries), air conditioning and ceiling fans, refrigerators/mini-bars, satellite television (6 channels), direct-dial telephones
Meals: Breakfast 8:30–10:00, lunch noon–2:30 in the poolside café or La Provence indoor/outdoor restaurant (dinner $70 to $90 for two); special Creole Buffet and barbecue nights; informal dress; room service to midnight
Entertainment: Bar/lounge

Sports: 2 beaches (one a manmade lagoon, neither of them especially inviting compared to their neighbors'), freshwater free-form pool, tennis (4 courts, lighted, pro shop)—all free; water sports are available at extra charge

P.S.: You may encounter groups of up to 175 participants

L'Habitation de Lonvilliers
St. Martin

☆☆ ♀♀♀ ➊➋➌➍ $$$$

At first glance, 200-plus rooms may seem too large to be a hideaway on an overcrowded island like St. Martin, but L'Habitation is lucky enough to have a secluded cove, or *anse*, all to itself; and while the original plans call for a 400-room sprawl, the resort as it now stands is tucked into just one corner of a spacious playground.

It's located on the northern shore of the island, a winding, weaving drive past Marigot and beyond Grand Case, up a steep hill and down a steeper hill. If that sounds like the back of beyond, it isn't. Marigot is really only about 20 minutes away (unless you get stuck, as I did twice, behind construction vehicles that couldn't make it through the narrow streets). It's worth the winding, weaving drive just for the setting: curve of soft sand, protective hills on either side, an inlet leading to a marina with some impressive white-hulled yachts, and high on one hillside one of the best sports complexes on the island (a separate operation known as Le Privilege, but officially part of the facilities).

The French owners proclaimed their designs as a contemporary version of traditional plantation architecture, but that's a bit farfetched even though the main lodge, with its steep roofline and its touches of gingerbread trimming, is vaguely reminiscent of a traditional Great House. The big, open, two-story lobby is awash in light marble, with a huge bird cage housing an obstreperous Venezuelan macaw named Coco who is likely to drive guests *loco*. Beyond, a paved pathway lined by lawns and guest rooms leads to the pool, poolside bar and, beyond that, to the palm-fringed beach. Give the plantings another few growing seasons, and the pastel colors of the buildings a few more winters to mellow, and it may all be quite grand.

Certainly the rooms are comfortable and stylish, with balconies or patios, louvered shutters so that you can let in the breezes without looking into the rooms opposite; luxury touches include mini-bars, hairdryers, and nifty bathrobes. Guests are not shortchanged in matters *sportif*—down to complimentary kneeboards and canoes. When you compare what you get here with rooms and facilities elsewhere on St. Martin/St. Maarten (especially at another newcomer like La Belle Creole) you'll find that L'Habitation takes the prize for value.

One of L'Habitation's major attractions, however, is dining. In the hotel itself you have the choice of two dining rooms by day plus a gourmet restaurant, La Belle France, in the evening; on the hill at Le Privilege sports complex, there's another restaurant with a spectacular view, and by the marina, there's a terrace café for light lunches and between-meal snacks. Moreover, although you're in a fairly isolated spot, you won't be held to ransom: Prices are as reasonable as any on the island, although the evening "theme" dinners (Russian, Caribbean, etc.) don't look like much of a bargain.

Name: L'Habitation de Lonvilliers

Manager: Paul Finnegan

Address: Anse Marcel, P.O. Box 230, St. Martin, FWI

Location: At Marcel Bay, on the northern corner of the island, about 30 minutes and $35 to $40 by taxi from Juliana Airport; 15 minutes and $20 by taxi from Marigot; complimentary shuttle bus to Marigot daily

Telephone: 590/87-3333

Fax: 590/87-3038

Reservations: Meridien Hotels, 800/543-4300

Credit Cards: All major cards

Rooms: 189 rooms, 12 junior suites, 49 one-bedroom Marina Suites, all with marble bathrooms (separate toilet, bathrobes, amenities baskets, hairdryers), remote-control television (U.S. channels), mini-bars/refrigerators, direct-dial telephones, balconies or lanais; Marina Suites have complete kitchens (with microwaves) and two balconies

Meals: Breakfast from 7:00 on, lunch noon–5:00, dinner 5:30–1:00 a.m., in one of three indoor/outdoor restaurants, plus a café at the marina and a restaurant in the hillside sports complex; dinner from $40 to $90 for two; informal dress; live music (guitar, piano) in La Belle France; full room service during dining room hours, extra charge

Entertainment: Live music every evening (in the lounge just off the lobby, for example, where the voltage practically knocks the bottles off the shelves), disco on the hill

Sports: Lovely sheltered beach, 2 freshwater pools, snorkeling gear, paddleboats, canoes, kneeboards, gymnasium, squash, racquetball, tennis (6 courts, with lights, pro shop)—all free, except for use of the lights on the tennis courts; waterskiing, parasailing, wave runners, jetskis, motorboats, banana rides, horseback riding (10 horses, one-half-day trail rides) at extra charge

P.S.: Some business groups, lots of children at holidays

P.P.S.: Just as this edition was going to press, L'Habitation was acquired by France's Meridien Hotels; an additional wing of 125 rooms and 20 suites is currently under construction (target opening, October 1991), to be known as Le Domaine, and including an additional restaurant and bar. A professional outfit like Meridien should bring big improvements here—unless they add too many rooms over and above Le Domaine

Alizéa Résidence de Tourisme

St. Martin

☆ ♀♀♀ ◑ $$$

Named after the trade winds (*les alizés*) that regularly waft over from the bay, this amiable inn is located in the Mont Vernon section of St. Martin. Small condo complexes and a large first-class hotel are sprouting on the neighboring hillsides, but the shore is nonetheless magnificent—a mile-long curve of white sand abutting a sea that is a dozen shades of blue.

Guests have their choice of 26 spacious rooms and apartments, the latter located in bungalows scattered up the hillside. There's nothing here out of the ordinary to rouse your senses: tiled floors, standard rattan furniture, white walls of rough-textured concrete. Whirring ceiling fans augment the breezes (air conditioning is available), and the bathrooms have big shower stalls rather than tubs, but the best feature is the oversized balconies, with views of the seas, and fully equipped kitchenettes.

However, once you've dined in the restaurant you'll be hard-pressed to put your private kitchen to use. It's not the restaurant's setting (a breeze-cooled terrace with too much concrete, peaked roof hung with eight paddle fans, and coral-and-canteloupe color scheme) or the service (friendly but a tad hesitant), but what has put Alizéa on the map—the food.

The chef is an alumnus of Moulin de Mougin, Roger Vergé's Michelin-starred restaurant situated in the hills of the Côte d'Azur, so it's not surprising that the entrées blend Mediterranean flavors and style of preparation with traditional Caribbean. The meals I consumed seldom hit a wrong note. There was calalou soup with spinach and coconut; a mixed salad with breast and egg of quail, served in a delicate red-wine sauce; filet of sole in a green sauce; and sea scallops in phyllo pastry, on a bed of tomatoes and herbs.

To work off all those calories, you can sail, ride horseback, snorkle, windsurf, and play tennis or squash at the neighboring L'Habitation de Lonvilliers (above), a five-minute taxi ride away. The nearest beach is a ten-minute stroll across a road and through a field—a great way to build an appetite for dinner.

Name: Alizéa Résidence de Tourisme
Manager: François Cambournac
Address: 25 Mont Vernon, 97150 St. Martin, FWI
Location: About 12 miles from Princess Juliana Airport (a 20- to 30-minute ride, $20 by taxi), in the hills behind Orient Bay
Telephone: 590/87-3342
Fax: 590/87-7030
Reservations: Direct, 590/87-3342
Credit Cards: American Express, MasterCard, Visa
Rooms: 26, 18 in the hotel, 8 in bungalows; all with private patios, air conditioning, ceiling fans, direct-dial phones, radio and cable television, kitchenettes
Meals: Breakfast, lunch, dinner (on terrace, with taped music; reservations required, approx. $110 to $120 for two)
Entertainment: Bar pavilion, television in lobby, live music
Sports: Freshwater pool, beach on Orient Bay a 10-minute walk away; snorkeling, sailing, windsurfing, horseback riding, tennis, squash nearby
P.S.: Closed September

Captain's Quarters
Saba

☆ ♀ ◑ $

You get a quick tour of this extraordinary island on the way to the inn. Saba is higher than it is long: It goes up, up, and up to 2,900 feet within a sea-level distance of less than a mile. The largest village, Windwardside, is about halfway up, teetering on a ridge between two precipitous flanks of the volcano, one of which drops in a blanket of greenery almost vertically to the sea. It's a hugger-mugger hamlet of whitewashed walls, red tin roofs, cisterns, and family graves in the backyards, a few churches, lots of goats, and an air of charming, total detachment. Back in the 1800s, a retired sea captain (by tradition the Sabans are, not surprisingly, great sailors) built a little square whitewashed cottage with a red tin roof and gingerbread veranda, just as his ancestors and neighbors had done, right on the edge of the ravine; he was joined a few years later by the village doctor, who built yet another small white house next door, practically swamped by hibiscus and orchids and snowflake. Several years ago the two homes were integrated and converted into the Captain's Quarters inn.

Coming upon Captain's Quarters is like discovering a New England inn on top of a magic volcano. All rooms are doubles (some have four-poster beds), with plenty of welcome cross-ventilation, modern tiled bathrooms with hot water, and balconies with great views over the green cliffs to the sea.

Meals are served family style, simply but elegantly, in an arbor pavilion beneath breadfruit, papaya, mammi, and mango trees. There's a pool perched on the edge of the ravine adjoining a sundeck, and a casual, shaded bar close at hand—and that's it. There's nothing to do here but relax and take great chugalugging gulps of fresh pine air. Maybe you'll hike up Mount Scenery, drive down to The Bottom (Saba's capital) or stroll through the winding streets of Windwardside. Divers have now discovered Saba in a big way, but most of the time you'll eat, have a rum punch in the sun, eat, snooze, take a dip in the pool, eat, make love.

Name: Captain's Quarters
Manager: Joseph L. Johnson
Address: Windwardside, Saba, NA

Location: At the top of the hill, $35 plus tip from airport or pier with a tour of the island thrown in
Telephone: 599/46-2201
Fax: 599/46-2377
Reservations: International Travel & Resorts, Inc.; Jacques de Larsay
Credit Cards: MasterCard, Visa, American Express
Rooms: 10, no air conditioning (up here you certainly don't need it), showers, balconies
Meals: Breakfast 7:30–9:30, lunch 11:30–2:00, dinner 7:00; informal dress (but bring along a jacket or sweater for the evening)
Entertainment: The other guests, library, parlor games—but the radio in the bar is insufferably loud for a setting like this
Sports: Tiny freshwater pool, tennis, hiking—all free; dive shops nearby
P.S.: In winter, expect lots of day-trippers around lunchtime; closed September

Juliana's
Saba

☆ ♀ ◑ $

Instead of just trying to imagine what it would be like to snuggle up inside one of those enchanting Saban cottages, check into Flossie's Cottage, a green-and-white two-roomer that's so reasonably priced you won't feel extravagant leaving the second bedroom undisturbed. There's a stone fireplace in the master bedroom (yes, in the Caribbean—at this elevation it can be a welcome addition). The cottage is full of island charm with lattice-work indoors and out. Three porches overlook Saban homes, including the Floral Cottage, one of the most painted and photographed places in Windwardside. Flossie's is part of a tiny complex called Juliana's, lovingly managed by its owners, a warm-hearted couple who recently expanded their small bed-and-breakfast into 10 comfy, pine-paneled rooms with private balconies (whose views are even better than those at Captain's Quarters, one street below). They may not have the charm of Flossie's Cottage, but these guest rooms are spacious and spotless, with contemporary decor and thoughtful touches like candles and umbrellas.

A small pool, light-fare restaurant, and recreation room are the only distractions. On land. Up here, anyway. You may find you have most of the place to yourself since many of the guests to this lofty aerie have come to the island to go diving down the deep spectacular Saba Wall.

Name: Juliana's
Owners/Managers: Juliana and Franklin Johnson
Address: Windwardside, Saba, Netherlands Antilles
Location: At the top of the hill, $35 by taxi from the airport
Telephone: 599/46-2269
Fax: 599/46-2389
Reservations: Medhurst Associates, toll free 800/344-4606
Rooms: 10, plus a 2½-room apartment and a 2-bedroom cottage, all with balconies, ceiling fans, showers, clock/radios, and coffee makers; fireplace in Flossie's Cottage
Meals: Breakfast, lunch, and poolside snacks; fine dining within walking distance
Entertainment: Rec room with TV, VCR, and board games
Sports: Small pool (under construction, February 1991)

The Old Gin House
St. Eustatius

☆☆ ♀♀ ☎ $$$

"We wanted to build a small inn that had island flavor, but we also wanted it to have good beds and good plumbing." So you'll find Sealy Posturepedic mattresses, modern bathrooms, and hot water behind the warehouse doors and louver windows (all hand-carved on the island). The bedspreads and curtains were hand-stitched by the women of the island, the armoires hand-carved by the men. Everything else is antique, mostly French or Welsh, mostly 18th century "and violently anti-Victorian"—tea chests, captain's trunks, and other pieces appropriate to a former trading post.

The first of the two inns, Old Gin House, consists of 6 guest rooms, sitting directly above the beach and 14 rooms facing the pool and courtyard. All rooms have showers and individual water heaters. (Rooms 22 and 23, by the way, are the favorites of Holland's—and Statia's—Queen Beatrix.) Breakfast and lunch are served beachside, on a trellised terrace lined with ferns and crotons, shaded by palm trees, cooled by the breezes off the beach, and decorated with ancient anchors and other doohickeys hauled from the crumbled warehouses beneath the water. This is where *le tout* Statia gather—swimmers, snorkelers, scuba-divers, other expatriate Americans, crews from the sailboats in the bay. So many visitors gathered here that John and his late partner, Marty Scofield, decided to produce a second dining room with island flavor, across the street in the tumbledown ruins of an old cotton gin factory at the foot of the cliff. The Mooshay Bay dining room is furnished in island style, an antique here, Haitian decoration there, even the door hinges, designed by Marty and crafted in the islands.

Evenings are passed in a leisurely, congenial manner in the raftered Publick House, sampling strawberry daiquiries or playing Scrabble in the library on the wooden gallery. The big clock on the wall is 200 years old, and it's working again because one of the regular guests fixes old clocks as a hobby and spent a vacation getting this one into ticking order. Soft candle-light glows on hardwood shutters and sturdy beams and walls of bare brick that once served as ballast on sailing ships. Which is more pleasurable—the setting or the hearty dinner? Both.

Name: The Old Gin House

Owner/Manager: John May

Address: St. Eustatius, NA

Location: On the beach, beneath Fort Oranje, among the ruins of the 18th-century port, a 10-minute ride from the airport, $3.00 per person by taxi; Statia, in turn, is 20 minutes by Winair from St. Maarten (longer via Saba)

Telephone: 599/38-2319

Fax: 559/38-8555

Reservations: E. & M. Associates, 212/599-8280 or toll free 800/223-9832

Credit Cards: All major cards

Rooms: 20, all with ceiling fans, antiques, quarry tile floors, showers

Meals: Breakfast 8:00–9:30, lunch noon–2:00, dinner 7:30 (4 courses, wine, $70 for two); informal dress, but not scruffy; no room service

Entertainment: Conversation or parlor games in the pubby bar or elegant lounge, tasteful background music (Bach, jazz, "whatever's appropriate")

Sports: Beach (maybe—most of the black lava sand had washed away on a recent visit, but it's expected back any time now), freshwater pool, hiking up the volcano; the dive shop—"Dive Statia"—has complete, profes-

sional snorkeling and dive facilities, including underwater cameras—
with several wrecks from several centuries only a few yards offshore (to
say nothing of the tumbled foundations of the old warehouses)

P.S.: Children are "discouraged in winter"; closed all of September
through October 15; as of this writing, the Old Gin House is expected to
change owners some time later this year

Added Attractions

Pasanggrahan Royal Guesthouse Hotel
St. Maarten

There are not many authentic old West Indian guesthouses still in business
but this is one of them—so authentic its very name is Indonesian for "guesthouse." This is the West Indies as they were back in the days when London
and Paris and, in this case, The Hague, had to build government lodgings
for roving royalty and officials because there was no other place to put them
up. Royalty doesn't stay here anymore, but you may find yourselves down-
ing rum punches in the company of publishers, art directors, executives,
professors, and students, all with a common predilection for a relaxed,
informal atmosphere.

Pasanggrahan is located on the cluttered main street in Philipsburg,
between the street and the beach. It's a pretty little oasis—with a deep white
porch, potted plants, rocking chairs, ceiling fans, and an antique-filled
lounge. Ahead of you, beyond the Dining Gallery, are the beach, the bay,
and the Garden Café—a cool jungle of knep trees and coconut palms,
almond and avocado trees. This is the most popular spot in the hotel by
day, particularly at tea time; after sundown, imbibers withdraw to the Evening Bar with its four rattan stools, cowhide chairs, four-bladed fans.

The original 12 guest rooms are in a two-story veranda-trimmed wing
(known as the West Wing) next to the Garden Café, screened from the
beach by trees and hanging plants. Probably the most romantic room is the
Queen's Room (21) on the second floor of the main house, up a private
spiral stairway wreathed with bougainvillea, a sort of tree house among the

birds. There are also six efficiency apartments in a new two-story wing on the other side of the Garden Café; these rooms are more comfortable (air-conditioned, too), but the price you pay for the extra touches is that you're closer to the garden. Despite the crowds and traffic on Front Street, Pasanggrahan is quiet and relaxing. 32 rooms. Doubles: $114 to $150. *Pasanggrahan Royal Guesthouse Hotel, P.O. Box 151, 13 Front Street, St. Maarten, NA. Telephone: 599/52-3588; fax: 599/52-2885.*

Grand Case Beach Club
St. Martin

Grand Case, the village, is the prettiest hamlet on the French side, its narrow main street lined with pastel-colored frame houses, boutiques, bistros, bistros, and more bistros. At the far end of town, where the main road makes a sharp right toward the French side's airstrip, you keep going straight ahead along a dirt road barely wide enough for a Toyota, aiming for the red rooftops of the seven-year-old Grand Case Beach Club.

What this lovely, quiet corner of the island calls for is a low-profile inn such as, say, Pasanggrahan or Mary's Boon, but what the Beach Club presents is an ungainly three-story facade, in a narrow 6½-acre plot between path and beach. That said, the rooms and studios are comfortably furnished in upholstered rattan and freshly decorated with batiks and Haitian flat-iron sculptures; each has a balcony or patio a few feet from the placid bay, and most of them have serene views of the village and bay (803, 809, and 810 are billed as "garden view"). The location, compared to most of St. Maarten/St. Martin, is certainly secluded, and there are few distractions to intrude on your relaxation. This is another place worth considering if you want seclusion *and* condo-style wall-to-wall comforts and convenience, including fully equipped modern kitchenettes. Also, it's within walking distance of the fashionable bistros, so you, unlike everyone else, don't have to worry about parking. 76 units. Doubles: $200 to $315 CP. *Grand Case Beach Club, Grand Case 97150, St. Martin, FWI. Telephone: 590/87-5187; Fax: 590/87-5993.*

The Queen's Leewards

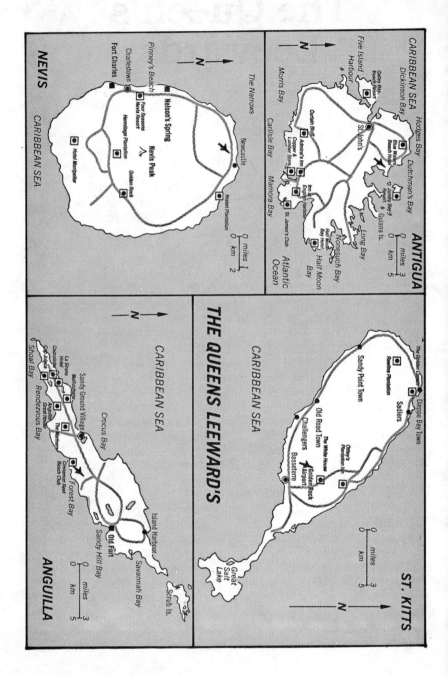

The Queen's Leewards

The five islands that make up this group are, with one exception, former British islands that now owe allegiance to Queen Elizabeth as head of the Commonwealth. The exception is Anguilla, whose citizens decided to secede from the St. Kitts/Nevis partnership and remain a Crown Colony, governed directly by London.

Antigua claims that lovers can spend a year on the island and visit a different beach each day. Maybe so, but once you see the beaches at, say, Half Moon or Curtain Bluff you'll wave good-bye to the others. Most of the tourist resorts are in the northwest, vaguely between the airport and St. John's, the capital; with the exception of the newly deluxed Blue Waters and the offshore Jumby Bay, all the hideaways in this guide are toward the south of the island, where the country is lusher, the hills higher (all the way to 1,319 ft. at the curiously named Boggy Peak), and picturesque English Harbour fairly oozes with memories of those dashing young 18th-century officers about town, Commander Horatio Nelson and Prince William Henry, Duke of Clarence. Apart from Nelson's Dockyard, forget the sightseeing, enjoy the beaches, even if you don't make it to all 365 of them.

St. Kitts, alias St. Christopher, may not be the most gorgeous island in the Caribbean and you have probably seen more romantic beaches; the central part has been developed (hotel, condos, golf, casino) for a mass tourism that has yet to mass, but the mountainous western half is authentic Caribbean, foothills of sugarcane, narrow coast-hugging roads, huddled villages. Two attractions worth the bumpy drives: the spectacular fort perched on Brimstone Hill (take a picnic) and Romney Manor, a batik workshop in a lovely old plantation house.

Nevis—now there's a fabulous little island. Slightly mystical, slightly spooky, with centuries-old plantations, tumbledown hamlets, rain forests, a mountain with its head in the clouds (hence Columbus's designation—*nieves*, or snow). Alexander Hamilton was born here, the illegitimate son of a Scottish planter (his restored home is now a museum); Fanny Nisbet lived here with her husband until he died, and she was later wooed, won, and wed by Nelson in the parish of Fig Tree. If they returned for a reunion, they'd find their island hadn't changed all that much—people still seek solace in the mineral baths where England's aristocracy came to frolic.

Anguilla is set apart from the others by geography as well as politics. It's just to the north of St. Martin, a 20-minute ferryboat ride from Marigot. It's long and flat and physically as undistinguished as the eel for which it's named, but if you want beautiful beaches here are beautiful beaches. And unaggressive, friendly people. In the past two or three years, a few new hotels have made people sit up and take notice, and another luxury resort is on the way. But Anguilla is a long, long way from being overdeveloped or crowded or spoiled—although there are now four traffic lights on the island and a smart new bungalow-size terminal at the airport.

Montserrat, 15 minutes by air southwest of Antigua, is one of the least visited of the Antilles—yet it's one of the lushest and prettiest, with its steep hills and dales, glens and glades. Some people compare it to Ireland (early settlers were Irish and the shamrock is the island's emblem). They wish. If Montserrat had beaches as beautiful as those in Ireland, we might have heard more of Montserrat.

How to Get There   For Antigua, Continental and BWIA from New York; Pan Am and BWIA from Miami; American from Orlando and Washington; Air Canada and BWIA from Toronto. For St. Kitts, BWIA operates two flights a week from New York and two a week from Miami via Antigua; otherwise fly to St. Maarten, St. Croix, or Antigua, then connect with LIAT, Windward, or American Eagle. To Nevis, there are a few flights daily on LIAT from Antigua or St. Kitts, but the island's inns recommend (and arrange) shared-seat charters on Carib Aviation; it costs a few dollars more, but it saves a lot of time and anguish. There is also ferryboat service between St. Kitts and Nevis, a one-hour trip, twice daily each way (no service on Thursday).

For Anguilla, first fly to St. Maarten and connect with Windward flights (10 minutes), or to San Juan to connect with nonstop, 40-minute flights on American Eagle. There are also small ferryboats several times a day between the island and Marigot on the French side of St. Martin.

⊂⟂⟩

Malliouhana

Anguilla

☆☆☆☆☆ ♈♈♈♈ ☯☯☯ $$$$$

When I first saw Anguilla's Mead Point in the early 1980s, it was a craggy coral headland flanked by two dream beaches—one a cove, one a ribbon of white sand—where "someone was planning to build a luxury hotel more beautiful than La Samanna." Ho-hum. How many times had we heard that over the years?

The next time I went there, someone was building a hotel. The stark headland was now a stark construction site, and during my tour of the cinder blocks and piled pipes, I met a young couple who had come over for the day from La Samanna just to see this new place they'd heard

about. They were so impressed they left behind a $1,000 deposit for the following February, for a room that didn't exist in a hotel yet to be built. I knew then that I was present at the birth of a legend.

From the day it finally formally opened in November 1984, people have clamored to get a room at Malliouhana. And most of the people who go there book on the spot for the following year. And who wouldn't want to return as often as possible to Malliouhana's delights? Thirty flowery acres with royal palms for shade, sea bean for greenery, purple and yellow allamanda for splashes of color, night-blooming jasmine for fragrance. Two beaches, one almost a mile long, the other a secluded cove, both with beach bars and loungers (the hotel assigns eight members of the staff just to look after two beaches!). A 30,000-bottle wine cellar, a kitchen headed by a Michelin two-star chef from the French Riviera. Villas whose bathrooms rival other hotels' bedrooms for size and appointments.

Step into the grand open-sided atrium lobby with its arched galleries and imposing paintings by Haiti's Jasamin Joseph and you feel like you're in a sort of Caribbean chateau. Settle into the plethora of pillows in the lounge's plump banquettes and admire the intricate raw silk tapestries and hand-carved wooden figurines (mostly lions in honor of owner Leon Roydon). The playground just beyond is a stunning landscape rather than a multilevel swimming pool.

The Roydons, on the spot day and night keeping an eye on things, have pulled out all the stops for their guests. Guest rooms are a carefree, non-bed-bumping 20 by 18 feet (a couple of feet larger in the villas) with decks only a few feet smaller. Interiors were designed by the esteemed Larry Peabody, with the same sensuous ambience he contrived for the much-lamented Habitation LeClerc in Haiti. Filtered sunbeams dapple hardwood louvers and quarry tile floors. Blossomy vines spill in profusion over balcony balustrades. Soft indirect lighting transforms lush planters and leafy ficus into mini-Edens. It's an atmosphere calculated to induce instant indolence. In addition, each villa comes with its own service pantry, a godsend for those of us who enjoy dawdly bathrobe breakfasts on the balcony, attended by not one but two maids—the first to set up the table and flowers, the other to serve piping hot croissants and pour freshly brewed tea. Granted, such a breakfast will set you back a tidy sum, but think what it does to set you up for another day of dallying.

Interiors are basically the same throughout the hotel, but location may make a minor difference. Assuming you have a choice (which might mean going in, say, June or July), rooms 109, 209, 110, and 210 would be my choices, although Leon Roydon's favorite is 101, above the bar but with a particularly large balcony. The most popular villas are those on the cliff beyond the pool, for the view; the two directly on Mead's Bay are for people who are water sprites. I spent time in a Garden Villa (i.e., looking at the hotel rather than the sea but surrounded by flowers) and didn't feel deprived in the slightest. The newest (1990) accommodations are six enormous two-terrace junior suites on the bluff above the cove—quiet and secluded, but that much farther from the dining room and tennis courts (farther—all of three minutes' stroll).

Many people travel much more than three minutes, of course, to dine here (if they can get a reservation), for the terrace restaurant is one of the undoubted lures to Malliouhana. Again, Leon Roydon wanted the best, and since one of his longtime friends was none other than Jo Rostang of the Michelin two-star La Bonne Auberge in Antibes, he invited him to direct the Malliouhana kitchen. Now even a Jo Rostang can't work miracles: Anguilla is no Riviera with an infinite supply of fresh produce. But given the shortcomings of a Caribbean island, Rostang and his corps do a commendable job of creating an Antillean Antibes. The setting helps immensely: an open fan-shaped pavilion above a sparkling sea, a hardwood canopy rising over giant ginger and stephanotis trees, with that final touch of civilized well-being—the pleasures of a well-endowed wine list (up to $400, but most are in the $20 to $30 range), the product of Leon Roydon's long-standing oenophilia.

All of which may make dining at Malliouhana sound like a stuffy activity. Far from it. The cuisine may be French, the china Limoges, the crystal French, and the cutlery Christophle, but the guests are as casually, but stylishly, dressed as they would be in St. Tropez. And the resort as a whole is as sports oriented as it now is luxurious—and now almost all the sporting activities are available at no extra charge. Including the smart new gymnasium/exercise pavilion on a bluff above the bay, its walls open to the sea and sky. You'd expect to find a place like this on the French Riviera, but on an unspoiled Caribbean backwater such as Anguilla it's a marvel.

Name: Malliouhana
Owners/Managers: Leon and Annette Roydon
Address: P.O. Box 173, Anguilla, BWI
Location: On Mead's Bay, on the northeast shore of the island, about 10 minutes and $12 by taxi from the airstrip, 6 or 7 minutes and $10 from the ferryboat pier at Blowing Point
Telephone: 809/497-6111
Fax: 809/497-6011
Reservations: David B. Mitchell & Company, Inc.
Credit Cards: None

Rooms: 34 rooms, plus 18 one- or two-bedroom suites, in the main building or villas, overlooking beach or garden, all with ceiling fans (all but 3
of the villas have air conditioning), balconies and/or lanais, stocked
refrigerators, telephones

Meals: Breakfast anytime in your room, lunch 12:30–3:00, dinner 7:00–
10:30 (approx. $90 to $100 for two, served in the breeze-cooled dining
terrace above the sea), also, lunchtime snacks in a new beach bar for hotel
guests only; informal but stylish dress; room service 7:30 a.m.–11:00
p.m. (special menu)

Entertainment: Elegant bar/lounge, two television rooms (cable and
video), library, backgammon, chess, cribbage

Sports: 2 beautiful beaches (1 long and public, 1 virtually private cove,
both with beach bars, good swimming and snorkeling), 2 freshwater
pools (chlorine-free but not for laps), tennis (4 courts, Peter Burwash
pro, lights), Sunfish and catamaran sailing, windsurfing, waterskiing,
exercise room (Nautilus devices, Aerobicycles, weights), trips to adjoining islets—all free; massage, scuba-diving, 35-ft. powerboat for fishing
available on the premises at extra charge

P.S.: One-week minimum stay in season

Cinnamon Reef Beach Club
Anguilla

☆☆☆ ♈♈ ◑◑ $$$

Take your pick: beach or bluff—either way you'll wallow in spacious sur-
roundings at the Cinnamon Reef's 40 beachside acres. All in individual
bungalows, they're suites rather than rooms, all with big patios, dressing
rooms, and high ceilings. Half of them are set beside the beach, the remain-
der on a bluff on the opposite side of the clubhouse. Otherwise, all the
suites are identical, with those lovely big patios, loungers, ceiling fans, sit-
ting areas with sofas and coffee tables, two double beds, and tiled sunken
shower stalls (no baths).

Architecturally, the Cinnamon style is eclectic, white poured concrete
that falls somewhere between Blockhouse Traditional and Mediterranean
Fanciful, all arches and portholes and cathedral doors. Patios are shaded by

arbors draped with wood rose, and when the bougainvillea blooms the bungalows are more Mediterranean than Blockhouse. The "clubhouse" (there's no significance to the word *club*) is a long, white arched temple abutting the bay, open to the breezes (but with electric-powered windows for those occasions when the breezes are too stiff), Italian tiled floors, pine-and-wicker and bamboo-and-canvas furnishings.

Pleasant setting, pleasant dining. The menu treads cautiously between Antillean and Manhattan, but is mostly seafood. There's entertainment (delightful, not obtrusive) most evenings by one of several local bands. Across the courtyard, the cavernous water tank provides an elevated foundation for the hotel's playground—a 40-by-60-foot pool, a snack bar, three tennis courts, and a new Jacuzzi in the poolside gazebo.

It's a shame that on an island with so many beautiful beaches, Cinnamon Reef has to make do with a modest curve of sand at the end of a pondlike harbor; on the other hand, the reef creates a lagoon-smooth bay and is one of the best spots on the island for sailing and windsurfing.

Name: Cinnamon Reef Beach Club
Manager: Norman Luxemburg
Address: Little Harbour, Anguilla, BWI
Location: On the south coast, at Little Harbour, 5 minutes and $5 by taxi from the airstrip and the ferryboat dock
Telephone: 809/497-2727
Fax: 809/497-3727
Reservations: Ralph Locke Islands
Credit Cards: American Express, MasterCard, Visa
Rooms: 14 bungalows and 8 suites, all with spacious bathrooms, including step-down tile showers and hairdryers, stocked mini-bars, telephones, patios, hammocks
Meals: Breakfast 8:00–10:30, lunch 11:30–2:30 in the main dining room, pool bar, or courtyard, afternoon tea 4:00, dinner 7:30–10:00 (approx. $60 to $70 for two), "long trousers for gentlemen in the dining room" in the evening; room service for all meals
Entertainment: Taped music, live music ("that is, evenings the musicians show up"); Friday night barbecue, backgammon, chess, Scrabble, dominoes, and Chinese checkers
Sports: Small beach, others nearby; 2 Deco-turf tennis courts, freshwater pool, Jacuzzi, windsurfing, Sunfish sailing, sailboats, paddleboats, floats, snorkeling, fishing gear—all free; island tours, sails, and picnic lunches can be arranged
P.S.: No children under 12 during peak season

Cap Juluca
Anguilla

☆☆☆☆   ♈♈♈♈   ◑◑ $$$$$

Let's start with the bathrooms, all 18 feet by 19 feet of them. Tubs for two (complete with headrests and Italian ceramic faucets) are separated from a sunbathing garden-patio by a wall of glass; floors and walls are marble, doors are louvered Brazilian hardwood, the walk-in closets could accommodate Elizabeth Taylor's wardrobe (well, her swimsuits anyway), and dimmer lights and ceiling fans underscore the romantic touch.

The bathrooms are the most striking feature of the Cap Juluca lodgings but even if you had only a shower and a john these accommodations would stand out from the crowd. For a start, they're spacious. Sitting rooms measure 27 feet by 19 feet, with banquettes piled high with pillows and walls of louvered hardwood shutter doors leading to enormous patios, partly shaded, partly in the sun, their arches framing a dazzle of flowers and the blue sea beckoning just beyond the hammock slung between the sea grape trees. Bedrooms are only slightly smaller, with king-size beds, more louvered doors opening to patios, bedside controls for the air conditioning and for setting the appropriate level of lighting. Decor throughout, without drawing attention to itself, plays tasteful variations on the resort's overall Moorish theme with Moroccan artifacts and antiques—ceremonial wedding belts, inlaid cabinets, antique saddlebags—all artfully framed and hung on stark white walls.

Potentially, this is one of the most romantic (grandest, even) resorts in the Caribbean. It's located on the leeward side of the island, on a heart-stoppingly beautiful mile of white sandy beach called Maundys Bay, with another mile or so, Cove Bay, on the other side of a low headland; 179 acres of land and lagoon screen the resort from any future development in Anguilla (although you will, alas, pass just such an abandoned project near the entrance to Cap Juluca). The master plan for these 179 blessed acres calls for 66 hotel rooms in 10 two-story Moorish–Patmos–Xanadu villas, all arches and mini-minarets, with a few million-dollar private homes tucked away at the far end of the beach.

As of this writing, though, what we have is a handsome restaurant and the first eight villas with a total of 48 rooms; another cluster of villas is being built a couple of hundred yards away and most of the time the work should not be a distraction for guests, except for occasional sounds of hammering, maybe an occasional cloud of dust.

Cap Juluca (the name comes from the ancient Arawak Indian rainbow god) is the brainchild of Robin and Sue Ricketts, an English couple with decades of innkeeping experience, who conceived Malliouhana and brought it to fruition; and who applied very un-Caribbeanlike energy, experience, and doggedness to their new dream. To say nothing of imagination. To say nothing of a flair for romance.

The resort's 74-seater white-on-white-on-blue restaurant with Moorish lines and a British name, Pimm's, is an Arabian Night's fantasy of white arches, domes, and palm trees, a mirage set on a rocky point beside the beach and sea. *Very* romantic. Guests dine off Hutschenreuther china, and the food and service here can now hold their own against many of the highly touted bistros across the channel on French St. Martin (in fact, many of Pimm's patrons come by ferry from Marigot).

Much of the appeal of a deluxe resort like this is service with a capital S. Among the flourishes are island cooks to prepare West Indian dinners in guest rooms; light meals served in rooms for guests arriving late and exhausted; signing in and settling bills in your room rather than in the lobby; pre-check-in of luggage and tickets at the airport on St. Maarten (not Anguilla), which allows you to spend an extra hour sunning rather than standing in line—and well worth the small extra fee.

And with 2½ staff members per room, Cap Juluca can service well above the Caribbean norm.

Name: Cap Juluca
Manager: Peter Shepherd
Address: P.O. Box 240, Anguilla, BWI
Location: On the leeward coast, about 15 minutes and $16 by taxi from the airport, $13 from the ferry dock (the resort meets guests at the airport)
Telephone: 809/497-6666
Fax: 809/497-6617
Reservations: Direct, toll free 800/323-0139; Flagship Hotels & Resorts
Credit Cards: American Express
Rooms: 48 rooms, studios, and suites in 8 two-story, Moorish-style villas (18 more rooms and suites to follow), all with lavish bathrooms (some with double bathtubs, patio-gardens, separate WCs, bidets, and dressing rooms), king-size beds, terraces or patios with hammocks or loungers, stocked refrigerators/icemakers, air conditioning and ceiling fans, room safes, direct-dial telephones; some with kitchenettes (micro-

waves and blenders), rooftop sun terraces with refrigerator, and barbecue grills; 2 suites with private plunge pools; VCR and music cassettes for rent

Meals: Breakfast served in villas any time after 7:30 (each villa has a maids' pantry), lunch noon–2:30 and dinner 7:00–10:00 in Pimm's beachside restaurant (approx. $65 to $75 for two), informal dress, but generally stylish; some live music and dancing in winter; room service from Pimm's at extra charge, and local cooks will, with 24 hours' notice, prepare West Indian dinners in rooms

Entertainment: Chatterton's Bar at Pimm's, library of cassettes

Sports: 2 mile-long beaches, snorkeling gear, windsurfing, waterskiing, HobieCat and Sunfish sailing, tennis (3 courts, lights, pro)—all free; scuba-diving and sailboat trips can be arranged

P.S.: 7-night minimum in winter, 10 nights at Christmas; closed September and October

Coccoloba

Anguilla

☆☆☆☆ 🍷🍷🍷 ◐◐◐ $$$$

If what you have in mind is a quiet unspoiled island and a quiet small resort where you can lounge on a patio a few paces from a beautiful beach and a beckoning sea, this may be the answer.

It's located on a low coral headland between two postcard-pretty beaches, with the main lodge perched on the promontory and the guest rooms in cottages arranged in a series of V's stretching along the bluff above the beach. Coccoloba is new in the sense that it reopened five years ago with a new name (it means "sea grape tree," I'm told), under new owners and new management. Those of you who know Anguilla may be thinking it sounds suspiciously like the former La Sante. You're right—but you should see what's been happening here.

The original La Sante opened many years ago as the last word in health spas and quickly turned into the last word in flops. The architecture was eccentric, the decor funereal. It wasn't so much an ugly duckling as a silly goose: The offices (not the bathrooms, the offices) were lined with marble; the peak-roofed main lodge looked more like the chapel in the valley than a rejuvenating spa; the dining terrace had a superb view of the sea so the owners built a kitchen on the point of the headland. Then along came a group of investors who have plowed millions into their 30 acres—including a quarter million on landscaping and a half million on a completely new kitchen. Manager Martin Flaherty has restyled the place (a thankless task), softening the harshness of the main "chapel," dispelling gloom in his inimitable way, creating an appealing indoor/outdoor dining terrace with yellow and white raftered ceiling, canvas awnings, and judicious clusters of potted plants, and he has removed the barbecue kitchen and installed terraces with tables and chairs.

The revamped guest rooms have a modified split-level layout, with a sitting area up front, double beds and dresser at the rear. There are lots of nice touches here: three Cannon sheets per bed, turndown service, bathrooms stacked with fluffy white towels and bathrobes, shower stalls with lots of shelves for soaps and shampoos from the amenities tray. The refrigerator is stocked with goodies, on the house (you pay only to have the items restocked). Because of the V-type setup of the layout, some of the rooms are less desirable than others since their arbor-decked patios are too close to the footpath; ask for one of the following rooms: 106 through 111, 115, 117, 121, 122, 124, or 125—all set back from the path but still with sea views. There are also six rooms in a two-story villa known as the Great House, at the far end of the beach, some with very generous balconies or patios; there's also a second swimming pool one floor up.

One of the most impressive features of the resort is its kitchen, not only because of the physical plant (La Sante's doctors could have performed operations here, it's so spotless) but because of the classy cuisine of chef Patricio Herrera, a Rockresort alumnus, like Martin Flaherty. Memorable dishes include Anguilla lobster Coccoloba style (that is, with cucumber puree and mild garlic, a hint of Pernod and olive oil) and grilled veal chop with shallots and port.

In a new hotel, on an island with no hotel school and few restaurants, dining room personnel have to be trained from scratch, but obviously someone has taken a lot of trouble to coach the young staff. Maybe even overcoach: Coffee was poured so carefully, you often ended up with only half a cupful, lest it spill over. But it's so refreshing to be served by people who are trying, really trying—and so friendly you'll quickly learn how happy they are to have you on their island and hope that you will have a wonderful time enjoying their beautiful beaches. And that goes for everyone in the hotel—all 100 of them.

You can't turn a silly goose into a proud peacock overnight, but now that the lantana and stefanotis, the jasmine downey and pink vine and bird's nest fern are establishing themselves, Coccoloba has become one of the most relaxing, most inviting hideaways in the islands.

Name: Coccoloba

Manager: Martin Flaherty

Address: P.O. Box 332, Barnes Bay, Anguilla, BWI

Location: Between Barnes Bay and Meads Bay, 20 minutes from the ferry or airport (by taxi, $13 from ferry and $15 from airport); the hotel will help you arrange flights by small plane to Anguilla from San Juan or St. Maarten

Telephone: 809/497-6871

Fax: 809/497-6332

Reservations: Direct, toll free 800/833-3559 or 203/230-0011

Credit Cards: American Express, MasterCard, Visa

Rooms: 51 rooms, including 2 suites, most of them in beachside cottages, except for 6 in a beachside villa; each with sea view (some more so than others), patio, sitting area, 2 double beds, bathrobes, stocked refrigerator, air conditioning, direct-dial telephone, ceiling fans, hairdryers, wall safe, walking cane and umbrella, amenities tray

Meals: Early-morning coffee 7:00–8:00, breakfast 8:00–10:00, poolside lunch 12:30–2:30, afternoon tea 4:00–5:00, dinner 7:00–9:30 ("reservations, please") in the indoor/outdoor pavilion; 4-course dinner $100 for two; room service for continental breakfast only; informal dress ("After 6 p.m., we suggest gentlemen wear slacks and comfortable shirts"); West Indian buffet once a week, some background music (mostly classical tapes)

Entertainment: Live music in the lounge/bar on weekends; library, game room with backgammon, chess, etc.; TV/VCR lounge; horticultural tours

Sports: 2 beaches (each about a mile long), large L-shaped pool with swim-up bar, whirlpool, exercise room, massage, sunfloats, tennis (2 courts, lit, ball machine, Peter Burwash pro), windsurfing, Sunfish sailing—all free, except for tennis lessons; other water sports and sailboat trips to outlying islands can be arranged

The Mariners
Anguilla

☆☆ ♈♈ ◑◑ $$$

This hotel, bless its unprepossessing heart, strives to be true to its West Indian heritage: verandas trimmed with gingerbread, lattice screens and louvers, two-toned shutters, tray ceilings and wood moldings, showers rather than baths, ceiling fans and breezes rather than air conditioners. And the hotel dining room is just what you would hope to find in a backwater such as this—island-style, indoor-outdoor architecture, planter-and-driftwood decor, and a wooden beachside gallery with views of outlying islets—Salt, Dog, and Prickly Pear.

Located on 8 acres beside a crescent of beach adjoining the salt ponds and a somnolent, one-street hamlet called Sandy Ground, the Mariners' rooms and suites are now divided among cottages and 2 two-story buildings. Each cottage is ingeniously arranged so guests can have simply a double room or a studio with kitchen or a one-bedroom suite or the entire cottage (a two-bedroom suite), each unit with its own entrance (interior double doors enhance privacy). They're arranged basically in an arc around the beach and sea grape trees, with others closer to the cliff; the setup and rate roster are confusing—Beachfront, Beachfront Special, Cliffside, Cliffside Special. The first two categories are best.

You'll probably see more than your cottage mates in the newly expanded, split-level dining room—it's a popular spot for guests in other hotels as well as day-trippers from St. Maarten because it's so moderately priced.

But even if the dining room is busy there's still the lovely peace of your veranda awaiting, where you can retire for the evening and think lazily about tomorrow.

Name: The Mariners
Owner/Manager: Clive Carty
Address: P.O. Box 139, Sandy Ground, Anguilla, BWI
Location: In the village of Sandy Ground, $8 by taxi and 5 minutes from the airstrip
Telephone: 809/497-2671, 2815
Fax: 809/497-2901

Reservations: Direct, toll free 800/848-7938 or International Travel & Resorts, Inc.

Credit Cards: American Express, MasterCard, Visa

Rooms: 65 studios, rooms, and suites; all with unstocked refrigerators, telephones, ceiling fans, some with kitchenettes and air conditioning

Meals: Breakfast 7:30–9:30, continental 9:30–10:30, lunch noon–2:30, snacks/afternoon tea 2:30–6:00, dinner 7:30–9:30 (approx. $40 to $45 for two) in beachside restaurant or poolside grill; informal dress; room service for continental breakfast 7:30–10:30, for bar service 10:30 a.m.–7:00 p.m.

Entertainment: Live music (amplified) 5 nights a week; buffet on Thursdays, West Indian Night on Saturdays; video/TV in the conference room

Sports: Beach, Jacuzzi, windsurfing, Sunfish sailing, snorkeling equipment, tennis (1 court, lighted)—all free; catamaran and picnic excursions to nearby Sandy Island, Little Bay, or Prickly Pear at extra charge

P.S.: Some small groups and conferences

Anguilla Great House
Anguilla

☆ ♀ ◐ $$$

If it's reminiscent of the pastel-and-gingerbread daintiness of The Mariners, it's no accident: Some of the same owners and planners were involved with both hotels. This newcomer sits by the edge of Rendezvous Bay, at the end of an as-yet unpaved road, its bungalows arranged in an inverted U around a swimming pool and still sparsely planted gardens. Give it another year or two and it should be an appealing spot. For one thing, the rooms are pleasantly designed and furnished. The exteriors echo the lines of a plantation great house; the interiors are trimly and simply fitted out with island Victorian mahogany, print fabrics, traditional tray ceilings overhead, and white ceramic tile underfoot. The verandas come with comfy padded deck chairs and, in a few months, their trellis fences will be entwined with hibiscus and bougainvillea. In the evening, guests can watch the twinkling lights of St. Maarten as they sit in the beachside pavilion and dine on creole conch and grouper, West Indian style.

If you hanker after a very quiet, unpretentious, laid-back, moderately priced hideaway beside the beach, the Great House could be your great place.

Name: Anguilla Great House
Manager: Cecil Niles
Address: P.O. Box 157, Rendezvous Bay, Anguilla, BWI
Location: On Rendezvous Bay, about 15 minutes and $12 from the airport or ferry
Telephone: 809/497-6061
Fax: 809/497-6019
Reservations: Anguilla Tourism Information, toll free 800/553-4939
Credit Cards: American Express, MasterCard, Visa
Rooms: 25 rooms, including 10 studios (another 40 are planned, but probably won't materialize for another couple of seasons); studios can be combined with the rooms to make one- or two-bedroom suites; all rooms have private bathroom, ceiling fan, veranda, small kitchen (studios and suites only)
Meals: Breakfast 7:30–9:30, lunch noon–2:30, dinner 6:00–9:30 (approx. $40 to $50 for two), casual dress; some taped music; no room service
Entertainment: Local string band on Friday nights during the peak season
Sports: Lovely beach, freshwater pool; various water sports activities can be arranged just along the beach

La Sirena Hotel and Villas
Anguilla

☆☆ ⚲ ◑ $$

It may not have the cachet of Malliouhana or Cap Juluca—neighbors that are two of the classiest, most expensive resorts in the Caribbean—but this small, friendly hotel has other charms. First of all, with a room rate under $200 a night, it's much easier on the pocketbook. Second, many couples seeking to get away from it all may actually prefer the casual, more relaxed beach ambience of La Sirena. You don't have to worry about staining the chair cushions with suntan oil, and the rooms, each with a balcony or patio, are spacious enough to function as comfortable retreats. Best of all, the beach—a mile-long, half-deserted, glistening white strand—is only a two-minute stroll away. It's the same beach used by high-paying guests at Malliouhana, and to get to it all you have to do is stroll a hundred yards down the hill, past a scattering of private homes.

The three-story hotel rises above a spread of lawns, gardens, and a large swimming pool; stone pathways lead through the gardens to the three villas, a Jacuzzi, and a second, more secluded pool. The Spanish-Mediterranean architecture—white walls and arches, wooden balconies, ochre-tiled roofs—is complimented inside by a decorating scheme of wicker and terra-cotta tile floors.

Each of the 20 guest rooms in the hotel has a mini-bar concealed in a light wicker chest, a bed with an arched wicker headboard, and contemporary accoutrements such as a floor lamp and a clock/radio. The balcony or patio is furnished with a canvas deck chair and table. The bathrooms have large tiled showers and fine toiletries. Only the closets are a bit skimpy; the Swiss owners must assume that their guests travel light.

For the best views and highest ceilings, reserve a room on the upper floors; two of the rooms on the third floor have wraparound views and lead to a roof terrace. Those seeking absolute privacy and more space should check out one of the three villas, two with two bedrooms and one with three bedrooms. Each costs about the same as a single room at many of the more exclusive resorts.

True, the service here is rather lackluster, and the dining room, presided over by a Swiss chef, is uninspired. However, since meals are optional, if you want to dine in style I suggest you head for the more elegant dining rooms at Malliouhana, Cap Juluca, and Coccoloba. The latter is only a five-minute walk away, and the lower room rate you're paying at La Sirena will enable you to splurge at the dining table without guilt.

Name: La Sirena Hotel, Restaurant, and Villas
Manager: Rolf Masshardt
Address: P.O. Box 200, Mead's Bay, Anguilla BWI
Location: On mile-long Mead's Bay, 10 minutes and $15 by taxi from the airport
Telephone: 809/497-6827
Fax: 809/497-6829
Reservations: International Travel & Resorts, Inc.
Credit Cards: American Express
Rooms: 20, in addition to 3 villas, 2 with two bedrooms and 1 with three bedrooms, all with balcony with deck chair, tile floors, telephone, clock/radio, ceiling fans
Meals: Breakfast, lunch, dinner (in dining room, approx. $60 to $70 for two); casual dress; villas have kitchens and barbecue equipment; no room service
Entertainment: Sunday brunch with live music, taped music in bar/lounge, cable television, videos for rent
Sports: Two freshwater pools; tennis, waterskiing, windsurfing, day trips to adjoining islands available
P.S.: Some children, especially on weekends

The Golden Lemon
St. Kitts

☆☆☆☆ ♈♈♈ ●● $$$

Take a 17th-century French manor house, in a walled garden beside a grove of coconut palms, and fill it with antiques and bric-a-brac. Paint the exterior a bright lemon yellow, tuck a tiny pool into a corner of the leafy garden, and you'll have a handsome country inn in the tropics.

But you still wouldn't have the legendary Golden Lemon.

The Golden Lemon is, indeed, all of these things—a 17th-century manor of volcanic stone with a wood-framed upper floor, an 18th-century addition, surrounded by a gallery with a wide-plank floor. From the gallery you look out to unspoiled Caribbean—a reef, a lagoon, a beach of black sand, and the palm trees, tall and spindly and well into their second century. In the walled garden, loungers and hammocks invite guests to relax among the trees, and white tables and chairs set on the arcade beneath the gallery beckon for a punch or lunch. All very romantic for escapists who want to savor authentic Antillean surroundings (the inn is located at the end of a narrow street in a simple fishing village). But there's more to The Golden Lemon than that.

It was the old manor's good fortune to be spotted by a connoisseur with a sharp eye who could recognize the house's thoroughbred qualities in its then dilapidated state. At the time, Arthur Leaman was an editor with

House & Garden magazine, who also happened to be an avid collector with an eclectic array of antiques—four-poster beds, mahogany tables, Blue Delft tulipieres from Holland, clocks from Italy.

Leaman has an extraordinary and enviable ability of taking a castoff and, by deft juxtaposition or downright alchemy, turning it into an heirloom. Each room at the Lemon is different, each a masterpiece of composition and color (I have a hunch that if you stood on your head in one of the rooms here you'd still have a picture-perfect interior). I can never decide which is my favorite—the Hibiscus Room with its two white canopy beds, the Batik Room with steps up to the big antique double beds, the Victorian Room for its ornamentation, the Turtle Room for its carapaceous doodads. Every detail reflects Leaman's refined sense of style, so much so that you're so busy admiring the grace notes in the bathrooms you don't even notice you're stepping into a prefab plastic shower stall. Rooms on the upper floor, it should be noted, are wood framed and not infallibly soundproof, but your compensation for keeping your voices down or overhearing extraneous sounds is breakfast on the gallery. First the maid announces its arrival by the sounds of a table being set with a trayful of playful lemon-motif mugs and plates; then she returns with pewter dishes of homemade preserves, perfectly browned toast, perfectly timed scrambled eggs, a Thermos of coffee—all served course by course. It gets your day off to a very slow, very stylish start—just the way life should be at The Golden Lemon.

For guests who want more substantial accommodations, Arthur Leaman recently built two wings of one- and two-bedroom townhouses across the garden, beside the volcanic shore: some with decks overhanging the sea, most of them with small private pools. The interiors, needless to say, are exquisite: some with canopy beds, some with bull's-eye orrery windows that dapple sunlight on the ceramic tile floors. The prices are extravagant at first glance, but, considering the setting and surroundings, not outlandish.

Evenings have always been special at The Golden Lemon. For one thing, the walled garden setting out front and the junglelike garden at the rear become quite magical with soft lighting and soft breezes. The antique-filled dining room sparkles in the soft light of candelabra and chandeliers. Traditionally Arthur Leaman hosts a sort of captain's table, but tables are also set for twos and fours, with place cards (which Leaman discreetly rotates to give everyone a chance to mix, if that's what they want). But his patrician presence and wit still turn evenings into house parties. Especially since the guests next to you in the bar may be paying their 20th visit in 20 years. Dinner is a fixed menu, with the inn's five young cooks always coming up with something to look forward to; but repeat guests know to look ahead to Sunday brunch and the inn's West Indies Rum Beef Stew, liberally laced with Mount Gay.

The Golden Lemon, let me quickly add, is not for everyone. Its devotees are mostly designers and writers, young Kennedys, young Washingtonians, people in the theater, people who probably will not be startled to find suitless sunbathers around the pool. Gracious Arthur Leaman may be, but he doesn't want his inn (and the solitude of his guests) disturbed by cruise ship passengers, young people under 18, and because, he claims, "you can take only so much of paradise," no one is allowed to stay longer than two weeks.

Name: The Golden Lemon
Owner/Manager: Arthur Leaman
Address: Dieppe Bay Town, St. Kitts, St. Kitts and Nevis, WI
Location: In the village of Dieppe Bay Town, on the northeast coast, about 30 minutes and $20 by taxi from the airport (let the hotel know when you're arriving and they'll arrange for a dependable driver to meet you)
Telephone: 809/465-7260
Fax: 809/465-4019
Reservations: Caribbean Inns Ltd.; Jacques de Larsay
Credit Cards: American Express, Visa (personal checks accepted)
Rooms: 18, in 2 buildings, all with private bathrooms, ceiling fans, balconies or patios; kitchens in the 16 new condo units, one with shared pool, the others with private pools
Meals: Breakfast 7:30–10:00, lunch noon–3:00 in the patio, afternoon tea 4:00 ("real tea, *not* bags"), dinner 7:00–9:00 ($40 to $60 for two, in the fan-cooled main dining room); informal dress ("no wet bathing suits at lunch"); room service, no extra charge
Entertainment: The bar, quiet taped music, backgammon, parlor games
Sports: Beach, 20-ft. by 40-ft. freshwater pool (plus private pools in the annex), new tennis court, snorkeling gear, "tremendous reef"—free
P.S.: "No young people under 18"; stays limited to 1-week minimum, 2-week maximum

Rawlins Plantation
St. Kitts

☆☆☆ ♉♉♉ ◑◑ $$$

Don't be put off by the bumpy, hilly dirt road that meanders through the fields of sugarcane. Granted, 260 acres of the sweet stuff are hardly a romantic introduction to a hideaway, but press on up the hill and around one last bend and you arrive at a 12-acre oasis of clipped lawns and clumps of croton, breadfruit, and African tulip trees. Up ahead, the cane fields rise to the foothills of forest-clad Mount Misery; behind you, the fields fall off to the sea and distant views of St. Eustatius.

At 350 feet above the sea, Rawlins is exactly the sort of cool, calm place you relish returning to after a sticky day at the beach, or a hike through the rain forest foothills beneath canopies of trailing vines and wild orchids. Some guests actually make it all the way up to the peak, 4,000 feet above the sea, where Misery must seem like Cloud Nine. The Walwyns will arrange picnic outings up the mountain, part of the way by Jeep, the rest on foot, fortified by their special rum punch. They've also flattened a corner of their lawn as that rarity—a grass tennis court.

But essentially, this is an inn for relaxing. You'd never get me near the beach or up a hill. Sit on the picket-fenced porch of Mount Pleasant House and read a hefty book. Dunk in the spring-fed pool that was once the mill's cistern. Sit on the veranda of the great house at sundown, gin and tonic in hand, and chat with fellow guests or simply dream sundown dreams. Check out the library. Watch the sunset's glow on Statia. Listen to the birds and tree frogs. This is what people have in mind when they dream about a place to unwind, really unwind.

The inn still looks like a gentleman's plantation—white great house at the center, cottages for managers and overseers in the gardens, a white lattice gazebo beside the pool. The circular stone base of the 17th-century windmill is now a duplex suite, much favored by honeymooners—pretty red and white sitting room downstairs, white cast-iron double bed upstairs; another pink and pretty suite, brand new, has a king-size bed, and semi-sunken bathroom with semi-sunken tiled bath. The remaining guest rooms reflect the ambience of colonial times, mahogany floors and rush rugs rather than fitted carpet, ceiling fans rather than air conditioning, wicker and rattan rather than leather, mosquito nets for decoration rather than protection. It's very tasteful and low-key. No television, no telephones. Plumbing and electricity are the sole concessions to the 20th century.

The former boiling room, where the cane was converted to molasses, is now a flower-draped, stone-floored patio where guests gather for drinks before moving to the new indoor/outdoor dining salon. Dining has always been especially pleasurable here. Rawlins has never promised "the finest continental cuisine" or any of the fatuous claims of some island inns. What Claire Rawson and her local cook serve are perfectly prepared local dishes with their own local embellishments and Claire's "lightly French accent." Thus, guests gathered on the veranda can while away sun-dappled noondays while nibbling on flying fish fritters, rice with ackee and dill, soups (breadfruit, eggplant, or cucumber with fresh mint), curries garnished with garden-fresh avocados and pawpaws. In the evening, candles sparkle on gold-and-white Royal Doulton and servings of, say, crab and callaloo soup, St. Kitts shrimp with orange butter, roast lamb with mango sauce, and, for dessert, bananas in puff pastry with local mountain oranges.

Between them, Rawlins and Golden Lemon have created a haven for lovers of fine foods, who wend their way to this unspoiled corner of the Caribbean year after year—Rockefellers, Cabots, Rothschilds, peers of the realm, doctors and lawyers and writers

Name: Rawlins Plantation

Owners/Managers: Paul and Claire Rawson

Address: P.O. Box 340, St. Kitts, WI

Location: At Mt. Pleasant Estate, near Dieppe Bay Town; directly across the island from the airport, about 30 minutes and $28 by taxi (let the Rawsons know when you'll arrive and they'll send a driver to meet you, "probably Dash, who'll wait forever in case your flight is late")

Telephone: 809/465-6221

Fax: 809/465-4954

Reservations: Own U.S. office, 617/367-8959; Jacques de Larsay

Credit Cards: None

Rooms: 10, in various cottages, including the Sugar Mill Suite and 2 two-bedroom cottages with shared sitting room, all with breezes and ceiling fans, private bathrooms, hairdryers, balconies or patios

Meals: Breakfast from 8:00 on, buffet lunch 1:00–2:00 on the veranda, afternoon tea 4:00, dinner at 8:00 (approx. $70 for two, fixed menu, in the dining room); informal dress, but no shorts; room service for breakfast only, no extra charge

Entertainment: "Good conversation," parlor games, library with more reading material than you can handle on one vacation

Sports: Small spring-fed pool, croquet, tennis (1 grass court, cramped, no lights), snorkeling gear, transportation to the beach at Golden Lemon—free; full-day cruises on catamaran to Nevis and crater trips by Jeep and foot can be arranged

P.S.: Some children, but they have their own supper hour

Ottley's Plantation Inn
St. Kitts

☆☆☆ ♉♉ ◐ $$$

The Ottley sugar plantation was founded in the early 1700s and the Great House was built in 1832, but its career as an inn didn't begin until just last December. It was bought by the Keusch family, former bookstore owners in New Jersey, who saw the tumbledown estate as the perfect means for fulfilling their dream of becoming Caribbean innkeepers. After a year of scraping paint, hammering, chipping, and (to say nothing of a month or two of **re**-renovation after Hurricane Hugo paid a brief call), their fantasy has finally come true.

The Great House, a two-story manor of brimstone walls, has a wraparound veranda, yellow storm shutters with white trim, and Brazilian hardwood doors—features that give the structure the appropriate tropical flavor. It sits on 35 acres of splendid grounds, with a row of coconut palms in the front and a rain forest out back in the foothills that lead to the peak of Mount Liamigua. Stone paths lead past crumbling statuary, allamanda-draped terraces, silk cotton and cinnamon trees, and massive strangler figs to a mango orchard.

In the inn itself, overstuffed rattan chairs and paisley Sheraton sofas on the veranda and in the Great Room are an invitation for afternoon tea-taking or just plain lounging around. Stunning Portuguese rugs accent the hardwood floors, and an antique Chippendale-style bar in the Great Room sets just the right tone for sundown socializing. A small anteroom with a television set and VCR functions as an entertainment center and library.

Ottley's 15 guest rooms are all variations of an overall style that's a cross between English Country and New Jersey Suburban, enhanced by wicker and rattan, floral chintz bedspreads and upholstery, antiques, and bric-a-brac. Island prints decorate the white walls, while Portuguese scatter rugs cover the white plank floors. Thoughtful touches include reading lights beside the comfy armchairs (the touch of a former bookseller), gardenia potpourri, and plentiful supplies of beach towels. Some of the rooms are quite large for a plantation-style inn, with high-peaked ceilings and floor dimensions of 24 by 24 feet. Several of the bathrooms are also unusually generous, with separate dressing areas and tiled bathtubs and showers. A favorite with privacy seekers is the Stone Cottage, the former cotton house, which has mullion windows, a separate sitting room, and a small patio looking out to sea. In a former incarnation, Princess Margaret reputedly stayed here. All the rooms are cooled by breezes and ceiling fans (air conditioning is available as well).

The owners' daughter, Nancy Lowell, and her husband, Martin, run a tight ship with a staff of 40 (a guest-to-staff ratio of almost one to one). The inn's restaurant, The Royal Palm, is already popular with Kittitians. Overnight guests have first dibs on the 15 tables, set up beneath ceiling fans and with a folding wall opening on to the swimming pool.

Name: Ottley's Plantation Inn

Managers: Nancy and Martin Lowell

Address: P.O. Box 345, Basseterre, St. Kitts, WI

Location: About 30 minutes from Basseterre, 20 minutes and $15 from the airport (let the hotel know your flight number and they'll send a reliable driver to meet you)

Telephone: 809/465-7234

Fax: 809/465-4760

Reservations: Direct or through U.S. office, 609/921-1259; Jacques de Larsay

Credit cards: All major cards

Rooms: 15, 9 in the guesthouse, 6 in cottages, all with private bathroom, air conditioning and ceiling fans, balconies or lanais, direct-dial telephone

Meals: Breakfast, lunch, afternoon tea on the terrace, dinner in the pavilion, known as the Royal Palm Restaurant ($70 for two); informal dress; beach barbecue once a week at Friar's Bay, with music ($40 for two); Sunday buffet brunch; room service for breakfast only

Entertainment: Bar/lounge, TV room with VCR, parlor games, in-house movies; live music once a week

Sports: 60-ft.-long spring-fed pool, hiking trails from the back door through a mango orchard and past allamanda-decked ruins to the rain forest; beaches nearby (transportation daily); tennis, golf, horseback riding, and sailing can be arranged

The White House
St. Kitts

☆☆☆ ♟♟ ◑◑ $$$

With its white-picket fence, broad lawns, and gardens blooming with alla-manda and bougainvillea, this airy, 250-year-old Great House is thoroughly at home on its hill overlooking the capital, Basseterre. There's a swimming pool in the front garden, and somewhere among the mango and bay trees, a grass tennis court and croquet lawn.

But the main attraction here is the galleried, peak-roofed manor house itself, the former home of a colonial plantation owner whose fields of sugar-cane once covered the nearby slopes. The house remained in the hands of the original family for more than 200 years, then was sold to a couple from London before being bought as an inn by Malcolm and Janice Barber in 1989. They had just finished restoring the house when Hurricane Hugo struck, tearing off part of the roof, uprooting an enormous banyan in the front yard, and delaying the opening until January 1990.

So far, it's been The White House's only snafu. You'd never guess, judg-ing from the style and attention to detail, that the owners are novice inn-keepers (in their former lives, Malcolm was a developer and Janice sold medical supplies). Now they expertly supervise the staff, go to market, drive guests to the beach or shops, and even provide full room service for recluses (let them know in advance, though, since there are no phones in the rooms).

Every last floorboard and panel is scrupulously polished. The cushions are plumped, and vases of fresh flowers and artfully arranged antiques fill the rooms. In each of the 10 guest rooms, a four-poster bed is comple-mented by Laura Ashley fabrics and floor tiles. The bathrooms feature new shower units. The second-story rooms are slightly more spacious, with higher ceilings and better views. But the keynote of all the rooms is a won-derfully refreshing simplicity: There are no radios, televisions, or air con-ditioning (with its ceiling fans and 18-inch walls, the house remains cool even at midday).

The original freestanding kitchen, transformed by gleaming 20th-century equipment, is still the place where meals are prepared. On any given night, dinner might be shrimp brûlée, chilled watermelon or orange soup, a choice of fillet of beef in rum and black pepper or swordfish in white wine, and mango or coconut ice cream. It's served by candlelight in a dining room dominated by an enormous mahogany table, in a salon at the rear, or in a tented pavilion overlooking the twinkling lights of Basseterre.

The dedication of the Barbers and their staff make it easy to unwind at The White House. If you could own your second home in the Caribbean, this is probably what it would be like—slow-paced, quiet, shaded, comfortable, unmistakably tropical.

Name: The White House
Owners/Managers: Malcolm and Janice Barber
Address: Box 436, St. Peter's, St. Kitts, WI
Location: In the foothills above Basseterre, the capital; 10 minutes by car from the airport (the owners provide round-trip transportation)
Telephone: 809/465-8162
Fax: 809/465-8275
Reservations: Direct
Credit Cards: American Express, MasterCard
Rooms: 10, 2 of which are suites, all in the Great House, with private bathrooms, ceiling fans
Meals: Breakfast 8:00–10:00 (on garden terrace), lunch noon–2:00 (on garden terrace), afternoon tea, dinner 8:00–9:30 (in fan-cooled dining room, family style, in the salon, or in tented pavilion, $80 for two); informal dress; full room service available with advance notice at no extra charge
Entertainment: Taped classical music in evenings
Sports: Pool, grass tennis court, croquet—all free; daily shuttle to nearby beaches; water sports, horseback riding, golf can be arranged
P.S.: Children are not encouraged

Nisbet Plantation Beach Club
Nevis

☆☆☆ ♈♈ ◑◑ $$$

Under new owner David Dodwell of the Reefs resort in Bermuda, this inn has undergone extensive changes in the past year. The first difference returning guests will notice is that the tiny pink cottage with gingerbread

trim, called Gingerland, has been turned into a boutique. Next to it is a
pavilion housing an airy reception lobby.

But that's just the beginning. There is a new complex on the beach, with a
freshwater pool and a restaurant called Coconuts. To my mind, this addition is unfortunate; one of Nisbet's attractions has always been its location
on a primitive, windward beach—providing a delightful contrast to the
dinner-party sophistication of The Great House, a quarter-mile away.
However, the new open-air restaurant does give guests the opportunity to
dine beneath the stars, with the rumbling of the surf just a few feet away.

Then there are the new lodgings. The two-story, pale yellow villas that
house the 12 new Premier rooms are somewhat obtrusive, given that all the
other plantation buildings are one story, and half-concealed by the shrubbery. Inside, however, the rooms are large and pleasant, with wet bars and
refrigerators, king-size beds on elevated platforms, and sitting areas with
comfortable sofas. One wall of each bathroom is devoted to closets, and
each has an elevated bathtub. The walls, ceramic floor, rafters, and wicker

furniture are white; wooden window louvers and ceiling fans help keep the rooms cool.

The Great House, connected to the beach by a 200-foot-long *grande allée* lined with coconut palms, has been rejuvenated, with new shutters around the screened veranda and a bright floral fabric on the sofas and chairs. Thankfully, the atmosphere of a gracious, peaceful, generations-old country house, complete with antiques-filled salons that function as dining rooms, has been retained. The square two-story dwelling is a sterling example of a traditional Nevisian plantation: It's built of native stone with a screened porch reached by an imposing flight of steps. In bygone days, when Nevis was wall-to-wall plantations, this was the estate of a Mr. William Nisbet, who lived here with his lovely young bride, Fanny (a few years later, she was widowed and went on to more universal fame as the wife of Horatio Nelson). The house is not the one in which the Nisbets lived, but rather an authentic-looking reconstruction.

All of the hotel's original gingerbread cottages, scattered under the coconut palms, have been spruced up with lighter furniture, stocked refrigerators, and bathrobes. The layout in most of these is two rooms per bungalow, arranged so that bathrooms rather than bedrooms abut each other, and so that porches face away from their neighbors. Furnishings are island-simple but comfortable and relaxing, and the newer bungalows have screened porches.

Despite the changes, Nisbet, which I first saw some 20-odd years ago, will always have a place in my heart. True, its original 12 rooms have mushroomed to 38 and the inn is no longer the same, but first-timers seeking a romantic escape will probably not be disappointed.

Name: Nisbet Plantation Beach Club
Manager: Tim Thuell
Address: St. James Parish, Nevis, WI
Location: On the northeast coast, just 1 mile from the airstrip, $5 by taxi, and 8 miles and $12 by taxi from Charlestown
Telephone: 809/469-9325
Fax: 809/469-9864
Reservations: Direct, toll free 800/344-2049
Credit Cards: All major cards
Rooms: 38, 12 in new two-story villas, 26 in cottages and bungalows, all with private bathrooms (some with showers only), ceiling fans, safes, porches
Meals: Breakfast 8:00–10:30 (on the veranda or at the beach bar), lunch 12:30–2:30 (at the beach restaurant; box lunches available with advance

notice for those going on an excursion), afternoon tea 4:00–5:00 (in the lounge), dinner 7:30–8:30 (in fan-cooled dining room); informal but stylish dress; room service for continental breakfast, no extra charge

Entertainment: Beach bar (open 10:00–5:00) Great House bar (open from 3:00 to late evening), library, backgammon, Scrabble

Sports: Beach, beachside freshwater pool, snorkeling, tennis (1 court, no lights)—all free; other water sports about 3 miles down the road at Ouali Beach; golf nearby; boat trips, horseback riding, taxi tours, air charters to other islands can be arranged

Hotel Montpelier
Nevis

☆☆☆ ♉ ◑ $$$

Horatio Nelson married Fanny Nisbet beneath a silk cotton tree on this hillside plantation, a few miles from Fig Tree Church where visitors can still see the couple's names in the wedding register. Or so goes tradition, and there's no need to ponder it too deeply as you lounge here, content in the shade of your own silk cotton tree. The estate now belongs to James and Celia Milnes Gaskell, and it was James who transformed the 100-acre estate and former sugar works into an inn in the early 1960s. "We made our home here and our life in the garden," he writes in his brochure. "We love it and you will, too."

The hub of the inn is the flower-draped gray stone great room, open to the breezes but with a cheery, floral-print clubhouse feel to it. This is the evening social spot; by day, guests tend to gather around the big swimming pool with its tropical murals and landscaping and the attendant bar/lounge/terrace, or they hop on the shuttle bus for a day at Montpelier's beach and beach bar. Dinner is served on a covered, candlelit terrace with views through flood-lit palms; the British chef is classically trained, but favors fresh local produce and recipes.

The 16 guest rooms, newly spiffed up post-Hugo, are comfortable and efficient in a sort of traditional island way, located in 8 cottages angled and staggered in such a way that each patio or terrace has plenty of privacy and views across the estate or the surrounding hills and the sea. Regular guests (a cross-section of Americans and British) don't come to Montpelier for *House & Garden* styling—they come to enjoy the quiet, courtly tone set by the Gaskells and the calm, unhurried air of bygone days.

Name: Hotel Montpelier
Owners/Managers: James and Celia Milnes Gaskell
Address: P.O. Box 474, Nevis, WI
Location: By taxi, 30 minutes and $15 from the airport
Telephone: 809/469-3462
Fax: 809/469-1932
Reservations: Ray Morrow Associates; Jacques de Larsay
Credit Cards: None
Rooms: 16 in 8 bungalows, all breeze-cooled, showers only, patios
Meals: Breakfast 8:00–9:30, lunch 1:00, afternoon tea at 4:00 (not included in rate), dinner at 8:00, on the covered patio (approx. $70 for two); informal; limited room service
Entertainment: During the winter season, evenings of dancing to The Honey Bees native band; beach barbecues with beach cricket
Sports: Large pool, games room, tennis (1 court, no lights, rackets and balls), free transportation to beach and water sports center
P.S.: Some children; closed August 21 to October 7

Golden Rock
Nevis

☆☆☆　♈♈　◑　$$

The seeds of sandbox trees no longer pop above your head since the old-timers were toppled by Hugo, but orchids grow in the stone patio, hummingbirds flit from blossom to blossom, from saman tree to saman tree. You're a thousand feet above the sea here, in a flowering 25-acre garden surrounded by 150 private acres of tropical greenery, with a misty rain forest an hour's hike from the pool.

Golden Rock is a 200-year-old sugar estate, its counting house converted into a guest cottage, its old stone stable now two new guest rooms, its original windmill an unusual duplex suite with stone walls, *three* antique four-posters, and a private sun deck at the rear. The remaining rooms, in pastel-colored bungalows widely spaced among the allamanda and hibiscus, have one-of-a-kind bamboo canopy beds (designed and made by Leonard the bartender) and verandas with views of unspoiled country-side and unending sea. Three new rooms were added within the last few years, between the rose garden and the herb garden, a few feet down the hill but still with that stunning view.

The dining room is a garden porch in the old vaulted "long house," where candlelit dinners might include pumpkin soup, lobster on the half shell or curried lamb with hot Nevis sauce, mango mousse or banana cream with meringue. There are also burgers with "a touch of coconut" served at the beachside Carousel restaurant.

It's an unhurried life up here, at the end of a long bumpy driveway lined by poinsettia and flamboyant. Unhurried breakfast on your ve-randa, unhurried lunch on the patio, unhurried drinks in Leonard's bar, unhurried dinner in the garden porch. This is a place for reading (in the "secret garden" orchid courtyard, for example). For backgammon or Scrabble. Maybe a game of tennis, surely a dip in the big spring-fed pool. Twice a day Pam Barry offers her guests a trip to the beach or town, and twice a day many of them decide not to leave the garden or gazebo. A couple of evenings a week the gardener picks up his bamboo flute and leads his group, The Honey Bees, through their repertoire of local airs.

But most of the time the loudest noise is the birds or the sighing of the breeze in the sanau trees.

Name: Golden Rock
Owner/Manager: Pam Barry
Address: Box 493, Nevis, WI
Location: In the parish of Gingerland, a thousand feet in the hills, give or take an inch or two, about 25 minutes and $20 by taxi from the airfield
Telephone: 809/469-3346
Fax: 809/469-1106
Reservations: International Travel & Resorts, Inc.; Jacques de Larsay
Credit Cards: None
Rooms: 16, including the Sugar Mill Suite (which can sleep 4), all with verandas, showers only (limited supplies of hot water), bamboo four-poster beds; the Sugar Mill Suite has an additional sleeping gallery, stone-walled shower, and huge antique four-posters (king size upstairs, 2 queens downstairs)
Meals: Breakfast 7:30–10:30, lunch noon–2:30 (both al fresco on the terrace), complimentary afternoon tea at 4:00, dinner at 8:00 (in the indoor garden pavilion, fixed menu, $40 for two); informal, but jackets

not inappropriate (partly because of the elevation); room service for breakfast, lunch, and afternoon tea, no extra charge; lunch is also served at the beach bar

Entertainment: Bar/lounge, parlor games, billiards, darts, some taped music in bar ("never in the dining room"), live music Tuesdays (calypso) and Saturdays (native band), telescope for stargazing

Sports: Spring-fed pool, tennis (1 court, recently resurfaced but with constricted alleys) in the garden, transportation to the inn's private 11-acre beach property twice daily, snorkeling masks, windsurfing—all free; hikes through the rain forest; other water sports can be arranged nearby

P.S.: "Not really suitable for children"

Hermitage Plantation
Nevis

☆☆ ♈♈ ◕ $$

Alexander Hamilton found it to his liking, we're told. So did Horatio Nelson. And so today do bevies of contemporary knights and lawyers, actors and low-key rock singers. Certainly the place has been around long enough to have welcomed Nelson and Hamilton: The Great House is something like 250 years old, all shingles and rafters and in remarkably fine if somewhat fragile fettle for its age. Its book-laden foyer leads to a roomy, raftered lounge furnished with Victoriana and assorted period pieces, the setting for house party–style gatherings before the pumpkin fritters and shrimp in vodka sauce or after the last crumb of key lime pie has been plucked from the plate; the trellised dining veranda, just off the lounge, blends nicely with its venerable surroundings.

The Carriage House, in traditional Nevisian style, houses a quartet of the guest rooms. The remaining lodgings are in a pair of new concrete villas in the garden, up the hill a few paces behind the stone-surrounded swimming pool. Decor features four-poster canopy beds (on wood-and-foam bases), Schumacher bedspreads with pastoral patterns, frilly pillowcases and sturdy wardrobes, and showers rather than tubs in the bathrooms. The newest quarters also have small kitchenettes.

Like so many Nevis plantations, Hermitage sits high in the hills, in a garden terraced by handcut stone, flowering shrubs, and tangerine, lime, tamarind, and soursop trees. Owners/managers Maureen and Richard Lupinacci built a reputation for fine cooking and cordial hospitality when they ran nearby Zetlands Plantation: Their infectious charm brings their guests back year after year, and they now have a loyal following, turning the Hermitage into the tropical cousin of a quiet little country inn in Vermont—or, I should say, Pennsylvania's Bucks County, the Lupinaccis' original home. It's so peaceful here that movie producers have been known to settle in for a week or two to work on scripts and shooting schedules. It's moderately priced, too, a fact that wouldn't be lost on Scots-descended Alexander Hamilton if he were around today.

Name: Hermitage Plantation
Owners/Managers: Maureen and Richard Lupinacci
Address: Nevis, WI
Location: In the parish of St. John Figtree, in the hills about 30 minutes and $16 by taxi from the airport
Telephone: 809/469-3477
Fax: 809/469-1481
Reservations: International Travel & Resorts, Inc. or Robert Reid Associates
Credit Cards: American Express, MasterCard, Visa
Rooms: 12, all different, in 3 separate garden villas; all with showers, ceiling fans, balconies or patios, four-poster canopy beds, antiques, electric kettles; 4 with pantries
Meals: Breakfast "anytime after 8," lunch 12:00–2:30, afternoon tea at 4, dinner at 8:00 in the covered veranda draped with flowering vines ($70 for two); informal dress; room service during meal hours; West Indian buffet with music on Wednesday evenings
Entertainment: Conversation around the bar, parlor games, TV room, scores of paperbacks
Sports: Pool, walking, trips to the beach by shuttle van
P.S.: Some children but not many

Four Seasons Nevis Resort
Nevis

☆☆☆ ♈♈ ①①①① $$$$

I've been carping about this place ever since I first heard that one of my favorite coconut groves was going to be carved up for a luxury resort (and, of course, it was no fault of Four Seasons that Hurricane Hugo came along in the midst of the construction and did its own thorough job of scything still more trees). Farewell, densely planted grove! What are we left with?

For starters, a breathtaking golf course. Since the surrounding landscape is virtually unspoiled nature, these fairways benefit from the happy confluence of forest and sea and gullies set off by the mystical backdrop of a perfect volcanic cone wreathed in clouds.

Then, too, we have Luxury with a capital L. Four Seasons didn't earn its present preeminence with no-frills lodgings, so here we have the lot—1,300-square-foot bathrooms with acres of marble, separate showers, and soaking tubs and toilets; closet safes; stocked refrigerators; direct-dial telephones; credenzas with concealed 15-channel television and VCR; ceiling fans and air conditioning; spacious screened porches. (There are several suites, but given the size and amenities of the regular rooms, I can't see any reason for upgrading.)

The public rooms are just as grand: a soaring lobby/lounge accented with antiques; a wood-paneled library-style lounge/bar; two high-ceilinged, chandelier-and-crystal dining rooms, each seating about 140 diners indoors and air-conditioned; or outside. The cuisine exceeded island norms, the breakfast and luncheon buffets are diet-busters, and the breads and pastries were freshly baked. So what's my problem, then?

For my money, it's all more Four Seasons than Nevis. It just seems such a shame that with all the resources of Four Seasons (the budget for this resort was said to be $75 million), with all their proven good taste, with all that talent at their disposal, they could not have come up with the perfect small resort for a perfect small island. Instead, we have 10 cottages that could be plopped down in Colorado or Maui with only minor adjustments, despite lavish trimming with gingerbread and giving each one an island plantation name. The interiors seem to have been inspired less by a sense of place than by the corporate manual. No Four Seasons fan will find anything out of place; island lovers may wake up discombobulated, wondering where the hell they are.

The Four Seasons people, to their credit, have been very concerned from the start about fitting into their new surroundings, aware that they were making an unusual impact on the delicate social, professional, and environmental balance of Nevis by moving in, on an island hitherto known only for modest inns, a world-class resort with a guest count that doubled the island's capacity overnight, with a championship golf course on an island that can count players on one hand, and with potential wages beyond the average Nevisian's dreams. So they went to extraordinary expense and care to adapt to Nevis, and mounted an impressive program we needn't consider here, other than noting that they shipped their rookie staff off to learn about luxury service in various Four Seasons hotels in the States.

Right from the start, they installed a manager, John Stauss, with Caribbean experience (that may seem obvious, but you'd be surprised at the number of corporations that overlook such a basic point). Stauss and his Four Seasons cadre have worked wonders in knocking raw recruits into shape, instilling motivation and esprit and a rather touching eagerness to please (in a resort where tipping is not allowed). Even so, service here is a long haul from Four Seasons levels in, say, Beverly Hills or San Francisco. One waiter was flummoxed when I told him I wanted to ask questions about items on the menu before ordering a drink—his formula was knocked out of sync.

But service is what Four Seasons is all about, after all, and here it has many refinements: a staff of 450, a golf cart patrolling the fairways with light refreshments, chilled towels for sunbathers and tennis players, an immigration form enclosed with the guests' room confirmations, jogging gear for guests' use, a tap room with darts and billiards for rainy days, a nurse, a nanny, a masseuse, and staff at the airport to meet you.

Accessibility is likely to be a major drawback, I suspect. Nevis is a favorite hideaway for many simply because you have to put in that little extra effort to get there. Here again Four Seasons tackles the problem with thoroughness: Since most guests are likely to be arriving via St. Kitts, Four Seasons people meet their flight there, transfer you by air-conditioned mini-bus to a private waterfront lounge, where you check in, sip a rum punch and, if you wish, book court time, tee times, and massages; then you board a private 65-foot launch that conveys you direct to the resort's pier, where you are again greeted by staff and escorted directly to your room, with your luggage arriving before you've had a chance to wash your hands. Not just any old launch, of course: This is a custom-designed, rather rakish twin-hulled vessel, with twin GM motors, air-conditioned lounge, open deck, and bar. There will be two of these launches, costing a cool $900,000 each.

Very impressive—and it's a beautiful trip, with volcanic peaks fore and aft, one on St. Kitts, one on Nevis. But next time I'll fly on a puddle-hopper direct to Nevis's rinky-dink airfield.

Name: Four Seasons Nevis Resort

Manager: John Stauss

Address: P.O. Box 565, Charlestown, Nevis, WI

Location: On Pinney's Beach, just outside Charlestown, 15 minutes and $10 by taxi from the airport, 40 minutes by launch from St. Kitts

Telephone: 809/469-1111

Fax: 809/469-1040

Reservations: Four Seasons U.S., toll free 800/332-3442; Canada, toll free 800/268-6282

Credit Cards: All major cards

Rooms: 196, including 10 Four Seasons and 2 Presidential Suites, all with screened porches, air conditioning, ceiling fans, stocked refrigerators, remote cable TV/VCR, direct-dial telephones, closet safes

Meals: From 7:00 A.M. on, in the Dining Room, Cabana, or Clubhouse, dinner 7:00–10:00 in the Dining Room or Grill Room (approx. $90 to $100 for two); "gracious informality . . . after sunset, we would recommend collared, buttoned shirts and closed-in footwear for gentlemen"; 24-hour room service

Entertainment: Lounge/bar, pub-like Tap Room (billiards, darts), movie library

Sports: 2,000 ft. of beach, freshwater free-form pool, freshwater lap pool, croquet, exercise room (Lifecycles, Stairmasters, sauna, whirlpool)—all free; golf (18 holes), tennis (10 courts, clay and all-weather, with lights, pro shop), small-boat sailing, pedalos, windsurfing, waterskiing, snorkeling gear, aquacycles, paddle cats, massage—all for a fee; scuba-diving by arrangement

P.S.: Some children (they're tucked away in their own game room and have separate dining hours), some executive seminar groups

Jumby Bay Resort
Antigua

☆☆☆☆☆ ♈♈♈ ➊➋ $$$$$

A private islet just off the northern coast of Antigua, Jumby Bay is one solution for escapists who want a resort that is at once secluded and accessible. Secluded because its 300 acres are shared by only 76 guests and a flock of wild sheep. Accessible because you take a taxi, 3 minutes, to the resort's dock, then, assuming schedules gel, a boat ride of 12 minutes to the island, with the crew dispensing rum punches and registration cards on the way. When you arrive, a mini-van or electric buggy takes you past trim lawns and the 200-year-old estate house direct to your room.

You have your pick of two styles of accommodation: the original octagonal guest cottages scattered around the cillamont-shaded lawns or the new two-story mission-style Pond Bay House at the far end of Jumby Beach. The rondavel cottages, two rooms to each, are draped in tropical foliage that screens the private porches from passersby and wafts the scent of tropical blossoms through the rooms; cathedral ceilings and anterooms with daybeds/sofas create a sense of space and comfort. The Pond Bay House lodgings are virtually mini-suites, designed on a sumptuous scale with raftered cathedral ceilings, Brunelleschi terra-cotta tiles, fabrics that are custom-designed and hand-painted, outline quilted bedspreads ("8 ounces," as the proud decorator points out, "not the usual 4 ounces"), striking showers with louvered doors opening onto private, planted patios.

Pond Bay House or rondavel cottage, all rooms have a few of those extra little touches that separate the memorable from the merely good: scads of big fluffy towels (18 per room!), cuddly terrycloth robes, golf umbrellas, walking sticks, wall safes. The welcome includes a refreshment tray with a bottle of Antiguan rum, cans of Coke, a bottle of Villa Banfi wine, and bottles of Riunite cooler. Banfi? Riunite? Right, but let me back up a little. The resort, then known as Long Island, was started by the island's owner, Homer Williams, about six years ago. In 1986, he sold 80% to New York's Mariani brothers, who built a company called Villa Banfi into the largest wine importers in the United States. They have their own vineyards in Italy, and one of their best-sellers is the aforesaid Riunite. It's there, so they say, simply to cool you down after a hot set of tennis and not to test your palate as an oenologist.

The new owners, to their credit, have set aside a nature preserve for hawksbill turtles, the endangered *Eretmochelys imbricata* (a cool $5 million worth of prime beachfront real estate, to put it in material terms), and sponsor a full-time marine biologist who patrols the beach every night in the nesting season to make sure all is well with the turtles. (Don't even think of asking your waiter for turtle soup—it's not considered funny.)

In the past few years, the owners have also installed a 23,500-foot nursery and planted some 5,000 trees and shrubs to add some shade here, a splash of color there, a tropical aroma beside your patio.

Not least of Jumby's attractions is the beach known as Pasture, on the windward side of the island, accessible only on foot or by bicycle, a real Robinson Crusoe place with hammocks strung between the sea grapes and a conveniently placed cooler with soft drinks, beers, rum, and ice. On the house.

Also on the house are cocktails from the bar, wine (Villa Banfi) with lunch and dinner, laundry, launch service, stamps for your postcards, most water sports, and tennis. And, of course, nature: several beaches, five miles of walking trails, and bike paths snaking through the box briar and pink cedar, through groves of turpentine and loblolly.

But you pay a price for Jumby Bay's accessibility; once or twice a day jets leaving the airport lumber upward close to the island, intruding on the tranquility, and once or twice a week a London-bound jumbo overflies Jumby late at night and has been known to awaken slumbering guests. Awakened myself one night, I decided I couldn't really give Jumby Bay a five-star rating, but next morning, surrounded by its ravishing attraction, I opted for the top rating. It's undoubtedly one of the Caribbean's finest resorts.

Name: Jumby Bay Resort
Manager: Paul Zuest
Address: P.O. Box 243, Long Island, Antigua, WI
Location: On an offshore islet, 12 minutes by 48-ft. boat from the mainland (no charge); if your flight misses the scheduled ferry, you can have drinks at the hotel beside the dock, but it's hardly a deluxe establishment
Telephone: 809/462-6000
Fax: 809/462-6000 (ask for fax)
Reservations: Direct, toll free 800/421-9016
Credit Cards: None (personal checks accepted)

Rooms: 38, in cottages and two-story Pond Bay House, all with ceiling fans, louvered walls or windows, porches or lanais, wall safes, wet bars, bathrobes, hairdryers, showers only; plus several villas for rent

Meals: Breakfast 8:00–9:30, continental breakfast to 10:00, lunch 12:30–2:00 (at the beachside terrace), afternoon tea at 4:00 in the Great House, dinner 7:30–9:30 (in the arcaded patio of the Estate House); weekly barbecue dinner and Caribbean Night at beach terrace; dress informal but elegant; limited room service; box lunches for picnics on Pasture Beach

Entertainment: Bar/lounge, library, backgammon, cribbage, etc.

Sports: 2 beaches (one leeward, one windward), windsurfing, Sunfish sailing, waterskiing, snorkeling, safaris, putting, croquet, 100 bicycles, tennis (3 courts, 2 with lights, pro), nature trails, boat trips to mainland—all free; scuba-diving and sport fishing can be arranged (as can golf, but hardly worth the effort)

P.S.: No children under eight; some small seminar groups in the off-season; closed September and October

Blue Waters Beach Hotel
Antigua

☆☆ ♈♈ ◑◑ $$$

For years, this quiet, family-owned, family-run resort had been a dependable 46-roomer, with first-class facilities but accommodations that were outdazzled by all the flora and shrubbery. Several years ago, Blue Waters acquired a new owner ("a butcher's boy from London," is how he styles himself, but in fact a successful entrepreneur who went from butcher to processor to tycoon), with juicy plans to hoist the hotel into the luxury category, then fill the rest of his 10 hillside/coveside acres with condos.

What remains is the lovely botanical-garden setting—down the steep hill, into the circular, tree-shaded driveway, through the open lobby to the flowering terrace, pool, and beach, with two-story wings of rooms fanning off on either side. Balconies are festooned with bougainvillea and plumbago; lawns are shaded by Antigua palms and flamboyants. There are so many plants and trees here that there are botanical walks through the

grounds, and 10 gardeners toil full time to keep everything spruce and dandy.

What remains, too, is the friendly, congenial atmosphere nurtured over a quarter of a century by the Kelsick family. Many of the senior staff are still holding fort, Chef Mannix is still in the kitchen, but now the team is headed by a highly regarded manager, Keith Woodhouse, from the island's Half Moon Bay Hotel.

He, in turn, has installed his own concept of comforts and services. A classy, à la carte restaurant has been tucked into an air-conditioned salon off the lobby. Meals are more inventive, well prepared, well presented (but Mannix's famed Sunday curry brunch is still the culinary highlight of the week for many guests). New superior rooms have been made larger simply by extending the rooms to the edge of the original balconies and adding new ones. And all rooms now come with stocked refrigerators, individual safes, and cassette radios (but you have to bring your own cassettes).

The new rooms and sprightlier decor notwithstanding, what still sets Blue Waters apart is the confluence of sea and beach and gardens (maybe the profusion of flowers is why it's so popular with the British), and the opportunities to appreciate the setting in romantic ways. Stroll past the plumbago and tamarinds to the breakwater known as North Point. There's a tiny gazebo there, just big enough for two, where you can get away from the chatter and laughter. Listen to the waves. Marvel at the water—maybe you'll discover yet another shade of blue.

Name: Blue Waters Beach Hotel
Manager: Keith Woodhouse
Address: P.O. Box 256, St. John's, Antigua, WI
Location: On the north shore, 15 minutes and $14 by taxi from the airport in one direction, from St. John's in the other
Telephone: 809/462-0290
Fax: 809/462-0293
Reservations: David B. Mitchell & Company, Inc.
Credit Cards: All major cards
Rooms: 46 in two-story wings, all with balconies or loggias facing the beach, all with air conditioning and louvers, stocked refrigerators, closet safes, amenities trays, radios, telephones; plus 21 deluxe rooms and suites in 8 two-story villas, some with kitchens, all with refrigerators/bars
Meals: Breakfast 7:30–10:00, lunch 12:30–2:30, afternoon tea 4:00–5:00, dinner 7:00–10:00 (approx. $70 for two, on the veranda or in the air-conditioned Cacubi Restaurant); barbecue Tuesdays, buffet Fridays, curry brunch Sundays; "casual but elegant" dress; room service during dining room hours, no extra charge
Entertainment: 2 bars, dancing, library, video room, dancing under the stars to live music 8:00–11:00 ("the bands have been chosen for how *quietly* they play"—which will be fine as long as the amplification plays as quietly as the band)
Sports: 2 beaches and a beachside manmade sandy terrace, freshwater pool, snorkeling, Sunfish sailing, HobieCats, windsurfing, pedalos, canoes, tennis (1 court, with lights)—all free; waterskiing you pay for; scuba, yachting, golf nearby
P.S.: Some children occasionally

Galley Bay Beach Resort
Antigua

☆☆☆ ♈♈ ◑◑ $$$

Old Antigua hands may wonder about the name: Yes, it *is* the former Galley Bay Surf Club. Yes, it has a new owner (English) and manager (Swiss). But despite a half-million dollars spent on renovating and rehabbing, the essential Galley Bay lives!

You still enter along a bumpy dirt track, through a grove of coconut palms and sea grape trees, with the gentle surf on one side and a placid lagoon on the other.

Guests who like to step from their rooms straight onto the sand (or nod off to the sound of the surf) check into the beachfront bungalows; romantics bed down beside the lagoon in thatch-roofed, Polynesian-style quarters called Gauguin Villas. The beachfront bungalows are attractive but not very different from beachfront rooms elsewhere, so it's the Gauguin Villas that put Galley Bay in a romantic class by itself. They're not exactly villas: Each consists of a pair of rondavels, neither of them very large but very sensibly arranged, one for sleeping, the other for showering and dressing, with a covered breezeway-cum-patio between the two. They're kooky and romantic but also very practical: You come in from the sea and sand, head for your shower hut without tracking sand all over your bedroom; then, all fresh and shiny, you can skip across your private breezeway to bed—or lounge around *deshabillé*, since all the breezeways have neck-high lattices that screen out intruders but let the breezes waft through. Don't let the word "hut" fool you—they're neat little whitewashed rooms, dressed with lace curtains, floral bedspreads, and island wall hangings.

The beachside lodgings are one-story, flat-roofed bungalows, two guest rooms to each; the new owners have installed a few grace notes like heavier towels, bathrobes, hairdryers, mini-fridges, and coffee machines, and each room is now entered through bamboo arbors draped with bougainvillea.

This Polynesian fantasy was put together about 20 years ago by a legendary innkeeper/hostess named Edie Holbert, from Bucks County, Pennsylvania; she has now retired to the other side of Antigua but her personality lingers on, and the new owners have been smart enough not to fiddle with the ambience and laid-back style. Guests still gather beneath a cone-shaped pavilion of local hardwoods and cedar shingle, which serves as the bar, lounge, dance floor, tea room, and rendezvous. Old-timers are smart enough to get there early to get first dibs on the traditional planters' chairs—wood and canvas armchairs with straps for putting your feet up and wide armrests for holding your rum punch. The adjoining dining room is likewise open to the breezes, part outdoors with market umbrellas set up beneath coco palms and sea grapes, part indoors in an open-sided pavilion decorated with Antillean paintings, native coal pots, and fans.

It's still Galley Bay. Just smarter.

Name: Galley Bay Beach Resort
Manager: Peter Hoehn
Address: Five Islands, P.O. Box 305, St. John's, Antigua, WI
Location: About 10 minutes from the capital, at the end of an unpaved road that discourages casual sightseers; about 15 minutes and $18 by taxi from the airport
Telephone: 809/462-0302
Fax: 809/462-1187, 0302
Reservations: Robert Reid Associates
Credit Cards: American Express, Diners Club, MasterCard, Visa
Rooms: 30 rooms, including 5 deluxe beachfront suites (larger, but otherwise not much different from the regular rooms) and 13 Gauguin Villas; all with showers, ceiling fans, bathrobes, hairdryers, baskets of toiletries, coffee makers, refrigerators, patios
Meals: Breakfast 7:30–9:30, continental breakfast 9:30–10:00, lunch 12:30–3:00, afternoon tea 4:30–5:00, dinner 7:30–9:30, all in the beachside pavilion (5-course dinner $60 for two); informal dress ("but we do request that guests do not wear jeans, T-shirts, or shorts after 7 p.m. in our bar and restaurant"); room service for breakfast only, no extra charge
Entertainment: Bar, live music two or three evenings a week (unamplified), chess, backgammon, and other parlor games
Sports: Half-mile beach (good swimming and snorkeling most of the time), hammocks, tennis (1 court, no lights), windsurfing, Sunfish sailing, bicycles—all free; waterskiing nearby
P.S.: Children eight years and older are accepted during the peak season except in February

Curtain Bluff
Antigua

☆☆☆☆☆ ♉♉♉ ❶❷❸ $$$$$

Behold: one of the loveliest settings in the Caribbean. A 12-acre headland, lagoon-smooth beach on the leeward side, breezy surfy beach to
windward, rocky bluff at the tip. The flowers are brilliant, the trees tall
and stately, the lawns primped to the nearest millimeter. And with rooms
for just 122 vacationers, there's more garden than there are guests.

Curtain Bluff also happens to be one of the most consistently dependable, top-drawer resorts in the islands, thanks largely to the personality of
its owner, the inimitable Howard Hulford. Thirty years ago, when he was
piloting planes around the Caribbean for oil company executives, he used
to fly over and lust after this south-coast headland, vowing that one day he
would build a dream home there. In 1985, he and his wife, Chelle, moved
into a *spectacular* dream home on the very tip of the bluff; but in the

intervening 25 years he had opened, modified, perfected his stylish resort and welcomed people to Howard's Headland year after year, decade after decade.

For some people, though, Curtain Bluff seems to be too cultivated, too country-clubby. You're expected to dress for dinner every evening, including Sunday, and judging by the sartorial splendor guests must send their togs ahead on container ships. Dinner is a serious affair, in an elegant garden pavilion surrounded by lawns, a gazebo, the Sugar Mill Bar, and a dance floor beneath a tamarind tree. Add to that a well-rounded wine cellar that wouldn't look out of place in Beaune and you may decide that dining here is the sort of event that makes all the dressing up worthwhile. Of course, you may also decide to forego the dining room and the combo tootling Gershwin and have your dinner shipped to your private balcony or patio.

The suites are located in villas built step-fashion up the leeward side of the bluff. Living rooms measure a generous 17 by 20 feet, bedrooms a few feet more; each room (not suite, room) comes with a comfy balcony overlooking the sea, and the suites with duplex configurations also have open dining terraces and secluded patios strung with hammocks. Everything in the suites seems to come in multiples. Two ceiling fans per room (again not suite, but room), plus another in the bathroom. His and her lighted closets, twin vanities, two double beds. Three, sometimes four, telephones to a suite. The one-bedroom suites are fitted with 18 light switches—for fans, vanities, dimmers, terraces, and the track lighting that pinpoints gallery-caliber artwork, most of it commissioned for the Bluff. Fabrics and rugs are in delicate pastels, glass doors and screens positively *glide*, oversize rattan sofas and chairs billow with 18 cushions; Italian marble covers the walls and floors and separate shower stalls of the sumptuous bathrooms. Chelle Hulford designed and decorated these suites with great good taste—and has conjured up some of the grandest accommodations in the Caribbean. The grandest of these is probably the Terrace Room, at the top of the bluff, with a king-size four-poster bed and huge terrace.

The remaining rooms, superior and deluxe, have more traditional proportions and accoutrements. They too have had their own dose of prettifying, and now look all spic and span with rattan end tables and chairs, jollier fabrics, circular headboards, and new tiled bathrooms and balcony screens. To celebrate the resort's 30th anniversary, the Hulfords have added an international squash court and an exercise room. It's all very relaxed and genteel here (there are no room keys and no one ever asks for them), but despite its country-club flavor Curtain Bluff is far from being a pasture for geriatrics.

It's actually one of the sportiest small hotels in the Caribbean (see listing below). And, into the bargain, one of the best values despite what at first glance might seem like stiff rates. All meals and all drinks are included; most sports facilities are available at no extra charge. Even waterskiing. Even scuba-diving. All you pay extra for is sport fishing or day sails on the resort's yacht *Tamarind*. From its decks, Curtain Bluff looks even more stunningly lovely than it did from the air all those 30 years ago.

Name: Curtain Bluff

Owner/Managers: Howard Hulford (owner), Robert Sherman (managing director), Calvert Roberts (general manager)

Address: P.O. Box 288, Antigua, WI

Location: On the south coast, next to the village of Old Road, 35 bumpy minutes from the airport ($20 by taxi)

Telephone: 809/462-8400, 8401, 8402

Fax: 809/462-8409

Reservations: Own office, 212/289-8888

Credit Cards: American Express

Rooms: 61, in two-story wings and the 6 one- and two-bedroom suites, all beachfront with balconies or lanais, bathrooms (amenities trays, bathrobes, and bathtubs, except in superior rooms, which have showers only), ceiling fans, louvers and screened glass doors, telephones, wall safes, refrigerators in suites

Meals: Breakfast 7:30–9:30, continental 9:30–10:00, lunch 12:30–2:00 (in the open-sided garden pavilion or Beach Restaurant), dinner 7:30–9:30 (in garden pavilion, approx. $70 per person); beach barbecue buffet on Wednesday; "we do request jacket and tie for the gentlemen after seven o'clock"; room service, no extra charge

Entertainment: Bar, lounge, library, parlor games, live music for dancing in the dining room every evening (combos, native bands, etc., amplified but not loud), steel band with beachside buffet

Sports: 2 beaches (1 windward, 1 leeward), hammocks, snorkeling, scuba, waterskiing, Sunfish sailing, seascopes (for fish watching), reef trips, tennis (4 courts, pro shop, 2 with lights), squash court, exercise room, croquet, putting green—all free; sport fishing and day sails on the resort's own 47-ft. sailboat cost extra

P.S.: "Please, no children in the bar after seven"; mid-May features a very popular pro-am tennis tournament

Copper & Lumber Store
Antigua

☆☆☆ ♈♈ $$

Four of the Caribbean's most stunning, most unusual suites can be found, not beside a beach, but in a dockyard—Nelson's Dockyard.

Don't let that faze you. No cranes and clatter, no grease and goo here—this is the National Park kind of dockyard, the former headquarters of Britain's navy back in the days when Lord Nelson was still Captain Horatio.

The revered hero/admiral is commemorated in a wood-frame mansion (now a museum), between the engineers' workshop (now the Admiral's Inn) and the warehouse that is now the dockyard's second inn, the Copper & Lumber Store. On a hillside across English Harbour stands Clarence House, the home of Nelson's buddy, the Duke of Clarence (Princess Margaret stayed here on her honeymoon); higher up the hill, on Shirley Heights,

the former barracks have been restored as a museum, and on the battlements there's a pleasant pub/restaurant with panoramic views of mountains and yacht-filled harbor. For yachting buffs, Nelson's harbor is the Caribbean's most popular, best-equipped marina and revictualling base.

Throw open your shutters in the morning and you look out on a stunning setting of bollards and capstans, masts and rigging. The pride of the world's yacht builders spread out all around you—classic schooners from Maine, sleek 70-foot ocean cruisers from Cowes, mammoth power boats laden with antennae, radar scanners, flying bridges, and unseamanlike names. Most of them are charter yachts, and many of the people staying or dining at either of the dockyard's inns are waiting to ship out—or have just returned from a cruise, unsteady of gait, getting back to normal before returning to the 20th century.

The Copper & Lumber Store, in its current incarnation, is a sturdy, two-story structure in Georgian/Admiralty style, built of native stone and hefty rough-hewn timbers that wouldn't have looked out of place on a ship-of-the-line.

In keeping with its heritage, the creator of the Copper & Lumber Store is, in Winston Churchill's memorable phrase, "a former naval person"—Commander Gordon Gutteridge R.N., Retired. In true mariner manner, young Gutteridge ran away to sea aboard a sailing ship, the *John and May Garnett* out of Chester; later he was an experimental (and not unheroic) diver in the Royal Navy; most recently he ran an industrial gas operation from the British Virgins. Apparently his wife, Gill, had a hankering for running a country house hotel in Wales but their navigation was flawed and they ended up in Antigua. With his bushy seadog eyebrows and commanding air, the Commander comes across to some people as gruff, but he is, in reality, a congenial, entertaining host and he and his wife run a tight ship. The Gutteridges recently sold their inn and returned to the BVI; the new owners (Stevens Yachts) have been making a few changes, but on the whole maintaining, even enhancing, the spirit of the place.

The "office" is a desk under the stairs. Not just any desk, but a sturdy 17th-century *escritorio* carted off as booty from a Spanish galleon. The lobby (weathered brick floor and walls, Oriental rugs, beamed ceilings, buttoned red leather wing chairs, breezes fore and aft) serves as an informal lounge/bar and opens onto the cloisterlike patio restaurant, its warehouse doors opening to the lawns and marina. In the adjoining pub the menu features traditional English items such as Scotch eggs, Cumberland sausages, mango chutney, pickled onions, and assorted cheeses. A welcome bargain, too, for these parts—$4.50–$8.50.

All the guest rooms have views of the harbor and yachts in one direction or another; all are furnished with antiques and period pieces accenting the basic decor of raw brick and ceiling beams. Gill Gutteridge herself did all the hand stenciling and sewed most of the fabrics, but there's nothing "homemade" about the interiors. Even Nelson didn't live in such style.

The *pièces de résistance* are the seven Georgian suites, each named after one of Nelson's ships. Africa, for example, a one-bedroom suite, is adorned with 200-year-old paintings, 400-year-old charts, and a display of antique Wedgwood. The floor sports hand-stenciled pineapple motifs, the paneling is Philippine oak, the wallpapers and fabrics are replicas of 200-year-old patterns, and the document chest is made of camphor wood on a steel frame. In the sleeping loft all the furnishings are authentic Chippendale, except for the double beds, which are replicas. What sets these seven suites apart, though, are their bathrooms—paneling of Honduras mahogany, washbasins of Argentine brass, shower stalls of Welsh slate. It's all done with a sympathetic feeling for authenticity.

Although most people who stay here are overnighting, before or after cruises, these are suites to settle into for several days. Take time to explore the battlements on foot, for the five-minute boat trip to the beaches in the outer harbor, to visit Shirley Heights for lunch, to row among the yachts at sunset. English Harbour was a "hurricane hole" for sailing ships, but the fact that it's so sheltered doesn't necessarily mean it's going to be hot and sticky; you can spend time there even in the summer without feeling uncomfortable.

There are several restaurants within walking distance of the Copper & Lumber (none of them, frankly, outstanding but at least they have some atmosphere); but there's less reason than hereto for eating out, now that the Copper & Lumber gives you the convenience of private pantries *and* a new restaurant.

Name: Copper & Lumber Store
Managers: Jill and Andrew Gallacher
Address: P.O. Box 184, St. John's, Antigua, WI
Location: Anchored in the middle of Nelson's Dockyard in English Harbour, 25 minutes and $25 by taxi from the airport or St. Johns
Telephone: 809/460-1058
Reservations: Direct, 809/460-1529
Credit Cards: American Express, MasterCard, Visa
Rooms: 14, all suites (including 3 studio suites and 7 deluxe Georgian suites), all different, all with private bathrooms (showers only), kitchens (refrigerators stocked on request, commissary nearby), ceiling fans, antiques
Meals: Breakfast 7:30–11:00, lunch 11:30–2:30, afternoon tea, dinner 7:00–10:00 in the new pub or courtyard restaurant cooled by breezes

and ceiling fans; pub lunch for two approximately $14, dinner for two $18 to $30; informal dress (but no shorts in the evening); taped classical 18th-century music; room service for breakfast only

Entertainment: The bar/lounge of the inn is popular with visiting yacht people, and it's not unknown to have an erudite conversation on Reaganomics continue into the wee hours; parlor games (Scrabble, wari, chess, darts, cribbage, shoveha'penny, backgammon)

Sports: Beaches nearby (the inn will supply beach towels and arrange for a launch to the beach of the Inn at English Harbour, 5 minutes away across the bay); boats for rent nearby, boat tours of harbor, scuba and snorkeling from the Dockyard, tennis/squash courts just outside the Dockyard

P.S.: "Not really suitable for children"; closed in September

The Admiral's Inn
Antigua

☆ ♈ $$

In Nelson's pre-admiral days as commander-in-chief of the dockyard, this two-story weathered brick structure was an unglamorous corner of his domain—the storehouse for turpentine and pitch. You'd never suspect it today. It's now a lovely 30-year-old inn in a most unusual setting. A well-worn stone patio, set with tables and chairs, shaded by sun umbrellas and casuarina trees, leads to a lawn that ends at the water's edge. Just off to the right, a row of sturdy but stunted stone pillars are all that remain of the former boathouse, decapitated in a long-ago earthquake, and just beyond that another section of the dockyard has become an annex with four more guest rooms. Yachts lie at their moorings a few oar strokes offshore, and somewhere behind you the market women of English Harbour have draped the old stone walls with batiks and T-shirts, necklaces and baubles.

The inn's lobby is a tiny desk beneath the stairs in a beamy lounge, bar on one side facing French doors that lead to the dining terrace. A dart board adds the right Royal Navy touch, the burgees of 100 yachts and yacht clubs remind you that the Admiral's Inn is a favorite gathering place for sailing buffs. If the Flying Dutchman were to come ashore again one of these days, this would be a sensible place for him to come ashore and search for a latter-day Senta.

Being a gathering place for yachtsmen and yachtswomen, the inn may not be the serenest of hideaways, but it has a lot of charm and camaraderie. Guest rooms are small, simply but tastefully furnished, decked with Williamsburg fabrics by Schumacher, cooled by ceiling fans or air conditioners. The prime nest (indeed, one of the prettiest in all of Antigua) is number 1, a large corner chamber with lacy curtains, khuskhus rugs, and canopied four-poster king-size bed (all the others are twins). Since it's right at the head of the stairs, number 1 gets a certain amount of inn traffic outside its doors, and since it's directly above the bar it picks up some of the chatter and jollity from rendezvousing voyagers. But the carousing generally ends around midnight, and then all you hear when you throw open the window shutters is the clank of the rigging on the sailboats.

The four rooms across the boatyard are a shade quieter—smallish in floor space but with high ceilings, whitewashed stone walls, built-in dressers, modern plumbing, fans, and air conditioners. Room A is the biggest, and being at the harbor end of the row with louvered windows on three sides, is also the brightest and breeziest.

Even if you don't have time to stay here, stop in for a drink on the broad terrace. Or a meal—indoors beneath iron chandeliers, outdoors beneath the lacy casuarinas. The service is sometimes as laid-back as the clientele, the meals sometimes disappointing, but the surroundings are delightful, the welcome friendly. It's another century. Even if the yachts have aluminum rather than wooden masts.

Name: The Admiral's Inn

Manager: Ethelyn Philip

Address: English Harbour, P.O. Box 713, St. John's, Antigua, WI

Location: In Nelson's Dockyard national park, on Antigua's south coast; 16 miles directly across the island from the airport (40 minutes and $18 by taxi) and 14 miles from St. John's (30 minutes, $20 by taxi)

Telephone: 809/463-1027, 1534

Fax: 809/463-1534

Reservations: American International

Credit Cards: American Express, MasterCard, Visa

Rooms: 14, all with private bathrooms (showers only); 8 with air conditioning, all others with ceiling fans, some with patios

Meals: Breakfast 7:30–10:00, lunch noon–2:00, dinner 7:30–9:00 (approx. $55 for two, served indoors or on the terrace); casual dress (but not scruffy, despite the proximity of all those yachts); room service by special arrangement

Entertainment: Combo Thursdays (in season), steel band Saturdays, dancing, some taped music, darts

Sports: Snorkeling gear, Sunfish sailing—free; windsurfing, paddle boats, beach, water sports, boat trips, tennis, scuba-diving, and golf nearby

P.S.: Some (sometimes lots of) cruise ship passengers, since you're right in the middle of what tourists come all the way across the island to see; especially busy during Sailing Week (late April, early May) and charter yacht review week (early December); closed for a few weeks during September and October

P.P.S.: The Inn's sister establishment, Falmouth Harbour Beach Apartments, is located 10 minutes away on a small beach in the next bay; 28 twin-bedded apartments come with kitchenettes, private verandas, and maid service—and bargain rates ($106 double in winter 1990). A larger beach is a 5-minute walk away

The Inn at English Harbour
Antigua

☆☆ ♈♈ ◐◐ $$$

Rather than follow the low road to English Harbour take the road to Shirley Heights. Up there, among the fortress ruins and the dramatic views of the outer harbor, you'll also find a tiny sign with 18th-century script identifying the inn. Turn off, go down the hill and there, among the flowering shrubs and fruit trees, you come upon a lodge with a few cottages nestled among the trees. Actually, this is only the upstairs of this upstairs/downstairs inn, with the bulk of the rooms all the way down the hill beside the beach. No, you won't have to trek all the way up again for a drink or a lunch: There's a bar/restaurant on the beach. And when it's time for dinner upstairs, the lodge will send a mini-bus to collect you.

Hilltop or beach, the rooms don't vary much in terms of decor or facilities: island-style rush rugs, a blend of wicker and contemporary furniture, bathrooms with separate showers and vanities, ceiling fans and balcony or patio, all brightly spruced up in 1988. But where you unpack your bags can make a difference: If you want breezes and view—hilltop; if you want the sea a toe-skip away—the beach; if you want to isolate yourselves as much as possible from fellow guests—hilltop cottages or rooms 28 or 29 in the beach cottages (which have no second floor).

Not that there's anything unwelcome about your fellow guests. Judging by all the magazines lying around the lounge and the darts and skittles in the pub, most of the guests here seem to be English. And if you want to waft yourselves to Cornwall rather than Antigua, listen to the accents during the traditional afternoon tea.

One of the Inn's most famous guests was actually a Welshman, whose honeymoon visit is commemorated by the Richard Burton Memorial Table on the terrace, on its own little promontory, screened by a palm tree and with a majestic view over the entire harbor, the hills, and the seas beyond.

Given the choice, I'd opt for staying with the view and making occasional forays to the beach, rather than vice versa.

Name: The Inn at English Harbour
Owner: Peter Deeth
Address: P.O. Box 187, St. John's, Antigua, WI

Location: On the bay called English Harbour, on the south coast, 16 miles, 40 minutes, and $16 by taxi from the airport, slightly less from St. John's

Telephone: 809/463-1014

Fax: 809/463-1603

Reservations: American International, Robert Reid Associates

Credit Cards: American Express, Discover, MasterCard, Visa

Rooms: 28, 22 on the beach, 6 on the hill, ceiling fans and breezes; tiled bathrooms, balcony or patio

Meals: Breakfast 7:30–10:30, lunch 12:30–2:30, afternoon tea 4:00, dinner 7:30–9:30 (approx. $60 for two, on the hilltop terrace, or indoors on breezy nights); informal dress (but no shorts at dinner); room service 7:30 a.m.–11:00 p.m., for a small extra charge

Entertainment: Taped music, barbecues (Wednesdays), live music Saturday and Tuesday

Sports: Beach, snorkeling, windsurfing, Sunfish sailing, dinghy to Nelson's Dockyard—all free; tennis, scuba, sailboat trips, deep-sea fishing, waterskiing, and horses nearby

P.S.: Closed September 15 to October 25

Half Moon Bay Hotel

Antigua

☆☆ ♀♀ ◑◑◑ $$$

On an island famed for its extravagance of beautiful beaches, here is one of the most beautiful. Fortunately for us all, these pristine sands were spotted back in the forties by zillionaire Paul Mellon, who chose an adjoining headland for his members-only Mill Reef Club, which preserves one end of the half moon. At the other, this less snooty but tasteful, low-key resort.

Obviously, with a beach like this, Half Moon is heaven for sun worshippers—idle or active. If you want calm waters, flop down in front of the hotel. If you want breezes and surf, walk half a mile along the soft white sand and you've got what you want, without having to share it with more than a few other couples.

But Half Moon is also a mecca for tennis buffs. Singer Elton John often drops in during the January Tennis Weeks, which attract stars from two continents. Regular guests have a chance to attend clinics with the stars— or play in their pro-am tournaments.

That's not the end of Half Moon's sporty attractions, either; there's also golf. Not on the scale of Dorado Beach or Casa de Campo, of course, just a challenging but hardly exhausting nine holes up and down the slopes above the beach.

In such a setting—palm-fringed beach, a 150-acre estate—a hotel doesn't have to draw attention to itself with stunning architecture and this one certainly doesn't do that. Four two-story guest wings flank a breezy core built around a glistening free-form swimming pool. The poolside bar and lunch terrace lead to a lounge (popular with card players) and separate games room (the pool table looks a bit scrawny), then to a two-tiered dining room dressed in the hotel's trademark blues and whites.

Most of the guest rooms face the beach, with a few yards of lawn between your private patio and the sand; and of these, the best are in the new streamlined wing. Stylish furnishings don't seem to be high on the list of musts for Half Moonies, who keep coming back year after year (in winter, most of the guests are repeaters, mostly American). What they *are* interested in is dependable service, and this they get—many of the 190 people on the payroll have become virtually personal retainers for the guests they've been attending to for generations.

Half Moon is not as classy as Curtain Bluff or as luxurious as Jumby Bay or as chic as St. James's Club, but it has its own charms. Not least of them, of course, that expanse of soft white sand.

Name: Half Moon Bay Hotel
Manager: Hiram Warner
Address: P.O. Box 144, St. John's, Antigua, WI
Location: On Half Moon Bay, on the island's southeast coast, 17 miles from the airport (45 minutes, $20 by taxi), about the same from St. John's
Telephone: 809/460-4300, 4301, 4302, 4303, 4304, 4305
Fax: 809/460-4306
Reservations: Robert Reid Associates
Credit Cards: American Express, Diners Club, MasterCard, Visa
Rooms: 100 in two-story wings plus 2 suites and 1 two-bedroom cottage, all with ceiling fans, showers only in most bathrooms
Meals: Breakfast 7:30–9:30, lunch 12:30–2:30, dinner 7:30–9:30 ($70 to $75 for two), all served in an airy, glass-enclosed room overlooking the beach; informal dress (but no shorts or T-shirts), jacket and tie

customary on weekends in season; room service for breakfast only, no extra charge

Entertainment: Music every evening (mostly live, steel band, guitarist, combo, piano), dancing, some taped music, limbo dancing, barbecues and buffets (the St. James's Club is 20 minutes away if you want to go gambling)

Sports: Crescent-shaped beach (calm waters at one end, surf at the other), 78-ft. freshwater pool, snorkeling (gear provided), Sunfish sailing, windsurfing, tennis (5 Laykold courts, 1 with lights, pro shop), golf (9 holes, par 34)—all free; certified windsurfing instructor and simulator (extra charge), scuba and boat trips available nearby

P.S.: Closed September; no children under 5 during peak season

St. James's Club
Antigua

☆☆ ♈♈ ➊➋➌ $$$$

"I don't collect antiques, I don't collect art, I enjoy having clubs and sharing them with people who like the things I like," explained Peter de Savary. The youthful English tycoon is probably wealthy enough to spend the rest of his days lounging on the deck of his America's Cup yacht; instead he invested millions of dollars and lots of time and labor into making the Antigua club as chic and luxurious as its tony namesake in London.

The St. James's Club opened with great fanfare in 1985 and the staff had a chance to polish their act in front of inaugural celebrities such as Joan Collins, Michael York, and Liza Minnelli. Elton John, David Frost, and the Duke of Kent checked in shortly afterward and ever since the glitzy flow has continued more or less unabated—even with de Savary out of the picture and a new owner, Amin Dalhawi, at the helm. What's the big attraction? At first glance, it's hardly the physical plant, which started out in the sixties as a formula two-story resort, first class rather than deluxe. Hardly an architectural gem, with little romantic character, the mildly Polynesian rooflines notwithstanding. But the owners have managed to transform this unpromising assortment of structures into a club worthy of the name St. James with 60,000 flowering shrubs, trees, and plants carted in for camouflage. Indoors, however, all is spic and span and shipshape. Custom fabrics, bamboo étagères with bird figurines, bamboo four-posters, and Dominican paintings add a dash of distinction to these basically standard-size rooms. In the suites, the double doors between bedrooms and sitting areas have been turned into graphic eye-catchers with hand-painted tropical flowers.

Luxury touches include specially milled and wrapped soaps, fluffy white towels woven with the club insignia, and white kimonos for each guest. Of the St. James's three residential blocks your best bet is probably Poinciana (rooms 180–190), if you want privacy, with balconies looking out to sea; Hibiscus (rooms 100–109), if you prefer to be close to the ocean beach and the tennis courts (but avoid the ground floor rooms or you'll have a steady stream of sun worshippers trotting past your balcony); Bougainvillea (rooms 160–179), if you want a sea view but still like to be close to bars and restaurants. If you'd rather have breezes than air condi-tioning, be warned that some of the lower rooms have a restricted flow of air. The quietest rooms of all are 14 and 15, in a string of villas known as the Frangipani Rooms, with none-too-private patios on a small peninsula facing a sheltered lagoon. The best quarters in the hotel, for anyone with moolah to spare, are in the Roof Garden Suite, on the upper floor of the Poinciana block—the terrace is as large as the suite itself, ideal for very private sunbathing.

Three years ago, the resort decked the hillside behind the lagoon with 73 new villas, all two-bedroom, full-kitchen units, more plushly furnished than the hotel rooms. Since these villas are priced for foursomes rather than twosomes (and since they're somewhat huddled together), you'll probably still prefer the hotel itself. But that still leaves the question: What do all these additional accommodations do to the overall ambience of the club? They don't help, that's for sure, unless you're interested in more action. With the additional rooms come a larger lagoon (twice the size of the original, or so it seemed to these eyes), more water sports equipment, two more tennis courts (for a total of seven), and a striking new multilevel bar/restaurant, Piccolo Mundo, for breakfast and dinner.

To motivate the staff (not the easiest of projects in these parts) manage-ment operates a system of bonuses: Each day, a few tokens are distributed among the guests, who are invited to pass them along to waiters, maids, whoever, for exceptional performance. Since the tokens carry a cash bonus but the staff have no idea which guests will be making the decision, everyone is, at least in theory, treated like a VIP.

A few drawbacks aside (the food in the main dining room is disappoint-ing, the Dockside Terrace is much more fun) few resorts offer guests so many diversions. Some may have horseback riding, but how many can boast stables with a dozen Texas quarter horses? Or seven tennis courts *and* lights? Or a full-fledged marina? Or a casino? A small casino, for sure, but restricted to hotel guests and a few local members, this being in theory a private club. So for vacationers who want more than a patch of sand and the shade of a palm, the St. James's hundred acres would seem to be as generous as they come—especially when you consider that most of the facilities come at no extra charge. Tennis champ Martina Navratilova came here to learn to scuba-dive, liked the diving and the resort so much she bought one of the villas. Now she's the club's official touring pro.

Name: St. James's Club
Manager: Audrey Ballantyne
Address: P.O. Box 63, St. John's, Antigua, WI
Location: At Mamora Bay, on the south coast, 30 minutes and $20 by taxi from the airport (the club has a rep at the airport to meet guests)
Telephone: 809/460-5000
Fax: 809/460-3015
Reservations: Prime Hotels & Resorts, toll free 800/274-0008 or 212/486-2575
Credit Cards: All major cards
Rooms: 105, including 15 suites, 5 villas (studios, 1 or 2 bedrooms) plus the 73 new 2-bedroom hillside condominium villas in what's called The Village, all with balconies or patios, air conditioning and ceiling fans, telephones, bathrobes, television, mini-bars, safes, amenities trays; suites with refrigerators, villas with full kitchens; also 4 three-bedroom homes, with private pools and cars, on the hill
Meals: Breakfast 7:30–10:00, lunch 11:30–3:30 (by the pool or beside the dock), dinner 7:30–10:30 (anywhere from $30 up, in one of three restaurants); casual in the restaurants, but "guests are expected to be attractively attired at all times"; 24-hour room service
Entertainment: Something every evening—cocktail piano or combo in the restaurant every evening, disco, casino (blackjack, roulette, 30 slot machines)
Sports: 2 beaches (1 ocean, 1 lagoon), 2 freshwater pools (1 Olympic-size), Jacuzzi, gymnasium (Nautilus, weights, etc.), snorkeling, wind-surfing (Mistral instruction), Sunfish sailing, catamarans, Lasers, ped-alos, waterskiing, tennis (7 Laykold courts, lights, pro shop), croquet— all free; massage, horseback riding (with guides), scuba-diving, and sport fishing extra
P.S.: Expect some parties of cruise ship passengers during the day—in the restaurant, in the pool, on the beach or tennis courts

Added Attractions

Croney's Old Manor Estate
Nevis

At Croney's Old Manor Estate, you'll be whiling away your hours in a romantic, almost sultry hideaway burgeoning with monkey-no-climb and gooseberry trees. Owner Vicki Knorr and her son, Gregg, have revitalized the place, said to be the island's oldest continually inhabited plantation, with weathered gear wheels and pistons, the metal sculptures from another era, dotting the grounds.

Guest rooms are grouped around the Sugar Mill and the Great House; number 3 in the Admiral's House is a terrazzo-floored duplex with a king-size bed draped in mosquito netting; number 4 in the Executive House (the former blacksmith shop) is a cheery stone-walled suite, also with marble terrazzo and a bed tucked away in a cozy alcove.

When you tire of hiking around the slopes of Mt. Nevis or lolling around the Croney's tropically foliaged 40-foot pool, you may start to think about dinner. And you're in the right place. Croney's is lauded for its dining room (the Knorrs even grow their own spinach and lettuce in what used to be the settling tanks).

In the breezy Cooperage Dining Room, surrounded by flamboyant trees, you can enjoy a tasty dish of shrimp dipped in coconut and sautéed with fruit juice and soy sauce, followed by a "sinful pie," coffee mousse with whipped cream and walnuts. Lobster is on the menu as much as possible (there's a special Friday night lobster and steak buffet). With such popular dining facilities, Croney's is probably the least "clubby" of the island's inns, especially in the evenings. 10 rooms. Doubles: $195, room only. *Croney's Old Manor Estate, P.O. Box 70, Charlestown, Nevis, WI. Telephone: 809/469-3445; fax 809/469-5388*

Ocean Terrace Inn
St. Kitts

This is not exactly what you would call a romantic hideaway but it has a lot of island atmosphere in its role as a crossroads for dedicated island-hoppers, traveling either for pleasure or on business. The Ocean Terrace overlooks the town of Basseterre and the sweep of South Friar's Bay, packing 30 comfortable guest rooms, 6 two-bedroom and 2 one-bedroom apartments into a well-tended garden, with an additional 11 efficiency apartments across the street in the bayside Fisherman's Village. The multilevel garden has two freshwater pools, one of them with a swim-up bar and a grotto-like Jacuzzi.

The inn's dining room and terrace bars are popular spots for lunch with both sightseers and Kittitians, but in the evening they have strong competition from Fisherman's Wharf, the barbecue restaurant at the hotel dock. Another option is Turtle Beach Bar & Grill, located on the southeastern peninsula. Open for lunch and dinner, the restaurant is a 20-minute bus ride (free transportation is provided) from the hotel. Free snorkeling equipment and Windsurfers, Sailfish, and acqua eye boards are available on the beach. Winter rates range from $95 to $200 for two, room only. *Ocean Terrace Inn, P.O. Box 65, St. Kitts, WI. Telephone 809/465-4121, 4122; fax 809/465-1057.*

Vue Pointe
Montserrat

The view is coastline, black sand beach, a nine-hole golf course among the coconut palms, a few private villas on the hillside across the valley. The hotel consists of hexagonal rondavels on a grassy slope above the sea, each individual unit with fifties furniture, sitting area, shower and deck screened by flowering shrubs. It's comfortable, sensible—the Caribbean in its unspoiled simplicity. The main lodge houses a large bar/lounge/terrace and so-so dining room. Don't come here for haute cuisine but for peace and quiet and friendly folks. Since the owner is an eager tennis player, the hotel has two of the best-kept tennis courts in the Caribbean—with lights! There's a water sports facility on the beach, a pool on the hill, and that uncrowded little golf course in the valley. 28 rooms. Doubles: $120 to $180 EP. *Vue Pointe, Olde Town, Montserrat, WI. Telephone: 809/491-5210; fax: 809/491-4813. Reservations toll free 800/223-6510.*

Covecastles Villa Resort
Anguilla

So distinctive is its postmodern architecture that Covecastles leaps out at you as you fly over Anguilla. From the coastline of St. Martin, just across the channel, it looks like a battery of bunkers and you half expect anti-aircraft guns to pop out and ratatat. The stark-white sculptural forms presumably make some kind of statement, but if the architecture is too un-Caribbean for these parts, even the most ardent traditionalist is likely to be seduced by Covecastles' secluded setting, dazzling half-mile beach, refined luxury, and attention to detail—from the champagne on ice awaiting your arrival and the exquisite hand-embroidered linens that caress you at night to the raw-silk upholstery on the rattan loungers and the inviting Pawleys Island hammocks on the oversized terra-cotta verandas.

Originally, Covecastles consisted only of two- and three-bedroom villas, which always posed problems for lovers—that is, which couple gets the master bedroom, the other rooms having too many drawbacks. Now there are also villa suites, more suitable for twosomes, with ceiling fans and acres of louvers (some bedrooms with air conditioning), cable television, radio, telephone, and kitchens that give new meaning to the words "fully equipped." Not that you yourself have to bother with all the gadgetry, since the resort will assign a maid/cook to prepare your meals.

There is a small restaurant on the premises, too (for a resort with lodgings for fewer than 40 guests!), open for dinner only, but its kitchens are available for room service throughout the day. Sports facilities include two lighted tennis courts and Sunfish sailboats. 12 villas and villa suites. Doubles: from $540 to $980, winter 1991–92, room only. *Covecastles Villa Resort, P.O. Box 248, Shoal Bay West, Anguilla, BWI. Telephone: 809/497-2801; fax: 809/497-2801. Reservations: 800/348-4716.*

K Club
Barbuda (Antigua)

The would-be swankest of all would-be exclusive hideaways—at something like $1,000-a-day for suite, breakfast, and dinner—may or may not be open on Barbuda at the time you're thinking of taking your next vacation. There is a resort there (quite beautiful, in fact), and I know colleagues who have dined there, but it has suffered from erratic owner-managership (it was created, not without boo-boos, by a leading Italian fashion designer). When I called to ask them to send me a brochure and let me know when the resort would be operating, they duly noted my name and address but never got around to sending me anything, and they didn't really know when the place would be closing for the season or when it would be reopening. Obviously, I am not recommending K Club, and I mention it here only because some observant reader or reviewer might otherwise note its absence from these pages and think "how come this guy considers himself some kind of expert on the Caribbean when he doesn't even know about the K Club?" *K Club, Codrington, Barbuda, Antigua WI; tel. 809/460-0300 or 212/752-3525.*

The French West Indies

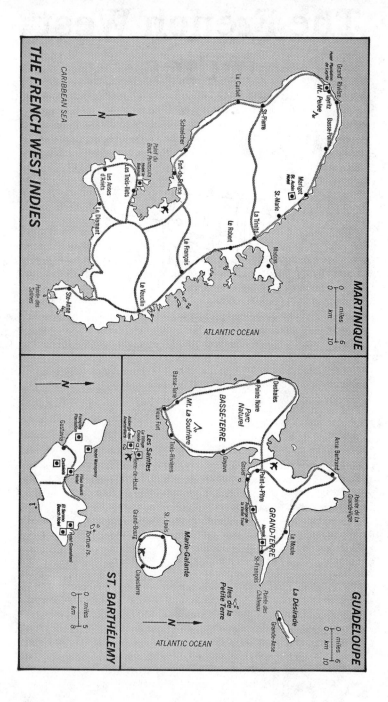

The French West Indies

The *tricouleur* flutters over and micro-bikinis wiggle on Martinique, Guadeloupe, St. Martin (the French half of the island otherwise known as Sint Maarten), St. Barthélemy and a few out-islands; French *savoir-faire* and *joie de vivre* have been transplanted intact—in fact, they may even have gained from overlays of tropical sensuousness. You'll find some of the best eating in the Caribbean here, some of the sportiest highways, the most stylish dressers, and, on the nudist beaches, the most enthusiastic undressers. These are great islands, or integral political units, of *la belle France.*

The largest of the islands is Martinique (50 miles long and 22 miles wide), a lush, mountainous land with rain forests, plantations, fishing villages, and masses of wildflowers. It has enjoyed centuries of renown for its dusky maidens: Napoleon's Josephine is the most famous, but Martinique has also provided queens and consorts for a dozen other rulers—including Louis XIV and the Grand Turk of Stamboul. Fort-de-France, the capital, is an intriguing mishmash of West Indies seaport, the latest Peugeots, fishing boats, yachts, open-air markets, high fashion, and gourmet restaurants; but the most interesting part of the island for my money is the spectacular north around Mont Pelée, especially the tower of St. Pierre, once known as the Paris of the Caribbean, before it was destroyed when Pelée erupted one Sunday morning in 1902. The highway/road/path along the rugged northeast coast to remote Grand'Rivière is also worth an excursion and picnic.

Guadeloupe (from the Spanish "Guadalupe" and the Arabic "Oued-el-Houb," meaning River of Love) is really two islands, Grande-Terre and Basse-Terre, linked by a short bridge. The capital is also known as Basse-Terre, away in the south, shut off from the rest of the island by the magnificent Natural Park of Guadeloupe. But the action is up around Pointe-à-Pitre, which is rapidly beginning to look like a suburb of Paris. When *les citoyens* of Pointe-à-Pitre want to get away from it all, they board a ferryboat for the 60-minute ride to Terre-de-Haut, one of the islets that make up the Les Saintes islands. It's about as quiet and unspoiled as they come, with an atmosphere that's French Antillean to the last Gauloise. This is one place where you may need an acquaintance with French beyond *bonjour* and *merci.*

Technically, St. Barthélemy, or St. Barts, is part of the *département* of Guadeloupe, although it's closer to St. Martin. *"Nudisme est interdit à* St. Barthélemy" is the first sign that greets you at the airstrip, but despite the ominous interdiction (which many people seem to ignore anyway), St. Barts is really a friendly little place. It's the tiniest (about eight square miles) of the French islands and something of a curiosity: It's the only island in the Caribbean with a predominantly white population (mostly descendants of the original Breton settlers), and its picture-postcard port of Gustavia was formerly an outpost of Sweden. Despite its modest size, St. Barts manages to accommodate 60 restaurants.

How to Get There   From New York to Guadeloupe and Martinique: American to San Juan where you connect with American Eagle service to Pointe-à-Pitre and Fort-de-France (there may also be direct service in winter on Air Minerve); from Miami and San Juan, direct service by Air France; from Montreal and Toronto, direct service by Air Canada. You can also make connections at Antigua (Air Guadeloupe to Pointe-à-Pitre), St. Maarten (to both islands), and Barbados (Air Martinique to Fort-de-France).

For St. Barthélemy, the most convenient connection is via St. Maarten, on Windward or Air St. Barthélemy, 16 flights a day; the latter also has regular flights from San Juan with seven-seat Cessnas, or nine-seaters from St. Thomas. For the fainthearted, who may prefer not to endure the modified kamikaze approach to St. Barts' airstrip, there are also several sea crossings from St. Maarten's Philipsburg. The St. Bart Express links the island with Marigot *and* Philipsburg on St. Maarten, three days a week. *Reminder:* If you are flying to St. Barts from St. Maarten, be sure to buy your ticket before you leave home to avoid paying the outrageous stamp duty slapped on airline tickets by the St. Maarten authorities.

Note: Hotels on St. Martin, the French half of the dual St. Maarten/ St. Martin, are listed under St. Maarten in the chapter on the Dutch Windward Islands.

‿❀◠

Castelets
St. Barthélemy

☆☆☆ ♆♆♆ ◑ $$$$

Perch by the edge of the tiny triangular pool, feet dangling in the water, champagne glass dangling from your fingers. Far below, one of the most breathtaking vistas in the Caribbean unfurls in a montage of silver beaches, rocky promontories, mini-mountains, craggy islets, and scudding sails. It's like watching a movie while sitting in the balcony (remember *big* movie screens?), but without the soundtrack.

This panorama alone may well be worth foregoing a beachfront lair, but there's more to Castelets than the view. Is there ever! *La cuisine*, for example. The menu is a leatherbound volume the size of a citation, inviting leisurely browsing and the careful planning of dinner. *Chausson de Camembert au cumin* (hot Camembert flavored with cumin in a popover) or *demoiselle des îles à la crème d'avocat* (lobster medallions with avocado), *paupiette de mérou au crabe* (grouper rolled and stuffed with crab) or *medaillons de veau plantation* (veal cutlets with banana garnish), *îles flottantes aux amandes* (soft meringue with vanilla cream and crushed almonds), or *millefeuille* (thin flaky pastry layered with cream filling). There are, it should be noted, two dining rooms here: the fireplace room, (where you may wind up sharing the refectory table with other diners) and the small enclosed terrace where—with the appropriate advance notice of four or five days—you can probably reserve a window table for two.

On this Antillean hilltop, the inn seems more of a *gentilhommerie* that echoes the backroads of Burgundy, its dining salon resplendent with hefty refectory tables and chairs of wrought-iron and leather, the circular stone fireplace sports a canopy of copper, and the walls glow with antiques and prints. Summon a vintage chateau-bottled wine from the extensive cellar ("we allow the wines to rest a good month and a half before serving," to let the Pommard and Château Margaux recuperate from their transoceanic voyage).

Each of Castelets' 10 guest aeries is different, with a few common themes such as Breton-style trundle beds and rope balustrades, upholstered wicker and doors of Guayana greenheart, decorations of framed silk squares by Hermès and antique maps of the Lesser Antilles. The least expensive (and smallest) rooms are identified as Bistro West and Bistro

East, meaning they're in the main lodge, above the restaurant; the remaining rooms and suites are in small villas, some with duplex sitting rooms and marble floors, bathrooms with fitted carpets, refrigerators, and tape decks. Villa 2 is the favorite of Mikhail Baryshnikov (Castelets is popular with dancers and musicians—Paul Taylor is another regular—most of whom reserve their favorite rooms a year in advance).

Four years ago Castelets sprouted a new room—tiny 2A, at the rear, with white walls and blue-gray trim and its own entrance from a small garden patio shaded by a flamboyant tree.

Each time I've come to Castelets over the past 13 years, it's been with a *frisson* of trepidation. Not because of the road that twists and curls its narrow way up the hill at an angle you wouldn't even want to experience in a biplane. No, but because of what *may* have happened in the interim to alter its *ambiance agréable*.

Fortunately, this little gem has turned out to be one of the most dependable inns in the entire Caribbean. The delightful Geneviève Jouany is still there to greet guests in her polished Parisian way; chef Michel Vaily is still tending the kitchen; the family of bananaquits is still nesting in the chandelier in Villa 3.

Only one thing seems to have changed: Over the years I've watched *le jardin Jouany* blossom and bloom (with the help of a local gardener with a distaste for pruning) and it's now luxuriant by the standards of St. Barthélemy.

This is another Caribbean up here among the Jouany jasmine and hibiscus, lignum vitae and poirier, high on the coolest hill, with the bedazzling Baie de St.-Jean spread out beneath you.

Name: Castelets
Owner/Manager: Geneviève Jouany
Address: St. Barthélemy, FWI
Location: In the hills above Gustavia, about 15 minutes and $7 by taxi from the airstrip
Telephone: 590/27-6173, 27-7880
Fax: 590/27-8527
Reservations: Jane Martin, New York, 212/319-7488
Credit Cards: None (American Express, MasterCard, and Visa in the restaurant)
Rooms: 10, in the main house and garden villas, all with breezes or fans, private bathrooms, some with tape decks
Meals: Breakfast 8:00–10:00, lunch noon–2:00, dinner at 7:00 or 9:00 (two sittings, approx. $80 to $100 for two), in main dining rooms; restau-

rant closed all day on Tuesdays and for lunch on Wednesdays; informal dress, but no shorts; room service for continental breakfast only
Entertainment: Parlor games, tape decks in villas
Sports: Tiny plunge pool; beaches and water sports just 7 minutes away
P.S.: "Not too suitable for children"; closed July and August

François Plantation
St. Barthélemy

☆☆☆ ♀♀♀ ◑ $$$$

For 20 years or thereabouts, François Beret has been one of St. Barts most esteemed restaurateurs, so his longtime fans have dutifully followed him to his new hillside inn. They applaud his restaurant, his cuisine, his wines, but his eyes really light up when you compliment him on his *garden.*

. In this flowery mini-jungle you'll find lantana and mangot, palmier and amandier, filao and caoutchou, "probably one of every type of tree that grows on the island" and 20 types of hibiscus in exquisite colorings, which M. Beret arranges in joyous bouquets to decorate his veranda. There are so many flowers and trees growing in this luxuriant garden that you barely see the inn and its dozen cottages until you're practically on the doorstep and walking beneath the whitewashed pergola into the lounge.

François Plantation sits on a cool hillside near the hamlet of Colombier (not far from where the Rockefellers built their private hideaway), with sweeping views from the veranda and most of the cottages, the grandest panorama reserved for the hilltop swimming pool with its sunbathing "island."

The pastel-colored cottages, too, are designed in traditional Antillean style—square wooden frames with steeply pitched roofs, raftered ceilings, terrazzo tile floors, chunky pencil-post beds crafted of mahogany, with rattan stands to house refrigerators and television sets.

The veranda doubles as lounge and restaurant, the former furnished with cushioned rattan and plump sofas in shades that echo M. Beret's hibiscus, and the latter in Georgian-style mahogany tables and cane-seated chairs. Lavish greenery in pots and planters and the leafy garden just beyond the white balustrade give the place an authentic colonial look, while the fabrics and pastel prints add a dash of sophistication.

François Beret, although still the mastermind behind the menu and upholder of standards, now functions as boniface-in-chief, handing the kitchen brigade over to an alumnus of Robuchon in Paris, Thierry Alix. What issues forth from the kitchen certainly merits the corkscrew drive uphill. *Coupe de poisson maison* and *panache de poissons au fenouil et pistil de safron* are two of the house specialties that entice most islanders, but we were delighted with *minute de taza mariniere de legumes* and *magret de canard au citron et miel*. The *tarte tatin chaude* and *fondant chocolat raisin et sa crême de Kahlua*, while delectable, may be too hearty for tropical evenings.

One can't fault the quality of the cuisine or presentation; the service is friendly and attentive (English versions of the menu are available, the waiters speak English well)—but even if the service were lethargic, you probably wouldn't mind just enjoying the pleasant setting.

Name: François Plantation
Owners/Managers: François and Françoise Beret
Address: Colombier, 97133 St. Barthélemy, FWI
Location: In the hills, about 10 minutes and $12 from the airport or the main town of Gustavia
Telephone: 590/27-7889
Fax: 590/27-6126
Reservations: WIMCO in Rhode Island, 401/849-8012 or toll free 800/932-3222; Jacques de Larsay
Credit Cards: American Express, Visa
Rooms: 12 colonial-style cottages, each with marble bathroom (twin vanities), air conditioning and ceiling fan, direct-dial telephone, stocked mini-bar, cable television, wall safe
Meals: Breakfast 7:30–9:30 on the veranda; no lunch; dinner 7:00–10:00, also on the veranda (approx. $100 for two), dress informal, some quiet background tapes; room service for breakfast only
Sports: Freshwater pool, sundeck; beaches nearby (within walking distance downhill, but you really need a car)
P.S.: Closed September and October

Hotel Manapany

St. Barthélemy

☆☆ 🍷🍷🍷 ◐◐ $$$$

The Manapany is tucked away on one of the few coves left on St. Barthélemy with no hotel—Anse des Cayes—among unkempt, typically Antillean landscape. Nonetheless celebrities such as Mick Jagger, Peter Allen, Gianni Versace, and tennis ace Yannick Noah have sussed it out and local cognoscenti praise its Ballahou Restaurant as one of the island's finest. Given the competition, gourmet and otherwise, on St. Barthélemy, that's saying quite a bit.

The Manapany's cottages are designed in traditional island style with red shingle roofs and gingerbread trim, and each consists of a suite with terrace and room with balcony. The rooms are small, but the suites are spacious and ideal for lounging and relaxing, with 20-foot screened terraces fitted with wicker sofas, armchairs, coffee table, dining table and chairs, and full kitchenette. Soothing pastel fabrics set off white-on-white walls, ceiling, and floors. Beachfront rooms cost more, but since most of them tend to look out on other cottages (try to avoid the Lapis Lazuli and Chrysalite suites), you may want to opt for one of the upper cottages clinging to the steep, terraced hillside. They impose a bit of a hike down a somewhat precipitous path to get to beach, pool, or restaurant, but they do afford more breezes and a stunning view. But the choice quarters are now the 12 Club Suites, with larger bathrooms and porches with refrigerators and two-ring burners (four beside the beach, eight on the hillside).

Whether you walk down the hill, Minimoke it, or just step over from your beach cottage, it's worth the effort when you're bound for dinner at the Ballahou (French nouvelle) or the glass-enclosed Ouanalou (Italian nouvelle). The Ballahou is attractive, with a bar at one end, its gingerbread trim fashioned from a single piece of timber about 40 feet long and decorated with lobsters, seahorses, and crabs. The Ouanalou curves around the big pool by the edge of the beach that seems to be one of the most congenial spots on St. Barts.

Name: Hotel Manapany
Owner/Manager: Guy Roy
Address: Box 114, 97133 St. Barthélemy, FWI

Location: On the bay known as Anse de Caye, about 5 minutes and $5 from the airstrip

Telephone: 590-27-6655

Fax: 590/27-7528

Reservations: Mondotels

Credit Cards: All major cards

Rooms: 52, including 20 rooms, 20 junior suites, 12 new Club Suites, all with air conditioning and ceiling fans, balconies or patios, private bathrooms (showers only, baths in Club Suites, bathrobes, wall-mounted hairdryers), clock radios, color TV (in-house movies, English and French), direct-dial telephones, pantries in suites

Meals: Breakfast 7:30–9:30, lunch noon–3:00, dinner 7:00–10:00 (approx. $50 to $70 for two), in the Ballahou or Ouanalou; informal dress; 24-hour room service (including full menu during restaurant hours), $2 per person extra charge (for waiter); piano player or taped background music

Entertainment: Bar/lounge/terrace with piano, taped music (*quel horreur!*), a big TV set on the bar "for Americans who want to watch football"; chess, Scrabble, backgammon; to say nothing of oodles of bars 10 to 15 minutes away by Minimoke

Sports: Beach (windswept, with coral, not especially good for swimming or windsurfing), large egg-shaped freshwater pool with island deck for sunbathing, whirlpool (solar-heated, sometimes lukewarm), tennis (1 court, pro, lights), snorkeling masks, exercise room with Universal equipment—all free; boat trips (with hotel-prepared picnics), scuba-diving, and sailing can be arranged

Filao Beach Hotel
St. Barthélemy
☆☆☆ ☲ ☾ $$$$$

The ambience around here is pure Côte d'Azur—but most resorts on the French Riviera would give an arm and leg to have a beach like the Filao's.

This plush little hideaway is on one of the prime locations on St. Barthélemy, right on fashionable (and usually topless) St. Jean Bay, on that talcum-fine strand between the island's toy-town airstrip and the rocky promontory known as Eden Rock.

Hugging its plot of precious beach, the hotel meanders back along well-marked paths through gardens of sea grape trees livened with white hibiscus, allamanda, and red cattail. Red-roofed bungalows house 30 guest rooms, each named for a château in France, with the name (Villandry, Montlouis, whatever) etched on a ceramic owl above the door. Each room is generously furnished with double bed, daybed/sofa, plenty of chairs and tables, television, refrigerator, both air conditioning *and* ceiling fan. The roomy bath incorporates tub, shower, and bidet.

All 30 rooms have recently been restyled and rejuvenated with new furnishings and fabrics; but it's in the niceties that Filao scores—fresh flowers in all the rooms, continually replenished supply of bottled water in the fridge, an electric hairdryer in the bathroom, and redwood chaises covered with comfy cushions in blue and white stripes on each private terrace. You'll probably do more snoozing than sunning on your terrace because of the copious shade from the sea grapes, but almost certainly you'll have breakfast there, seated at the glass-topped table decorated with an island chart, poring over the topography of St. Barthélemy's, deciding which beach to visit once you've scooped up the last flakes of croissant.

After a morning's swim you can look forward to a pleasant lunch at the Filao's beachside bar/restaurant, a peak-ceilinged pavilion with lazily turning fans. It opens directly onto a raised wooden deck and an angular swimming pool, with the flags of France, Sweden, the United States, and Filao Beach fluttering fraternally in the trade winds above the topless sun-worshippers. The Filao's light lunches (no, not the topless bathers) draw a crowd from all over the island to nibble on the freshest lobster (someone's brother-in-law is a lobsterman), sip Sancerre, and look out across the sand to the far-off reefs.

Afterward, if you're feeling too sated for much else, you have to walk only a few steps to the beach and settle into a molded plastic lounger for a siesta. For something more active, the waters off St. Jean Bay, protected by those scenic reefs, are ideal for windsurfing—and there's a windsurfing concession right there to rent boards and offer instructions.

Name: Filao Beach Hotel
Manager: Pierre A. Verdier
Address: BP 167-97133, St. Barthélemy, FWI
Location: On St. Jean Bay, about 1 mile from the airport, free shuttle for guests
Telephone: 590/27-6484

Fax: 590/27-6224
Reservations: David B. Mitchell & Company, Inc.; Jacques de Larsay
Credit Cards: American Express, Diners Club, Visa
Rooms: 30 (8 Deluxe Beachside, 10 Deluxe, 12 Garden), all with ceiling fans and air conditioning, refrigerators, hairdryers, TV, video, and safe-deposit box
Dining: Breakfast and lunch only, and the bar closes at 8:00; room service for breakfast only; there are lots of restaurants within walking distance
Sports: Freshwater pool, beach swimming, snorkeling masks and wind-surfers for rent
P.S.: Closed September 2 through October 12

Hotel Guanahani
St. Barthélemy

☆☆☆ ♉♉♉ ◐◐◐ $$$$$

A dozen swimming pools. A couple of tennis courts. St. Barts has never had it so lavish.

After a false start as Le Warwick, the island's largest resort finally opened its doors in December 1986 with a new name and new owner—the AXA Insurance Company of Paris. Whatever you may feel about insurance companies as hotel keepers, there can be few misgivings about Guanahani's setting: bay and beach, reef and islet, headlands and blue but breeze-whipped sea. The resort sprawls over several acres of landscaped hillside tucked into one corner of Grand Cul-de-Sac Bay, a reef-protected beach, with the low-profile but snazzy El Sereno Hotel on one side, a grove of coconut palms belonging to Edmond de Rothschild on the other.

Although it's the island's largest resort, Guanahani still has well under a hundred rooms, deployed two or three to a villa. Furnishings and decor are more or less standard in all rooms—tasteful and luxurious but not overdone, Antillean with a dash of Rive Droite, white pencil-post beds with paisley sheets. All suites come with kitchenettes and have private pools. Kitchen and pools aside, your options boil down to location—whether or not you want to be beside the beach and steps from the water or on the hillside to catch the breezes and views. Tennis buffs might enjoy

rooms 10, 11, and 12, overlooking one of the resort's two courts and sharing a pool for après-match dunking. (Conversely, those three rooms are less than ideal for late sleepers who prefer not to be awakened by thonk-thonks and assorted blasphemies.) Rooms 39 and 41 are particularly attractive because they're at the edge of the property, overlooking the Rothschild coconuts; at the Sereno side of the resort, room 61 has an exceptionally large and secluded terrace with uninterrupted views of the entire bay.

No one, private bank or private moneybags, can hope to run a successful hotel on St. Barts without paying almost as much attention to the kitchen as to the decor. Maybe even *more*. The most popular pastime on this island is not sunning but dining—here, there, everywhere, so that at times the entire island seems to be a stream of scooters and Minimokes puttering their way to the latest eatery.

You can sample Chef Jean-Louis Chezeaud's efforts in two restaurants. The Indigo, beside the beach, adjoining the pool, is a French-style casual café for luncheon grills to accompany bottles of Chablis or Muscadet; the Bartoloméo, a few terraces above the beach, sets a classier tone, with handsome mahogany-trimmed decor, tables set with fine china and silver candleholders. It looks expensive—and it is (a fact of life on St. Barthélemy). But what appears on the table has a level of refinement you don't often find in the Caribbean. The service is professional and friendly, without, on the whole, the stumbling block of languages.

If you do leave Guanahani to dine elsewhere, it is probably because Bartoloméo's 40 seats have been snapped up by people from other hotels, who have scootered and Minimoked here to sample Chezeaud's *petit loup grillé au fenouil, parfumé au Ricard.*

Name: Hotel Guanahani
Manager: Bruno Hill
Address: Anse de Grand Cul-de-Sac, 97133 St. Barthélemy, FWI
Location: On the Atlantic coast on Grand Cul-de-Sac Bay, about 15 minutes from the airstrip in courtesy air-conditioned mini-bus
Telephone: 590/27-6660
Fax: 590/27-7070
Reservations: Leading Hotels of the World, Crown International Marketing, or WIMCO
Credit Cards: All major cards
Rooms: 68 rooms and suites in 30 villas, each with fans *and* air conditioning, bathtubs, terrace/patio, refrigerator, satellite TV, radio, telephone; some with kitchenettes, wall safes, and/or Jacuzzis
Meals: Breakfast 7:00–10:00, lunch 12:30–3:00 in the beachside Indigo Café, dinner 7:00–10:00 in the fan-cooled Bartoloméo Restaurant (approx. $100 to $120 for two); informal but stylish dress ("shorts, T-shirts, swimsuits, or other similarly casual clothing are inappropriate after dark in the dining room and bar"); "soft music" every evening in Bartoloméo; room service for continental breakfast and dinner only
Entertainment: Weekly barbecues on Saturday (with music), video films
Sports: Beach (with a second swatch of sand on the other side of the Rothschild coconut grove), 11 individual swimming pools (private or semiprivate), large pool and Jacuzzi beside the beach, snorkeling, tennis (2 courts, hard court, with lights)—all free; beach concession offering windsurfing, HobieCats; deep-sea fishing, sailing by arrangement

El Sereno Beach Hotel
St. Barthélemy

☆☆☆ ♕♕♕♕ ☻ $$$$

Despite the attraction of a secluded beach and protected bay, of a glamorous tiled swimming pool with sunbathing "islands," *dining* is the high point of a stay at this delightful little hotel on St. Barts' Grand Cul-de-Sac.

The Sereno's managers, Marc and Christine Llepez, are also the owners of a popular brasserie in Lyon, Le Café du Marche. They recently brought in a Paris-trained Lyon chef to oversee the glittering dining room of El Sereno, Restaurant La Toque Lyonnaise. Chef Andre Chenu not only knows his way around a *beurre blanc* but also embraces local seafood and produce with gusto. Lobster ravioli and truffles in cabbage butter share space on the menu with red snapper and mashed christophene. He even serves the traditional Lyonnaise green salad with poached egg, country bacon, and garlic croutons. But figure also on Lyon prices—$100 for dinner for two, with wine.

The setting for all this gourmandizing is an open pavilion beside the beach and the pool, newly restyled with teal-trimmed wicker armchairs, teal rafters, and ceiling fans. In the evening the dining room takes on its fairyland quality. Tiny lights set into the deck twinkle in the twilight; the mirror-encased chimney refracts the light from all directions; chicly clad guests lounge on comfortable sofas covered with Jean-Yves Fromant fabrics or around the bar where Marc and Christine welcome everyone to what appears to be a vivacious house party.

Visually, the hotel complements the restaurant—it's equally stunning. Set among low palm trees, it's a dazzle of free-form white walls, royal blue lampposts, and the red and blue shiny tiled pool. Guest rooms surround a sandy center courtyard, each with a fragrant, private patio-garden of hibiscus and laurier and latanier. The rooms are all alike indoors—whitewashed, blue-beamed but small, with cot beds, closets in the bathrooms, and like the dining room newly renovated with brighter color schemes and wicker furniture. Terraces have chaises, hammocks that look like trampolines, and tables and chairs for your morning croissants—and since the foliage and wall offer some protection you don't have to be too fussy about dressing for breakfast.

Unfortunately, the cross-ventilation may prove something to fuss about—there isn't much, despite the sliding glass door that divides the rooms from the terraces. And since there are still no ceiling fans, you'll probably have the air conditioner running more often than you'd like, although prime rooms 1, 2, and 6 get a few more riffles of breeze than the others since they face the bay (of these, 2 is the most private).

But don't let the lack of ventilation keep you away from El Sereno. You'll be skimpily attired indoors or out most of the time—paddling in a bay so shallow it's still no more than shoulder high some 200 yards out, sunning yourself on those "islands" in that stunning pool, lunching lazily on the trellised porch—or dozing on the beach, eying that dazzling dining room and dreaming of *Matelotte de langouste* and *feuillantine à la banana*.

Name: El Sereno Beach Hotel
Owners/Managers: Marc and Christine Llepez
Address: BP 19, 97133, St. Barthélemy, FWI
Location: On Grand Cul-de-Sac Bay, about 3 miles from the airport, about $12 by taxi
Telephone: 590/27-6480
Fax: 590/27-7547
Reservations: International Travel & Resorts, Inc.; Jacques de Larsay
Credit Cards: American Express, MasterCard, Visa
Rooms: 20, each with patio-garden, showers only, satellite TV (VCR upon request), wall safe, air conditioning, refrigerator, direct-dial phone, hairdryer
Meals: Breakfast and lunch on the beachside glass-enclosed terrace, Le Lagon Bleu; La Toque Lyonnaise is open for dinner only (dinner for two approx. $100); dress code "elegantly casual" in the evening; room service for breakfast only
Entertainment: The bar, or video movies in your room
Sports: Swimming, freshwater pool; windsurfing, pedal boats, tennis nearby
P.S.: Closed September 1 through October 15; restaurant closed June 1 through October 15

Hamak

Guadeloupe

☆☆☆☆ 🍷🍷🍷 ◕◕◕◕ $$$$

Hammocks, hammocks everywhere. One waiting on your front patio. Eight more swinging over the bar. And embossed on every towel, plate, and ashtray as well. The message here is clear: relax.

On an aquamarine lagoon where a perpetual ocean breeze cools the sunshine even at high noon, this is a place for doing everything or nothing in great style. A technicolor botanical garden of 10,000 (the gardener keeps count) exotic trees and flowers undulates around 56 cabana suites. The glass wall of your bedroom opens into a private walled garden with a locked gate to which only you and the maid have a key. Along with hummingbirds, bougainvillea, and beach chairs, each garden has a tiled open-air shower big enough for your own private splash party. But this is one of the few Caribbean resorts where you can do your topless tanning anywhere. For Hamak has both an openness and a privacy few other places have mastered.

A hundred other guests are here—somewhere. In their walled gardens. On a little scallop of private beach in front of their cabanas. Or out to sea waterskiing, pedal boating, Sunfishing, windsurfing, etc. But the only spot where you're likely to encounter more than one body at a time is in the middle of Hamak's main beach, and most of them make very pleasant scenery. Even the adjoining sweeping Robert Trent Jones golf course is blessedly free of both crowds and the island's famous *yen-yens* (nasty gnats that make a buzzing sound just like their name as pronounced by a Frenchman).

As all good things usually do, Hamak's sophisticated simplicity emanates from an owner who runs the place strictly to his own tastes. What Jean-François likes *you* had better like, too. And why not?

Every last matchbox and dinner napkin has been chosen with bull's-eye taste. And there's not a polymer in sight. Creamy stucco and poured concrete, dark woods and terrazzo tiles are the stuff everything's made of. The cabanas are simply but thoughtfully done: 10 feet of soft sofa in the sitting room, floor-to-ceiling mirrors beside the king-size bed, roomy bath, nearly silent air conditioning, and refrigerator.

But the instant you want to get away from it all, the hotel provides jitney, powerboat, or private plane to take you where you want to go. With a landing strip right on the property, you can arrange to go on a day's island hop to St. Martin and St. Barthélemy (both in one day), to the nearby islets known as Les Saintes, or all the way to Mustique for lunch and a swim at the Cotton House.

Name: Hamak
Owner/Manager: Jean-François Rozan
Address: 97118 Saint-François, Guadeloupe, FWI
Location: On the beach, about 20 miles and $35 by taxi from Pointe-à-Pitre and the airport
Telephone: 590/88-5999
Fax: 590/88-4192
Reservations: David B. Mitchell & Company, Inc.; Jacques de Larsay
Credit Cards: American Express, Diners Club, MasterCard, Visa
Rooms: 56, in garden bungalows, all suites, all with garden patio, extra shower on patio, terrace with hammock, air conditioning, refrigerator, pantry, wall safe
Meals: Breakfast 7:00–10:00, lunch noon–3:00, dinner 7:30–11:00 (approx. $65 to $75 for two); informal dress; room service
Entertainment: Taped music, "mood music" combos; casinos and shopping nearby
Sports: 3 virtually private beaches, waterskiing, Sunfish sailing, windsurfing, tennis (2 courts, with lights, at nearby club); golf (Robert Trent Jones design, 18 holes, guaranteed starting times for Hamak guests *twice* a day); snorkeling gear for rent; excursions by boat and twin-engined plane can be arranged

Auberge de la Vieille Tour
Guadeloupe

☆ ♈♈ ◑◑ $$$

Some travelers choose great hotels with a decent restaurant attached. *French* travelers choose great restaurants with a decent hotel attached. Hence, the never-ending popularity of this fifties-style hotel. Yes, it has nice beaches, pool, tennis, boats, and refurbished guest rooms—but the real attraction here is what comes steaming out of the kitchen every night.

Delicately prepared local fish in perfect sauces. Pink and tender lamb. A rolling silver cart of crisp, fresh Caribbean antipasto. Bries and Camemberts. Rum cordials with a headiness inherited from the exotic fruits you find lurking at the bottom. So, although that handsome 18th-century sugar-mill tower at the entrance is what gives the *auberge* its name, as soon as you step into the lobby you sense that eating is the main sport here.

Since the rate for every room here is precisely the same, reserve early and get a good one. Number 77, for example, is actually a bungalow; it sits all the way at the end of the garden completely refurnished and with a tiny terrace right over the beach. Its three matching neighbors aren't quite so private but otherwise have all the same advantages. Another stretch of 18 guest rooms has also been redone from stem to stern in simple white cottons and natural wood. Each has a vest-pocket refrigerator stocked with champagne, Schweppes, beer, and fruit juice.

If the three tiny beaches get too crowded for you, the hotel will send a boat around to take you to a nearby island where you can establish your own beachhead, break out a picnic lunch supplied by the hotel chef, and still be back in time for one of Vieille Tour's outstanding dinners.

Name: Auberge de la Vieille Tour
Manager: Thierry Demart

Address: 97190 Gosier, Guadeloupe, FWI

Location: About 10 minutes and $17 by taxi from the airport, or from Pointe-à-Pitre

Telephone: 590/84-2323

Reservations: Pullman International Hotels, 212/757-6500

Credit Cards: American Express, Diners Club, MasterCard, Visa

Rooms: 80, with mini-bars, air-conditioning, balconies, and sea views

Meals: Breakfast 7:00–10:00, lunch noon–2:30, dinner 7:00–10:00 (in the air-conditioned dining room, approx. $110 for two); dress is moderately formal—jacket (maybe) but no tie; room service, 7:00 a.m.–9:00 p.m., no extra charge

Entertainment: Piano bar daily, steel band and Caribbean ballet on Thursdays, dancing, orchestra from 8:00 to midnight Wednesday through Saturday; casino nearby

Sports: Beach, freshwater pool, tennis (1 court, lights)—free; snorkeling, scuba, sailing, boat trips, golf (18 holes) nearby

P.S.: Occasional small groups, lots of outside guests for dinner; most of the staff speak English

P.P.S.: An extension of 80 rooms and suites is currently being constructed, which may result in some unwanted noise. Ask for a quiet room, away from the construction site. The extension is scheduled to open next winter.

Auberge des Anacardiers

Terre-de-Haut, Guadeloupe

☆ ♀ ◑ $

Until recently, most visitors came over to Terre-de-Haut for the day because the few hotels on the island were barely the kind to tempt people to stay longer. That has changed somewhat in the past few years when several new lodgings opened, the most engaging of them run by Robert Joyeux, who has simply converted his modest hilltop home into an amiable 10-room *auberge*.

Named for one of the many fruit trees that ring the house, this little plant-filled, tile-roofed charmer sits at the top of a hill with an unbeatable view of the bay. Even with the occasional language puzzles, you get the feeling that guests are cordially invited to feel at home. So settle back. Admire the view from the arbor out front. Peek into the cages aflutter with prize French pigeons and the technicolor parrot. Sample *le punch* the mayor loves to concoct with native rum and the fruits plucked from his garden—the bar sports apothecary jars filled with this heady stuff.

The inn's interior is simple, in keeping with the unspoiled ambience of the island, featuring lots of wood paneling and sturdy hand-carved wooden rockers that are a specialty of local artisans. The front parlor is now a pretty little dining room in traditional French Provincial style. As you might expect, the kitchen's specialties come from the surrounding sea, but the menu also offers *filet de boeuf* or *entrecôte*, and the same grill that sears *langouste* or *mérou* can also produce a tasty *brochette* of beef. Breakfasts (included with lunch or dinner in the rate) are generous—*café, thé, chocolat, pamplemousse, ananas, goyave, oeufs au plat, oeuf brouille, pain frais et grillé.*

Guest rooms are small, as you might expect, but comfortable, with efficient plumbing (and air conditioning, although that's something you can be without most of the time at this elevation). Four of the rooms have bathrooms just outside in the hall (but each reserved for a specific room, so still private)—and priced at bargain rates as a result. Rooms 1 and 2 (with fully private bathrooms) have the advantage of doors opening to the terrace beside the pool.

Everyone here, whether they speak your language or not, takes special care of you, running you into town or to the beach, doing your laundry, plying you with *le punch*. The *auberge* is a taste of a bygone, more personal Caribbean—all served with inimitable French flair.

Name: Auberge des Anacardiers
Owner/Manager: Robert Joyeux
Address: La Savane, 97137 Terre-de-Haut, Les Saintes, Guadeloupe
Location: In the hills, 5 minutes by hotel mini-bus from the dock (the island itself is 1 hour by ferryboat from Pointe-à-Pitre, 30 minutes from Trois Rivières, 15 minutes by Air Guadeloupe)
Telephone: 590/99-5099
Fax: 590/99-5488, attn. Anacardiers
Reservations: Direct; Jacques de Larsay
Credit Cards: All major cards
Rooms: 10, all with air conditioning, 4 with private baths in the hall
Meals: Breakfast 7:00–10:00, lunch 12:30–2:00, dinner 7:30–9:00 (approx. $50 for two); informal; no room service
Entertainment: Taped background music, TV set in parlor

Sports: Pool, free transportation to beach; bikes, snorkeling gear, water
　sports for rent nearby
P.S.: Not all the waiters and chambermaids speak English

Le Village Creole
Les Saintes

☆ ◑ $$

Look straight ahead and there's a bay, some yachts bobbing at anchor, an
islet with a fort on top—Fort Josephine. Turn around, look up, and there,
somewhere above you, is another fort—Napoleon. The relative newcomer
(it opened in 1987) sits on a 3½-acre waterfront site, but rather than a
beach you have a garden with tropical flowers and lawns. The 11 cottages
are designed in the island vernacular—small and square with pointed
rooflines and garden patios. Interiors have separate bedrooms and living
rooms with kitchens in a duplex arrangement, and one extra-swank suite
has a Courrèges bathroom in light blue. Furnishings are comfortable and
practical, and if you're looking for someplace well off the beaten track,
someplace quiet and uncrowded, someplace unpretentious, consider
checking into this *domaine*. 　　　　　　　　　　　　　　　　˙

Name: Le Village Creole
Owner/Manager: Ghyslain G. Laps
Address: Pointe Coquelet, Terre-de-Haut, 97137 Les Saintes, FWI
Location: About 15 minutes on foot from the town dock (occasional
　shuttle bus from hotel)
Telephone: 590/99-5383
Fax: 590/99-5555
Reservations: Direct
Credit Cards: MasterCard, Visa
Rooms: 11 cottages, 22 suites, all with air conditioning, ceiling fans,
　direct-dial telephones, kitchens, TV available for rent
Meals: No restaurant, plenty of places within walking distance, includ-
　ing one next door
Sports: None on the premises, watersports nearby

Hotel Plantation de Leyritz
Martinique
☆ ♀ ◑ $$

You know there's got to be something special about a place when all the other hotels in the country (including Club Med, a three-hour drive away) send their guests here by the bus load. For Martinique has two glorious sights: the volcano Pelée and Leyritz.

Born before Mozart, before the steamboat, before even the United States, it is a living, working banana plantation three centuries old and as close to unspoiled as a national treasure can be that's not locked behind glass. The guardhouse, the slave quarters, the grand manor house are all intact—but now instead of *planteurs* bedded down in them, you find guests. The former chapel and sugar factory have been transformed into beamed, stone-walled dining rooms with stenciled ceilings. And at the bottom of a long emerald lawn, a swimming pool with fountains sparkles like a big, cool sapphire.

Accommodations here are comfortable but far from luxurious. What wins Leyritz its rating is that overworked catchall word, charm. Forget you ever saw it before. This is the place for which it was invented.

Everywhere you go, a miniature stone canal splashes fresh mountain water along your route. Through the garden, past the guest rooms of the carriage house, cascading over the walls. Engineered by the first French colonial owner to bring water down from the rain forests to the coffee and spices he grew here, the canal's role now is to provide water music for the guests.

Some people who come back to Leyritz year after year make a point always to choose different quarters—they say it's like staying at a different hotel each time. For instance, the 14 tiny cottages that once housed the plantation's slaves provide the most privacy—snug little bamboo-roofed warrens with foot-thick stone walls and windows discreetly screened by tropical flowers and mango trees. Rooms in the carriage house all have sun decks and the easiest route to the swimming pool is 250 grassy feet down the hill; the smallest rooms are the newest—in a one-time dormitory. But probably the two most unusual places to hang your sun hat at Leyritz are what once served as the guardhouse and the master's kitchen. Now each gives you your own stone cottage surrounded by guava trees and manicured lawn.

Although it hasn't cooked up a meal in a hundred years, the kitchen cottage is still called Pan by the present lady of the house (but after the satyr, she says, not the utensil). Three-hundred-year-old beams crisscross above your bed, and if you hear a whistle it's only the ghost of a long-departed scullery maid. (The master demanded that the help always whistle in the kitchen—so he could be sure they weren't stealing a bite of his dinner.)

The guardhouse cottage gives you the best of both worlds: inside a cool and shadowy stone-walled bedroom with slit windows just wide enough to poke a musket through, and outside your own tiled patio with nothing in sight but a few million banana trees.

As to what to do between siestas, the main sport here is wandering. To the tiny village next door, where the local people always have a welcome mat—and a cold rum punch—for any guest of Leyritz. Or by car down to the beaches and fishing villages below, especially Grand'Rivière at land's end, where the fishermen have devised their own ingenious navigation system for sailing against the breaking waves. Saint-Pierre, "the Paris of the Caribbean" before being wiped out by Mont Pelée in 1902, is a short drive away. Or go on a Tarzan and Jane adventure in one of the gorgeous gorges of the surrounding rain forests. Leyritz has one right on its own estate, but as of this writing it is impassable to anyone but a mountain goat, thanks to the last hurricane. However, there's an even more spectacular climb down the Gorges de la Falaise nearby: under giant fern trees and wild orchids and up a racing river of mossy rocks and icy pools to a 200-foot waterfall you can have all to yourself.

By the time you make it back to the real world, trade winds will be rocking the birds to sleep in Leyritz's ancient mango trees, and the candles will be lit for a dinner of baby lamb and *papaya gratinée*.

Name: Hotel Plantation de Leyritz
Manager: Christian Lecat
Address: 97218 Basse-Pointe, Martinique, FWI
Location: In the north, 35 miles from Fort-de-France, or $55 and an hour's drive by taxi from the airport; most people rent a car to get there, but if you will be arriving after dark, let the hotel know and they'll arrange to have a reliable taxi driver waiting for you at the airport (you pay the fare, of course)
Telephone: 596/78-5392
Fax: 596/78-9244
Reservations: Jacques de Larsay and International Travel & Resorts, Inc.
Credit Cards: American Express, MasterCard, Visa
Rooms: 53, 4 in the main building, the remainder in former plantation annexes, all with telephones, some with air conditioning
Meals: Breakfast 7:30–10:00, lunch noon–2:00, dinner 7:30–8:30 in dining pavilion (approx. $45 to $55 for two); informal dress; room service for breakfast and drinks only; a new restaurant, with capacity for 800 guests, is currently under construction
Entertainment: Dancing to live music twice a week, some local folklore groups or bands
Sports: Pool, tennis, walks through the plantation; beaches 30 minutes away
P.S.: Tour groups for lunch almost daily (eat early or late or request seating in the smaller room adjoining the noisy main dining room); several staff members speak English, but you can expect a few verbal hitches

Hotel le Bakoua
Martinique

☆ ♟ ➊➊ $$$

The distinctive feature of Le Bakoua is a cluster of orange conical roof-tops representing the *bakoua*, or conical native hat, for which the hotel is named. They cap a colorful, open dining pavilion seating 500 (that is, two and a half times the guest count), where fresh anthuriums and crotons climb the columns, the table linen matches the anthuriums, and wait-resses in local costume serve the Bakoua's French and Creole delicacies (Sunday is "lobster night," with island crustaceans cooked half a dozen different ways). Expect distractions, though—the dining area abuts a dance floor covered by an orange and yellow awning, next to a circular open bar.

Le Bakoua, now a part of the Sofitel chain, is probably your best bet for a resort hotel in Martinique, a ravishing island short on refined lodgings. It's surrounded by gardens of frangipani and coconut palms. The rooms are comfortable, amply equipped, recently refurbished with spanking new tiled bathrooms. The 20-odd compact *casitas* between the garden and the sea are probably the best buy, with modern fitted wall units, balconies, sliding screen doors, tiled floors, tiled showers, and double beds.

Originally sole guardian of a quiet peninsula, Le Bakoua has managed to keep its calm and its distance through all the development on its doorstep and now offers the best of both worlds. If you want beach, you have a beach, of sorts, and lots of water sports and tennis; if you want a disco or casino, they're just a stroll away in the big hotels; and if you want the markets, shops, and nightlife of the city, they're just across the harbor, a 20-minute trip by *vedette*. And if you want a good dinner and a quiet drink on your own terrace, you can have that, too.

Name: Hotel le Bakoua
Owner/Manager: Claude Chevauché
Address: Pointe du Bout, 97229 Martinique, FWI
Location: Across the harbor from Fort-de-France at Pointe du Bout, 20 minutes and $2.50 round trip by ferry, but 30 minutes and $32 by taxi from the airport ($42 between 8 p.m. and 6 a.m.)
Telephone: 596/66-0202

Fax: 596/66-0041
Reservations: Accor/Resitel, 914/472-0370, or toll free 800/221-4542
Credit Cards: American Express, Diners Club, MasterCard, Visa
Rooms: 140 rooms and suites, some on the beach, the remainder in three-story wings with sea view, each with balcony or patio, air conditioning, telephone, radio
Meals: Breakfast 7:00–10:00, lunch noon–3:00, dinner 7:30–10:00 (in the big open dining terrace, approx. $80 for two); informal dress, but no shorts in the evening; room service 6:00 a.m.–3:00 p.m. and 7:30 p.m.–10:00 p.m., $1 extra
Entertainment: 2 bars, dinner dancing nightly to local live music; folklore dance show on Fridays; steel band and show Saturdays; discos and casino nearby
Sports: Beach, freshwater pool, tennis (2 courts, lighted, free by day, $6 an hour with lights); snorkeling gear, scuba, waterskiing from the beach (extra charge); golf 5 minutes away (18 Robert Trent Jones holes), horseback riding nearby
P.S.: Some groups, some children, most of the staff speak English

St. Aubin Hotel
Martinique

☆ ♈♈ ◑ $$

Could it have been a playful time warp—or an addled travel agent? You get on a jet for Martinique and end up on a Louisiana bayou plantation complete with miles of filigreed veranda and sunny sugarcane fields.

But look again, and beyond the cane you see blue sky meeting even bluer sea. St. Aubin has recently been restored, if not to its original French colonial grandeur, at least to a night's colorful, comfortable stopover.

Nobody comes to Martinique to flop in just one spot. There's probably no more glorious ride between California's Big Sur and the Riviera's Grande Corniche than along this island's west coast. So rent a car, ooh your way up the Caribbean side, aah it down the Atlantic side, and you'll find St. Aubin a handy half hour from the airport. The second-floor rooms all open on the veranda (most have sea views-cum-breezes). And the pretty pool near the garden is the perfect refresher after a day in the car.

As for dinner, the owner himself, who previously ran the best restaurant in Fort-de-France, will prepare for you three courses of French Creole cooking to remember, served with a fine chilly bottle of Muscadet.

Name: St. Aubin Hotel
Manager: Guy Foret
Address: Petite Rivière Salée, B.P. 52 97220 Trinité, Martinique, FWI
Location: 30 minutes from the airport, about 19 miles from the capital
Telephone: 596/69-3477
Fax: 596/69-4114
Reservations: International Travel & Resorts, Inc.
Credit Cards: Diners Club, Eurocard, MasterCard, Visa
Rooms: 15, all with private bathrooms
Meals: Breakfast 7:00–9:30, no lunch, dinner 7:30–8:30 (approx. $30 for two) for hotel guests only; no room service
Entertainment: Eating
Sports: Freshwater pool; swimming and other water sports nearby

Added Attractions

Hôtel l'Hibiscus
St. Barthélemy

From your private hillside terrace you look down on an authentic Old West Indian harbor. Red tin rooftops line a rectangle of *quais*, interisland freighters creakingly unload their cargoes, and charter yachts bob at their moorings. The beach may be a five-minute walk away, over the hill, but all of Gustavia's lively bars, boutiques, and bistros are right there at your feet. If, on the other hand, you prefer to stay around your terrace and enjoy the view, just fasten the rope with the *occupé* sign across the path to your cottage and your enjoyment will be undisturbed.

L'Hibiscus is the best place to stay if you want to savor the charm of Gustavia. Its dozen white-walled cottages cover a terraced hillside draped with, of course, hibiscus. Rooms are modern and efficient, with contemporary island decor of native hardwoods and rattan, with television, VCRs, and telephones. Each has a view of the harbor from a private terrace, but what may appeal to many visitors is the outdoor Pullman kitchen (eye-level oven, two-ring cooker, refrigerator, china and cutlery for six), transforming your deck into an intimate outdoor dining room.

The core of the Hibiscus is a midlevel terrace decorated with wicker elephant planters and macrame hangings, with sun deck and pool at one end; at the other, a bar and dining room where you can sample the continental and Creole cuisine prepared by the Belgian *patron*. 12 units. Doubles: $360 EP. *Hôtel l'Hibiscus, P.O. Box 135, Gustavia 97133, St. Barthélemy, FWI. Telephone: 590/27-6482; fax: 590/27-7304.*

Village St. Jean
St. Barthélemy

A hillside garden full of rooms (6) and villas (20), with kitchenettes (except for 4, which have only refrigerators), air conditioning and fans, telephones, television, comfy furniture, terrace or garden, and maid service (including dishwashing). Food critic Craig Claiborne vacations here every December—he even leaves his own set of pots and pans here. It's a steep hike up the hill from the beach (say, 5 minutes down, 10 up); pool, Jacuzzi, open-air restaurant, boutique, comissary, reading/game/video room. The attraction is the rates, from approximately $108 to $310 with breakfast in winter, just $65 to $170 in summer. 26 rooms and suites. *Village St. Jean, 97133 St. Barthélemy, FWI. Telephone: 590/27-6139; fax 590/27-7796.*

Emeraude Plage
St. Barthélemy

Another garden full of bungalows, this time by the edge of the beach. All 30 rooms have kitchenettes, sun decks, and maid service; the atmosphere is totally beachcomber and there are water sports facilities on the doorstep. Season rates are approx. $155 to $265, room only, in winter. 30 rooms. *Emeraude Plage, B.P. 41, St. Barthélemy, FWI. Telephone: 590/27-6478; fax: 590/27-8308.*

Taiwana
St. Barthélemy

It's one of those hearsay hideaways that no one I know has ever actually stayed in—small site, tucked into one corner of a good but not great beach. There's one sexy suite almost in the surf; the remaining four units (all smaller) are on an elevated terrace behind the parking lot, minuscule pool, and stylish dining pavilion. Outlandishly expensive and terribly chic; but why celebrities would want to seek seclusion and anonymity in a tiny enclave where outsiders can come to lunch and swim in "their" pool is a mystery. Service, if not quite sullen, is not exactly outgoing (at least, not to noncelebrities). Owner Jean-Paul Nemegiey doesn't solicit guests and accepts only those referred by other guests. Let them have their privacy. 5 suites. *Taiwana, St. Barthélemy. Telephone: 590/27-6382.*

Jardins de St. Jean
St. Barthélemy

Perched on a hillside, with stunning views over the Bay of St. Jean, this cluster of un-formula condos includes 12 one-bedroom apartments (some duplex), all with terraces, kitchenettes; some have private gardens; some have television. Each apartment is furnished differently (1B is particularly attractive); some of them are no match for the view, but they're comfortable and convenient. There's a shopping mall at the base of the hill, water sports and restaurants across the street. Rates, by St. Barts' standards, are reasonable, the management friendly (they speak English). 20 rooms and apartments. Doubles: $140 to $225 EP. *Jardins de St. Jean, 97133 St. Jean, St. Barthélemy, FWI. Telephone: 590/27-7019; fax: 590/27-8440.*

Hotel Carl Gustaf
St. Barthélemy

This is another superdeluxe nook to watch out for—scheduled to throw open its shutters for winter 1991–92. But only if you're in the market for an $800-a-night room (with breakfast) in a hotel that's not on a beach on an island of beaches. Granted the view from the terraces is stunning (a broad panorama of the bay and harbor of Gustavia) and the sumptuously furnished suites come equipped with full kitchen, private plunge pool, satellite television/VCR and fax machine—but $800 a night with breakfast? (For that kind of money Jumby Bay and Curtain Bluff on Antigua will give you all your meals, all your drinks, water sports, and tennis.) Public facilities will include an elegant restaurant and health club. 14 suites. Doubles: winter 1991–92, approximately $800 to $1,000, with breakfast. *Hotel Carl Gustaf, Gustavia, 97133 St. Barthélemy, FWI. Telephone: 590/27-8283 or 27-7343; fax: 590/27-8237.*

Fregate Bleue
Martinique

Last year Yveline de Lucy Fossarie, owner of one of the Caribbean's most romantic inns, Plantation Leyritz (see page 237), opened a second property, the Fregate Bleue, a simple modern house with gingerbread trim. Although it is much more modest than Leyritz, the seven-room hotel is nonetheless an enticing hideaway. Part of its appeal is the setting: on a hilltop overlooking the sea, dotted with islets and reefs where islanders like to wade in the morning while sipping a cool drink. Behind the building there's a swimming pool shaded by trees and perfumed by flowers. Each of the seven rooms is furnished in a tasteful assortment of antiques, with four-poster beds and Persian rugs on the floor. Each has a balcony with an ocean view, ceiling fan (with air conditioning as a backup), cable television, wet bar, and kitchenette. 7 rooms. Doubles: $220 to $245, winter 1991–92. *Fregate Bleue Hotel, 97240 Le Francois, Martinique, WI. Telephone 596/54-5466; fax: 596/54-7848. Reservations: Caribbean Inn Ltd., toll free 800/633-7411.*

The Queen's Windwards

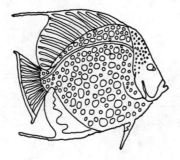

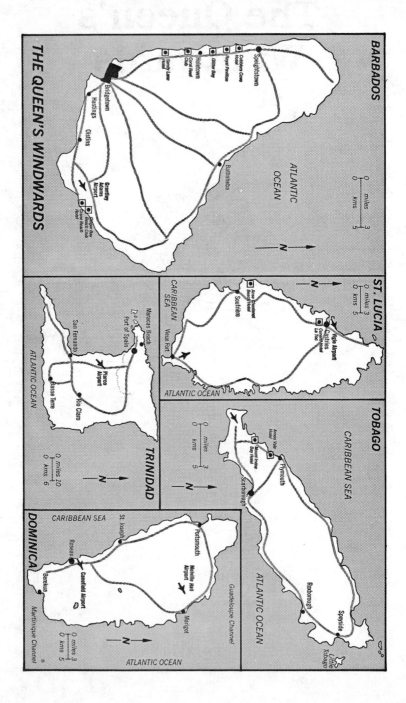

THE QUEEN'S WINDWARDS

BARBADOS

Speightstown
Cobblers Cove Hotel
Royal Pavilion
Glitter Bay
Holetown
Coral Reef
Sandy Lane Hotel
Bridgetown
Hastings
Oistins
Bathsheba
Grantley Adams Airport
Sailors Bay Beach Club Hotel
Silver Beach

ATLANTIC OCEAN

0 miles 3
0 kms 5

N

ST. LUCIA

CARIBBEAN SEA
Anse Chastanet Beach Hotel
Soufrière
Vieux Fort
Vigie Airport
Castries
Cunard Hotel
La Toc

ATLANTIC OCEAN

0 miles 3
0 kms 5

N

TRINIDAD

Maracas Beach
Port of Spain
San Fernando
Piarco Airport
Basse Terre
Rio Claro

ATLANTIC OCEAN

0 miles 10
0 kms 6

N

TOBAGO

CARIBBEAN SEA
Arnos Vale Hotel
Mount Irvine Bay Hotel
Plymouth
Scarborough
Roxborough
Speyside
Little Tobago

ATLANTIC OCEAN

0 miles 3
0 kms 5

N

DOMINICA

CARIBBEAN SEA
St. Joseph
Portsmouth
Roseau
Melville Hall Airport
Canefield Airport
Berekua
Marigot

Guadeloupe Channel
Martinique Channel

ATLANTIC OCEAN

0 miles 3
0 kms 5

N

The Queen's Windwards

Dominica, St. Lucia, Barbados, Trinidad, and Tobago are not, strictly speaking, a geographical entity, and any sailors who think of them as "windwards" may find themselves way off course; but for lovers and other romantics this is a convenient, if grab-bag, grouping. What these islands have in common is that they were all at one time British dependencies.

Of the group, Dominica is the most fascinating—the Caribbean as it must have been at the turn of the century, or, once you get into the mountains and rain forests, as it must have been when Columbus arrived here one *dominica* in 1493. This is an island for travelers rather than vacationers, with real me-Tarzan-you-Jane countryside—untamed, forbidding landscapes, mountains a mile high, primeval forests, waterfalls, sulphur springs, lava beaches, and communities of the original Carib Indians. But for lovers I haven't been able to find a suitable hideaway since my previous favorite was wiped out by a hurricane.

St. Lucia has much the same topography as Dominica, but somehow this one is a gentler island, its landscape softened by mile after mile of banana, spice, and coconut plantations, by bays and coves of white sand beaches. The new road from the international jetport takes you along the windward Atlantic shore and across the mountains, but if you have time, return to the airport by the old road down the west coast. It winds and snakes and twists and writhes forever, but the scenery is impressive, and you pass Marigot Bay (good lunch stop), Soufrière, the famed Pitons, with possible side trips to volcanoes, sulphur springs, or rain forests. The problem with this idea is that you'd have to rent a car, trot round to the police station to get a local driving permit (I also got zapped for a donation to Police Week), and when you leave the car at the jetport, you may be asked to pay an outrageous drop-off charge. But I'm almost persuaded it's worth the effort and expense.

Barbados is hardly a St. Lucia or Dominica in terms of scenery (it's relatively flat and pastoral except for a hilly region in the northeast), but it has a cosmopolitan air that few other Caribbean islands have, maybe because it has always been a favorite with the English gentry. Its main attraction, of course, is its scalloped western coastline, each cove with a lagoonlike beach. It may be rather crowded these days, but it still shelters most of the island's finest resorts. When it's time to take a break from sunning and swimming, however, Barbados rewards the leisurely tourist with a variety of sights, from caves and flower forests to plantation houses and forts and venerable churches. There's even a house where George Washington slept when he visited his brother Lawrence.

Trinidad you can keep. At least as a lovers' hideaway. This island seems to get by on the strength of its carnival and, to some extent, the bustling, swinging, melting-pot qualities of its capital, Port of Spain. Its airport would be high on the list of places to avoid at all costs, if it weren't for the fact that you have to transit there to get to a gem—Tobago.

Tobago is another story: 114 square miles of lush mountains, backwater fishing villages, beautiful beaches, and Buccoo Reef. This is the sort of island where the local bobbies hitch a ride in your taxi because they can't afford patrol cars and their chief is using the official bicycle. It's certainly worth the trouble it takes to get there, if you want someplace offbeat and secluded.

How to Get There   Barbados's Grantley Adams International Airport is one of the major gateways to the Caribbean, from North America and Europe, so there are daily nonstops from New York (American, Pan Am, BWIA); Miami (Pan Am, BWIA); and frequent nonstops or direct flights from Washington/Baltimore (Pan Am); Boston (American, Pan Am); Montreal (Air Canada); and Toronto (Air Canada, BWIA).

St. Lucia needs a little more attention, because it has two airports: Hewanorra International in the south for jets, Vigie in the north for small planes. Otherwise, there's a lengthy drive (at least an hour) from Hewanorra to the hotels near Castries and beyond. You can get to Hewanorra on BWIA from Miami, New York, and Toronto, and on American from San Juan. You can also make connections to Vigie via San Juan (American Eagle), via Barbados (LIAT, several times a day), or via Antigua about 10 times a day.

For Tobago, you must first fly to Trinidad's Port of Spain, which is served from New York by Pan Am and BWIA, from Miami by Eastern and BWIA (some nonstops in each case). From Canada, there are direct flights on BWIA and Air Canada. BWIA also operates the 20-minute jet flights from Trinidad to Tobago. Leave yourselves plenty of time to negotiate the tediously officious formalities at Trinidad; even with a confirmed ticket try to check in for the Tobago flight a full hour before departure, especially on weekends when everyone in Trinidad, it seems, is heading for Tobago. Some of the North American flights arrive too late to make the Tobago connection; your best plan in that case is to head straight for the Trinidad Hilton.

Cunard Hotel La Toc and La Toc Suites

St. Lucia

☆☆☆ 𝒴𝒴𝒴 ❶❶❶❶ $$$$

Judging by the àccents all around you, you could be in Brighton or Blackpool, but step out into the sun, look at the expanse of pinkish beach and the free-form pool with the tree in the middle and you know you're nowhere near England's favorite resorts. This is the Caribbean with a capital C. Palm trees, soft trade winds, clear water, blue skies. Nevertheless, La Toc breaks so many of my yardsticks (see Introduction) it almost shouldn't be included in these pages: It's big, it hosts cruise ship passengers, and it indulges in "crab-racing" and other buffooneries to keep its guests amused. And yet . . . La Toc has so many attractive features that

you'll probably be happy to overlook any shortcomings and enjoy its comforts and facilities—not least, the new deluxe suites.

The owners, Trafalgar House Investments, are London-based property development specialists (they also own the Cunard Line, hence the name). Their property here is a valley of 100 acres opening onto a half mile of curved beach, protected on either side by low headlands and the entrance to Castries harbor; their development consists of a cantaloupe and white hotel, a cottage colony, a nine-hole golf course, tennis courts, and a few score private homes dotted around the valley and the golf course. It all sounds overwhelming, and in fact your first glimpse of the four-story Tower Wing from the top of the hill hardly signals "hideaway," but when you get into the swing of things you don't really notice the hotel's size. You can thank nature a lot for that; in St. Lucia's fertile climate a matchstick can grow into a coconut palm, and here at La Toc the grounds are vivid with red ixorra, Christmas candle, and purple eranthemum. Despite the size and the slabs of cantaloupe stucco, you're never far from the sounds of tree frogs, crickets, and birds.

There was a time, a few years back, when La Toc lapsed into the doldrums. Maintenance was slack. Staff was surly. The beach was often overrun by passengers from Cunard's cruise ships. But then the Cunard people spotted the trend to Caribbean Deluxe and decided to spend millions refurbishing the entire property. Especially the pastel-colored villas. Into the sea went the concept of self-catering, and with it went the kitchens. They've been replaced by stocked refrigerators and wet bars. Stylish new furnishings include cabinets with television and VCR.

The best of these villas have private plunge pools just outside the windows. In theory, all the villas have ocean views, some more so than others; but the choice locations are those farthest from the hotel—beside the beach or up on the bluff (identified as "Luxury Sea View" suites). Over here you not only have a splendid sea view and cooler breezes, but you're also screened from the comings and goings at the hotel; yet one of the hotel's two large pools, the Crow's Nest Bar, and Les Pitons (the smartest of the resort's three restaurants) are within easy walking distance—on lazy days you can always call for the mini-bus to come to collect you. Cunard refers to its new villa suites as "a hotel within a hotel"—you don't check in at the main desk; you're simply whisked directly to your suite to sign in at your convenience.

And the service is what you might have expected sailing transatlantic on the old *Queen Mary*. Maybe better. Your stewardess unpacks and irons your clothes; your dark blue bathrobes and white kimonos are waiting for you on your bed, folded like a fan and topped by a hibiscus; comfy slippers are neatly lined up on the dhurry rugs on either side of the bed;

the amenities basket of oversize vials includes fabric wash, moisturizer, and suntan lotion; turndown treat is a miniature of Bailey's Irish Cream or Courvoisier. At night, you can switch on the floor lights that shine romantically through the plants; in the morning you can step from your bed, slide open the glass doors, and hop right into your private pool.

The remaining revampings are decided improvements, especially the smart new Crow's Nest Bar and Les Pitons Restaurant. The kitchen has improved; the staff is sharper and friendlier. And the Cunard people, realizing that you can't have a top-of-the-line resort swarming with day-trippers, have decided to bite the bullet and restrict the number of cruise ship passengers visiting La Toc. And then make those visitors pay for water sports.

Overnight guests, of course, enjoy the sports facilities at no extra charge. With a wide array of water sports, a dandy little golf course, and five tennis courts—to say nothing of its 46 plunge pools—La Toc Suites (which gets three stars—the hotel itself would be two or three) now has to rate as one of the classiest sporting resorts in the islands.

Name: Cunard Hotel La Toc and La Toc Suites
Manager: Michael Prantz
Address: P.O. Box 399, Castries, St. Lucia, WI
Location: Just south of Castries, the capital; 10 minutes and $10 from Vigie Airport, 1½ hours and $40 by taxi from Hewanorra Airport
Telephone: 809/452-3081, 3089
Fax: 809/452-1012
Reservations: Cunard, New York, toll free 800/222-0939
Credit Cards: All major cards
Rooms: 155 rooms and 12 suites in the hotel, 46 luxury rooms or suites in garden villas, all rooms with air conditioning, patios or balconies, direct-dial telephones; all suites with patios or balconies, stocked refrigerators, wet bars, cable TV/VCR, ceiling fans, some with private plunge pools
Meals: Breakfast 7:00–10:00, lunch noon–3:00, afternoon tea 3:00–5:30, dinner 7:00–10:00 ($40 to $70 for two, in one of 3 breeze-cooled dining rooms); informal dress, but stylishly so in Les Pitons; live music with dinner at the main terrace; room service 7 a.m. to 11 p.m., no extra charge
Entertainment: 3 bars, tennis club pub, library (with VHS tapes), movies, live entertainment every evening—quiet guitar at Les Pitons, amplified combos, folklore shows, etc. in the main hotel
Sports: Sandy beach (good swimming), 2 freshwater pools, 46 plunge pools, fitness center, snorkeling, Sunfish sailing, windsurfing,

waterskiing, tennis (5 courts, Omnicourt and clay, 3 with lights, pro shop), golf (9 holes, par three, pro shop)—all free; scuba-diving, sport fishing, and horseback riding can be arranged

P.S.: Some children, some cruise ship passengers (but they now have to pay to use the beach and facilities, which effectively cuts down on the numbers)

Anse Chastanet Beach Hotel
St. Lucia

☆☆☆☆ ♈♈ ◑◑ $$$

Don't come here for three-speed showerheads and Porthault sheets. The luxuries at Anse Chastanet run deeper, and dearer. First, there's the Caribbean's most spectacular view, a Bali Ha'i of jagged mountains soaring out of the sea that would have sent Gauguin diving for his umbers and indigos. Then there's the hotel's simple good taste, from handmade mahogany bed tables to the twist of immaculate madras on every waitress's head.

But you find something else here that is all too rare in the Caribbean these days: a caring and a closeness not just between owner and guests or staff and guests, but with the whole tiny community—taxi drivers, schoolgirls, fishermen, banana cutters. Consider what happened to the guests here on Christmas Eve. As they sat sipping their after-dinner cognacs high above the darkened beach, suddenly a flaming torch appeared in the sea. Then another and another and another. The villagers had come to sing carols from their canoes. No hats were passed; no bows were taken. It was just to say Merry Christmas.

Artfully tucked away in one of St. Lucia's remotest back pockets, Anse Chastanet proves hard to get to even once you get there. Its private roadway rocks and rolls you up and up and up until at the end of it all you discover the beginning of the hotel, spiraling down the other side of the mountain to the sea.

Octagonal, whitewashed guest cottages cantilever from the hibiscus like vacationers who can't get enough of that Gauguin view. The style is Beach Functional: wraparound windows and terraces, paddle fans, island-crafted furniture of local wood, crisp madras and muslin at the windows

and on the beds, no-frills showers. All of it born of the theory that beach houses are for sleeping. (Best views, by the way, are from rooms 5, 6, and 7.) In December 1990, Anse Chastanet introduced 11 new suites a notch or two up the hill, ranging from 900 to 1,600 square feet, some with ceilings soaring 20 feet, and some with bathrooms larger than most hotel rooms. Each of the new suites has a breathtaking view, whether it's facing north across the luxuriant dell and beach or south to the Pitons. Suite 7B has a perfectly framed view of the peaks; in 7E, the bed has been set at an angle for a classic view of the Pitons; 7F has an enormous terrace with a 180-degree vista and a *shower* with a perfect Piton view; suite 14B, slightly futuristic in looks with soaring ceiling, sports a free-form stucco shower open to the breezes with a tree in the middle; 15B suggests a sort of treehouse with its wraparound louvers opening onto dense foliage. The 12 spacious rooms tucked behind the beach are handsome and luxurious (room 11 is best in terms of privacy) and some of them will, at some point in the future, compensate for what could be a breezeless location with private plunge pools. For the rest, there is a series of multilevel open-air terraces, dining rooms, and bars—and, at the bottom of a long hillside stairway, a graceful quarter-mile beach of fine volcanic sand the color of pussywillows.

But who says you have to be a stay-at-home? Take a picnic lunch to the hotel's private waterfall. Get a native guide to paddle you around the neighboring mountain islands. Give your camera a workout in Soufrière, a tumbledown fishing village as picture-perfect as a movie set. Tour an authentic French colonial banana plantation. Soak your weary bones in the hot mineral baths of a tropical rain forest. Visit a volcano you can drive into (and *out* of). And in the evening, try the Hummingbird. It's one of the West Indies' best restaurants, and it's right at the start of Anse Chastanet's roadway.

Then, if all this hasn't exhausted your pluck, leave in grand style. Skip the tortuous taxi ride to Vigie Airport and take the *Family Bible* instead. It's a pirogue, a dugout canoe owned by a local fisherman who cheerfully takes you and your luggage the 25 miles in one sea-breezy hour right to the terminal's front door. Just remember not to wear your Guccis—it takes a few steps in the ocean before you step into the terminal.

Name: Anse Chastanet Beach Hotel
Owners/Managers: Nick and Karolin Troobitscoff
Address: P.O. Box 7000, Soufrière, St. Lucia, WI
Location: On the southwest coast, 75 minutes and $35 by taxi from Hewanorra airport, 2 hours and $50 from Vigie or Castries (the fare is included in the weekly scuba package or escape package); the hotel will have someone meet you at the airport if you let them know when you'll be arriving
Telephone: 809/454-7000, 7355, 7354
Fax: 809/454-7700
Reservations: Ralph Locke Islands
Credit Cards: American Express, Diners Club, MasterCard, Visa
Rooms: 48, 11 in spacious new hillside villas, 25 in the hillside cottages (of which 5 are suites), 12 in three plantation-style villas at beach level, all with ceiling fans, balconies or patios
Meals: Breakfast 7:30–9:30, lunch 11:30–3:30 (at the beachside bar), dinner 7:30–9:30 (approx. $50 for two, in one of two hillside terraces);

informal dress; coalpot barbecues Friday evenings, Creole buffet Tuesdays; room service for breakfast only, $1 extra

Entertainment: Quiet taped music, folklore shows, dancing, local "shake-shake" band, steel band, pool table, library

Sports: Beach (volcanic sand), snorkeling, windsurfing, Sunfish sailing, pirogue trips to the Pitons, tennis (1 court, no lights)—all free; complete scuba facility with 3 dive boats and photo lab extra (no spearguns—the sea around here is about to be declared a national preserve)

Ginger Bay Beach Club
Barbados

☆ ♈ ◑ $$

To get to the beach here you walk through the garden gate, along a stone path to a cavelike gash in the coral cliff, then down, down 64 wooden steps *through* the coral cliff.

Sounds like work? Maybe. Especially on the return trip. But in either direction the hike is well worth the huffing and puffing since this is the northern end of Crane Beach, probably the island's loveliest (some reporters list it as the most beautiful beach in the world but that's fanciful).

Built in 1984, the Beach Club (a club in name only) sits romantically atop the coral cliff, three two-story villas all dressed up in coral pink. The suites (no rooms, just suites) come with air-conditioned bedrooms, wet bars, and living rooms. But you may find yourselves spending most of your nonbeach hours on the spacious lanai, lounging in your hammock, listening to the surf pound the coral far below, and watching the moonlight shimmer on the sea. Suites 5, 6, 9, and 10 have two-sided balconies, but you can skip suite 4 since it has no ocean view.

Furnishings and fabrics are more English country house than Barbados resort—fitted carpets, wingback armchairs, double beds topped with forest green spreads, and baldachins with floral motifs—although most of the suites are showing signs of their windswept location and badly need perking up.

There's a more tropical flair about the hub of the club—a compact courtyard given over to free-form pool and whirlpool, kiosk bar, and open dining pavilion, with patio furnishings, umbrellas, and even the bottom of the pool embellished with a stylish representation of the ginger lily, the hotel's insignia.

Ginger's, the club's pavilion-restaurant, puts you even more in an island mood: gray-stained hardwood beams and columns, candles in terra-cotta replicas of traditional Bajan homes. The menu has not forgotten its Bajan roots, featuring flying fish or dolphin smoked over pinewood, callalloo, breadfruit "vichysoisse," lobster and chubb from the reef beyond your windows, prepared with ginger and lime.

Ginger Bay set out to be grand luxe, but it has since reined in its ambitions and is now a modest, moderately priced resort—in a stunning location.

Name: Ginger Bay Beach Club
Manager: Mark Springer
Address: St. Philip, Barbados, WI
Location: On the windward southeastern shore, 10–15 minutes from the airport, $15 by taxi
Telephone: 809/423-5810
Fax: 809/428-6343
Reservations: International Travel & Resorts, Inc.
Credit Cards: American Express, MasterCard, Visa
Rooms: 16 one-bedroom suites, all with ceiling fans and air conditioning, balconies or lanais, direct-dial telephones, radios
Meals: Breakfast 7:30–11:00, lunch noon–3:00, dinner 7:00–9:30 (approx. $50 for two); informal dress; room service at no extra charge
Entertainment: Bar
Sports: 1 mile of beach (good swimming and snorkeling, depending on the surf), freshwater pool, tennis (1 lighted court)—free; other sports by arrangement

Crane Beach Hotel
Barbados

☆☆ ♀ ◑◑ $$$

Once the only thing that stood on this airy bluff was a gigantic wooden crane that handed down bales of sugarcane to British schooners bobbing in the sea below. By the turn of the 18th century, the gentleman who

owned the crane had done so well that next to it he built himself a very
small, very grand manor house. Close to 200 years later, that mini-
mansion of gray-white coral stone is the east wing of the Crane Beach
Hotel.

You can usually count on a couple of centuries to take their toll, especially in a windswept, spumeswept spot like this. But the miraculous thing
about the old Crane is that its original seigneur would probably still feel
right at home—even with the addition of a new wing in the 19th century
and a swimming pool in the 20th.

This pool, a spectacular Roman affair with Ionic columns, is scooped
right out of the edge of the cliff with a backdrop of sea and beach and a
full-blown coconut grove. It's the kind of vista that dreams are made of
(although some purists might cringe at the columns).

Unfortunately, it's also the kind of vista that attracts parties of sightseers in mini-buses. Good-bye tranquility, farewell serenity, especially on
weekends. These trippers usually arrive at midday for drinks on the
terrace, lunch in the terrace dining room—where, if the wind blows and
the windows are closed, the noise level can be jarring. Escape *is* possible.
Your breezy balcony or patio, for a start. And since a few rooms have
kitchenettes (but no stoves) you may be able to rustle up your own light
lunch without setting eyes on a single day-tripper.

The guest rooms may be outshone by the hotel's setting—but only just.
And the dreary reception area might tempt you to zoom right back to the
airport without checking in. The guest rooms are closer to a country
auberge than an Antillean resort. Floors of gleamingly polished wide-
plank pine or cooling quarry tiles. Canopy beds and 16-foot ceilings. Walls
a foot thick, of coral stone or old brick. Antique chests and wardrobes.
Tiled baths with both overhead and hand-held showers.

Some favorites: Room 3 may be the most intimate of all the Crane's
romantic nooks and crannies; it has simple beachy furniture, a refrigerator and honor bar, and a flowery brick patio. Above, Room 10A has a
balcony that gives you a two-way view—along the picture-book beach and
east out to the reef and sea. Rooms 1, 2, 7, 8 have four-poster beds.

For going the whole hog, there's no place like Suite 8. Beyond the
gleaming foyer waits a sitting room worthy of a governor-general: a
burnished wood ceiling, silken sofas, glass-doored bookcases imag-
inatively stocked. Beyond that is a *House Beautiful* kitchen, and beyond *that*
a bedroom full of splendid antiques. In the middle of it all, on a carpeted
platform of blue, looms a huge canopied bed from which, on a clear day
with the wooden louvered shutters pushed aside, you can view the same
sunny sea lane that those ancient sugar schooners followed home to
Liverpool.

A pair of caveats, however. One: The Crane Beach dining rooms are not the most attractive in Barbados and the cooking is nothing special, so you may want to dine in the island's restaurants, most of which involve trips of 30 minutes or more (except for nearby Ginger Bay Beach Club or Sam Lord's Castle). A car will be useful, but during the winter months you'd better reserve your wheels when you reserve your room. The hotel will take care of both reservations. Two: The hotel was acquired in 1988 by a Canadian organization, Go Vacations, which still plans to add 80 rooms, a "fantasy" pool, a restaurant, and a nine-hole golf course. Check on the status of these projects before you make your reservations—you don't want to vacation in a construction site.

Name: Crane Beach Hotel
Manager: Timothy C. Boyce
Address: The Crane, St. Philip, Barbados, WI
Location: On the southeastern corner of the island, 15 minutes and $15 by taxi from the airport, 30 minutes and $25 from Bridgetown (bus to town in winter)
Telephone: 809/423-6220
Fax: 809/423-5343
Reservations: Direct
Credit Cards: American Express, MasterCard, Visa
Rooms: 20, including 10 suites, all with ceiling fans (they're talking about adding air conditioning) and telephones, most with balconies or with pantries, some with four-poster beds and antiques
Meals: Breakfast 7:30–10:00, lunch noon–2:30 in the glass-enclosed cafeteria overlooking the beach and reef, afternoon tea 2:30–6:00, dinner 7:00–10:00 in the breeze-cooled, tented dining room with the beach floodlit 60 ft. below (approx. $70 for two); informal dress; entertainment for lunch and dinner seven days a week; full room service from 7:00 a.m.–10:00 p.m.
Entertainment: Taped classical music in lounge, four-piece amplified dance band on Saturday
Sports: 1,000 ft. of white sand beach (down spiral steps), freshwater pool (with 160,000 gallons, every drop from a private well), snorkeling, tennis (4 courts, no lights)—free; horseback riding, sailing nearby
P.S.: "Not suitable for young children"; three-night minimum in winter, seven at Christmas/New Year

Sandy Lane Hotel
Barbados

☆☆☆☆ ♀♀♀ ◕◕◕◕ $$$$$

Physically, Sandy Lane is one of the class acts. An imposing driveway curves beneath enormous mahogany and tamarind trees, past terraced gardens with cherub fountains and flowerbeds, down to the Palladian porte cochere and main lodge of pink gray, hand-cut coral stone. And you know you're in class surroundings when the resort's two vintage Rolls-Royces pull up beneath the porte cochere after shuttling to and from the airport with lords and ladies who have just arrived from London. The Mercedes station wagon tags along, too—for the luggage.

But even classics, even stars sometimes fade. Sandy Lane in recent years has been coasting along on its past reputation. Some reputation, of course. A new history of the resort's first 30 years is peppered with the names of celebrities and aristocrats who have vacationed here. One of the winter regulars is none other than Lord Forte, whose Trusthouse-Forte group owns Sandy Lane. Apparently he has seen the light. For a thirtieth birthday treat he is giving the hotel a facelift. A major project. As this edition goes to press, every room in the main beach wing is being enlarged to accommodate more spacious marble bathrooms, broader balconies, wet bars, cable television, and an array of amenities and niceties.

The project is the dream of Sandy Lane's new manager, Richard Williams, known to readers of this guide as the wiz who turned around nearby Cobbler's Cove, and the resort's first Barbadian-born manager (his ancestors came from the United Kingdom some 200 years ago).

Another promising Williams innovation is the installation in the kitchen of chefs from Jo Rostang's La Bonne Auberge in Antibes (who perform the same function for Anguilla's Malliouhana, of course, but also for Manhattan's Plaza-Athenée, another Trusthouse-Forte hotel). The Rostang family will supervise the Sandy Lane kitchens, but Bajan chefs will also fly to the Riviera for training at *la source*. As it is, even before the official arrival of Rostang's *brigade*, Sandy Lane was showing a considerable improvement in the caliber of its cuisine and the bounty of its buffets (I liked particularly the bottle of Moet champagne on the breakfast buffet, uncorked and ready for lovers of a morning mimosa).

But the most noticeable improvement at Sandy Lane since the last edition of this guide is the service. A lot of the old-timers, biding their time until pension day, seem to have been edged out and replaced by a younger team more in sync with Williams's ideas of motivation and initiative. Certainly, the welcome is friendlier, the front desk staff is on its toes, the dining room staff is more alert, and the housekeeping people behave like a bunch of doting grandmothers. It now functions like an intimate 50-room inn rather than a 110-room resort.

Things are definitely looking up here. "I plan to make this one of the 10 best resorts in the world," says Richard Williams. I'll settle for one of the 10 best in the Caribbean.

Name: Sandy Lane Hotel

Manager: Richard Williams

Address: St. James, Barbados, WI

Location: On the west coast, 25 minutes from the airport (you can have one of the vintage Rolls-Royces pick you up for $90, the Mercedes for $45); 20 minutes and $12 by taxi from Bridgetown

Telephone: 809/432-1311

Fax: 809/432-2954

Reservations: Leading Hotels of the World or Trusthouse Forte, toll free 800/225-5843

Credit Cards: All major cards

Rooms: 110 rooms and suites in 3 two-story and four-story wings (even if you save a few dollars, avoid the Garden View, since the beach views are so stunning); all with balconies or lanais, bathrobes, hairdryers, wet bars, refrigerators, wall safes, clock/radios, cable television

Meals: Breakfast 8:00–10:00, lunch 12:30–2:30, (to 5:00 in the poolside café), dinner 7:30–9:30 (approx. $80 to $90 for two), in two classic beachside pavilions draped with pink and white awnings and open to the breezes; informal but dressy most of the time, (black tie is optional but jackets and ties are required on Wednesdays and Saturdays in winter); room service during dining room hours, no extra charge

Entertainment: Terrace bars, lounge with big screen for VCR movies, live music every evening, dancing under the stars on the Starlight Terrace, some floor shows and folklore shows (including the inescapable limbo, which you'd think regular guests would be bored with by this time)

Sports: Long, long stretch of beach (public, of course, so sometimes bustling with folks from cruise ships), freshwater pool at the tennis club, tennis (5 courts, lights, pro), golf (18 championship holes, shared with local club members), snorkeling gear, waterskiing, windsurfing,

HobieCats, mats, and floats—all free; scuba-diving, yacht trips, and horseback riding can be arranged

P.S.: Member of Elegant Resorts dine-around program; some children, some executive seminars in the off-season

Coral Reef Club
Barbados

☆☆☆ ♟♟♟ ◑◑ $$$$

You stay in bungalows with names like Petrea and Allamanda and Cordia, and you walk to the beach past splashes of blue petrea and yellow allamanda and orange cordia.

You swim a few leisurely breast strokes to the coral reef offshore.

You dine off flying fish mousse and marlin pâté, tipsy trifle and coconut meringue pie.

Above all, you relax.

The Coral Reef Club is the sort of place where people go to wind down rather than dress up, where entertainers like Engelbert Humperdinck and Tom Jones or Olympic skating stars like Torvill and Deane go to find undisturbed seclusion. This clubby but unstuffy inn has been a standard-bearer among Barbados resorts for over 30 years, a prototype of the small Barbados retreat built around a coral-stone villa. And because it was there before the others, it managed to snare more beachfront acreage—more than a dozen acres of tropical greenery. Space enough for most of the rooms to be in semiprivate bungalows, spread out among cannonball and mango and mahogany trees.

The other attraction that sets Coral Reef apart is the O'Hara family. Budge and Cynthia O'Hara started the place all those 35 years ago (after a stint at England's famed Lygon Arms) and they haven't missed a year since, greeting every guest, overseeing gardens and kitchens, buying gifts for everyone staying at the club at Christmas. (Question: What do you get Engelbert *and* Tom when they're *both* guests over the same holiday? Answer: Each other's records.)

Now the torch has passed to a new generation of equally dedicated O'Haras. With the long-serving staff (some of whom have been with Budge since Day One) it all adds up to a special, warm feeling you can never find at a Sandy Lane, with its track record of what seems to be a different corporate manager every year. (How many resorts, for example, let you have continental breakfast any time between 8:00 and noon?)

The family feeling overflows to the large and airy guest rooms, which lean to almost defiantly *non*designer decor. Until last year, that is. Lounge areas and guest rooms were recently given a touch-up, but before devoted Coral Reefers have palpitations, it should be pointed out that the place hasn't changed all *that* much, since the designers themselves are family. A few new fabrics, a new sun terrace beside the dining room, the addition of ceiling fans and refrigerators in most rooms. Nothing major. Guests still have their own toasters, their own shelves of paperbacks, and, if they're lucky enough to be in a bungalow (specify Poinsettia, Frangipani, Cordia, or Petrea to be closest to the beach), their own terraces draped with vines to match the name of the room—petrea or frangipani or cordia or whatever. In the original Great House, my favorite quarters would be the newly restyled and enlarged rooms known as House 3 and House 4.

Name: Coral Reef Club
Owners/Managers: The O'Hara Family
Address: St. James, Barbados, WI
Location: On the northwest coast, 25 minutes and $19 by taxi from the airport, 20 minutes and $13 from Bridgetown (free shuttle to town weekdays at 9:30 a.m.)
Telephone: 809/422-2372
Fax: 809/422-1776
Reservations: Ralph Locke Islands
Credit Cards: All major cards
Rooms: 75, in garden bungalows, the Clubhouse, or in a two-story wing, all with private bathrooms, refrigerators, hairdryers, patios or balconies, air conditioning and ceiling fans, direct-dial telephones, toasters, wall safes, shelves of paperbacks
Meals: Breakfast 7:00–10:30, continental breakfast until noon, lunch 1:00–2:30, afternoon tea 4:00, dinner 7:30–9:30 (approx. $70 for two) in the breeze-cooled beachside pavilion; Monday evening Bajan buffet; jacket and tie three evenings in winter, informal the remainder of the year; 24-hour room service at no extra charge
Entertainment: Live music and dancing seven evenings a week year-round (amplified "but not loud"), weekly folklore show and beach barbecue, parlor games, VCR
Sports: Good beach, good swimming and snorkeling, freshwater pool, tennis (two all-weather courts, no lights, across the street and a five-minute walk), Sunfish sailing, windsurfing, waterskiing, cocktail

cruises, snorkeling gear—all free; HobieCats, scuba-diving for a fee; golf at nearby Sandy Lane; horseback riding and deep-sea fishing can be arranged

P.S.: "Children welcome except from January 15 through March 15 when those under 12 years cannot be accommodated"; member of Elegant Hotels group, with dine-around privileges at eight other resorts (see Cobblers' Cove)

Glitter Bay
Barbados

☆☆☆ 🍷🍷 ⬤⬤ $$$$

The glitter comes from the play of sun on sea, but when the Cunard family of steamship fame took over the estate in the thirties, the *guests* were the glitter—Noël Coward and Anthony Eden, assorted lords and

ladies and merchant princes. Ocean-going Cunarders putting into Bridgetown often found their ships' orchestras shanghaied to play for Sir Edward's garden parties. All very romantic.

Today, the sea still glitters, lords and ladies still winter here, and at least one Arab prince has settled in for six weeks on more than one occasion, accompanied by an entourage of 25. But Sir Edward Cunard's original coral-stone Great House is now the centerpiece of a small resort, created eight years ago by an Englishman, Michael Pemberton. He made his bundle in amusement arcades and real-estate developing, but with his prime Caribbean estate he has opted to develop it in the style of Andalusia rather than the Antilles—white stucco buildings rising three or four stories above the lawns, their ocher-tiled rooftops eye-to-eye with the coconut palms, their balconies and terraces angled for sea views. By confining the rooms to one side of the garden and by building up rather than out, Pemberton avoided that pitfall of so many of the newer beachside resorts in Barbados—rooms looking into rooms.

The rooms are attractively tropical with Mediterranean overtones: scatter rugs to brighten the quarry tile floors and (nice touch) cushioned banquettes on the stucco balconies. Since the resort was conceived originally as a condo operation, most of the accommodations are suites with kitchenettes, in versatile configurations of duplex suites, penthouse suites, and nests with one to three bedrooms.

But Glitter Bay is almost two distinct resorts, because the most appealing rooms, for my money, are located not in the new Andalusia-style villas but in the beachside villas known as Beach House, a coral-stone replica of the Cunards' palazzo in Venice, with five luxury suites.

Glitter Bay also gives you a sense of space rare in Barbados—22 acres tended by a dozen gardeners, lawns shaded by royal palms and cannonball trees, pathways lined by frangipani and lady-of-the-night, sturdy saman trees embraced and entwined by traceries of wild orchids.

The old Great House sits well back from the beach, while the remaining structures are grouped around a split-level swimming pool with a wooden footbridge and waterfall. Down by the beach, the restaurant, Le Piperade, enjoys fresh sea breezes and lavishes attentive service on its diners (the young staff are forever checking if everything is fine, heating plates for entrées, whisking plates away promptly). Prices are reasonable (for food *and* wine), and the menu runs the gamut from fried flying fish sandwich and fish cakes with spicy tomato sauce to *escalope de veau Cordon Bleu* and *noisette d'agneau.*

Glitter Bay evenings begin with cocktails in the Great House, the original Cunard mansion, now with extensions and icy air conditioning, but still a gracious gathering place (gone, I'm happy to say, are the gaudy slot machines, but the grand piano has been joined by an oversize video screen). Complimentary drinks are served here in the evening—a pleasant prelude to a stroll across the lawns to the restaurant, along those winding pathways lined by frangipani and lady-of-the-night.

Name: Glitter Bay
Owner/Manager: Stephen Grant
Address: St. James, Barbados, WI
Location: On the northwest coast, 25 minutes and $20 by taxi from the airport (you can also arrange to have the resort's Daimler sedan collect you, for $50), 20 minutes and $12 from Bridgetown
Telephone: 809/422-5555
Fax: 809/422-3940
Reservations: International Travel & Resorts, Inc.
Credit Cards: All major cards
Rooms: 83, in three- and four-story wings or beachside villas, all with air conditioning and fans, terraces or patios, mini-bars, direct-dial telephones, hairdryers, radio; suites also have kitchenettes
Meals: Breakfast 7:30–11:00, lunch 12:30–6:30, and dinner 7:00–10:00, in the breeze-cooled, beachside restaurant (approx. $70 for two); afternoon tea in the air-conditioned Great House lounge (where you can also have complimentary drinks at cocktail hour); informal dress (but no shorts or T-shirts in the evening); room service during dining room hours; snacks around the clock; meals can also be charged at the Royal Pavilion (below)
Entertainment: Beachside bar, live amplified music for dancing, some folklore shows, cable TV and VCR in lounge (TV sets can also be rented)
Sports: Cove beach, raft, 2-tiered free-form freshwater pool, windsurfing, snorkeling masks, Hobie 16s, waterskiing, tennis (2 courts, with lights)—all free; sailboat and speedboat cruises and scuba can be arranged at the beach hut, golf and horseback riding 10 minutes away
P.S.: Expect lots of children during holidays (but they have their own planned activities) and a few seminar groups in the off-season

Royal Pavilion
Barbados

☆☆☆☆ ♈♈♈ ●●● $$$$

When Mike Pemberton of Glitter Bay told me that he had bought the old Miramar Hotel, next door, and planned to turn it into a deluxe resort, I thought the midday sun had finally befuddled his English brain. How could anyone take that dumpy motel and transform it into anything remotely luxurious?

Well, Pemberton has shown us how.

First you call in Glitter Bay's landscape architect extraordinaire, Fernando Tabora, to work his green-thumb magic on the seven acres of grounds. Next you summon Ian Morrison, the architect who designed Glitter Bay, to work his visual magic—adding a tower here, a turret there, primping the facades with fretwork motifs, knocking down a wall here, adding an archway there to create a pink palace out of motel-like squatness. Morrison's *pièce de résistance* is the resort's Palm Terrace, a capacious beachfront room for lounging, sipping, chatting, and dining—about as elegant, comfortable, and eye-pleasing as any room in the islands. The two-story, vaulted ceiling of pickled pine is specially designed to let in the 20% of sunlight Tabora needs for the nourishment of 20-foot McCarthy palms and other plants that turn the terrace into a mini-conservatory. Five pink stucco archways along the front of the room open to the sea, with graceful arches along the sides encasing renaissance-paned windows. On the pink marble floors sit natural-stained wicker furniture plump with cushions and pillows covered in a striking water-splashed gray and pink fabric. Even the lighting is carefully contrived, with some bulbs reflecting up pink stucco columns, others focusing downward from the eaves. Ceiling fans add the right tropical touch and yet the overall elegance of the room allows the ebony grand piano to seem very much in its rightful place.

The entrance to all this elegance is an impressive buildup after passing through several plant-filled patios with crested tiles on the walkways and gouaches by an Englishman named Adam Smith on the walls. There's also a small arcade along some of the walkways with very fancy boutiques.

The oversize rooms (referred to as junior suites) come with oversize terraces with divans and breakfast tables facing the beach. They are plushly decorated, with king-size beds, small sofas, and coffee tables in the sitting areas, dressing areas beside the bathroom, and (the best part) walls of glass that open fully to each terrace. With the drapes pulled back and the glass doors wide open, your room feels bathed in space, Caribbean breezes, and gentle surf sounds. (It's a pity that the rooms don't have ceiling fans in addition to the air conditioners.)

Since the guest rooms are essentially identical, the choice is in location. Those on the third floor are not only the most private but they also have pickled pine ceilings with beams that add a nice sense of space and warmth. Those on the first floor, though, score by having a garden-patio in addition to a large terrace—a semiprivate front yard, as it were, with a low wall separating it from the beach. Top or bottom, though, a room in the north wing offers the most privacy.

Fernando Tabora's landscaping is lush and often breathtaking. There's a gigantic travelers' palm beside the pool (artfully lit at night), an amazing bearded fig tree behind the north wing, and hardly a vista or nook that is not accented by flowering flourishes. No wonder Pemberton honored his gardener by naming one of the hotel's restaurants Tabora's. It serves light fare; at the more ambitious Palm Terrace, your best bet is to stick to simple preparations like broiled fish or steaks, although the cuisine *has* improved in the past year.

Nitpicks apart, the Royal Pavilion has vaulted right into the front rank of Barbados resorts, attracting guests like Michael Caine and John Cleese; and it could easily become number one on the island when they improve the cuisine and banish the wave-runners.

Name: Royal Pavilion
Manager: Julia Seymour
Address: Porters, St. James, Barbados WI
Location: On the northwest coast, 20 minutes and $12 by taxi from Bridgetown, 30 minutes and $20 by taxi from the airport (you can also have one of the Pemberton Daimlers meet you at the airport, about $50 one way)
Telephone: 809/422-5555
Fax: 809/422-3940
Reservations: Robert Reid Associates
Credit Cards: All major cards
Rooms: 75 junior suites, all beachfront, all with balconies or patios, air conditioning, direct-dial telephones, clock radios; plus 1 beachfront penthouse and 1 villa for six
Meals: Breakfast 7:30–9:45, lunch/dinner noon until midnight, both in

Tabora's, the casual beachfront dining pavilion, afternoon tea 3:00–5:00, dinner 7:00–9:45 in the Palm Terrace (approx. $90 for two), informal dress; room service; some live music most evenings, barbecue Wednesday in the Palm Terrace; guests can also charge bills at the Piperade in Glitter Bay or on the "dine-around" program with nearby resorts

Entertainment: Some form of live music, as mentioned, most evenings, classical or light classical piano at teatime

Sports: Half-mile beach, pool, tennis courts (two lighted, one grass), waterskiing, HobieCats, windsurfing—all free; golf and horseback riding nearby

P.S.: No children under 12 during the high season

Cobblers Cove Hotel
Barbados

☆☆☆☆ ♈♈♈ ☎ $$$$

Claudette Colbert lives two villas along the beach and when, a few years back, Ronald Reagan came a-calling and a-swimming, quiet little Cobblers Cove found itself awash with paparazzi and a perspiring Secret Service.

Next day, it was back to being its cozy, relaxed self. Just 38 suites, 76 guests. A stately drawing room. A charmer of a wood-framed dining pavilion beside the beach. A mini-swimming pool and a quarter-mile of unspoiled palm-fringed cove—with just the resort at one end, a fleet of fishing boats at the other, and Claudette Colbert in the middle, screened by a mass of sea grape.

The most northerly of Barbados's small hideaways, Cobblers is a world apart, the unsung rendezvous of actors from the United Kingdom, CEOs from the United States, professionals and romantics from hither and yon. For some it may be too small—three acres of garden with 10 two-story shingle-roofed cottages, 4 suites to a cottage, arranged in a V around an 81-year-old castellated villa that looks like a setting for a Gilbert and Sullivan opera.

If the property is a tad cramped, the recently renovated and restyled accommodations most certainly are not: suites only, each with a big hardwood balcony or patio, living room with a louvered wall that folds back, kitchenette, bathroom, and air-conditioned bedroom, all stylishly designed and furnished. Suites located at the bottom of the V may have less privacy than you prefer (also, suites 19 and 20 may pick up some traffic noise from the road just beyond the garden wall); the best are the most expensive, closer to and, in most cases, facing the beach—1 through 8 and 33 through 36 (with even numbers—and higher ceilings—on the second floor). The latest addition is the spacious, very private Camelot Suite, with king-size four-poster bed, whirlpool bath, terrycloth bathrobes, and a 16-by-14-foot lounge with wet bar and a spiral cordstone stairway to a totally secluded rooftop deck, private plunge pool, and a second wet bar. Camelot indeed!

But whatever your suite, you'll find a welcoming, instantly at-home feeling to Cobblers Cove. Hamish Watson is very much an on-the-spot, hands-on manager; his staff is pleasant and efficient (with maybe a couple of grumps out of a roster of 61). The kitchen has improved immensely, to the point where what was once a nice hotel with a fine kitchen is getting a reputation as an outstanding kitchen with a nice hotel attached.

So on balmy, candlelit evenings with the sea foaming just inches away, guests of the Cobblers now sit down to tempting dishes you might expect on St. Barts rather than Barbados—*rillette de canard et papaye marinée, langouste a la vanille au rhum,* and *rosette d'agneau aioli a la menthe.*

Ronald Reagan couldn't have dined more splendidly at the villa along the beach.

Name: Cobblers Cove Hotel
Owner/Manager: Hamish Watson
Address: St. Peter, Barbados, WI
Location: On the sheltered northwest coast, adjoining the village of Speightstown (pronounced "spiteston"), 45 minutes and $23 by taxi from the airport, 15 minutes from Bridgetown (free shuttle/mini-bus daily or $13 by taxi)
Telephone: 809/422-2291
Fax: 809/422-1460
Reservations: Robert Reid Associates
Credit Cards: American Express, MasterCard, Visa
Rooms: 38, all suites, with private bathrooms, air conditioning and ceiling fans, louvered doors, kitchenettes, mini-bars, hairdryers, balconies or patios, direct-dial telephones; plus the stunning new Camelot Suite
Meals: Breakfast 8:00–10:00, lunch 12:30–2:30, snack menu 2:30–6:00, afternoon tea 4:00–5:00, dinner 7:00–9:00 (approx. $60 for two), in the beachside pavilion; barbecue buffet Tuesday, "elegantly casual" dress; room service during dining room hours, no extra charge (dine-around plan with nearby resorts)

Entertainment: Lounge/bar, occasional live music (not too loud, not exactly pianissimo either), radio or TV for rooms available

Sports: Lovely beach and lagoon-smooth bay, small freshwater pool, snorkeling gear, waterskiing, windsurfing, Sunfish sailing, new Omni tennis court across the street (with lights)—all free; scuba-diving, picnic sails, tennis and golf can be arranged, at extra charge

P.S. Some families with small children (they have their own dining hour—6:00–6:30 and are not allowed in the bar after 7:00)

Arnos Vale Hotel
Tobago

☆ ♈ ◑ $

When you sit down for afternoon tea, a giant flamboyant shades you from the sun, and a sprawling sea grape tree cools you when you sip a punch on the beachside terrace. You stroll to and from your room along pathways hugged by oleander and frangipani. Bananaquits come to filch tidbits from your breakfast, and you lunch to the cries of parrots and jacamars, mockingbirds and motmots.

"We wanted the place to look as little like a hotel as possible," said the original owners. They certainly succeeded. What you see when you step through the lobby is an arena-shaped botanical garden, solid greenery accented with splashes of color, the sea glittering beyond the foliage. Look more carefully and you notice a building or two here and there at different levels, up there on the hillside, down there by the cove. The shingled, cut-coral cottage housing the lobby, lounge, and dining veranda, is perched at the 100-foot level. Follow the footpath 20 feet higher and you come to six rooms in three cottages, including an aerie called the Crow's Nest Suite. The remaining rooms are by the beach and pool, each different, but simply furnished with few frills, even though they come in two categories, standard and superior.

The most romantic suites are right on the beach, with local fishermen's dugout canoes hauled up at the foot of the tiny stone stairway that leads to a small private terrace. Back in the days when Arnos Vale was a sugar plantation this was part of the storehouse where the cane was stacked before being shipped to England. What makes a real difference between the rooms is location—whether you want to be close to the beach and pool, or up in the hills with the birds and breezes.

There are plenty of paths to follow through virtually unspoiled tropical forest. Your best plan would be to ask the bartender to make up a flask of rum punch, then follow the path up the hill to Sunset Point, where you'll find a bench for two, strategically placed to face the sun.

Since the original owners left, so has much of the tender loving care a place like this needs to keep it spic and span, but it's still a place for true solitude. Maybe too much so—I met an Englishman there once who claimed, in impeccably clipped accents, that he could actually talk to the motmots.

Nowadays you'll hear fewer English accents since the resort has been taken over by an Italian tour operator, who usually fills the place in winter.

Name: Arnos Vale Hotel

Manager: Giobata Pescio

Address: P.O. Box 208, Scarborough, Tobago, Trinidad & Tobago, WI

Location: In a tropical vale beside a quiet cove on the southwest coast, 20 minutes and $18 by taxi from Crown Point Airport

Telephone: 809/639-2881, 2882, 3247, 3251

Fax: 809/639-4629

Reservations: Direct

Credit Cards: American Express, Diners Club, MasterCard, Visa

Rooms: 30, divided between the hilltop main lodge, hilltop cottages, and beachside wings (8 of them new in 1988), all with balconies or terraces, telephones, air conditioning, and showers

Meals: Breakfast 8:00–10:00 and lunch 1:00–2:00 on the beachside terrace, dinner 8:00–9:00 (on the veranda of the main lodge, approx. $35 for two); barbecues at lunchtime; informal dress (but trousers rather than shorts for men after 6:00)

Entertainment: Taped music in the dining room, local entertainment nightly, TV on terrace adjoining the dining room (spewing forth "Down by the River Side" in the middle of the afternoon, with not even a bananaquit watching it)

Sports: Sheltered beach, freshwater pool, tennis (one court, newly resurfaced, lights)—free; snorkeling gear for rent, fishing, scuba-diving, golf, excursions to Buccoo Reef and bird sanctuaries can be arranged

Mount Irvine Bay Hotel
Tobago

☆☆ ♉ ◑◑◑◑ $$$

It's constructed around an old sugar mill, fitted with a shingle-roofed ramada and stylishly transformed into an open bar and dining terrace.

A two-story wing of balconied guest rooms forms a protective L around a big blue-tiled swimming pool with a swim-up bar in one corner. Other rooms (46 out of 100) are housed in little square bungalows engulfed in heliconia and thumbergia. But what makes this 1970s resort so attractive is the setting—27 acres of tropical flora surrounded by 130 acres of fairways and coconut palms, laid out on a bluff above the curve of Mount Irvine Bay, with the famed Buccoo Reef breaking the sea just beyond the headland.

Most of the balconies and loggias are sited to make the most of the gardens and the views, and without the views the rooms would be fairly conventional. New owners (a Trinidadian company) who took over the resort six years ago have recarpeted the rooms and cottages, replaced the plastic slat patio furniture with tubular loungers and chairs in tropical colors. In

celebration of its 20th anniversary, the hotel is currently undergoing a $2 million refurbishment, including new furniture and satellite television in the rooms; upgrading of the Golf Club; and a new seafood restaurant, Le Beau Rivage, located on the fairways.

With the exception of the standards, the rooms are quite large, with double the usual closet space. The bungalows, the priciest accommodations, have large loggias that are virtually breezy outdoor living rooms with terrazzo floors and khuskhus rugs; the bedrooms, with beige-plum wall-to-wall carpeting, are smaller and probably need the air-conditioning units stuck in the walls.

The *pièce de résistance* of Mount Irvine is its Sugar Mill Restaurant, especially in the evening with the candlelight flickering, its raftered ceiling, its gray stone walls softly lighted, the scent of jasmine wafting in from the garden. (On my last visit the new owners were talking about installing a second air-conditioned restaurant for quote, gourmet dining, unquote, but my bet is you'll prefer the open terrace.)

For guests who enjoy a round of golf, earnest or casual, the Mount Irvine might rate high there. Not because its lovely, rolling fairways are a challenge for players of all handicaps. Not because the green fees are a mere $24 *a day*. But because anytime I've been there I had the fairways and greens (and, alas, traps) almost to myself. Even if you're not a golfer, take a walk or bike ride along the courses' winding pathways to enjoy the views of the bay and the reef and the tropical greenery.

Name: Mount Irvine Bay Hotel
Manager: Carlos Dillon
Address: P.O. Box 222, Scarborough, Tobago, Trinidad and Tobago, WI
Location: 10 minutes and $14 by taxi from the airport
Telephone: 809/639-8871, 8872, 8873
Fax: 809/639-8800
Reservations: Utell International, toll free 800/448-8355; Robert Reid Associates; Golden Tulip Reservations system, toll free 800/344-1212.
Credit Cards: American Express, Diners Club, MasterCard, Visa
Rooms: 110, including 64 superior rooms in the main building; the remainder in 2-room bungalows; all with private bathrooms (tub and showers), air conditioning (cross-ventilation in bungalows only), balconies or loggias, telephones, wet bars and refrigerators in bungalows
Dining: Breakfast 7:00–10:00 (continental breakfast to 10:30), lunch noon–3:00 (the quietest spot is the golf course clubhouse), snacks at the beach pavilion all afternoon, dinner 7:00–10:00, at the open-air Sugar Mill Terrace of the air-conditioned Jacaranda Room; dinner $40 for two;

jacket and tie in the Jacaranda, informal on the terrace, but "we do believe that informality has its acceptable limits within a hotel and house rules do not permit T-shirts or sleeveless vests in the public areas after 6:00 p.m."; room service 7:00 a.m.–10:00 p.m., $2 extra; taped music or radio on terrace, possibly live music in the Jacaranda Room

Entertainment: Steel bands, calypso and limbo shows, movies in video room, live entertainment in the Jacaranda Room

Sports: So-so beach across the road, with beach bar, snack bar, chaise longues, changing rooms, and local fishermen and their boats (there are better beaches nearby), freshwater pool with swim-up bar, tennis (2 courts, with lights), sauna—all free; snorkeling gear, bikes and scooters for rent, golf (18 holes, $24 a day green fees); excursions (to Buccoo Reef to watch the fish, to Grafton's estate to watch the birds) can be arranged

P.S.: The hotel can handle groups of up to 200, but they are usually low-key

Added Attractions

Sandpiper Inn
Barbados

Owned by the O'Hara family of the esteemed Coral Reef Club (see page 263), the Sandpiper is located beachside just a few miles south. Recently renovated, upgraded, and enlarged, it now has 46 rooms and suites, in a trim-and-tidy garden setting at right angles to the sea; decor is rattan and wicker, pickled pine woodwork, colorful island fabrics, and ceramic tile floors, while amenities include refrigerators or kitchens, air conditioning, and ceiling fans. Garden-level apartments have French doors opening to not-very-private patios, but spacious enough for two rattan loungers, coffee table, and chairs; second-floor suites have roomy balconies and high ceilings. Restaurant, tennis, water sports, freshwater tiled pool. 46 rooms and suites. Doubles: $450 to $510 MAP, winter, 1991–92 *Sandpiper Inn, St. James Beach, Barbados, WI. Telephone: 809/422-2251; fax: 809/422-1776. Reservations: Ralph Locke Islands.*

Treasure Beach
Barbados

The ownership of this 24-suite hideaway in the fashionable parish of St. James has passed from Charles and Mary Ward to a partnership headed by Tony Bowen, until recently manager of Glitter Bay. The restaurant here has always been distinguished, and the new menu is equally ambitious and innovative: locally smoked black marlin and flying fish with a ragout of pawpaw and melon, or grilled fillet of dolphin in a mango and green peppercorn sauce. Meals are served in a pleasant, raftered pavilion open to the breezes. Lodgings are one-bedroom, air-conditioned, kitchen-equipped suites, newly restyled and redecorated, housed in two-story wings along each side of the garden but, as so often happens in these Barbadian beachside enclaves, with rooms facing rooms rather than the sea, except for four Deluxe Oceanfront suites (Garden View suites, though, should be shunned unless you're counting your dollars). Service is friendly, housekeeping immaculate, the beach uncrowded, with facilities for water sports on the premises. No children under 12, music a couple of evenings a week. 24 suites. Doubles $325 to $410, with breakfast, winter 1991–92. *Treasure Beach, St. James, Barbados, WI. Telephone: 809/432-1346; fax: 809/432-1094. Reservations: Robert Reid Associates.*

Coconut Creek Club Hotel
Barbados

The setting here is modified Barbados—the usual quiet cove and sandy beach, but this time with a few coral cliffs added. And, of course, some coconut palms to justify the name. A few of the rooms and suites are perched on the coral, with balconies facing the sea; the remainder are grouped around the central pool area; they are comfortable but unremarkable. A dozen of the newer rooms are the Club's most luxurious and attractive—done in Moorish style with tiles and columns, walled flower gardens, posh rattan furniture, and solid mahogany captains' chests. The striking feature here is the drinking-dining enclave, a cross between an adobe hacienda and an English pub, its walls decorated with Britannic nostalgia—pewter mugs, dart board, cricket bats, and photographs of ships of the Royal Navy. You will be regaled with music most evenings of the week (steel bands, guitarists, combos), while you dine on *callaloo* soup or chilled cream of christophine, Creole carp imperial or roast shoulder of pork. We sat down to lunch recently at the awkward hour of three but the service was friendly, courteous, and attentive—one of the specialties of the Coconut Creek. 50 units. Doubles: $250 to $290 MAP. *Coconut Creek Club Hotel, St. James, Barbados, WI. Telephone: 809/432-0804; fax: 809/422-1726.*

Dashene
St. Lucia

Waking up here in the morning is like being present at the Creation. Immediately below, an amphitheater of hillside thick with tropical greenery drops off precipitously to a coconut plantation; then the Caribbean glistens and glitters all the way to the horizon. And framing the view, the picturesque Pitons, those postcard-perfect twin volanic cones soaring straight from the sea to about the same height as your bed, 1,200 feet above the yachts bobbing at anchor in the bay. You don't even have to open the windows or push back shutters to enjoy the view since your hilltop aerie has no west wall. In some suites, you can *ooh* and *aah* at the panorama without even getting out of bed. Alas, here's another spot that was closed (sort of) at presstime, in this case in the throes of litigation. Nevertheless, keep your eyes peeled for news of new management taking over, because this is one of the loveliest, most idyllic spots in the Caribbean. Since each villa is privately owned, decor varies considerably, mostly variations on bamboo and wicker, colorful fabrics, and tropical flora; some suites have plunge pools, some four-poster beds. The small public area includes a cliffside swimming pool and lounge/dining room in Polynesian style. 18 suites and villas. *Dashene, Soufrière, St. Lucia, WI. Telephone: 809/454-7444.*

Le Sport
St. Lucia

The former Steigenberger Cariblue, that pink palace of a resort that fills a cove at the northern end of the island, has new St. Lucian owners who have transformed the place into an all-inclusive spa featuring thalassotherapy treatments (said to be a first for the Caribbean). Treatments include seawater baths and showers, high-pressure sprays and sea-mud packs, herbal wraps and eucalyptus inhalations. The resort also features a piano bar, a full complement of water sports, tennis, golf, and horseback riding. Almost everything (even beauty treatments and the ride to and from the airport) is included in the daily rate—about $220 to $360 for winter 1991–1992. For more information, call 800/221-1831 or 800/223-5652. 102 rooms. *Le Sport, Cariblue Beach, P.O. Box 437, St. Lucia, WI. Telephone: 809/452-8551; fax: 809/452-0368.*

East Winds
St. Lucia

Resorts don't come more beachcomberish than this one—on a virtually private bay with sea grape and coconut palms separating the powdery sand from a peaceful garden of casuarinas and wood rose. Somewhere among the oleander and orange trees you come upon a series of small hexagonal cottages, each one with a wood-cone roof, *bohio*-shaded patio, ceiling fan, king-size bed, and refrigerator and pantry with hot plate. New owners have taken over here, too late to review the resort in full before presstime, but it's a place to keep in mind when you're in the mood for a real back-to-basics, lolling-around, barefoot vacation. 8 rooms. Doubles: $165 FAP. *East Winds, P.O. Box 1477, Castries, St. Lucia, WI. Telephone: 809/452-8212; fax: 809/452-5434.*

The Royal St. Lucian Hotel
St. Lucia

Yet another luxury resort with acres of marble, satellite television, air conditioning, bathrobes, lavish pool—everything but personality. Granted, it was barely finished when I saw it (February 1991), but even lavish landscaping is unlikely to disguise the cookie-cutter, three-story architecture. It happens to be on the island's grandest expanse of beach, which it shares with its sister hotel, The St. Lucian (popular with package groups), but only a few of its suites actually face directly across the beach to the sea and some of them have enormous terraces. The Royal St. Lucian could be anywhere, and when it names its coffee shop *La Nautique* and its dining room *L'Epicure*, someone is sticking a neck farther than this resort can afford to go. 98 suites. Doubles: $290 to $435, winter 1991–92. *The Royal St. Lucian Hotel, P.O. Box 977, Castries, St. Lucia, WI. Telephone: 809/452-9644; fax: 809/452-9639.*

Jalousie Plantation
St. Lucia

Jalousie, the plantation, is a dense grove of coconut palms in a lush amphitheater of hills between the island's landmark Pitons. There are many people on the island, captivated by the magic of the setting, who claim that it should have been set aside as a nature preserve. Instead it is now being carved into a 325-acre resort by a Geneva-based Iranian who has never set foot on the island. The first phase of 150 bedrooms was scheduled to open for winter 1991–92. When I walked the property in February 1991, the project was well underway, and much effort had gone into landscaping, even to installing eight hydroponic tunnels for growing vegetables. But the architecture seemed uninspired given the unique setting; the rooms looked skimpy (hard to tell, granted, when things are not completed) and were designed to have air conditioning and ceiling fans, wet bars, and "probably no TV," although the site is wired for cable. Some of them have private plunge pools.

Public facilities include a large Great House with restaurant, bar, and exercise room; four tennis courts beside a large mango tree; and a water sports center. Maybe it will turn out to be wonderful. More likely people will be wishing it *had* been left in its natural state. *Jalousie Plantation, 16 Bay Street, Soufrière, St. Lucia, WI. For updates, call 809/454-7138.*

Windjammer Landing Villa Beach Resort
St. Lucia

Here are some of the most appealing lodgings on St. Lucia, even if they are in a condo development and even if the project has been a revolving door for managers since it opened three years ago. Most of the suites are in villas designed in Mediterranean-Spanish white-stucco red-tile manner, but with lots of grace notes and refinements that set them apart from run-of-the-mill condos. The latest section of the 55-acre multilevel estate is a collection of one-bedroom suites halfway up the hill, with a separate hillside pool and dining pavilion. Each of these 1,300-square-foot suites comes with a complete kitchen (including microwave), television, ceiling fans, and bedroom air conditioning. Some of the tiled bath/showers have ramada sun-shades and the same coastal views as the balconies. Elsewhere on the estate many of the two- and three-bedroom Beach Villas also have private plunge pools and extra-spacious terra-cotta–tiled patios.

The public areas, too, are among the most attractive on the island: split-level bar/lounge, poolside bar, and beachside dining pavilion, all done in pickle-pine and designer fabrics. The food (nouvelle cuisine with St. Lu-cian accents) is innovative and appetizing; the young staff members are unusually welcoming and eager to please. The beach is not the greatest but is adequate (they're talking about lugging in additional sand); there are enough water sports facilities to fill your days, four freshwater pools, and two tennis courts with lights. The drawback for many visitors may be the terrain: steep hills that can really be negotiated only with jitneys (no cars are allowed), so you may find yourself fidgeting for transportation, unless you spend most of your time in your suite or villa—not out of the question given the comfort and refined decor. 11 villas, including 56 one-bedroom suites. Doubles: $285 ($360 with private pool), winter 1991–92. *Windjam-mer Landing Villa Beach Resort, P.O. Box 1504, Labrelotte Bay, St. Lucia, WI. Telephone: 809/452-0813; fax: 809/452-0907. Reservations: toll free 800/243-1166.*

St. Vincent–Grenadines and Grenada

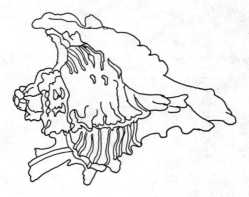

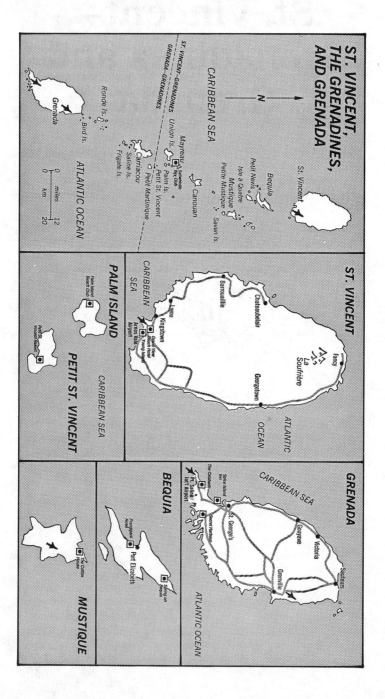

St. Vincent–Grenadines and Grenada

The most desirable islands, like the most desirable lovers, make extra demands. That's how it is with the Grenadines; they'll reward you with seclusion, serenity, and privacy, but you first have to get there, switching planes at least once, maybe twice. These islands are really part of the British Windwards, but they're so special, so totally Caribbean, that they deserve a category all to themselves.

They are, in fact, two quite separate and independent nations—St. Vincent–Grenadines (consisting of, for the purposes of this guide, St. Vincent, Young Island, Bequia, Mustique, Palm Island, Petit St. Vincent, and Union, which is the transit airstrip for Palm and PSV) and Grenada.

St. Vincent is a mountainous island, lushly forested, incredibly fertile, brimming with pawpaws, mangoes, and breadfruit. The bustling capital, Kingstown, is in the south, surrounded by towering hills, but the main scenic attractions are day-long excursions along the Leeward Highway to the foothills of 4,000-plus-foot Mount Soufrière or via the Windward Highway to Mesopotamia and Montreal—all very picturesque.

Bequia is a dream. The only way to get there is by boat. Not a big, powerful cabin cruiser or twin-hulled ferry, but by cargo/passenger ferryboat or island sloop stacked with chickens, toilet paper, kerosene, Guinness stout, Heineken beer, bags of cement, a carburetor, more Guinness, more Heineken. If you see a man get aboard carrying bags of money accompanied by a guard with a discreet gun, you know you're on the "bank boat." The trip takes about an hour, and you arrive in one of the most beautiful and most sheltered harbors in the Caribbees, in the town of Port Elizabeth. There's not much more to Bequia than the hills you pass on the way into the harbor, but it's one of the most charming, most idyllic islands of all. Nothing much happens here, except once or twice a year when whales are spotted, and the men go out in their small boats armed only with hand harpoons—the only remaining fleet of hand-harpooners in the world.

Mustique, Palm Island, and Petit St. Vincent are privately owned and

285

when you read about their hotels you're reading about the islands themselves.

Grenada, like St. Vincent a lush volcanic island, is the largest of the group (21 miles long, 12 miles wide) and scenically one of the most beautiful of all the Antilles. Still—despite the efforts of modern firepower to wipe the island off the charts. You remember the events of October 1983? Some people called it an invasion, others a rescue mission. The official island description is a diplomatic "United States/Eastern Caribbean Intervention." Whatever, not much has changed, give or take a pock-marked wall or two. The Grenadians are pro-American (they always have been); the Holiday Inn is now a $15-million Ramada Renaissance; and some of the roads have been resurfaced, mostly those between Government House and the new airport. The major improvement these days is, of course, the airport, Point Salines International, which started it all. It's located in the southwest, near the hotels, thus eliminating the hour-long drive from the old Pearls Airport. Does this mean cheaper taxi fares? No. Taxis serving the airport belong to a special association, most of whose members still live in villages near the *old* airport, and since they now have to drive all the way across the island to the *new* airport, visitors—a.k.a. you—have to pay through the nose. Why, you might ask, don't they use taxi drivers who live near the *new* airport? Because those taxis belong to another, ineligible association—either the "hotel" association or the "cruise ship" association. It's all very simple. If you're a taxi driver. But these are inconsequential matters if you're simply planning to find a great little hideaway and flake out—and Grenada has plenty of pleasant, friendly places for doing just that. Into the bargain, to try to lure back their old North American clientele (the British kept on coming), the local hotels have been raising their rates by minuscule smidgens, so you may find your vacation dollars will go further here.

How to Get There   There are some direct flights from New York and Miami to Grenada (by BWIA and American), but otherwise to get to any of these islands you have to switch planes at Barbados or Antigua. (You can also catch connections at Trinidad but I don't recommend that because it's such a hideous airport, or at St. Lucia, where you may waste time because of the difference between the international and regional airports.) Barbados is the simplest route—nonstop or direct on American, Pan Am, Air Canada, and BWIA. From there you can catch a scheduled LIAT flight to St. Vincent, Mustique (occasionally), Union, and Grenada. But, as mentioned in the introduction to the guide, your best bet is to allow your hotel to arrange seats on a shared charter, probably on Air

Mustique, most likely a nine-seater Islander or a five-seater Beach Baron. This arrangement costs a few dollars more but can save a lot of aggravation. (Just trying to determine the LIAT schedule is aggravation enough.)

Bequia involves a trip across the waters—either by charter launch (which your hotel can probably arrange, but it's expensive) or by the *Admiral I* or *Admiral II*, the ungainly but efficient Danish coasters that shuttle back and forth between St. Vincent and Bequia two times a day on weekends and four times a day during the week. The last departure from St. Vincent is 7:00 p.m., on Saturdays and weekdays, which allows at least some passengers from North America to get to Bequia the same day. You can also go the romantic way—on one of the 35-foot interisland sailing sloops. If you find you have to spend the night in St. Vincent, Grand View Hotel is a convenient address. In town, the Heron Hotel has local color and tends to be rather noisy but within walking distance of the jetty, if you're not carrying too much luggage. On the other hand, an airstrip *is* under construction on Bequia and by the time you read this it may be possible to fly there direct from Barbados.

Young Island

St. Vincent

☆☆☆☆☆ ♈♈ ◑◑ $$$$

A Carib Indian chieftain, they say, once kept his harem on this islet, and generations of Vincentians used it as their vacation escape from the "mainland," a couple of hundred yards away across the lagoon. Now Young Island is 35 acres of petaled Polynesia. Half a million plants clamber up the hillsides. It took almost as long to landscape the grounds as it did to build the cottages and pavilions, but that was 25 years ago and now the island garden luxuriates. White ginger and giant almond trees soften the sun's rays as you stroll along stone pathways to quiet benches where twosomes can enjoy the breezes and sunsets. Swimming in the free-form pool, canopied by bamboo and fern and mango, you half expect Lamour and Hope to go floating by. And you're still shrouded by shrubbery and flowers when you rinse the sand off, because each room has an open patio shower screened by neck-high bamboo fences.

Two hundred yards may not sound like much of a journey but once you

board the dinky water taxis for the three-minute voyage, you could be on your way to Bali Ha'i. Once guests step ashore and sip the zingy Hibiscus Special that's waiting for them on the dock, they usually find there's no compelling reason—not even the 200-year-old botanical garden, not the oddball 150-year-old cathedral—to board that dinky taxi again until it's time to head for home. (Actually, if they sip more than half of their Special they probably *will* see Lamour and Hope.)

Why escape tranquility? There are so many ways to enjoy the barefoot euphoria of Young when you put what's left of your mind to it. At the Coconut Bar, a thatched *bohio* on stilts about six strokes from the shore. Curled in a *bohio*-shaded hammock, within semaphore distance of the shorebound bar. Flat out on the sand. Climbing the hundred-odd steps to the peak of the island for an isolated stroll in one direction or the tennis court in another. For any guest who finds a 35-acre islet and some 50 guests claustrophobic after a while, owner/manager and 20-year veteran Vidal Browne has his boatmen whisk the guests over to the most romantic manager's cocktail party in the Caribbean—on the nearby chimney rock known as Fort Duvernette, complete with native bamboo band, barbecue, and flickering torcheurs.

But maybe the most sensuous way to enjoy the serenity of Young Island is to stay put in your own wicker wonderland: Guest rooms feature lots of rush matting, native fabrics, terrazzo and shell floors, screened windows with jalousies, and hardwood louvers. For anyone who has been to Young Island in the past, the rooms were refurbished in 1986–87, and although the overall Polynesian ambience remains, they're brighter, more inviting. The cottages are located on the beach and at various elevations up the jungly hillside, accessible by stone steps; the higher the cottage, the cooler the air but the wider the panorama. Of the beachside cottages, number 10 still has the fairest breezes and the most private of patios.

While the original rooms were being prettified, Vidal Browne was installing three new hilltop cottages, each a spacious luxury suite (a first for Young Island) with huge semicircular deck/terrace with loungers and hammock, living room with rattan sofa and swivel chairs, wet bar and stocked refrigerator, toaster, kettle, and the makings for a pot of coffee or tea. Each louvered bedroom has two queen-size beds, separate dressing room paneled with greenheart, with bathrobes and amenities, twin vanities, and open-to-the-breezes shower stall with its own water heater. The views are eye-filling, the breezes rejuvenating, the solitude complete. Just *how* far you've gotten away from it all is brought home to you when, thumbing through the welcome booklet, you come upon this sentence: "Keys for the cottages are available at the front desk, if this is considered necessary."

Name: Young Island
Owner/Manager: Vidal Browne
Address: P.O. Box 211, St. Vincent, WI
Location: Just east of Kingstown, 200 yards offshore, about 10 minutes and $6 by taxi from the airport, shuttle launch to the resort free at all times; the hotel can arrange a "shared seat" charter flight from Barbados to St. Vincent for about $10 more than the scheduled one-way fare
Telephone: 809/458-4826
Fax: 809/457-4567
Reservations: Ralph Locke Islands
Credit Cards: American Express, MasterCard, Visa

Rooms: 29, all cottages, some beside the beach, others on the hillside, 1 with air conditioning, all with ceiling fans, patios or verandas, indoor/outdoor showers, some with wet bars and refrigerators

Meals: Breakfast 7:30–9:30, lunch 1:00–2:30, dinner 7:30–9:30 (approx. $70 for two, in one of the breeze-cooled beachside pavilions); informal dress; room service for breakfast only, no extra charge

Entertainment: Live music 3 nights a week—steel band on Saturday, Bamboo Melodion Band on Tuesday and Thursday, at the spectacular lantern-lit cocktail party on Fort Duvernette ("no amplification ever . . . request guests not to use radios/tape recorders"—which, alas, does not deter the disco owners on the "mainland" from occasionally bombarding the world with heavy metal, regardless of the protestations and petitions of Vidal Browne and his guests)

Sports: Beach with offshore Coconut Bar, saltwater lagoon pool in the garden, snorkeling, Sunfish sailing, windsurfing, glass-bottom boat trips—all free; tennis (1 court, free by day, $5 per hour with lights); scuba, waterskiing, and cruises (to Bequia, Mustique) on the resort's 44-ft. yacht by arrangement

P.S.: No children under 12, no groups ever, a few (very few) cruise ship passengers and day-trippers on weekends

Grand View Beach Hotel
St. Vincent

☆ ♈ 🌑🌑 $$

Your Grand View grand view is made up of islands, lagoons, bays, sailboats, Young Island, a fort, mountains, headlands, and dazzling sea that turns into dazzling sky somewhere beyond Bequia. The hotel itself is a big, white, rather ungainly two-story mansion on top of a bluff (not on the beach, despite its name) between two bays, and surrounded by eight acres of bougainvillea, frangipani, palms, and terraced gardens. It's a beautiful location (breezes, flowers, birds, trees) if you don't mind climbing up and down to the beach. About 150 years ago it was a cotton-drying house, the private home of the Sardines, whose ancestors came over from Portugal; Frank Sardine, Sr., converted it into a hotel 17 years ago, and despite its longevity, it's in spanking fresh condition. It's homey, pleasant, and very relaxed, like the sort of small hotel Europeans would flock to on the

Riviera (and, in fact, the hotel gets lots of visitors from Europe); the guest rooms are plain and unadorned—but who needs decor when you have a view like this? Eight additional rooms, including two suites with whirlpool baths, are currently under construction. An added bonus is the Racquet & Fitness Centre, which opened last January and offers aerobics classes and equipment, a sauna, and massage.

Name: Grand View Beach Hotel
Owner/Manager: Tony Sardine
Address: P.O. Box 173, St. Vincent–Grenadines, WI
Location: At Villa Point, 5 minutes and $6 by taxi from the airport, 10 minutes from town
Telephone: 809/458-4811
Reservations: Robert Reid Associates in the U.S. and U.K.; Nina Chouvon in Canada (toll free 800/268-0424); Caribbean Inns, Ltd. in the U.S.
Credit Cards: American Express, MasterCard, Visa
Rooms: 12 rooms, 5 with air conditioning, private bathrooms, showers only
Meals: Breakfast 7:15–9:00, lunch noon–3:00, afternoon tea 4:30–5:30, dinner 7:00–8:30 (approx. $40 for two); casual dress; room service (no extra charge)
Entertainment: Pleasant lounge with wicker armchairs, a vintage radio, a few books; maybe a cocktail party once a week in season, depending on the guests
Sports: Beach at the base of the cliff, swimming pool; snorkeling gear for rent; tennis court ($20 an hour with lights), 31-ft. fishing boat, squash court, windsurfing, plus exercise classes, aerobic machines, sauna, and massage at the Fitness Centre (membership available to locals); sailing and scuba by arrangement

Spring on Bequia

Bequia

☆☆☆ 🍷🍷 ◐◐ $$

You're sitting on the terrace of your room, maybe lounging in a hammock, and looking across a valley of coconut palms toward a bay, a pair of headlands, and a sheltering reef. What you see is a working plantation

that produces mangoes and avocados and plums and melons—to say nothing of all those coconuts; and what you are staying in is a 10-room jewel on a very quiet hillside in a very quiet corner of a very quiet island.

The 250-year-old Spring Plantation was bought up about 18 years ago by an Iowa lawyer, who planned to build a few unobtrusive homes among the trees of the hillsides (they're there, but you may not see them!) and a small inn to house prospective buyers and visitors. Part Japanese, part Finnish, part Caribbean, the hotel's clean, contemporary lines enclose open-plan rooms with native stone walls, stone floors, furniture fashioned from wood right there on the plantation, khuskhus rugs, whole walls of purpleheart louvers that push back to bring the outdoors right inside. Spring now has electricity, so the stone-floored, stone-walled shower stalls gush hot water.

All the guest rooms, refurbished in 1988, are charmingly rustic. The four dozen rooms in the old plantation Great House, draped in frangipani and cordia, are close to the swimming pool and tennis court, but since they're also next to the kitchen some guests prefer to be higher up the hill in one of two cantilevered wings: Gull, with four rooms, halfway up the hill, or the Fort, with two and higher still. They're a stiff climb from the dining room, even more so from the beach; but if you've come here for seclusion, this is *seclusion*—with a beautiful view thrown in for good measure.

Spring's lobby/bar/dining room attached to the old Great House is open on two sides and overlooks the old syrup mill and slave quarters, a pleasant, breezy gathering place, with a rustic roof of beams and planks, walls of canvas, and matted bamboo screens. The bar stools are the stumps of coconut palms with purpleheart seats; the native stone walls are covered with vines and planters, decorated with turtle shells and anchor chains. But mostly the decor is the trees and the flowers and you're more aware of plantation than inn. Having dinner here is a bit like dining out in a cage of tree frogs and crickets—real Caribbean flavor. The home-cooked meals are no letdown, either.

The good news, of course, is that Spring is still there and receiving guests. Closed for a few years, it is now the pride of the Rudolf family from Minnesota (who attribute their fascination with inns to an earlier edition of this guidebook); daughter Candace may be the only innkeeper in the Caribbean who speaks fluent Chinese. Wish them well, since Spring is still one of the most romantic tiny inns in the islands—even with its new electricity and solar-heated hot water.

Name: Spring on Bequia

Manager: Candace Leslie

Address: Bequia, St. Vincent–Grenadines, WI

Location: On the southeast coast, but just 1 mile over the hill from Port Elizabeth; the inn will pick you up at the dock; for some guests, the inn is a pleasant 30-minute *walk* from town

Telephone: 809/458-3414

Reservations: Direct to the inn's U.S. office at 612/823-1202

Credit Cards: American Express, MasterCard, Visa

Rooms: 10, 4 in the main lodge, 2 in hillside cottages, with private bathrooms (showers only), breeze-cooled (now with electricity and hot water), most with balconies

Meals: Breakfast 7:30–9:00, lunch noon–2:00, dinner 7:00 (approx. $30 for two); informal; no room service

Entertainment: Parlor games, conversation

Sports: 500 ft. of virtually solitary sandy beach (with beach bar), about 5 minutes away along a pathway through the coco palms and Pride of Barbados, freshwater pool, tennis (1 court, rackets available), walking and hiking trails, snorkeling—all free; sailing trips to Mustique and the Tobago Cays

P.S.: "Not really suitable for children." Closed July through October

Frangipani Hotel
Bequia

☆ ♈ ◑ $

They used to build island schooners in the front yard here, the lounge was a ships' chandlery back in the thirties, and the sea captain who built it disappeared with his crew in the Bermuda Triangle—while his schooner sailed on. His son, currently prime minister of St. Vincent, turned this white-walled red-roofed family home into an inn back in the sixties, and it's now one of the most popular watering places in the Grenadines. It hasn't lost touch with its nautical heritage, either: Antique charts and seascapes decorate the lounges; the jetty at the bottom of the garden welcomes fleets of dinghies from the yachts moored just offshore; and sooner or later everyone who sails the Grenadines stops off at the Frangipani beach bar to greet old friends they last saw beating toward the Tobago Cays.

The Frangipani is a real wicker-decked West Indies inn. The half-dozen rooms upstairs are scantily furnished, with mosquito nets, partition walls, and a couple of shared bathrooms down the hall—like the deck of a schooner, functional rather than frilly. The exception is also upstairs, where two rooms have been blended into one charming, plank-floored nest with four-poster canopy bed and private, if tiny, toilet/shower. If you prefer bunking down in something more substantial, ask for one of the rooms in the stone and timber garden cottages—big comfortable cabins with big bathrooms, dressing rooms, grass mats, and louvers. Each of these five rooms has beams and furniture crafted from a different local hardwood; each has its own sun deck draped with jade vine, bougainvillea, or the inevitable frangipani.

There's absolutely nothing to do here, nothing but unwind. Evenings, you can nibble fresh seafood on the veranda or sit on the seawall and listen to rigging; you can swap a few fancy tales with yachters or listen to a folksinger or have another beer and watch the last sailors row off zigzaggedly to their yachts. In the morning, grab a cup of coffee and settle into a large, purpleheart armchair beside the beach. Watch the schooners and ketches weigh anchor for the Tobago Cays or Martinique. Don't even bother waving good-bye—they'll soon be back at Frangipani.

Name: Frangipani Hotel
Owners/Managers: Marie Kingston and Lou Keane
Address: Bequia, St. Vincent–Grenadines, WI
Location: On the waterfront, a 3-minute walk from the schooner jetty
Telephone: 809/458-3255
Fax: 809/458-3244
Reservations: Direct
Credit Cards: American Express, MasterCard, Visa
Rooms: 15, 9 with private baths and balconies in the garden cottages, 3 in main house with washbasins but sharing bath and toilets; mosquito nets, ceiling fans
Meals: Breakfast 7:30–9:00, lunch anytime, coffee, wine, snacks at "Gingerbread" café, or new "Clubhouse," dinner 7:30–9:00 (approx. $20 to $30 for two, served in the beachside patio bar/restaurant with harbor view); no room service; very casual dress
Entertainment: Barbecue and "jump-up" every Thursday, string band every Monday, guitar player or impromptu entertainment most evenings
Sports: "Along the bayside" at the hotel's Gingerbread complex is the center for "sun sports"—Mistral Windsurfers, NAUI and PADI scuba, tennis (1 hardcourt), Sunfish sailing, waterskiing—all extra, with a discount for guests
P.S.: Closed September. Lots of yachters, castaways, and beachcombers

The Cotton House
Mustique

☆☆☆ 𝅘𝅥𝅮𝅘𝅥𝅮 ◑◑ $$$$

It's that rare combination of informality and elegance, of pristine (well, relatively pristine) surroundings and civilization. Here you are, on a private tropical island with a permanent population of 300, a few coconut groves, a few citrus groves, a dozen deserted beaches.

You can spend an entire day here without meeting anyone other than your maid or waiter or gardener; you can disappear to a beach for a picnic lunch—not another soul in sight; you can spend hours snorkeling among fish that rarely if ever encounter *homo sapiens*. Then in the evening you

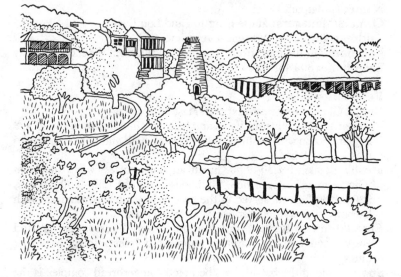

mingle with escapists who turn out to be cosmopolitan, urbane, and sophisticated—maybe even celebrated. And, at the end of the day, you hop into bed in a dreamy boudoir designed by no less a talent than the late Oliver Messel.

Mustique, unique Mustique, is small (3 miles long, ½ mile wide) and flat (about 400 ft. at its highest point); you arrive by air in a seven-seater that sweeps in between a pair of breastlike hills, to touch down in a pasture with a runway and thatch and bamboo terminal. When Reynolds, alias Snaky, the hotel's effervescent porter/majordomo/greeter/chauffeur/ guide, sees the plane coming in he jumps into his mini-bus, and by the time you've taxied to the toy terminal and cleared customs, he's there waiting to convey you to the hotel.

And what a hotel! The Cotton House itself is an 18th-century storage house of handsome proportions—two floors of mellowed stone and coral rimmed by deep verandas accented by cedar shutters and louver doors. A few yards away, on the peak of a knoll, Oliver Messel created a swimming pool surrounded by "Roman ruins," the sort of setting he might have designed for a Gluck opera at Covent Garden. Beyond the stone stump of the mill (now a boutique) a pair of handsome two-story Georgian-style villas house half the guest rooms, each room with a different decor and furnishings, but all with custom-designed bedspreads and matching drapes, plank floors with rush mats, ceiling fans, breezy balconies or patios. Color schemes are restrained and cool, with antiques and doodads adding delightful little touches of Messel charm. Other guest rooms are in three cottages fashioned in vaguely "island hut" style; in a new two-story wing in vaguely Motel Georgian style; and the newest of all, five guest rooms and suites in a villa, Cuoutinot House, formerly owned by the Guinness family (smaller bedrooms, but with a big open-to-the-breezes common room lounge/terrace), with decor and furniture that doesn't quite do credit to the memory of Messel. The latter are closest to the beach at Endeavour Bay, but the prime quarters have to be the original Oliver Messel rooms in the Georgian villas (recently refurbished with newly sanded floors, new wooden balustrades, and colors that recapture the originals).

But none of the guest rooms ever quite matched the exquisiteness of the main lounge in the Cotton House itself—with its raftered ceiling, its hand-carved bar, and masses of antiques—once one of the most beautiful rooms in the Caribbean. In the hemisphere. Alas, gone is the original Messel-designed acorn fabric, recently replaced by a run-of-the-mill *faux* batik; Lady Bateman's steamer trunks have been shunted off to a corner of the veranda, a tacky exhibit of art-for-sale lines one wall—red tags and all.

The veranda facing the sunset is given over to comfy armchairs and loungers. Another corner, shaded by shutters and foliage, is the dining room (recently enlarged, to the detriment of the overall proportions), where candles flicker on rustic tables and straw-seated chairs and the air is filled with the sound of tree frogs. In a setting as romantic as this, who cares if the cuisine is not three-star?

Mustique may be too quiet for some, no doubt. Yet, for all its isolation, the Cotton House can, on occasion, plunge its guests into nightlife that larger islands envy. For a start, there's Basil's Bar, a raucous wood and wicker deck on Britannia Beach, blaring rock-and-roll even at noontime, positively hopping at the Wednesday barbecue, popular with home-owners and yachters, so you might find yourselves at three o'clock some morning, beneath a full moon and a myriad stars, listening to bamboo flute and "shake-shake," mingling with princesses, viscounts, rock stars, fishermen, and CEOs masquerading as swingers.

Name: The Cotton House
Manager: Raymond Polynic
Address: Mustique, St. Vincent–Grenadines, WI
Location: On a private island, 35 minutes by twin-engined plane from

Barbados (the hotel will arrange space on a charter flight, approx. $170 per person, round-trip); there is also frequent scheduled service from Martinique, St. Vincent, and Grenada; the hotel, 4 minutes from the airstrip, will collect you by mini-bus, free of charge

Telephone: 809/456-4777

Fax: 809/456-4777

Reservations: Ralph Locke Islands

Credit Cards: All major cards

Rooms: 22 rooms and 5 suites, in villas, cottages, and a two-story wing, all with balconies or patios, ceiling fans, telephones, some with showers only

Meals: Breakfast 7:30–10:00 and buffet lunch 12:30–2:30 served poolside, afternoon tea 4:00, dinner at 8:00 (approx. $80 for two, on the candlelit veranda of the Great House); informal but "island elegant" dress; room service for all meals, no extra charge; some taped music, not always appropriate

Entertainment: Bar/lounge, parlor games, taped music, "Flambeaux" beach barbecue Saturdays (with steel band—and perhaps some of the island's other celebrity homeowners), weekly managers' cocktail party for hotel and villa guests, Caribbean buffet every Thursday, piano bar twice a week, "jump-up" at Basil's Bar every Wednesday

Sports: 12 beaches (free transportation, with picnic lunch), freshwater pool, tennis (2 courts, no lights), snorkeling, windsurfing, Sunfish sailing—all free; horseback riding, scuba, and cruises to Tobago Cays or Bequia can be arranged

P.S.: No cruise ships with more than 21 passengers

P.P.S.: In addition to the Cotton House, Mustique has 30-odd one-of-a-kind luxury villas for rent, some perched on hillsides, some beside the beach. None of them are designed for twosomes, but if you decide to junket with friends, this could be a memorable way to spend a vacation à la jet set. Mick Jagger's new wood and bamboo home may or may not be on the list of rentals, but Princess Margaret's is (although it's quite modest compared to some of the others). Among the most attractive *two*-bedroom villas: Blue Waters and Pelican Beach House (both on the water), Camylarde and Marienlyst (in the hills). Current rates are no longer outlandish compared with some of the Caribbean's new hotels: in 1991–1992 two-bedroom villas cost approximately $3,650 to $4,950 a week in winter, $2,750 to $3,950 in summer, in each case with full staff, Jeep, and laundry. Or, in other words, less than $200 per day per couple in summer. For details and a lavish color brochure, write to Mustique Villas; i/c Resorts Management, Inc.; 201½ East 29th Street; New York, NY 10016. Telephone: toll free 800/225-4255 or 212/696-4566. Fax: 212/689-1598.

Palm Island Beach Club
Palm Island

☆☆☆ ♀ ◑◑ $$$

The beach curves on and on for a mile and a half, and you get so spoiled for space here that if half a dozen other sun worshippers get to the strand before you tumble out of bed in the morning, you'll probably walk around the next bend to yet another uncrowded spot.

Not too many tides ago there weren't even half a dozen people here—and the island was no more than a ring of beach around a swamp, on the charts identified prosaically as Prune. Then along came John Caldwell. Alias "Coconut Johnny." "Tree planting is my hobby. . . . There's hardly an island in these parts where I can't go ashore and look at some trees I've planted." At Palm he can look at somewhere between two and three *thousand*.

Caldwell, now in his seventies, is a Texan who grew up in California, short, wiry, a mizzenmast of a man who bought a pair of shoes 15 years ago and has been seen wearing them once ("I've lived for 24 years on $1,200 a year"). Over 20 years ago he set out to sail single-handed across the Pacific and ended up on a reef off Fiji; somehow he continued to Australia, where he built a 45-foot ketch, loaded his wife and two young sons aboard, and set off again—this time smack into a hurricane in the Indian Ocean and then through the Suez Canal and across the Atlantic to the Grenadines. He spent five years there chartering; on each trip he came ashore on Palm/Prune Island with his charterers, and while they were having a picnic or swim he was planting his coconut palms. Before long, the swamp was a grove, the Prune was a Palm, and John Caldwell had started to plant a hotel. He and his sons designed and built the entire place from scratch, putting in power, water, roads, an airstrip, a dock—and 18 months later, in December 1967, they were ready to open Palm Island Beach Club.

The club (it's a club in name only—you don't have to join anything) at first sight appears to be a white beach sprinkled with coconut palms, casuarina, sea grape, and almond trees, dotted with brightly colored plastic loungers; a second look and you'll find that there are bungalows strung along free-form stone paths rambling through lanes of sun-dappled greenery, a few steps from the edge of Casuarina Beach. "It's small because we want to enjoy it ourselves." The dozen two-room bungalows are half stone, half hardwood, with two walls of wooden-slat vertical louvers, a third of sliding glass doors facing a patio. Some have open-air shower stalls, where you wash out the sand with water heated by solar power. John Caldwell designed and built his own furniture—in the no-nonsense, shipshape manner of a man who's fitted out a 45-foot ketch (although a recent restyling has added rattan furniture and television).

You spend your days at Palm Island Beach Club shuffling from your louvered room to the beach to the circular beach bar to the big open-air timber Polynesian longhouse for an informal Creole-dish dinner (note the ceiling, a superb piece of carpentry). Maybe at some point you'll grab your snorkeling mask and sneakers and go for a walk on the coral garden on the front beach, a hundred yards north of the beach bar. Maybe tomorrow you'll sail over to the Tobago Cays. Maybe you'll go diving. Maybe you'll join the visitors from the yachts at the beach bar for a tall, cool drink and a tall, salty tale. More likely you'll just lounge around in a couple of chaises and look at Union Island—one of those enticing mirages whose contours change with the passage of the sun, revealing unsuspected hamlets or coconut groves sparkling in the afternoon light.

By sundown, the loudest sound on Palm Island is the rigging of visiting yachts.

By nine o'clock, you're in bed—flicking flecks of sand from each other's cheeks.

Name: Palm Island Beach Club
Owners/Managers: John and Mary Caldwell and family
Address: Palm Island, St. Vincent–Grenadines, WI
Location: The Club *is* the island, and the island is 15–20 minutes by a new, 36-ft. launch (free) from Union Island; Union, in turn, can be reached by scheduled flight from St. Vincent by LIAT, from Martinique by Air Martinique, or by charter flight from Barbados (about $103 per person, and the hotel can help arrange the flight if you give them plenty of warning)
Telephone: 809/458-8824
Fax: 809/458-8804
Reservations: Caribbean Information Office, Chicago (toll free 800/621-1270; 312/699-7570, in Illinois); William Gardiner, New Jersey (toll free 800/247-2447; fax: 201/835-5783)
Credit Cards: American Express, Visa
Rooms: 24, in bungalows, breeze-cooled, refrigerators
Meals: Breakfast 7:30–9:30, lunch 1:00–2:00 (buffet), afternoon tea 4:00–4:30 on your patio, dinner 7:30–8:30 (family-style, barbecues Wednesday and Saturday); casual dress, barefoot if you wish; room service for breakfast, lunch, dinner at no extra charge

Entertainment: Barbecues twice a week, calypso night on Wednesday, Saturday evening "jump-up"; TV, video

Sports: 5 beaches, paddle tennis (1 untended court), games room, snorkeling gear, Sunfish sailing, windsurfing and "Highway 90," John's own aerobic fitness trail—all free; sailboats for rent; scuba equipment, diving off Palm or at nearby Tobago Cays; day sails to Tobago Cays and Mayreau on an Irwin 52 ketch

Saltwhistle Bay Club

Mayreau

☆☆☆ ⵏⵏ ◐ $ $ $

Real barefoot, flake-out, crash territory—an unspoiled bay on an unspoiled cay in the unspoiled Grenadines. To get there you first fly to Union Island, where you'll be met by the resort's launch, which will skim you across the channel past Saline Bay, then finally around a headland and into Saltwhistle Bay.

Tom and Undine Potter, a young Canadian/German couple, settled here almost a decade ago and built a beachside restaurant catering to passing yachts, then four years ago opened their hotel. When you sail into the bay, with its glistening semicircle of sand, and beyond the beach, dwarf palms and sea grape trees that part to reveal glimpses of another shining sea beyond, you may well wonder where *did* they build their hotel?

Go in a bit farther; it's all there nestled into 22 acres of coconut palms, more sea grapes, that great curve of soft white sand and a windward beach that's pure Robinson Crusoe.

Though the landscape may be lush, there's nothing plush or luxurious about the Saltwhistle's accommodations—but there's nothing uncomfortable about them either. The guest quarters are in sturdy native stone and timber cottages at one end of the beach, each with hardwood louvers, handcrafted furniture, ceiling fans, and showers supplied with water heated by the noonday sun. At the other end of the beach, there's a sprinkling of circular gazebos in matching stone with stone banquettes and palm-thatched shades. The two-room cottages share a spacious rooftop gallery with loungers, tables, and chairs. The Potters' dining room is an ingenious collection of circular stone booths topped by thatched canopies where you can stuff yourselves with local delicacies like curried conch, turtle steaks, and lobster, all fresh from the surrounding reefs.

There's not much to do at Saltwhistle—delightfully so. It is, as their brochure puts it, "an island where you start the day with nothing to do and finish it only half done." Of course, for the truly ambitious there's snorkeling gear, picnics to the wild and windswept beach with views of Palm Island and Tobago, fishing with the locals in their gaff-rigged sloops, a walk up the hill to the village for a warm beer and a sweeping view of all those cays and reefs, or a hike down to Saline Bay to watch the mail boat come in. And if any or all of these possibilities (or just the thought of them) exhaust you, there's always the lure of a good book, a rum punch, and a nice big hammock.

Name: Saltwhistle Bay Club
Owners/Managers: Tom and Undine Potter
Address: Mayreau, St. Vincent–Grenadines, WI
Location: South of St. Vincent, a few miles from the islands of Union, Petit St. Vincent, and Palm; to get there, you fly from Barbados to Union, where the hotel collects you by boat ($30 per person, round-trip), but since the Club (with advance notice) will make all the arrangements, all you have to do is get to Barbados
Telephone: Radio only, VHF Channel 16
Reservations: North American office, toll free 800/263-2780 (in Toronto, 416/430-8830); fax, 613/541-1787
Credit Cards: None
Rooms: 21, including 7 standard, 10 superior, 4 junior suites; all with sun-warmed showers, ceiling fans (and steady cross-ventilation); superior rooms also have shared rooftop decks
Meals: Breakfast 8:00–10:00, lunch noon–2:00, dinner 7:00–9:00 (approx. $60 for two), all served in beachside booths; occasional beach barbecues; casual dress; taped music; room service on request
Entertainment: Hammocks strung between the palm trees, conversation in the bar, darts, backgammon, a moonlit stroll on the beach
Sports: 300–400 yards of beautiful beach, snorkeling, windsurfing—all free; scuba-diving, boat trips to Tobago Cays, "sundowner" rum punch cruises, excursions with local fishermen at extra charge
P.S.: Closed September and October

Petit St. Vincent Resort
Petit St. Vincent

☆☆☆☆☆ 🍷🍷🍷 ◑◑◑ $$$$$

"Some of our guests never put on any clothes until dinnertime." Not in public, perhaps, but on their private terraces, because all but half a dozen of the rooms here are self-contained cottages, widely dispersed around this 113-acre private out-island. It may well be the most secluded, most private of the Caribbean's luxury hideaways.

It's certainly one of the most consistently dependable. PSV has no problems of revolving-door management. Any good resort manager knows where the pipes and power cables are, but in the case of Haze Richardson, he not only knows where they are but he put them there in the first place. He helped lay the cables and the pipes, helped quarry the stones for the cottages, installed the refrigeration in the kitchen, built a desalination plant, planted the fruit trees. Now the resort even makes its own fiberglass Jeeplike Minimokes. Richardson came to the island by way

of a 77-foot staysail schooner *Jacinta*, which he skippered. One of his charterers was the late H. W. Nichols, Jr., then the top man at a big corporation in Cincinnati, who bought this dinky Grenadine from a little old lady in Petit Martinique, the island just across the channel. They started building in 1966 and slaved for three years, working with whatever was available (mostly bluebitch stone and hardwood), planning the location of the individual cottages to make the most of the breezes and vistas.

It may sound simple and rustic, but it's really quite lavish in terms of solitude and seclusion—all that space for only 44 guests. And a staff of 75 to boot. The cottages follow a basic U-shaped pattern: big open sun deck, big shaded breakfast patio, big glass-enclosed lounge separated by a wall of bluebitch from a big sleeping area with twin queen-size beds, separated in turn from a stone-walled dressing room and bathroom with curtain-enclosed shower. There are no newfangled gadgets such as television or telephone. For room service there's the unique PSV semaphore system: a bamboo pole with a notch for written messages (e.g., "Two piña coladas fast," "afternoon tea for two") and two flags—red for "Do Not Disturb," yellow for "Come In." But the tactful maids and room service waiters first ring the little brass bell at the entrance—just in case you want to slip into your fluffy PSV-crested bathrobes.

Guest room interiors follow a basic style of bluebitch walls, purpleheart louvers, khuskhus rugs on red tile floors, new bathrobes, new fabrics—in soft islandy shades of yellow, turquoise, and terra-cotta.

Where the rooms differ is in location: up on the bluff for the best breezes and views, down on the beach by the lagoon, or on the beach beyond the dock. Cottage 1, on the bluff, is one of the most secluded, with a big deck overlooking a dazzling sea and the craggy silhouette of Union Island. For a beach right on your doorstep, cottages 6 through 11 look out on unspoiled castaway beach. For total detachment, turn your back on the entire resort and check into Cottage 18, where a few stone steps lead to a private patch of beach, and beyond that nothing but ocean—all the way to Guinea-Bissau or thereabouts. Some of the cottages are what passes in these lazy climes as a stiff hike (all of five minutes) to the dining pavilion, but you can always arrange to be picked up by one of the ubiquitous "mokes."

This hilltop bar/dining pavilion is the focal point of the resort, with soaring hardwood roof and indoor/outdoor patios overlooking the anchorage and Petit Martinique. Recently the owner added two additional open-air dining gazebos, with panoramic views of the bay and boats. Beautiful place to sit and savor the twilight while sipping a Banana Touch or mango daiquiri. PSV meals are above average for these parts (meats, for example, are personally selected by Julia Child's butcher, a regular PSV guest, and flown in specially for the resort); the dining room staff is particularly attentive.

Indeed, one of the main attractions of PSV, a feature that sets it apart from many of its peers, is its long-serving staff. They seem to care genuinely about making your vacation perfect. More often than not, Haze Richardson is at the dock to greet you with a rum punch when you arrive. The *Wakiva* skipper, Michael, is solicitous about getting you back to Union on time for your plane. There are totable beach chairs in your room in case you want to sample a nearby beach, but if you want to cart your *lounger* along, one of the roving stewards will pick you up in his Minimoke and transport you to whichever beach you choose (the one at the west end is particularly tranquil, with hammocks strung beneath thatch *bohios*). If you're bored with *that*, you can even have one of the boatmen transport you to PSR—Petit St. Richardson, a minuscule offshore cay with lots of sand and a solitary palm.

But why quit your own private deck in the first place—with or without swimsuits?

PSV may not be for everyone. You have to be your own entertainment. You have to forego the plushest amenities. You have to dine in the same dining room every evening, except one. But for anyone who genuinely wants a castaway setting with civilized comforts, who wants to get as far as possible from the everyday world without spending forever getting there, Petit St. Vincent is one beautiful, enchanting hideaway.

Name: Petit St. Vincent Resort
Owner/Manager: Haze Richardson
Address: Petit St. Vincent, St. Vincent–Grenadines, WI
Location: An inkblot on the charts, just 40 miles south of St. Vincent and 20 minutes from Union Island, the nearest airstrip, by PSV's 42-ft. Grand Banks yacht, *Wakiva* (the ride is free); the easiest way to get to Union is by shared-seat charter from Barbados (about $103 per passenger), which can be arranged by PSV; there are also scheduled flights to Union by LIAT and Air Mustique, from Grenada, Barbados, St. Vincent, and Martinique
Telephone: 809/458-8801
Fax: 809/458-8428
Reservations: Own U.S. office (513/242-1333 or toll free 800/654-9326, fax 513/242-6951), or Leading Hotels of the World
Credit Cards: None

Rooms: 22 cottages, all with bedrooms and sitting rooms, open *and* shaded patios or terraces, showers only (heated by the sun), amenities trays, bathrobes, hammocks, some with ceiling fans (otherwise acres of louvers take care of the cooling)

Meals: Breakfast 7:30–10:00, buffet lunch 12:30–2:00, afternoon tea 4:00–5:00, dinner 7:30–9:30 (all in the hilltop dining pavilion); Friday beach barbecue, with Grenadine flute band, when the staff carts the entire dining room—chairs, tables, *and* piano—to the lawn beside the beach; dress—informal but stylish (cover-ups required at lunchtime); room service all meals (including early morning coffee service), no extra charge

Entertainment: Quiet taped music in bar, occasional live music (guitar, folk), backgammon and other parlor pastimes

Sports: Virtually continuous beach (plus the offshore cay), snorkeling, Sunfish sailing, HobieCats, windsurfing (with instruction by shore simulator), tennis (1 court with lights), croquet, table tennis, fitness trail, foot path up 275-ft. Mount Marni (great view), snorkeling on 20-ft. island boat built from island cedar—all free; waterskiing, scuba-diving and day trips on Chester's high-speed powerboat or the 80-ft. ketch *Camelot* to Tobago Cays and Mayreau at extra charge

P.S.: Few children, no groups except maybe the crew from a passing yacht who stop by the bar for a drink

The Calabash
Grenada

☆☆☆ ♈♈ ◑◑ $$

You never have to worry about making it to the dining room in time for breakfast because you have a kitchenette and maid (who has her own entrance to let herself in without disturbing you). So leave your order in writing the night before, or wake up and whenever you feel like breakfast, just tell your personal maid. She'll serve it to you in bed, in the sitting room, or on your private patio. Eating, in fact, is one of the prime pleasures at The Calabash. Lunch and dinner are served in a pretty pavilion of native stone and local hardwoods, furnished with chairs and tables of polished saman. Flowering *Thunbergia grandiflora* dangles from overhead vines, threatening, it seems, to reach down and gobble up your lambis or swordfish pie Creole.

The Calabash is an old Grenada favorite—the British in particular have been wintering here loyally for a quarter of a century. The intimate little resort circles eight beachside acres, a "village green" dotted with lofty trees and fragrant shrubbery. The 22 suites perfectly capture island atmosphere, comfortable but not plush, rustic but snug. For my money, the best buys are the suites in the two-story cottages on the west side of the lawn, and preferably the higher-ceilinged units on the second floor: each suite subdivided with kitchenette, indoor sitting room, lazy breeze-cooled porch, small fan-cooled bedroom (showers only in the bathrooms). Room 1 is listed as a Honeymoon Suite, close to the beach, with a big hand-carved mahogany four-poster bed.

The prime quarters are now the two suites with private plunge pools, especially *the* Pool Suite, with a very large, very private indoor/outdoor living room, full kitchen, and a giant calabash tree in the garden. But what brings the British and others back year after year to The Calabash is the long-serving staff—friendly, willing, attentive but unobtrusive. They make The Calabash an inviting, relaxed hideaway.

Name: The Calabash
Manager: Chloe Barnes
Address: P.O. Box 382, St. George's, Grenada, WI
Location: At L'Anse aux Epines (Prickly Bay) on the south coast, about 10 minutes and $10 by taxi from the airport, $12 from St. George's
Telephone: 809/444-4234, 4334
Fax: 809/444-4804
Reservations: International Travel & Resorts, Inc., or GHA, toll free 800/322-1753
Credit Cards: American Express, MasterCard, Visa
Rooms: 22 suites, most with baths and showers, all with kitchenettes and porches, ground-floor rooms with air conditioning, ceiling fans throughout, telephones, 2 with private plunge pools
Meals: Breakfast anytime, lunch 1:00–2:30, dinner 7:30–10:00 (in the arbor-covered dining terrace or at the beach bar, approx. $50 for two); informal (but preferably trousers, rather than shorts, for men in the evening); room service at no extra charge
Entertainment: Some taped (or radio) music, steel band or country trio several times a week in winter, less frequently in the off-season

Sports: Beach, tennis (1 court, with lights), billiard room—all free; snorkeling, scuba, waterskiing, sailing can be arranged

P.S.: Occasional din of planes, rarely after 10:00 p.m.; some cruise ship passengers come to enjoy the dining and the beach

Secret Harbour

Grenada

☆☆ ♀♀ ◐◐ $$$

For lovers, the secret harbors at Secret Harbour may be the bathtubs—sunken, free-form, masses of colorful Italian tiles surrounded by masses of colorful Italian tiles, matching towels, potted plants, and an unglazed "wagonwheel" window that lets you listen to the lapping of the water below as you lazily lap the water on each other's back.

Secret Harbour is the dream-come-true of an expatriate English lady, Barbara Stevens, a chartered accountant, who closed her books one day about 20 years ago and set sail with her first husband to cross the Atlantic

in a 45-foot ketch; after spending four years chartering in the Grenadines, she decided Grenada was her island and Musquetta Bay her mooring. This is where she built her hotel back in 1970. The hotel has recently been acquired by a new owner, Club Mariner, which is a division of Charter Yacht Company.

It's more like a Spanish-Mediterranean village on a terraced hillside of gardens and greenery: a splash of red-tiled roofs, white stucco arches, and hand-hewn beams among lime and papaw trees, frangipani, and triple bougainvillea. At the top of the hill, the lobby-lounge and restaurant; the guest bungalows are a few feet above the water, and between top and bottom there's a big, tiled free-form pool as colorful as your bathtub.

Secret Harbour, now owned by the Charter Yacht people, welcomes you with luxury—but luxury in keeping with the Spanish-Mediterranean theme: a big, semicircular balcony overlooking the bay, with padded loungers and enough room for a dinner party; arched glass-paneled doors leading into a small sunny lounge foyer with bright two-toned banquettes; a pair of authentic four-poster double beds from island plantations; stained glass windows to cast spangled light, and candles with dimmer switches beside each bed to set just the right romantic mood. To say nothing of your tasteful bathroom.

Name: Secret Harbour

Manager: Len Nelson

Address: P.O. Box 11, St. George's, Grenada, WI

Location: On a quiet bay (Mount Hastman) on the south shore of the island, a few miles from the resort hotels along Grand Anse Beach, 10–15 minutes from St. George's ($12 by taxi), 10 minutes from the airport ($10 by taxi)

Telephone: 809/440-4439, 4548

Reservations: Direct

Credit Cards: American Express, MasterCard, Visa

Rooms: 20 suites in 10 cottages, all with air conditioning and ceiling fans and verandas

Meals: Breakfast 7:30–10:30, lunch 12:00–2:00, afternoon tea at 4:00, dinner 7:30–10:00 (approx. $50 for two); room service at no extra charge; informal dress (but slacks rather than shorts at dinner)

Entertainment: Piped music, amplified combos, steel bands occasionally

Sports: Small (private) beach, sunbathing terrace, pool; Sunfish sailing, windsurfing, scuba, waterskiing, snorkeling; trips by speedboat to nearby Hog and Calivigny islands

Spice Island Inn
Grenada

☆☆☆ ♊ ◐ $$$

Begin the day by slipping out of bed, sliding back the screens, and plopping straight into your private plunge pool. When the bell by the garden gate rings, it means the waiter has arrived with your breakfast, which he'll set up on your private, shaded breakfast patio. Dawdle over the fresh island fruits and cassava bread—the hot plate will keep your coffee piping hot. After breakfast, step down onto your private sunning patio and spread out on a lounger—the garden wall screens you from passersby, the doorbell guards you against maids and waiters, so you can shuck your bikini or robe or whatever you have half on, half off. Spend the entire day here—sunning, dipping, eating, loving, dipping, sunning, all in your own private little sun-bright world.

Your suite, if you take time to notice, is craftily designed: The terrazzo sun deck is in the sun all day; the breakfast patio is in the shade all day. In addition to your tiny garden and freshwater pool, your suite has tiled floors with soft scatter rugs, wicker chairs, and fitted dressers crafted from local hardwoods; the bathrooms are like locker rooms—big tiled sunken shower stalls, double washbasins, separate johns, magnifying mirrors. The 20 beach suites, the original 20-year-old accommodations, are less opulent, with a small inner garden patio that separates the sleeping quarters from the bathroom. All Spice Island's suites, beach or pool, have louvers and air conditioning for cooling and individual gas water heaters to give you reliable supplies of hot water. The resort has just emerged from a $2-million renovation that added 14 new suites equipped with whirlpools; 7 also have private pools. Along with the new suites, whirlpools have been added to the existing beach suites.

When you get curious about the rest of the world, stroll a few yards across the lawn, among the coconut palms and flowering shrubs, to Grand Anse Beach—2½ miles of fine white sand. Jog. Walk. Work up an appetite or thirst, both of which you can satisfy in pleasant surroundings in the inn's big bamboo and wood beachside pavilions. But no matter how tasty the breadfruit vichyssoise or nutmeg ice cream, no matter how jolly the music of the folk trio that serenades you, it's always a delight to slip off to your private patio and your private pool for a midnight swim beneath your private stars.

Name: Spice Island Inn
Manager: Augustus Cruickshank
Address: P.O. Box 6, Grand Anse, St. George's, Grenada, WI
Location: On Grand Anse Beach, 10 minutes and $7 by taxi from St. George's, 15 minutes and $10 by taxi from the new airport
Telephone: 809/444-4258, 4423
Fax: 809/444-4807
Reservations: International Travel & Resorts, Inc. in the United States, Robert Reid Associates in Canada, GHA (toll free 800/322-1753)
Credit Cards: American Express, Discover, MasterCard, Visa
Rooms: 56, including 17 pool suites, 39 whirlpool suites, all with air conditioning, ceiling fans, louvers, patios or lanais, mini-bars, clock/radios, telephones
Meals: Breakfast from 7:30, lunch 12:30–2:30, afternoon tea 3:00–6:00, dinner at 7:30 (approx. $60 for two); full room service; informal but stylish dress
Entertainment: Barbecues and steel bands, local bands; new open-air dance floor
Sports: 2½-mile beach (hotel's frontage about ½ mile), 17 private freshwater pools; tennis (1 court), snorkeling gear, Sunfish sailing and windsurfing—all free, a short walk along the beach; scuba-diving, waterskiing, and water sports nearby, at extra charge
P.S.: Children under five not allowed in season

Added Attractions

Twelve Degrees North
Grenada

Another spot worth looking into, although it's not a hotel: Twelve Degrees North, a group of eight self-contained apartments (six with one bedroom), each with its own maid, who prepares breakfast, lunch, fixes the beds, tidies up, and does your personal laundry. The apartments are immaculate, attractively decorated with simple island-style furnishings, and each has a large balcony or patio overlooking Prickly Bay. On the beach, at the foot of the hill, you'll find a Sunfish, 17-foot sailboat, 23-foot launch, two Wind-surfers, freshwater pool, and honor-system beach bar; up top there's a Plexi-Pave tennis court in tiptop condition (but bring your own rackets and balls). Twelve Degrees North, owned and operated by Joe Gaylord, the American who built it and keeps everything running like clockwork, is in the residen-tial area of L'Anse aux Epines, a short taxi ride from several good restau-rants. Children not encouraged. By the week only. 8 apartments. Doubles: $145 EP. *Twelve Degrees North, P.O. Box 241, St. George's, Grenada, WI. Tele-phone: 809/440-4580; fax: same as phone number*

Blue Horizons Cottage Hotel
Grenada

For many visitors to Grenada, this is the garden they pass through on the way to one of the island's finest restaurants, La Belle Creole. Diners have a hillside view over the bay as they sit down to conch scram and deviled langouste, recipes familiar to guests of Ross Point Inn (where the owners, the Hopkin brothers, learned the art of Creole cooking from their mother); beneath the newly decorated La Belle Creole, hidden among the saman and cassia trees and coral plants, are the cottages housing the guest rooms. The 32 suites, including 16 deluxe, have all recently been reappointed with new mahogany furniture, new kitchenettes, new beds, and even new hair-dryers; all have air conditioning, ceiling fans, and patios. Communal areas include a pavilion lounge beside a freshwater pool, shaded by a tall Bar-ringtonia that blossoms for two hours every evening at twilight. Two blocks from Grand Anse Beach, and ideal for lovers on a tight budget, although the restaurant, of course, is not inexpensive. 32 suites. Doubles: $120 to $150 EP, winter 1991–92. *Blue Horizons, P.O. Box 41, St. George's, Grenada, WI. Telephone: 809/444-4316; fax: 809/444-4807.*

Friendship Bay Hotel
Bequia

The location is superb—the flank of a low hill, overlooking a half-circle of bay and the islets of Sample Key, Petit Nevis, Île Outre, and Ramière, with a mile of sandy beach a three-minute walk from your room. You may even sight the whale hunters returning to Petit Nevis with a hapless cetacean. The island's largest hotel, Friendship Bay has been spruced up in recent years, transforming a once-floundering, once-cranky place into a welcoming rendezvous. The best nooks are the 10 cottages along the shore, with louvered windows, overhead fans, and batik wall hangings illustrating Bequia life in *naif* style. Dinner is served in a glass-enclosed dining pavilion above the bay. There are water sports, tennis, and a convivial beach bar for socializing with visitors and Bequians. 27 rooms. Doubles: $170 to $245 MAP, winter 1991–92. *Friendship Bay Hotel, P.O. Box 9, Bequia, St. Vincent–Grenadines, WI. Telephone: 809/458-3222. Reservations: toll free 800/233-9815.*

Sunny Caribbee
Plantation House Hotel
Bequia

There's been a hotel here for many years, but the original century-old main house burned down several seasons ago. New Canadian/Bequian owners have rebuilt it in its original two-story, colonial style with broad veranda, presently the bar and restaurant. There's more dining in the beach bar, between the kidney-shaped pool and the edge of the sea. Guest accommodations are in 17 individual wooden cabanas scattered around the 10-acre flower garden, each with private bathroom, ceiling fan, and veranda; there's also a three-bedroom suite beside the beach, and the second floor of the main house is now given over to five deluxe rooms with air conditioning. Don't expect sumptuous luxury here (look at the rates!), and don't expect much in the way of nightlife. What you do get in abundance is peace and quiet, and the nautical atmosphere of Admiralty Bay and all its sailboats and occasional yacht-size cruise ships. For active guests there's a tennis court and a complete dive shop with three instructors right on the premises. 25 rooms. Doubles: $230 and $245 MAP, winter 1991–92. *Sunny Caribbee Plantation House Hotel, P.O. Box 16, Admiralty Bay, Bequia, St. Vincent–Grenadines, WI. Telephone: 809/458-3425; fax: 809/458-3612. Reservations: toll free 800/752-1703 or 516/261-9606.*

The Dutch Leewards

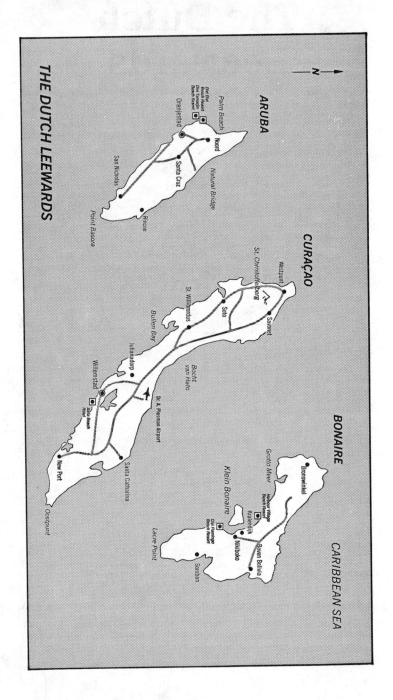

The Dutch Leewards

They're ledges of coral rather than volcanic peaks, they're covered with cactus rather than jungle, and they have a personality all their own—part Dutch, part Indian, part Spanish, part just about everything else. They even have their own language, *Papiamento*, which grabs a few words from any language that happens to come along, shakes them around like a rum punch, and comes up with something as infectiously charming as the people themselves. Thus, *Carne ta camna cabes abou, ma e sa cuant' or tin* means, "He is as innocent as the babe unborn," although the literal translation is "The sheep walks with its head down, but it knows what time it is"; or *stropi cacalaca*, which means "sweatheart" or "darling" although its literal translation means something quite unsuspected.

Bonaire is the loveliest of the trio, a coral boomerang 24 miles long and 5 miles wide, a world all its own, a world so bright, so luminous from coral and sand you practically get a suntan crossing the street. It has more goats than cars, and almost as many flamingos as people; one-third of the island is national park, and another large chunk is salt flats cultivated by Dutch seafarers a couple of centuries ago. The capital, Kralendijk, has 1,000 inhabitants, 1 discotheque, and 2 Chinese restaurants.

Curaçao is the largest of the three, and its main city, Willemstad, is the capital of all the Netherlands Antilles. Willemstad is utterly unique, almost a miniature Caribbean Amsterdam with gingerbread houses the colors of a coral reef. Of late, it has become a bit grungy and slightly overcommercial, so maybe you'd better skip town and head out to the *cunucu*, or countryside, to find yourselves a quiet cove for the afternoon.

Aruba is all beach, but a beach unsurpassed by any other island, with mile after mile of some of the whitest sand in the Caribbean. It's the smallest but the liveliest of the Dutch Leewards, with high-rise hotels, nightclubs, casinos, and lots of restaurants to keep you from enjoying the moon and the stars.

How to Get There From New York, American, Air Aruba, and Continental fly wide-body jets to Aruba, with Air Aruba and Continental continuing to Curaçao; from Miami, ALM and Air Aruba to both islands. ALM flies direct to Bonaire several days a week from Miami and Atlanta.

Otherwise, to get to Bonaire you switch at Aruba or Curaçao to an ALM jet.

Divi Divi Beach Resort

Aruba

☆ ♈ ◑◑ $$$$

There's probably more sand on this beach than there is on a half dozen other islands put together. Shimmering, glistening, beckoning sand. Sand about as white as a beach will ever be. It's called Eagle Beach at this point, and it sweeps into the distance on either side, one mile to the south, about six miles to the northern tip of Aruba.

The slightly Miami-ish Divi Divi appears in these pages by courtesy of this beach—and courtesy of its *casitas* and lanais. The *casitas*, 40 of them, are in staggered rows among tailored lawns and hibiscus in many hues; the 20 new lanai suites are next door to them, right on the beach.

Each *casita* has a patio on the lawn with a shaded breakfast alcove and a Spanish-Mexican interior, with tile floors, ceiling fans, Caribbean paintings, cane chairs, big tiled bathrooms, and fresh flowers on the *two* double Sealy Posturepedics with hand-carved headboards. The lanai suites have similar decor, with, of course, lanais facing the beach and a cool, quiet palm court.

Both the *casitas* and the lanais are to the left of the Divi Divi's open, breezy lobby; to the right there are a couple of two-story wings on the beach but in general appearances much like a motel; the focus of activity is the big, palm-encircled swimming pool off the main lobby and adjoining the bar and snack terrace. The public shenanigans here almost put the Divi Divi beyond the pale for lovers—there's music in some loud, amplified form or another almost every night of the week, often until 1:00 or 2:00 a.m. Fortunately, most of the *casitas* (except for those ending in 26, which are the noisiest, unfortunately, since they do have the best views) and lanais are upwind of the noise—you could be in a different hotel over there.

You could also feel like you're in a different hotel if you opt for the Divi Divi's deluxe hacienda-style rooms, known as Divi Dos. These three-story Spanish villas all have suites with windowed patios and ocean views; cool breezes, overhead fans, *and* air conditioning; full bathrooms and dressing rooms, pretty floral printed fabrics, lattice grillwork separating refrigerator/sink areas from the bedrooms. There's a separate whirlpool–swimming pool–lily pond–deck area for Divi Dos guests exclusively.

You have, actually, plenty of opportunities to escape the bustle and brouhaha—the beach is so vast a short walk will isolate you from just about everything except yourselves and the sand (turn left when you get to the beach, walk a few hundred yards, and you'll come to one or two great spots for coral and conch shells; turn right and you will pass a bit of construction inland).

Name: Divi Divi Beach Resort

Manager: Astrid Muller-Matthew

Address: Oranjestad, Aruba, NA

Location: On the west coast beach, adjacent to the Alhambra Casino and Shopping Bazaar, 10 minutes and $12 by taxi from the airport, 5 minutes from town, about the same from the casinos and nightclubs along hotel row (buses every 45 minutes, 90¢ a ride)

Telephone: 599/82-3300

Fax: 297/83-4230

Reservations: Divi Hotels own office, toll free 800/367-3484 or 607/277-3484

Credit Cards: American Express, Diners Club, MasterCard, Visa

Rooms: 202, including 40 *casitas* and 20 lanais, all with air conditioning, most with cross-ventilation, all with balconies or patios, satellite TV

Meals: Breakfast 7:30–10:00, continental breakfast 7:30–11:30, lunch noon–6:00, dinner 6:30–10:00 on the terrace or in the air-conditioned Red Parrott ($20 for two on the terrace, $60 for two in the Red Parrott); casual dress on the terrace and dining room

Entertainment: Piped music on terrace, live music most evenings, steel bands, folklore shows, barbecues, buffets, Sunday brunch, beach parties; sunset sails on the 76-ft. ketch, *Mi Dushi*; casinos and nightclubs nearby

Sports: Beach (and how!), freshwater pool, loungers (no extra charge), tennis (one court with lights)—all free; snorkeling gear for rent; scuba, sailboats, and waterskiing nearby

P.S.: Many groups in main hotel

Divi Tamarijn Beach Resort

Aruba

☆ 🍷 ◐ $$$

The Tamarijn is the kid brother of the Divi Divi Beach Resort, but costs a few dollars less, a point in its favor right there. Inspiration for its design is the typical country cottage you see in the *cunucu*, Aruba's scrubby countryside, but instead of individual cottages, the Tamarijn strings them together in three or four clusters, red-tiled and white-walled, strung along the beach. Interiors recently have been warmly refurbished—earth-colored tiles, orange wicker headboards, seashell colors on printed bedspreads and drapes; every room has two full-size double beds, small wall safes in the bathrooms, and sliding screened doors opening onto patios with *bohios* or balconies, all with ocean views. You may find the rooms in wings 17 through 22 quietest, and (lucky break) they're also the least expensive rooms because they're farther (two minutes, say, instead of one) from the lobby, bar, and dining terrace.

The hotel revolves around the Cunucu Terrace with its beachside/poolside bar, botanically boxed in by rows of cayena or hibiscus. Above you the palm trees, above the palms the stars, and with candles flickering on the table it would be one of the most romantic as well as one of the prettiest dining spots on the island if it weren't for the nondescript music blaring from the overhead speakers. (Make a point of avoiding the number 14 wing series—who needs to listen to an amplified combo version of "Feelings" when you'd rather sit quietly and feel the trade winds cool off your tan?)

Guests at either of these Divi resorts have access to the facilities of the other, and a golf cart known as the Panther shuttles between the two at regular intervals. There's also a paved path (a seven-minute walk); but if you decide to drink here and dine there, the thing to do is kick off your espadrilles, roll up your pants, and stroll along the edge of the sea.

Name: Divi Tamarijn Beach Resort
Manager: Astrid Muller-Matthew
Address: Oranjestad, Aruba, NA
Location: On the west coast beach, about 10 minutes and $12 by taxi from the airport

Telephone: 599/82-4150

Fax: 297/83-4002

Reservations: Divi Hotels own office, toll free 800/367-3484 or 607/277-3484

Credit Cards: American Express, Amoco, Carte Blanche, Diners Club, MasterCard, Visa

Rooms: 236, in beachside bungalows, with breezes, air conditioning, wall safes, patios or balconies

Meals: Breakfast 7:30–11:00, continental breakfast to 11:30, lunch noon–5:00, dinner 6:30–10:00 (approx. $30 to $35 for two, served in the garden terrace or in the recently remodeled air-conditioned Palm Court Restaurant); casual dress but "coats and ties are permitted, reluctantly"; room service from 7:30 a.m.–11:00 p.m., $1 per order

Entertainment: Piped music at dinner, steel bands, amplified combos in conical band shell

Sports: Freshwater pool, Ping-Pong; 1,000 ft. of virtually private beach (which is not as spectacular as the strand at the Divi Divi, a short walk away); tennis (2 courts, free by day, $5 per half hour at night); snorkeling gear for rent; waterskiing, scuba-diving, sailing, boat trips nearby

P.S.: Some charter groups, noticeable only at check-in and check-out times (mostly weekends)

P.P.S.: A time-sharing property, Dutch Village, has opened on the Tamarijn property, without much disruption in hotel services or environment. The studio, one-, and two-bedroom apartments all have air conditioning, full kitchens, cable TV, Jacuzzis, and patios or balconies, with lushly planted grottos in view. They have carved wood furniture, canopied king-size beds, big bathrooms.

Divi Flamingo Beach Resort and Casino

Bonaire

☆☆ ♈♈ ◑◑ $$$

What you slip into in the morning here is probably what you'll slip out of at bedtime—bikini, swim shorts, diving tanks (or snorkel for the uninitiated), maybe even a pair of sandals. This is a down-to-coral resort ("where toes are in and ties are out"), which reflects the unspoiled, uncomplicated lifestyle of the island of Bonaire and the zealous, underwater lifestyle of the divers who come here.

If you're one of the discerning band of Bonaire buffs who would grow gills if you could, you already know what I'm talking about. If you've never heard of Bonaire or have never checked an air tank, no matter. When you finish breakfast in the open-air Calabas Terrace, just take three steps down to the beach, don snorkel and fins, and float through schools of small-mouth grunts, listen to the spotlight parrotfish munch on some coral, keep an eye out for the shy royal blue, a real beauty. When you finally surface, you may want to pop over to the Flamingo Nest for an aqueous refreshment, a cool Mai-Tai perhaps, while you take in that stunning view: the multihued, multi*blued* Caribbean, the tiny coral mass, Klein Bonaire, the northern tip of boomerang Bonaire, and one spectacular sunset.

Just about the most formal place at the Flamingo Beach is the Chibi-Chibi, a wood-beamed, red-shingled two-story terrace restaurant overhanging the water. Shoes and shirts are considered formal. Here you can watch the tropical fish, even moray eels, frolic and fight over the crumbs I that drop through the wood-planked floors, while you savor a tasty Antillean *bouillabaise* or *keshi yena*, a local dish of chicken, spices and vegetables baked under a Gouda cheese dome. If you fancy wine, there's a surprisingly extensive French list.

Guests tend to retire early here, unless, of course, they're going to pay a visit to the "first barefoot casino in the world," just past the Calabas in a restored Bonairean mansion.

However directly or indirectly you do come to your rooms, you'll find comfortable accommodations when it's time for bed. Stay in the original cottages on the horseshoe path behind the terrace and you can relax on a patio shaded by gnarled old bean trees, behind a white picket fence of upended conch shells. All these cottages have recently been renovated to include new tile showers and sliding glass doors. The two-story oceanfront deluxe rooms beside the coral beach feature big, wooden-railed balconies built right over the gently lapping sea, and are tastefully appointed in wicker and batik, with double beds and half canopies. Over by the muraled, free-form pool and courtyard, superior rooms are done up Mexican style, with carved wooden bedposts and bureaus, tiled floors; some rooms have sea views; some are shaded by palms and overlook the gardens.

Recently the hotel completed a new wing of time-sharing units called

Club Flamingo, which may sometimes be available to the hotel's guests. The 40 units are in a self-contained, two-story L, just past the casino, and designed to blend in with the rest of the grounds—light latticework partitions separate the screened-in porches, the slanted roof is edged with Caribbean-style green gingerbread, and there's new landscaping and a blue-tiled pool and Jacuzzi. The studio apartments have kitchens, air conditioning, and custom-designed, light-colored Haitian furniture.

Despite the expansion, Divi's Flamingo Beach remains strictly a place for relaxing. Nothing but sea, sand, sun, sun, sand, sea; rum punches in the beach bar; lazy dinners in the pavilion with moonlight shimmering on the bay.

Name: Divi Flamingo Beach Resort and Casino
Manager: C. Alastair Mackellar
Address: Kralendijk, Bonaire, NA
Location: 3 minutes and $6 by taxi from the airport (although it's so close you won't be disturbed by aircraft noise)
Telephone: 599/78-285
Fax: 599/78-238
Reservations: Divi Hotels toll free 800/367-3484 or 607/277-3484
Credit Cards: American Express, Diners Club, MasterCard, Visa
Rooms: 150 rooms, all with air conditioning, many with cross-ventilation, half with balconies or patios, deluxe rooms have bath tubs, others showers only
Meals: Self-service breakfast buffet 7:30–10:00, continental breakfast 10:00–12:00, lunch noon–2:30, dinner 7:00–10:00 (approx. $45 to $55 for two, served in open pavilion beside the beach); no room service; "ties and jackets absolutely prohibited"
Entertainment: Trio 4 nights a week in winter, Antillean Night with steel band (slightly amplified), Calypso Night with combo on Saturday; casino with open-air Players Bar
Sports: Pool, Jacuzzi, small beach; snorkel gear, bicycles, boat trips to offshore islands for a small fee; sightseeing and sunset cruises on the 37-ft. trimaran *Woodwind*, extra; complete dive shop, underwater photo center, and car rental on premises
P.S.: Occasional small charter groups, some seminars, lots of scuba-divers

Harbour Village Beach Resort
Bonaire

☆☆ ♈ ◑◑ $$$

This is bonny Bonaire's first venture into the world of luxury lodgings. Oh, well. On the one hand, for luxury lovers these days you need things like lamps and desks, air conditioning that works, room service that gets the entire breakfast to your balcony in one attempt; for island lovers, on the other hand (and especially this beachcomber island), you need louvers and cross ventilation in the rooms and a lobby that doesn't feel like a refrigerator.

The harbor viewed is a yacht marina, part of a 100-acre resort development; the hotel itself is a 10-acre enclave tucked between the marina and a small beach, with a jetty jutting into the sea and fitted with a ship's wheel and Adirondack chairs as La Balandra Beach Bar—the most Bonairean part of the hotel. The rest is predictable two-story, canteloupe-and-coral stucco with arches, courtyards, and parquet brick walkways.

The pool, sun terrace, and dining terrace are attractive, with the right island touches, but they are assigned to a corner of the property behind the other buildings with only an intermittent view of the beach or marina. In the Kasa Coral dining terrace and La Balandra Beach Bar, the food is passable and the service is amiable.

For the record, Harbour Village started out as a Sonesta hotel, but the owner and Sonesta soon parted ways and it is now run by the family of the owner. Perhaps they can transform this near-miss into a near-hit if they have succeeded, since my visit, in fixing the following items in Room 223: toilet, bathroom light, air conditioner thermostat, balcony table, cutlery with room-service breakfast.

Name: Harbour Village Beach Resort
Manager: Patrick Poggi
Address: Kaya Gobernador Debrot, Bonaire, Netherlands, Antilles
Location: At Playa Lechi, on the edge of town, about 10 minutes and $10 from the airport

Telephone: 599/77-500
Fax: 599/77-507
Reservations: Toll free 800/424-0004 or 305/669-9646; fax 305/ 669-0842
Credit Cards: All major cards
Rooms: 63, including one-bedroom suites, all with balcony or terrace, air conditioning, ceiling fan, remote cable television
Meals: Breakfast 8:00–10:00, lunch 12:00–2:30, afternoon tea, dinner (in Kasa Coral) 7:00–9:00 (approx. $60 to $70 for two); informal dress; room service 7 A.M. to 11 P.M.
Entertainment: Lounge/bar, occasional live music
Sports: Small beach, freshwater lap pool; for a fee, windsurfing, water-skiing, small-boat sailing, scuba-diving, snorkeling

Avila Beach Hotel
Curaçao

☆☆ ♈♈ ◑ $$

The driveway with its jungle greenery and the glimpse of sun-dappled patio at the rear says "tropics," and so does the Avila's owner Nic Møller. "I like to give my guests a feeling of the tropics; I like to find things to make it interesting." *It* being a four-story colonial governor's mansion built in a time (1811) when ships had to fire gun salutes for the mansion as they bobbed down the coast to the harbor. The yellow, impeccably kept mansion with white trim and red-tiled roof, next to the octagonal home where Simón Bolívar used to visit his sisters, could still receive a governor at a moment's notice. And it's certainly *interesting*.

The lobby has been recently lightened and brightened with a cultivated Caribbean/European air: Pastel colors replace the heavy wood paneling, Oriental rugs blend with smart cane furniture, a grand piano stands ready for the occasional recital, and large mirrors are guarded by life-size ceramic dogs.

Follow the sun through this pleasant lobby and you come to a breezy patio/terrace with flagstones and ceramic lamps, a sunshade of twining palms and flamboyants, cacti and rubber plants, with white wooden chairs grouped around white wooden tables with cheery red cloths. Further down there's a second arbor shading rustic lounging chairs and the Schooner Bar, which is shaped like a ship's prow with a roof of thatch projecting from the mast. Then comes the beach. Well, something like a beach. The Avila is indeed on the seafront but on this stretch of the coastline there's precious little natural beach; so with typical Dutch ingenuity, someone has fashioned a small breakwater to create a small lagoon with a sandy beach in one corner, ringed by a sunbathing terrace with a layer of sand and shaded by half a dozen *bohios*. Two years ago, Møller added a string of iron-poled, orange-capped gas-lamp like lights to guide you to the end of the breakwater, perfect for private stargazing.

The Danish-born owner has been in possession of Avila for the last 12 years. All the rooms in the main house and its wings have recently been redone in crisp Scandinavian style—cool, striped cloth blinds, sleek-lined wooden beds and couches, framed antique maps or pretty little watercolors on the walls. The standard rooms are fairly small; if you have a choice and can afford a sea view, ask for rooms 125, 235, or 345, on the upper floors, facing the tankers and cruise ships maneuvering for the run into the harbor channel. Rooms 344 and 345 have terraces/balconies for afternoon sunning.

The Avila is by no means a plush hotel, but in its unpretentious, friendly way it has a lot of old colonial charm. Especially in the evening, when you're sitting around the Schooner Bar sipping an Amstel, the pelicans are diving for their suppers, a cruise ship passes like a wall of lights, and you'll soon be sitting down to a dinner of fresh fish smoked in the kitchen's spice room, topped off by homemade sorbet, all beneath the twining palms and flamboyants.

Name: Avila Beach Hotel
Owner/Manager: Nic Møller
Address: Penstraat 130-134, Willemstad, Curaçao, NA
Location: On a residential street beside the sea, a 10-minute walk from the shopping center, $11 by taxi from the airport
Telephone: 599/96-14377
Fax: 599/96-11493
Reservations: Utell International
Credit Cards: All major cards
Rooms: 45, all with air conditioning, direct-dial telephone, showers only (water warmed by the sun), television
Meals: Breakfast 7:00–10:00, lunch noon–2:00, dinner 7:00–10:00 (approx. $45 for two, served on the open terrace beside the beach); special Antillean night on Wednesday (with strolling trio) and barbecue

on Saturday with mariachi or steel band; casual dress; no room service
Entertainment: Schooner Bar beside the beach
Sports: Beach, loungers, free snorkeling gear
P.S.: Some cruise ship passengers, beach club families on weekends; mini-bus service to and from Willemstad in the mornings
P.P.S: Sometime in the fall of 1991, Avila Beach should have a new four-story wing with modern apartments (some for rental) and a tennis court

Added Attractions

The Point at Bonaire
Bonaire

Bonaire's second luxury hotel, it was still a construction site when I last saw it, but was well on its way to a spring 1991 debut. Since its co-owners, the Parker family, have been running the Concord Hotel in upstate New York for many years, and plan to manage this one, The Point probably has a better chance of making the grade and lasting the pace than Harbour Village (above). Despite the New York connection, the architects are Italian, and they've incorporated lobbies of Italian granite and lots of fountains, while fitting out the guest rooms with air-conditioning, ceiling fans, balconies, 3-cubic-foot refrigerators, and 26-inch cable televisions. The Point is located on 20 acres between town and the airport, alongside a half-mile curve of beach that's scheduled for a few boatloads of fresh sand; in addition to the usual water sports facilities and tennis, promised attractions include a 5,000-square-foot casino, five bars, giant-screen satellite television for major sports events, telecopying, and stock market quotations. Just what Bonaire needs. 174 rooms and suites. Doubles: $330 and up, room only, winter 1991–92. *The Point, Bonaire, Netherlands, Antilles. Reservations: toll free 800/926-6247.*

Caribbean Cruises:
Four Small Luxury
Ships

I know, I know. It says in the introduction that *Caribbean Hideaways* features only inns and resorts where you will not be overrun by hordes of unleashed cruise ship passengers. So what am I doing with a section on cruise ships? Well, these are *small* cruise ships: The largest carries fewer than 200 passengers, the smallest no more than 100. I have sailed on four of them and my experience is that when they hit a port only a dozen or so of the passengers head for a beach (except when the ships organize beach parties, which are usually on deserted or isolated beaches, far from resorts).

These ships are really oversize luxury yachts, the seagoing equivalents of, say, Malliouhana or Curtain Bluff, offering the camaraderie of an *intime* inn and the privacy of an exclusive resort plus the opportunity to visit *several* islands on one vacation without the hassles of unpacking and repacking every other day. In the case of the *Wind Star*, of course, and its sister ship the *Wind Spirit*, the comparison is more accurately with tall ships since they are four-masters with sails, which furl and unfurl automatically at the behest of the ships' computers. However, most of the time (at least on the *Wind Star* cruise I took) the ship just puttered along powered by its three engines, with the sails being set just for show (except, perhaps, during the night when there was time to kill between ports); moreover, the computers ensure that the ships will never list more than 7 degrees, so from the point of view of comfort they function like regular cruise ships. You rarely have even the slightest sense of *sailing*. It is an interesting experience, nevertheless.

Otherwise, how do the four ships stack up?

THE STATISTICS

These basic facts and figures give you a quick profile of each ship, arranged by fare, most expensive first. The fares are for comparison purposes only, a *daily* rate based on the ships' basic seven-day cruises; they have been culled from the cruise lines' brochures, but they can almost certainly be reduced by a few hundred dollars by talking to the right travel agents (in any case, you might want to check on special rates that include airfares and hotels before or after the cruises).

Seabourn Spirit/Seabourn Pride:
10,000 tons; 439 feet; 18 knots; 200 passengers; 140 crew. Daily rates for two, $734 to $1,196. *Telephone: toll free 800/351-9595 (U.S.) or toll free 800/527-0999 (Canada).*

Sea Goddess I/Sea Goddess II:
4,250 tons; 344 feet; 17.5 knots; 116 passengers; 86 crew. Daily rates for two, $660 to $1,180 (including all drinks and tips). *Telephone: toll free 800/458-9000 (U.S.) or toll free 800/268-3702 (Canada).*

Renaissance I/Renaissance II:
4,500 tons; 290 feet; 16 knots; 100 passengers; 65 crew. Daily rates for two, $462 to $748. *Telephone: toll free 800/525-2450.*

Wind Star/Wind Spirit:
440 feet; 5,350 tons; about 17 knots (under power); 148 passengers; 91 crew. Daily rates for two, $400 to $560. *Telephone: toll free 800/272-4550 (U.S.) or toll free 800/833-4550 (Canada).*

STATEROOMS

All staterooms on these ships are outside cabins. Cunard's Sea Goddess ships were the first of these yacht-like vessels and set the pace in cabin design, amenities, and comforts. Each stateroom (or suite-room, as Cunard calls it) is the equivalent of, say, a junior suite ashore, although a tad smaller, with a sitting area, mini-bar, television and VCR, and four-channel radio. With windows rather than portholes, the room is that much brighter, in addition to letting you see where you're going or where you've been; but the bed rather than the sitting area is next to the window, which is the wrong way round for my taste. The cabins on the Wind Star ships are similar in format (but with large portholes rather than windows).

The other ships learned from their predecessors: In each case, the sitting area is next to the window, although on the Renaissance ships the furniture is arranged in such a way that both the sofa *and* the bed are next to the window. In terms of visibility, the Seabourns get the nod because its windows are larger (about 5 feet wide) and lower, so that you can see the world pass by while sitting on your sofa, even while enjoying room service breakfasts or dinners. However, I found the Renaissance staterooms to be especially attractive: The Italian designers have used a laminate resembling highly polished mahogany, with lots of brass trim and mirrors, giving the stateroom a true yacht-like appearance (and its lighting was not merely functional—with the proper adjustment of spotlights and dimmers it could be downright sexy).

As for bathrooms, the Renaissance and Wind Star ships have showers only (the latter in an ingenious space-saving tube, the former a sensibly designed sauna-like stall); the Sea Goddesses have squeezed a tub/shower into a space that should have been tub only, so the best bathrooms are the tub-and-shower, marble-and-glass designs on the Seabourn ships, where you have space to towel off briskly without knocking the toiletries on the floor.

The Sea Goddess and Seabourn ships have a few cabins on their lower decks with portholes rather than windows, a popular trade-off for some passengers—less visibility but extra stability.

The ultimate way to go: The Sea Goddess and Renaissance ships have a few cabins with small, private verandas; Seabourn has a couple of suites with private verandas, but its four bow-facing super-deluxe Regal Suites are the grandest aboard any of this collection of ships (as they should be at $1,196 a day).

DINING

One attraction all these ships have in common is open seating in the dining rooms. In fact, their dining rooms function like regular restaurants, with passengers free to choose their times, tables, and table companions. No first and second seatings, here; no assigned tables; no risk of being stuck with bores for an entire voyage.

Open seating also encourages a higher caliber of cuisine, since dishes can be prepared à la minute rather than en masse. The cuisine in each case tends to be nouvelle continental with delicate accents from exotic lands that the ships and chefs have visited—Indonesian, Indian, Japanese, Polynesian.

The Seabourns claim to spend more on provisioning their kitchens than their competitors. Maybe yes, maybe no. Certainly the food on my *Seabourn Spirit* cruise was outstanding. But it was equally outstanding on the *Sea Goddess II*, which actually had one of America's star chefs on board to prepare a couple of special dinners, but whose efforts, it seemed to me (and several of my fellow passengers) were outshone by the ship's own chef. The *Renaissance II*, although significantly less expensive, came close to being on a par with the others; even the *Wind Star* served up fare that would compare with good shorebound Caribbean restaurants.

If I were to give any of them an edge on matters of dining, it would probably be the Seabourns because of their Veranda Cafés, indoor-and-outdoor dining spots all the way aft (but, alas, open only for breakfast and lunch); in terms of service, the restaurant of the *Sea Goddess II* had the most polished staff. (It should be noted that the Sea Goddesses serve complimentary wines with all meals—not great vintages, obviously, but a well-chosen variety from the prominent vineyards of France and California; if you're not impressed by their selections, you can always sip their complimentary champagne—or order other vintages from the ships' *cartes des vins*.)

The restaurants on each ship are roomy, restful, refined, elegant. Seabourn and Sea Goddess passengers are expected to dress for dinner every evening, with black tie affairs two evenings a week; the dress code is more casual on the other two (just as well in the case of the Wind Stars, where closet space is, well, yacht-like). The alternative to dressing up is to dine in your stateroom. All four ships have round-the-clock room service menus, but the Seabourns and Sea Goddesses allow you to order from the restaurant menu during regular dining hours; in each case, the coffee table in your stateroom is converted to a dinner table, set with fine china and crystal, and your meal is served course by course.

ENTERTAINMENT

Each of these ships has at least one small lounge that doubles as a disco/theater/nightclub/boite/casino; the Seabourns and Sea Goddesses also have piano bars. Live entertainment consists of a small combo for dancing (usually electronic keyboard and rhythm synthesizers, usually with the volume turned up higher than the acoustics warrant). They are augmented by vocalists, talented people, all of them, and an hour or two of Gershwin or Sondheim before or after dinner is certainly more welcome than a pseudo-Vegas pseudo-extravaganza.

These ships are blessedly free of talent shows and costume balls, and, with the exception of the Seabourns, that blight known as the ship's photographer, who always wants everyone at the table to pose when I'm getting to the punch line.

Chalk up a point for the Wind Star ships: While the others may organize an occasional buffet or postdinner dance on deck, only the *Wind Star* had a topside bar open after 6:00 every evening. Granted, because of its sails, it had more reason to entertain its passengers on deck than the others, but I'd happily settle for the moon and stars, sails or no sails.

SERVICE

In each case, overall service was above average for cruise ships, and well above the norm at Caribbean resorts. The top prize goes to Sea Goddess, by a short neck: You know you're dealing with a classy group from the minute your documents arrive in a burgundy leather wallet with matching luggage tags; and when you get to your cabin, the card key for your cabin and your ID pass are waiting in a matching leather card case. Moreover, the staff members seem to memorize names instantly and anticipate requests faster, which is not to downplay the other crews—but the Sea Goddess people have been around longer and their ratio of crew to passengers, 89 to 116, is probably the highest in the industry.

SHORE EXCURSIONS

Seabourn and Renaissance have snappy, custom-designed launches for tendering passengers to shore; the Sea Goddesses use their lifeboats— real old-fashioned lifeboats, not the last word in convenience or comfort but adequate since the ships are never farther than five minutes from shore. On the other hand, the Sea Goddesses offered the best tendering service, by lifeboat or inflatable dinghy, with the boats leaving whenever anyone wanted to leave, rather than operating half-hourly shuttles.

The cruise directors were, for my money, the weak links in the service of all four ships I cruised on: This is not to say that they are not willing attendants or congenial traveling companions, but you'll probably find you know more about the islands than they do. Too often they seem to be captives of the shore agents who actually arrange the excursions; thus, your ship may go into Marigot on the French side of St. Martin/St. Maarten, but since the shore agents have to do something and have to earn some revenue they arrange for buses into Philipsburg on the Dutch side, a wasted half hour each way since the shopping there is only marginally better and Marigot offers more charm, more cafés, and more fine restaurants just a few minutes from the dock.

However, there are some out-of-the-ordinary highlights among the shore excursions: Renaissance organizes Minimoke car "rallies" for its passengers on St. Barthélemy, a jolly event that everyone seems to enjoy; Sea Goddess arranges for passengers to race aboard twin America's Cup yachts (the real thing!) off St. Maarten.

Where these ships score with shore excursions is their beach parties— perhaps on an uninhabited island in the Tobago Cays, probably in the British Virgin Islands. The Sea Goddesses have the most famous of these outings—on the BVI's Jost van Dyke, complete with a dining tent, full buffet lunch, and waiters dressed up in proper uniforms and shorts who wade into the sea to serve your complimentary caviar and champagne.

SPORTS FACILITIES

All of these ships have water-level platforms aft and carry their own equipment for windsurfing, waterskiing, and small-boat sailing. The Seabourns, however, go one better with Star Wars contraptions that open up to become not just a deck but an outdoor protected swimming pool. However, it's such an elaborate affair to operate that it can be used only in the smoothest anchorages.

Both the Windstar and the Renaissance ships carry scuba-diving gear and certified instructors. In the case of the *Renaissance II*, scuba-diving facilities include instruction videos, compressors, 21 tanks and regulators. In addition, each ship has a small pool and whirlpool on deck (two whirlpools on the Seabourns); all of them have exercise rooms, the most spacious and best equipped being on the Seabourns and the Sea Goddesses (the latter operated by Golden Door at Sea Spas).

ITINERARIES

All these ships have unusually shallow drafts (as little as 12 feet in the case of the Renaissance ships), allowing them to negotiate channels and moorings where larger ships never venture. Nevertheless, they seem to spend much of their time cruising to and from routine ports of call like St. Martin/St. Maarten, Barbados, St. Thomas, and Antigua. Among the out-of-the-way destinations are places like Bequia, the Tobago Cays, Jost van Dyke, Montserrat, and the Iles des Saintes; and on islands like Antigua they may stop in Falmouth Harbour rather than St. Johns; on St. Lucia, Rodney Bay rather than Castries.

My problem with most of the itineraries is not the routine destinations but the fact that they have you in a different port (sometimes two ports) every day instead of treating you to one or two days at sea. It seems odd to provide ships with everything needed to keep passengers comfortable and amused at sea, then tie up in a harbor. Some of the Seabourn itineraries, however, do include two days at sea on a seven-day itinerary—something worth keeping in mind if what you are looking for is a real seagoing experience. For details of the specific itineraries, call the numbers listed above, in the section "The Statistics."

The Rates—and How to Figure Them Out

Before you go any further: *All the room rates quoted in this guidebook are for two people.*

Islands have different ways of establishing their rates, and individual hotels have their own little methods. The variables include twin beds versus double beds, rooms with bath or without bath, rooms on the beach or near the beach, facing the front or facing the back, upper floors versus lower floors, cubic feet of space. Some rooms may cost more because they have air conditioning, others because they have small refrigerators, and so on. It would be a lifetime's work to figure out all the odds. If you have any special preferences, let the hotel know when you make your reservations.

DIFFERENT TYPES OF RATES

Hotels in the Caribbean quote four different types of rates:

EP	European Plan	You pay for the room only. No meals
CP	Continental Plan	You get the room and breakfast (usually a continental breakfast of juice, rolls, and coffee)
MAP	Modified American Plan	You get room with breakfast plus *one* meal—usually dinner
FAP*	Full American Plan	You get everything—room, breakfast, lunch, afternoon tea (where served), and dinner
FAP+	Full American Plan with extras	You get room, all meals, afternoon tea, and items like table wines, drinks, laundry, and/ or postage stamps

* Sometimes known as American Plan and abbreviated to AP.

FAP and MAP rates may mean that you order your meals from a fixed menu, rather than from the à la carte menu; in some Caribbean hotels this is a racket because the choice you're offered is so limited or unpromising you're almost obligated to order the items that cost a few dollars more. That happens in only a few of the hotels in *this* guide; although in many of the smaller inns you will be offered a fixed menu for dinner, served at a fixed hour, often at communal tables (identified in these pages as "family style").

Which rate should you choose? They all have their advantages. Usually you're better off having the EP or CP rate, because this gives you the flexibility to eat wherever you want to eat—for instance, to sample a *rijsttafel* in Aruba or Curaçao, to dine in some of the bistros on Martinique. On the other hand, in many cases the hotel dining room may be the best eating spot on the island (in some cases the *only* spot), and you'd want to eat there anyway; or the nearest restaurant may be a $10 or $15 cab ride away on the other side of the island and not worth the fare. In the case of Casa de Campo, in the Dominican Republic, the MAP supplement is only $40 per person, which seems to me to be a real bargain.

On some islands, as in Barbados, some hotels have wisely banded together to arrange an exchange program—in other words, you tell your hotel that you want to dine in hotel B, in which case they arrange to have hotel B send the bill to them. On other islands, you encounter a tiresome attitude among hotel managers in which each one claims to have the best restaurant on the island and therefore "everyone wants to dine in his place anyway."

REBATES ON MEALS

Many hotels allow you a rebate on the dinner portion of your MAP or FAP rate—probably not a full rebate, but most of it, and only if you let them know before lunchtime that you're not going to dine there that evening.

The reason why hotels put you through this hassle is that their supplies are limited, and they have to know in advance how many dinners they must prepare (in the case of steaks, for example, how many they have to unfreeze), without entailing a lot of waste.

In the hotel listings elsewhere in this guide, I've included the price of dinner where a hotel offers a choice of EP or MAP/FAP rates. Usually, the cost of dinners on a one-shot deal is more expensive (a couple of dollars or so) than the MAP/FAP rates.

TAXES

Most islands entice you to their island and then clobber you with a tax, sometimes two. These taxes may go under any of several euphemisms— room tax, government tax, airport tax, departure tax, energy tax—but what it boils down to is that you're going to pay more than the advertised hotel rates. Some are as high as 8% on your total bill; some are 3% on your room only. If you're on a tight budget, or if you simply don't feel like being taken for a ride, choose an island with no tax. In any case, check out such things if you're watching your pennies. If you *are* concerned about your dollars, note that on the French Islands, taxes and service charge are almost always *included* in the rate.

SERVICE CHARGE

Most hotels in the Caribbean now add a service charge to your bill, usually 10%, 12½%, or 15%, ostensibly in lieu of tipping; in some hotels you may tip in addition to the service charge; in others it's positively forbidden to tip and any member of the staff caught taking a *pourboire* is fired on the spot. The system has its pros and cons: From your point of view, it means you can relax and not have to bother about figuring out percentages, sometimes in funny currencies; on the other hand, a flat fee doesn't reward individual feats of activity, initiative, and personal attention, and without that incentive service can be lethargic. But the chances are service will be lethargic either way. If tipping is included, don't encourage lay-abouts who hover around looking for an additional tip—send them on their way; and if service overall is so bad it almost ruined your sex life, just refuse to pay the service charge.

ADDITIONAL NOTES ON RATES

In the list of rates that follows, please remember that "off-season" is spring, summer, *and* fall: In other words, these seemingly horrendous peak-season rates are in effect only four months of the year, the lower rates the remaining *eight months*.

For most hotels, the peak season runs from December 15 through Easter, but this may vary by a few days; if you check into the matter carefully, you may find that in some hotels the higher rates do not begin until Christmas, or even until late January, and you can grab a few unexpected "peak" season bargains. Still others will give you a reduced rate during the *first two weeks in January*. A few of the hotels listed here have three or four seasons; keeping track of them for this guide would be a round-the-year vocation, so the range of rates for those hotels represents the lowest and highest for the two winter and two summer seasons *combined*.

Remember   The figures quoted are not the full story—to get a more accurate comparison of rates between hotels you should also check out the paragraph marked "sports" in the individual hotel listings, to determine what activities are *included* in the rates at no extra charge. For instance, Guadeloupe's Hamak and Jamaica's Half Moon Club give you free golf on Robert Trent Jones courses, Bitter End Yacht Club on Virgin Gorda includes virtually unlimited sailing.

SPECIAL PACKAGES

As I mentioned in the introduction, and remind you here, your wallet may benefit by looking into special packages offered by individual hotels and airlines to independent travelers. For example, Young Island in the Grenadines treats "Lovers" to their own special off-season rate that includes everything but drinks and postage stamps. American has an extensive selection of "Pleasure Islands" that includes three-night or seven-night stays (often including round-trip airport transfers, which can be costly otherwise). Check with your travel agent for details.

BEWARE

In the best of times, it's difficult for a hotel keeper to estimate rates for two seasons hence; in these inflationary times it's virtually impossible. Since most innkeepers wait until the last minute to publish their rates, I have simplified the process by taking the winter 1990–91 rates and adding 10%—a bit high, perhaps, but better to play it safe. So, alas and alack, some of these rates will be wrong by the time you get around to escaping. It's not my fault. It's not my publisher's fault. Blame it on oil sheiks, bankers, gold speculators, trade unions, fishermen, and the sailors who man the island schooners. In any case, the prices will still be valid as a *comparison* between hotels and resorts, even between islands. The differences shouldn't be more than a few percentage points, but always double-check the rates before you go.

The rates are arranged alphabetically by island and are quoted in U.S. dollars.

HOTELS	RATE/TYPE (U.S. $)	PEAK SEASON	SERVICE CHARGE	OFF-SEASON DISCOUNT

Anguilla (8% tax)

HOTELS	RATE/TYPE (U.S. $)	PEAK SEASON	SERVICE CHARGE	OFF-SEASON DISCOUNT
ANGUILLA GREAT HOUSE	$220–360 EP	12/15–4/15	10%	30%
CAP JULUCA	$430–880 EP	12/15–4/5	10%	30%
COCCOLOBA	$395–505 CP+		10%	45%
CINNAMON REEF BEACH CLUB	$250–330 EP	12/21–4/7	10%	40%
MALLIOUHANA	$495–740 EP	12/18–3/31	10%	35%
THE MARINERS	$235–425 EP	12/15–3/31	10%	30%
LA SIRENA HOTEL AND VILLAS	$180–215 EP	12/15–3/31	10%	40%

Antigua (7% tax)

HOTELS	RATE/TYPE (U.S. $)	PEAK SEASON	SERVICE CHARGE	OFF-SEASON DISCOUNT
THE ADMIRAL'S INN	$100–120 EP	12/15–4/14	10%	25%
BLUE WATERS BEACH HOTEL	$325–410 MAP	12/16–4/9	10%	25%
COPPER & LUMBER STORE	$175–310 EP	12/15–5/15	10%	40%
CURTAIN BLUFF	$545–875 FAP	12/19–4/14	10%	30%
GALLEY BAY BEACH RESORT	$295–$367 FAP+		(included)	30%
HALF MOON BAY HOTEL	$325–520 MAP	12/16–4/15	10%	50%
THE INN AT ENGLISH HARBOUR	$110–330 EP	12/15–4/24	10%	25%
JUMBY BAY RESORT	$985 FAP+	12/16–4/15	10%	25%
ST. JAMES'S CLUB	$495–1,045 MAP	12/20–4/15	10%	30%

Aruba (5% tax)

HOTELS	RATE/TYPE (U.S. $)	PEAK SEASON	SERVICE CHARGE	OFF-SEASON DISCOUNT
DIVI DIVI BEACH RESORT	$290–485 EP	12/19–4/9	15%	30%
DIVI TAMARIJN BEACH RESORT	$240–265 EP	12/19–4/9	15%	30%

Barbados (5% tax)

HOTELS	RATE/TYPE (U.S. $)	PEAK SEASON	SERVICE CHARGE	OFF-SEASON DISCOUNT
COBBLERS COVE HOTEL	$440–585 MAP	12/19–4/5	10%	25%

HOTELS	RATE/TYPE (U.S. $)	PEAK SEASON	SERVICE CHARGE	OFF-SEASON DISCOUNT
CORAL REEF CLUB	$340–595 MAP	12/16–4/5	7½%	25%
CRANE BEACH HOTEL	$210–395 CP	12/22–3/31	10%	30–40%
GINGER BAY BEACH CLUB	$220 EP	12/15–4/14	10%	N/A
GLITTER BAY	$335–505 EP	12/22–4/15	10%	25%
ROYAL PAVILION	$433–940 EP	12/22–4/15	10%	30%
SANDY LANE HOTEL	$590–1,360 MAP	12/19–4/15	10%	30%

Bequia (5% tax)

FRANGIPANI HOTEL	$55–110 EP	12/15–4/19	10%	25%
SPRING ON BEQUIA	$190 MAP	12/15–4/15	10%	30%

Bonaire (5% tax)

DIVI FLAMINGO BEACH RESORT AND CASINO	$100–220 EP	12/19–4/9	15%	30%
HARBOUR VILLAGE BEACH RESORT	$225–495 EP	12/19–4/6	10%	25%

Cayman Islands (6% tax)

HYATT REGENCY GRAND CAYMAN	$270–475 EP	12/19–4/14	10%	45%

Curaçao (5% tax)

AVILA BEACH HOTEL	$93–145 EP	12/16–4/30	10%	25%

Dominican Republic (11% tax)

CASA DE CAMPO	$255–385 EP	12/21–4/3	10%	50%

HOTELS	RATE/TYPE (U.S. $)	PEAK SEASON	SERVICE CHARGE	OFF-SEASON DISCOUNT
Grenada (7½% tax)				
THE CALABASH	$275–475 MAP	12/21–4/15	10%	45%
SECRET HARBOUR	$218 EP	12/20–4/15	10%	30%
SPICE ISLAND INN	$325–460 MAP	12/21–4/15	10%	30%
Guadeloupe (tax included in rates)				
AUBERGE DE LA VIEILLE TOUR	$325–408 CP	12/23–4/15	(included)	45%
AUBERGE DES ANACARDIERS	$110–148 MAP	12/15–4/15	(included)	N/A
HAMAK	$310–420 EP	12/19–4/22	10%	50%
LE VILLAGE CREOLE	$140–170 EP	12/15–4/15	(included)	30%
Guana Island (7% tax)				
GUANA ISLAND CLUB	$535 FAP	12/16–4/1	12%	40%
Jamaica ($12 per person per day)				
HALF MOON GOLF, TENNIS & BEACH CLUB	$275–420 EP	12/19–4/15	10%	30%
JAMAICA INN	$355–410 FAP	12/15–4/16	10%	30%
PLANTATION INN	$340–420 MAP	12/15–4/15	10%	30%
ROUND HILL	$275–450 CP	12/15–4/14	15%	30%
SANS SOUCI HOTEL CLUB AND SPA	$285–340 EP	12/21–4/15	10%	30%
TRIDENT VILLAS AND HOTEL	$365–485 MAP	12/16–4/15	(optional)	40%
TRYALL GOLF, TENNIS & BEACH CLUB	$275–350 EP	12/15–4/15	10%	40%
Martinique (tax included in rates)				
HOTEL LE BAKOUA	$245–305 CP	12/15–4/15	(included)	40%
HOTEL PLANTATION DE LEYRITZ	$140 EP	12/18–4/22	(included)	30%
ST. AUBIN HOTEL	$114 CP	12/14–4/14	(included)	10%

HOTELS	RATE/TYPE (U.S. $)	PEAK SEASON	SERVICE CHARGE	OFF-SEASON DISCOUNT

Mayreau (5% tax)

HOTELS	RATE/TYPE (U.S. $)	PEAK SEASON	SERVICE CHARGE	OFF-SEASON DISCOUNT
SALTWHISTLE BAY CLUB	$410 MAP	12/16–4/15	10%	30%

Mustique (5% tax)

HOTELS	RATE/TYPE (U.S. $)	PEAK SEASON	SERVICE CHARGE	OFF-SEASON DISCOUNT
THE COTTON HOUSE	$450–525 FAP	12/17–4/17	10%	35%

Nevis (7% tax)

HOTELS	RATE/TYPE (U.S. $)	PEAK SEASON	SERVICE CHARGE	OFF-SEASON DISCOUNT
FOUR SEASONS NEVIS RESORT	$385–1,200	12/15–4/15	10%	30%
GOLDEN ROCK	$190 EP	12/20–4/15	10%	45%
HERMITAGE PLANTATION HOTEL	$215 EP	12/17–4/15	10%	35%
MONTPELIER	$360 MAP	12/15–4/15	10%	45%
NISBET PLANTATION BEACH CLUB	$325–435 MAP+	12/15–4/14	10%	65%

Palm Island (5% tax)

HOTELS	RATE/TYPE (U.S. $)	PEAK SEASON	SERVICE CHARGE	OFF-SEASON DISCOUNT
PALM ISLAND BEACH CLUB	$350 FAP+	12/15–4/14	10%	40%

Petit St. Vincent (5% tax)

HOTELS	RATE/TYPE (U.S. $)	PEAK SEASON	SERVICE CHARGE	OFF-SEASON DISCOUNT
PETIT ST. VINCENT RESORT	$685 FAP+	12/22–3/20	10%	30%

Puerto Rico (6% tax)

HOTELS	RATE/TYPE (U.S. $)	PEAK SEASON	SERVICE CHARGE	OFF-SEASON DISCOUNT
THE HORNED DORSET PRIMAVERA HOTEL	$255–295 EP	12/20–4/15	—	30%
HYATT DORADO BEACH	$320–565 MAP	12/20–4/14	—	40–50%
PALMAS DEL MAR	$205–255 EP	12/19–4/30	—	N/A

Saba (5% tax)

HOTELS	RATE/TYPE (U.S. $)	PEAK SEASON	SERVICE CHARGE	OFF-SEASON DISCOUNT
CAPTAIN'S QUARTERS	$140 CP	12/15–4/14	15%	20%
JULIANA'S	$85 EP	12/15–4/14	10%	30%

HOTELS	RATE/TYPE (U.S. $)	PEAK SEASON	SERVICE CHARGE	OFF-SEASON DISCOUNT

St. Barthélemy (tax included in rates)

HOTELS	RATE/TYPE (U.S. $)	PEAK SEASON	SERVICE CHARGE	OFF-SEASON DISCOUNT
CASTELETS	$170–595 CP	12/20–4/10	10%	30–35%
EL SERENO BEACH HOTEL	$270–345 CP	12/19–4/16	(included)	25%
FILAO BEACH HOTEL	$525–635 CP	12/10–4/30	(included)	25%
FRANÇOIS PLANTATION	$305–425 CP	12/20–4/15	(included)	50%
HOTEL GUANAHANI	$360–410 CP	12/22–4/5	(included)	40%
HOTEL MANAPANY	$340–630 CP	12/22–5/1	(included)	25%

St. Croix (7½% tax)

HOTELS	RATE/TYPE (U.S. $)	PEAK SEASON	SERVICE CHARGE	OFF-SEASON DISCOUNT
THE BUCCANEER HOTEL	$190–390 EP	12/20–4/1	(optional)	30%
CARAMBOLA BEACH RESORT AND GOLF CLUB	$520–630 FAP	12/22–3/31	(optional)	25%
CORMORANT BEACH CLUB	$385–495*	12/21–4/31	10%	35%

*Price includes breakfast, lunch and all drinks before 5 p.m.

St. Eustatius (7% tax)

HOTELS	RATE/TYPE (U.S. $)	PEAK SEASON	SERVICE CHARGE	OFF-SEASON DISCOUNT
THE OLD GIN HOUSE	$165 EP	12/15–4/14	15%	25%

St. John (7½% tax)

HOTELS	RATE/TYPE (U.S. $)	PEAK SEASON	SERVICE CHARGE	OFF-SEASON DISCOUNT
CANEEL BAY	$340–560 FAP	12/20–4/16	(optional)	30%

St. Kitts (7% tax)

HOTELS	RATE/TYPE (U.S. $)	PEAK SEASON	SERVICE CHARGE	OFF-SEASON DISCOUNT
THE GOLDEN LEMON	$315–465 MAP	12/16–4/15	10%	20%
OTTLEY'S PLANTATION INN	$265–330 CP	12/16–4/15	10%	25%
RAWLINS PLANTATION	$410 MAP+	12/16–4/15	10%	N/A
THE WHITE HOUSE	$385 CP	12/16–4/15	10%	20%

St. Lucia (8% tax)

HOTELS	RATE/TYPE (U.S. $)	PEAK SEASON	SERVICE CHARGE	OFF-SEASON DISCOUNT
ANSE CHASTANET BEACH HOTEL	$160–240 EP	12/15–4/15	(optional)	30%

HOTELS	RATE/TYPE (U.S. $)	PEAK SEASON	SERVICE CHARGE	OFF-SEASON DISCOUNT
CUNARD HOTEL LA TOC AND LA TOC SUITES	$250–550 EP	12/16–4/20	10%	50%

St. Maarten/St. Martin (5% tax on Dutch side, $1 per person per day on French side)

HOTELS	RATE/TYPE (U.S. $)	PEAK SEASON	SERVICE CHARGE	OFF-SEASON DISCOUNT
ALIZÉA RÉSIDENCE DE TOURISME	$170–385 CP	12/21–4/15	(included)	25%
LA BELLE CREOLE	$380–785 CP	12/21–4/15	10%	30%
L'HABITATION DE LONVILLIERS	$330–480 EP	12/23–5/14	(included)	40%
MARY'S BOON	$165 EP	12/15–4/15	15%	40%
OYSTER POND HOTEL	$190–410 EP	12/15–4/14	15%	40%
LA SAMANNA	$550–790 EP	12/15–4/6	10%	20%

St. Thomas (7½% tax)

HOTELS	RATE/TYPE (U.S. $)	PEAK SEASON	SERVICE CHARGE	OFF-SEASON DISCOUNT
PAVILIONS & POOLS HOTEL	$250–280 CP	12/21–4/14	(optional)	10–20%
POINT PLEASANT	$240–460 EP	12/20–4/14	(optional)	25%

St. Vincent (5% tax)

HOTELS	RATE/TYPE (U.S. $)	PEAK SEASON	SERVICE CHARGE	OFF-SEASON DISCOUNT
GRAND VIEW BEACH HOTEL	$230 CP	12/15–4/14	10%	30%
YOUNG ISLAND	$360–575 MAP	12/15–4/15	10%	30%

Tobago (3% tax)

HOTELS	RATE/TYPE (U.S. $)	PEAK SEASON	SERVICE CHARGE	OFF-SEASON DISCOUNT
ARNOS VALE HOTEL	$210 FAP	12/15–4/15	10%	30%
MOUNT IRVINE BAY HOTEL	$195–230 EP	12/18–4/15	10%	30%

Tortola (7% tax)

HOTELS	RATE/TYPE (U.S. $)	PEAK SEASON	SERVICE CHARGE	OFF-SEASON DISCOUNT
LONG BAY HOTEL	$230–335 MAP	12/16–4/15	10%	25%
PETER ISLAND	$465–575 FAP	12/18–4/15	10%	30%
THE SUGAR MILL	$145–210 EP	12/15–4/14	10%	15%

HOTELS	RATE/TYPE (U.S. $)	PEAK SEASON	SERVICE CHARGE	OFF-SEASON DISCOUNT
Virgin Gorda (7% tax)				
BIRAS CREEK	$455–660 FAP	12/19–4/2	10%	25%
BITTER END YACHT CLUB	$350–770 FAP	12/19–4/10	$12 per person per day	25%
DRAKE'S ACHORAGE RESORT INN	$365–520 FAP	12/18–4/17	15%	30%
LITTLE DIX BAY	$615 FAP	12/20–4/16	optional	30%

Reservations and Tourist Information

THE REPS

Hotel representatives keep tabs on the availability of rooms in the hotels they represent, and handle reservations and confirmations at no extra charge to you (unless you wait until the last minute and they have to send faxes or make phone calls back and forth, in which case you'll be charged). The reps who have appeared most frequently in these pages are listed below; in the interests of simplicity, only the main offices are listed for each one. (The list is in alphabetical order in the sense that David B. Mitchell, for example, is listed under D rather than M.)

American International
1890 Palmer Avenue
Larchmont, New York 10538
914/833-3303, toll free 800/223-5695
Fax 914/833-3308

Caribbean Inns Ltd.
P.O. Box 7411
Hilton Head Island, South Carolina 29938
803/785-7411, toll free 800/633-7411
Fax 803/686-7411

David B. Mitchell & Company, Inc.
200 Madison Avenue
New York, New York 10016
212/696-1323, toll free 800/372-1323
Fax 212/213-2297

Divi Resorts
54 Gunderman Road
Ithaca, New York 14850
607/277-3484, toll free 800/367-3484
Fax 607/277-3624

Flagship Hotels & Resorts
43 Kensico Drive
Mt. Kisco, New York 10549
Toll free 800/235-3505 or 800/729-3524
Fax 914/241-6279

International Travel & Resorts, Inc.
4 Park Avenue
New York, New York 10016
212/545-8469, toll free 800/223-9815
Fax 212/545-8467

Jacques de Larsay
622 Broadway
New York, New York 10012
212/477-1600, toll free 800/366-1510
Fax 212/995-0286

Leading Hotels of the World
747 Third Avenue
New York, New York 10017-2847
212/838-3110, toll free 800/223-6800
Fax 212/758-7367

Mondotels
1500 Broadway, Suite 1101
New York, New York 10036
212/719-5750, toll free 800/847-4249
Fax 212/719-5763

Preferred Hotels
1901 South Meyers Road
Oakbrook Terrace, Illinois 60181
Toll free 800/323-7500
Fax 708/290-6172

Ralph Locke Islands
P.O. Box 800
Waccabuc, New York 10597
Toll free 800/223-1108
Fax 914/763-5362

Ray Morrow Associates
360 Main Street
Ridgefield, Connecticut 06877
203/697-2340, toll free 800/223-9838
Telex 962400

Robert Reid Associates
500 Plaza Drive
Secaucus, New Jersey 07096
201/902-7878, toll free 800/223-6517
Fax 201/902-7738

Rockresorts
501 East El Camino Real
Boca Raton, Florida 33432
Toll free 800/223-7637
Fax 407/368-1946

WIMCO
Box 1461
Newport, Rhode Island 02840
401/849-8012, toll free 800/932-3222
Fax 401/847-6290

TOURIST INFORMATION

The function of this guide is to give you facts and tips on where to stay, rather than what to see; there just isn't time or space to do both. In any case, with the exceptions of islands like Puerto Rico, Jamaica, and a few others, there really isn't much to see—a fort, a volcano, a native market or two. Many of the major sightseeing attractions (and a few offbeat sights) are mentioned in these pages; if you want more information on topics like shopping and sightseeing, I suggest you get in touch with the tourist office of the islands that interest you. The other possibility is to write to the Caribbean Tourism Association (20 East 46th Street, New York, NY 10017, 212/682-0435) for information on most of the islands.

If you wait until you get to the island, you'll find no shortage of publications and notice boards with up-to-the-minute details on shops, restaurants, sights, and tours.

INDEX

NOW, SAVE MONEY ON ALL YOUR TRAVELS!
Join Frommer's™ Dollarwise® Travel Club

Saving money while traveling is never a simple matter, which is why the **Dollarwise Travel Club** was formed 31 years ago. Developed in response to requests from Frommer's Travel Guide readers, the Club provides cost-cutting travel strategies, up-to-date travel information, and a sense of community for value-conscious travelers from all over the world.

In keeping with the money-saving concept, the annual membership fee is low —$20 for U.S. residents or $25 for residents of Canada, Mexico, and other countries—and is immediately exceeded by the value of your benefits, which include:

1. Any TWO books listed on the following pages.
2. Plus any ONE Frommer's City Guide.
3. A subscription to our quarterly newspaper, *The Dollarwise Traveler.*
4. A membership card that entitles you to purchase through the Club all Frommer's publications for 33% to 40% off their retail price.

The eight-page **Dollarwise Traveler** tells you about the latest developments in good-value travel worldwide and includes the following columns: **Hospitality Exchange** (for those offering and seeking hospitality in cities all over the world); **Share-a-Trip** (for those looking for travel companions to share costs); and **Readers Ask . . . Readers Reply** (for those with travel questions that other members can answer).

Aside from the Frommer's Guides and the Gault Millau Guides, you can also choose from our Special Editions. These include such titles as *California with Kids* (a compendium of the best of California's accommodations, restaurants, and sightseeing attractions appropriate for those traveling with toddlers through teens); *Candy Apple: New York with Kids* (a spirited guide to the Big Apple by a savvy New York grandmother that's perfect for both visitors and residents); *Caribbean Hideaways* (the 100 most romantic places to stay in the Islands, all rated on ambience, food, sports opportunities, and price); *Honeymoon Destinations* (a guide to planning and choosing just the right destination from hundreds of possibilities in the U.S., Mexico, and the Caribbean); *Marilyn Wood's Wonderful Weekends* (a selection of the best mini-vacations within a 200-mile radius of New York City, including descriptions of country inns and other accommodations, restaurants, picnic spots, sights, and activities); and *Paris Rendez-Vous* (a delightful guide to the best places to meet in Paris whether for power breakfasts or dancing till dawn).

To join this Club, simply send the appropriate membership fee with your name and address to: Frommer's Dollarwise Travel Club, 15 Columbus Circle, New York, NY 10023. Remember to specify which single city guide and which two other guides you wish to receive in your initial package of member's benefits. Or tear out the next page, check off your choices, and send the page to us with your membership fee.

FROMMER BOOKS
PRENTICE HALL PRESS
15 COLUMBUS CIRCLE
NEW YORK, NY 10023
212/373-8125

Date_____

Friends: Please send me the books checked below.

FROMMER'S™ GUIDES

(Guides to sightseeing and tourist accommodations and facilities from budget to deluxe, with emphasis on the medium-priced.)

☐ Alaska	$14.95	☐ Germany	$14.95
☐ Australia	$14.95	☐ Italy	$14.95
☐ Austria & Hungary	$14.95	☐ Japan & Hong Kong	$14.95
☐ Belgium, Holland & Luxembourg	$14.95	☐ Mid-Atlantic States	$14.95
☐ Bermuda & The Bahamas	$14.95	☐ New England	$14.95
☐ Brazil	$14.95	☐ New Mexico	$13.95
☐ Canada	$14.95	☐ New York State	$14.95
☐ Caribbean	$14.95	☐ Northwest	$16.95
☐ Cruises (incl. Alaska, Carib, Mex, Hawaii, Panama, Canada & US)	$14.95	☐ Portugal, Madeira & the Azores	$14.95
		☐ Scandinavia	$18.95
☐ California & Las Vegas	$14.95	☐ South Pacific	$14.95
☐ Egypt	$14.95	☐ Southeast Asia	$14.95
☐ England & Scotland	$14.95	☐ Southern Atlantic States	$14.95
☐ Florida	$14.95	☐ Southwest	$14.95
☐ France	$14.95	☐ Switzerland & Liechtenstein	$14.95

☐ USA $16.95

FROMMER'S $-A-DAY® GUIDES

(In-depth guides to sightseeing and low-cost tourist accommodations and facilities.)

☐ Europe on $40 a Day	$15.95	☐ Israel on $40 a Day	$13.95
☐ Australia on $40 a Day	$13.95	☐ Mexico on $35 a Day	$14.95
☐ Costa Rica; Guatemala & Belize on $35 a day	$15.95	☐ New York on $60 a Day	$13.95
		☐ New Zealand on $45 a Day	$14.95
☐ Eastern Europe on $25 a Day	$16.95	☐ Scotland & Wales on $40 a Day	$13.95
☐ England on $50 a Day	$13.95	☐ South America on $40 a Day	$15.95
☐ Greece on $35 a Day	$14.95	☐ Spain on $50 a Day	$15.95
☐ Hawaii on $60 a Day	$14.95	☐ Turkey on $30 a Day	$13.95
☐ India on $25 a Day	$12.95	☐ Washington, D.C. & Historic Va. on $40 a Day	$13.95
☐ Ireland on $35 a Day	$13.95		

FROMMER'S TOURING GUIDES

(Color illustrated guides that include walking tours, cultural and historic sites, and other vital travel information.)

☐ Amsterdam	$10.95	☐ New York	$10.95
☐ Australia	$10.95	☐ Paris	$8.95
☐ Brazil	$10.95	☐ Rome	$10.95
☐ Egypt	$8.95	☐ Scotland	$9.95
☐ Florence	$8.95	☐ Thailand	$10.95
☐ Hong Kong	$10.95	☐ Turkey	$10.95
☐ London	$10.95	☐ Venice	$8.95

(TURN PAGE FOR ADDITONAL BOOKS AND ORDER FORM)

0391

FROMMER'S CITY GUIDES

(Pocket-size guides to sightseeing and tourist accommodations and facilities in all price ranges.)

☐ Amsterdam/Holland	$8.95	☐ Minneapolis/St. Paul	$8.95
☐ Athens	$8.95	☐ Montréal/Québec City	$8.95
☐ Atlanta	$8.95	☐ New Orleans	$8.95
☐ Atlantic City/Cape May	$8.95	☐ New York	$8.95
☐ Barcelona	$7.95	☐ Orlando	$8.95
☐ Belgium	$7.95	☐ Paris	$8.95
☐ Berlin	$8.95	☐ Philadelphia	$8.95
☐ Boston	$8.95	☐ Rio	$8.95
☐ Cancún/Cozumel/Yucatán	$8.95	☐ Rome	$8.95
☐ Chicago	$9.95	☐ Salt Lake City	$8.95
☐ Denver/Boulder/Colorado Springs	$7.95	☐ San Diego	$8.95
☐ Dublin/Ireland	$8.95	☐ San Francisco	$8.95
☐ Hawaii	$8.95	☐ Santa Fe/Taos/Albuquerque	$10.95
☐ Hong Kong	$7.95	☐ Seattle/Portland	$7.95
☐ Las Vegas	$8.95	☐ St. Louis/Kansas City	$9.95
☐ Lisbon/Madrid/Costa del Sol	$8.95	☐ Sydney	$8.95
☐ London	$8.95	☐ Tampa/St. Petersburg	$8.95
☐ Los Angeles	$8.95	☐ Tokyo	$8.95
☐ Mexico City/Acapulco	$8.95	☐ Toronto	$8.95
☐ Miami	$8.95	☐ Vancouver/Victoria	$7.95

☐ Washington, D.C. $8.95

SPECIAL EDITIONS

☐ Beat the High Cost of Travel	$6.95	☐ Motorist's Phrase Book (Fr/Ger/Sp)	$4.95
☐ Bed & Breakfast—N. America	$14.95	☐ Paris Rendez-Vous	$10.95
☐ California with Kids	$16.95	☐ Swap and Go (Home Exchanging)	$10.95
☐ Caribbean Hideaways	$14.95	☐ The Candy Apple (NY with Kids)	$12.95
☐ Honeymoon Destinations (US, Mex &		☐ Travel Diary and Record Book	$5.95
Carib)	$14.95	☐ Where to Stay USA (From $3 to $30 a	
☐ Manhattan's Outdoor Sculpture	$15.95	night)	$13.95

☐ Marilyn Wood's Wonderful Weekends (CT, DE, MA, NH, NJ, NY, PA, RI, VT) $11.95
☐ The New World of Travel (Annual sourcebook by Arthur Frommer for savvy travelers) $16.95

GAULT MILLAU

(The only guides that distinguish the truly superlative from the merely overrated.)

☐ The Best of Chicago	$15.95	☐ The Best of Los Angeles	$16.95
☐ The Best of France	$16.95	☐ The Best of New England	$15.95
☐ The Best of Hawaii	$16.95	☐ The Best of New Orleans	$16.95
☐ The Best of Hong Kong	$16.95	☐ The Best of New York	$16.95
☐ The Best of Italy	$16.95	☐ The Best of Paris	$16.95
☐ The Best of London	$16.95	☐ The Best of San Francisco	$16.95

☐ The Best of Washington, D.C. $16.95

ORDER NOW!

In U.S. include $2 shipping UPS for 1st book; $1 ea. add'l book. Outside U.S. $3 and $1, respectively.
Allow four to six weeks for delivery in U.S., longer outside U.S.
Enclosed is my check or money order for $_____

NAME_____

ADDRESS_____

CITY_____ STATE_____ ZIP_____

0391